D1271972

My Mother's
Sabbath Days

Other Works by Chaim Grade
in English Translation

PHILOSOPHICAL DIALOGUE
My Quarrel with Hersh Rassayner

NOVELS
The Well
The Agunah
The Yeshiva, vol. I
The Yeshiva, vol. II, Masters and Disciples

NOVELLAS
Rabbis and Wives

MY MOTHER'S SABBATH DAYS

A memoir by

CHAIM GRADE

754

Translated from the Yiddish
by Channa Kleinerman Goldstein and Inna Hecker Grade

Alfred A. Knopf   New York   1986

THIS IS A BORZOI BOOK
PUBLISHED BY ALFRED A. KNOPF, INC.

Library of Congress Cataloging-in-Publication Data

Grade, Chaim, 1910–1982.
My mother's Sabbath days.

Translation of: Der mames Shabosim.
I. Title.
PJ5129.G68M3613   1986   839'.0933   86–45267
ISBN 0-394-50980-3

Manufactured in the United States of America

FIRST EDITION

Contents

Foreword

WHEN PLANS TO TRANSLATE *My Mother's Sabbath Days* became known, two very special people sent me priceless items from their personal archives. One is Chaim Grade's childhood friend who knew his mother, Vella, personally—the historian and archivist of Vilna, Leyzer Ran, editor/compiler of the multilingual encyclopaedia *Jerusalem of Lithuania*. The other is Yehoshua Misholi, the Israeli author and educator, and brother of Grade's first wife, Frumme-Liebe, or Frumme-Liebche, as she is called in this volume. Yehoshua Misholi sent me Frumme-Liebe's and Chaim's letters to her family, letters that shed much light on their life before and after the Soviet invasion of Vilna, which is described in the present volume. Leyzer Ran provided, among other historical documents, transcripts of clippings from Vilna Yiddish newspapers, dating back to 1934. Below is the text of one such clipping, which appeared on June 22, 1939, in the Yiddish daily *Unzer Tog*, reporting on what proved to be the last rabbinical convention ever held in Eastern Europe:

> Rabbi Regensburg, the octogenarian Rav of Zambrow, the grandfather of Grade's wife, speaks, summoning his last strength. His speech reminds one of the times when upon hearing such words, Jews were prepared for utmost self-sacrifice for the sake of the Holy Name. In the audience was Chaim Grade.

This article points to Chaim Grade's position in pre-World War II Vilna; the aged and venerable Rabbi Regensburg is introduced as "the grandfather of Grade's wife." For the reporters of *Unzer Tog*, a secular paper, it was a source of wonderment that Grade, who had broken away from Orthodoxy, should nonetheless attend their convention. The truth is that he attended it as an artist—not, to be sure, with any deliberate intention of describing the rabbis, but rather, led on by that curiosity and love that live side by side in the soul of an artist, curiosity about and love for his subject. He loved the world of rabbinical scholarship into which he had himself been born, and whose beautiful daughter, Frumme-Liebe, had become his wife.

Chaim Grade left numerous manuscripts yet to be published in Yiddish and eventually translated into English, and a number of major works already published in Yiddish, and scheduled for translation. The present volume, *My Mother's Sabbath Days*, is one of the latter, and I want to take this opportunity to express my gratitude to Melvin Rosenthal, who worked on this volume, as he worked on *Rabbis and Wives*, as copy-editor and coordinator. I am delighted that my co-translator of this volume, Mrs. Channa Goldstein, values Mr. Rosenthal's work as much as I do. And above all, to Chaim Grade's devoted editor, Ashbel Green, I wish to offer my heartfelt thanks for his invaluable assistance and for his unfailing kindness and courtesy.

In *My Mother's Sabbath Days*, Chaim Grade presents not much more than a sketch of his tragic father, the formidable Rabbi Shlomo Mordecai Grade, *maskil* (champion of enlightenment), Hebraist, and early Zionist, who was well known for challenging rabbinical rulings and was, indeed, at war with almost all of Orthodox Vilna. Rabbi Shlomo Mordecai did not defer even to the Ḥazon Ish, one of the greatest Talmudic authorities of all time, and a true saint who chose young Chaim as his personal disciple. The difficult relationship of the *maskil* Rabbi Shlomo Mordecai and the ultra-Orthodox Ḥazon Ish developed into a veritable duel for the heart and mind of a youth who was at once the favorite son of one and the favorite disciple of the other—with the victory going in the long run to the father.

In the present work, Grade portrays the frightful poverty of the Jewish working masses—for which reason, very much as in the under-developed countries of today, Communism had numerous followers. True, the Jewish Socialist Bund also had a considerable membership, as did the Zionists as well. But Communism was by far the most powerful move-ment. This was a source of great tragedy, not only because of the per-secutions carried out by the semi-Fascist Polish regime, but also because so many poor, unsuspecting youth were lured by the local Party bosses into crossing the border to find the "ideal" life in the Communist paradise. These border-crossers promptly found themselves arrested as "spies" and shipped without trial into Soviet concentration camps, where they became slave laborers. In the present work, Grade shows vividly the despair of the parents of such young people—notably, the hunchbacked Velvel the tailor and Zalman Press, stocking-peddler and frustrated poet. Miracu-lously, one couple, Leyzer Ran and his wife, Bathsheva, survived the ordeal of ten years in Soviet slave labor camps and Siberian exile, and now live in New York City.

Mr. Ran reported his gruesome experience on the Soviet side of the border at a banquet in honor of Chaim Grade in New York on May 20, 1962. His testimony completed the portrayal of the tragedy, which in *My*

Mother's Sabbath Days does not go beyond the border, since Grade is here concerned chiefly with what he himself witnessed and experienced. Playing on the title of Grade's very popular poem *Kraten* ("Prison Bars"), Ran labeled the Soviet Union—*Ratenfarband* in Yiddish—the *Kratenfarband*, that is, "Union of Prison Bars."

VILNA WAS A CITY strongly influenced by both Polish and Russian culture. In Polish as well as Russian society, the position of a poet was akin to that of a prophet. Each political party strove to have a poet on its side, and it was for this reason that the Jewish Communists of Vilna did all they could to woo Chaim Grade, whose popularity and authority as a poet were enormous. Their first severe disappointment came when Grade married Frumme-Liebe, "a clergyman's daughter of a Zionist family in Palestine." The Communists actually tried to disrupt the marriage—the two chief culprits in this regard being a certain Jona (Yankel) Gutkowicz and his friend, a man whom Grade later described in the novel *From Beneath the Ground*, under the name of Bentze Krasny (that is, Bentze "Red"). This second man still lives in Communist Poland, one of its last Jews, having held on to the bristles of the broom with which Polish Communists swept out their Jewish "comrades."

Frumme-Liebe's letters of 1939, even before the Nazi and Soviet invasions, reflect immense sadness. There is not a single word of complaint—only sadness, the same sentiment so prominent in Chaim Grade's poetry of this period. The city's Jewish Communists enveloped the couple in vile intrigues, and Frumme-Liebe was literally put on their "hit list." This entire pathetic experience haunted Grade for the rest of his life. Early in June 1982, he described it to me in detail, in the course of discussing plans for the novel in which he intended to record it, *The Jewish City*, which was to have dealt with Vilna on the eve of World War II.

WHEN CHAIM GRADE first joined secular, literary Vilna, the young Communist poet Kaczerginski (Czemerinski in *From Beneath the Ground*) sought, in 1934, to win him to the cause with a slogan: *"Hey, ḥaver Grade, hey, ḥaver Grade, ḳum shliss ziḥ on on der royter brigade, zol vern dayn lebn a royte ballade"*—"Hey, comrade Grade, hey, comrade Grade, come and join the red brigade, let your life become a red ballad."* The slogan became so popular with the Jewish youth of Vilna that they chanted it in the streets. According to Leyzer Ran, it inspired scores of parodies

---

* Kaczerginski, it should be noted, became a militant anti-Communist after 1940.

employing the easily rhymable name *Grade*, with *brigade* and *ballade* yielding place to *shokolade, marmelade, limonade, olimpiade*, etc. (Mr. Ran himself wrote one such parody, a copy of which he has kindly sent me.) To put an end to this, Grade composed a few lines in response to Kaczerginski, among them:

> *Mice devour the books in your bookcase,*
> *And time devours you, as the wave devours the beach,*
> *And in the dark graves turn and turn*
> *Your eternally lost days.*

Grade was then only twenty-four, but these lines strikingly echo those of Baudelaire in his lament about man's eternal enemy, Time:

> *—O douleur! O douleur! Le Temps mange la vie,*
> *Et l'obscur Ennemi qui nous ronge le coeur*
> *Du sang que nous perdons croit et se fortifie!*

AFTER THE SOVIET INVASION of Poland, the situation of Chaim Grade and Frumme-Liebe became extremely dangerous. The offices of the Soviet secret police were crowded by eager local Communists, Jews and Gentiles alike, denouncing their anti-Communist neighbors. Even the Soviet officials themselves eventually tired of the endless, macabre stream of denunciations. They knew from experience what the local Communists did not yet know: that once a wave of arrests began, no one could tell where it would end. It often happened that the denouncer shortly followed the one denounced, and that later the official who had accepted the denunciation would join the two of them in prison or concentration camp. The wheels of Soviet "justice" turned swiftly, efficiently, and without discrimination.

The Soviets entered Vilna for the first time in September 1939 and they left, temporarily, in December of that year, having turned Vilna over to Lithuania, destined with its fellow Baltic states to remain free for less than a year more. Lithuanian Jewish Communists accompanied their Soviet bosses to the Soviet "zone" in Bialystok, annexed from partitioned Poland. Chaim Grade was relieved and happy to see them go, yet when they returned in June 1940, after the annexation of the three Baltic republics, he knew that the Communists would regard his having stayed behind in Vilna as yet another transgression.

As *My Mother's Sabbath Days* describes, the Soviet occupation of Vilna plunged Chaim Grade into an apocalyptic mood. We see that Poles, even anti-Semitic Poles, mourning the fall of Poland at prayer in their churches and cathedrals, were closer to Chaim Grade's heart than the reckless Jewish Communist youth who, oblivious of the fate of so many comrades in the Soviet Union, fraternized and celebrated with the Soviet soldiers and officers in full view of the mourning Poles. For Chaim Grade the path to these Poles was barred by their anti-Semitism, and the path to the jubilant Communist youth was barred by the criminality of the regime which they celebrated and which eventually would destroy them. Chaim Grade did not join the celebrating Communists because he was a poet and an individualist, a "son of the Prophets." As Leyzer Ran stat·d in 1962:

> Grade inherited his social pathos and stormy protest against injustice from the Prophets Isaiah, Ezekiel, Jeremiah, Amos. No Marx or Engels was among his guides, neither they nor any of their Marxist "apostles." Grade has always spoken out against every repression, injustice, and violence, no matter whether the evil comes from the right or from the left.

During the year that followed under the Soviets, Frumme-Liebe and Chaim Grade lived in constant expectation of arrest, because of her "clerical-Zionist" connections and his various sins in the Party's eyes. And then came the beginning of what was to become his ultimate tragedy— June 22, 1941, the day of the German invasion of Russia.

It was the prevailing belief in the recently annexed Soviet territories that the Germans posed a danger chiefly to able-bodied men, whom they would round up for hard labor, but that they would not harm older men or women and children. Sharing this belief, Chaim Grade and Frumme-Liebe fled on foot. Soon rumors spread of the Germans' rapid advance, and to many it seemed more perilous to be overtaken by the Nazis than to remain and be found in one's own city. Grade insisted that Frumme-Liebe return to Vilna—a decision he later considered the most fateful of his life. He was certainly not the only one to allow himself to be deceived regarding the Nazis' intentions. Even a person as well informed, as sophisticated in political matters as Zivia Lubetkin, one of the leaders of the Warsaw Ghetto uprising, wrote in her memoir, *In the Days of Destruction and Revolt*:

> During the initial years of the war, when we were still unaware of the master plan to murder the entire Jewish population, there seemed to be a blossoming of social and cultural life within the ghetto. . . .

Such widespread unawareness existed in the face of Hitler's explicit statements of his plans in *Mein Kampf* and his radio broadcasts. People heard these statements, heard them repeatedly, but could not bring themselves to believe them.

A Professor at the Hebrew University of Jerusalem, Dr. Yeḥiel Szeintuch, once asked a Yiddish writer who had fled Poland for America on the eve of World War II, what had made him flee. The writer replied that *he believed every word of the German Führer, he believed that he would carry out his every threat*.

But Chaim Grade, like his friend Zivia Lubetkin, did not believe it. Even after the Holocaust, standing on the ruins of the Vilna Ghetto, he cried out his refusal to accept that what had happened could ever happen. To believe in the possibility of evil, he felt, one must carry within oneself a germ of evil. The greatest problem of his life was that he did not know how to deal with evil—or, at least, not with the kind represented by the Nazis. His rabbinical background had prepared him to be wary of the masked Soviet evil, but it left him helpless in the face of the unmasked Nazi evil. He knew that to protect himself against the Soviet evil, he had to be able to see through it. But what to do about evil unmasked, or rather self-unmasking? The truth seemed too monstrous to be true.

When Chaim Grade said good-bye to Frumme-Liebe in the village of Rukon, he had no way of knowing it was a final parting. A man from Vilna wrote me that people were convinced the Germans would be defeated within a week or two, so they fled with their apartment keys in their pockets. It was only after Grade crossed the old Polish-Soviet border on a military truck, apparently filled with deserters, found himself in Russia proper, and saw the horrendous devastation caused by just two days of war—only then did he realize that he had left his mother and Frumme-Liebe forever.

This experience marked for him the end of the old way of life, the end of the world into which he was born, and his entrance into the world of the unknown in the vastness of Russia. *My Mother's Sabbath Days* offers a detailed description of Grade's flight into Russia, on foot and on various transport trains. The readers will meet countless sharply etched characters, will vividly share Soviet experiences, will taste the Soviet reality as the train progresses deeper and deeper into the country.

Of these encounters, two are especially memorable. One is with the tragically disillusioned Jewish Communist Lev Kogan. Kogan, a local Party secretary in the Ukraine, had truly believed that Communism would do away with international hatred and establish a worldwide brotherhood of peoples. To men like him, Communism had appeared to be the solution to all problems, and this in their eyes justified its cruelty. The beginning of his undoing comes with the Hitler-Stalin Pact. Before then his wife, like the rest of the Soviet population, had been exposed to continuous anti-Nazi propaganda, which she believed. But the agreement with Hitler had shattered her faith, and she concluded that the anti-Nazi attacks must have been a sham. She had refused to leave with her husband for the safer eastern regions, convinced that the Germans would not wage war on women and children. As Lev Kogan's train moves further and further into eastern Russia, he realizes he has left his wife and children to face certain death. Also, it becomes clear to him that the war slogan is not "for the Communist World Proletariat," as he had expected, but "for Mother Russia." But to him, a Jew, "Mother Russia" is alien. It is all more than he can bear. He has lost his wife and children, lost his ideals, his faith; his life has ceased to have meaning. He commits suicide, and the only one who understands his tragedy and mourns him is the refugee from the west, Chaim Grade.

Among the victims of the Soviet regime that Lev Kogan had helped install is another of Grade's road companions: the *durachok*, or simpleton. The *durachok* is a young convict, one of a group of temporarily freed prisoners riding with civilians on the open platform of a train. As Chaim Grade contemplates these men, he realizes that the Soviets during just one year in the Baltic republics have populated the land with slave labor camps and he understands that, whereas the victims from the annexed regions have been shipped to central Russia and to Siberia, the victims from Russia proper were filling the new camps in occupied Latvia, Lithuania, Estonia. In the heat of June the convicts wear worn-out, dirty, quilted winter outfits. Grade also comprehends that at the outbreak of the war, aware that camp inmates might consider the Nazis their liberators, the Soviets were shipping them away from the front lines, even at the price of leaving behind a civil population eager to flee.

As the train moves eastward, the Soviet authorities institute a search for German spies who have parachuted ahead of their advancing army. Sure enough, the innocent *durachok*, who does not understand what is going on, is mistaken for a spy. Dumbstruck with terror, he is, like Melville's Billy Budd, incapable of uttering a word in self-defense. He cannot explain why he who owns only his winter clothes was tempted to pick up a fine bag lying on the road. In desperation, he jumps off the platform of the train and is shot dead by a guard. After the murder of the innocent *durachok* the other passengers fall into despair, and Chaim Grade comprehends "the law" of the land to which the Germans have driven him.

As his train moves deeper into Russia, he grows more and more acquainted with Soviet reality. He is dismayed by the sight of a Russian Orthodox Church turned into a barn, and even more saddened to realize that he is the only one who pays any attention to this "abomination of desolation." The resigned Russians accept it as a normal phenomenon. Even so, the faith and spirituality so deeply ingrained in the Russian people surge up at crucial moments. Women weep, pray, and cross their men going to war as their great-grandmothers had done centuries ago, as if the Soviet system never existed.

Chaim Grade survived his ordeal in Russia because of his respect for the spirit of the land, for the Russian people, for their suffering, for their spirituality, for their faith. People with genuine love for their own faith and traditions love and respect the spiritual heritage of others. This is especially true in the Soviet Union, where the persecution of religion gives people of faith a truly ecumenical education. Soviet society is thus divided between Communist atheists and the faithful of all denominations. Grade's Jewish faith was so strong, he was so secure in his awareness as a *national Jew*—I heard him use this phrase often—that he never felt threatened by other religions and cultures but approached them with openness, with the honest curiosity of a scholar, with the love of an artist and the goodwill of a humanist.

Although it is not Grade's goal in *My Mother's Sabbath Days* to give a detailed description of his life in Russia, nevertheless he offers a faithful picture of the plight of the Jewish refugees and of the Russian people during the war. We meet the once elegant and prosperous Warsaw attorney Orenstein, who becomes virtually a beggar, dies in a remote village in Central Asia, and is buried by strangers. There is the refugee from Lodz, Misha Troiman, who, unable to endure the thought of what is happening to his people, to his wife and son in Nazi-occupied Poland, decides that in order to go on living he must start a completely new life, with new ties—and is killed as the result of an accident.

And there is the good man Yankel Grot, sick, melancholy, ekeing out a living by selling home-rolled cigarettes in the market. This "business"—private enterprise, by Soviet standards—nearly lands him in jail. And yet he manages to help other refugees even less fortunate than he. Yankel Grot has a dream: to survive the war and reach the Holy Land. And there is the local Jewish shoemaker, who speaks only Bukharian, who has neither leather nor thread to mend Grade's all-but-disintegrated shoes, but who lovingly polishes them. He shows Grade with pride a prayerbook, a *sliha*, printed in Vilna and, since it is the eve of Rosh Hashanah, he gives him a pomegranate as a "new fruit" of the season.

Grade left Russia with great love for its people. His experience corroborates that of Nadezhda Mandelstam, wife of the poet Osip Mandelstam, who perished in Stalin's Gulag. She wrote that there is no anti-Semitism among the Russian people, that it is imposed from above, by the government, Imperial or Soviet, but always by the government. In

My Mother's Sabbath Days Grade does not report a single instance of anti-Semitism during his stay in Russia.

UPON HIS RETURN TO VILNA, Chaim Grade was confronted by the total destruction of what had been Jewish Vilna, with the destruction of European Jewry, with the violent death of his mother and of Frumme-Liebe, When Grade had married her, he was fascinated by her name, Frumme-Liebe, or "Pious Love," which in combination with his surname, Grade, "straight" in Yiddish, is "Straight Pious Love." This is precisely what Frumme-Liebe meant to him. Her death, no less than the death of his mother, became to him the symbol of the destruction of European Jewry, of the end of the European Diaspora. In the lamentations of the shoemaker Balberishkin—the only dweller of the ruined Ghetto, who has survived through his gentile looks and his knowledge of White Russian—for his murdered family, especially for his young daughter, little Yentele, Grade embodies as well the lamentations of Frumme-Liebe's father, the Rav, over his murdered daughter. By a peculiar twist of fate, the Balberishkins had been Frumme-Liebe's neighbors in the Ghetto, and as a nurse she had attended the sickly Yentele.

Within the walls of the ruined Grand Synagogue of Vilna, Grade was destined to have yet another unforgettable experience: an encounter with a young Orthodox rabbi on a mission from America, whom he contemptuously calls "dos Rebele," "the little Rabbi"—"one of those fine young men with a little black rabbinical beard"—and who stuns him with the arrant presumption of his avowal that the national Jewish tragedy had occurred because of the Jews' lack of piety, their "wickedness." Grade's experience with the rabbi from America would prove prophetic.

CHAIM GRADE ALWAYS FELT that he inherited from his father his nature of a philosopher who questions everything, but had taken from his mother his artistic, poetic nature, his all-encompassing ability to love that enabled him to endure all, to survive, to create. As her son describes her, Vella Grade was tiny, very thin, desperately hardworking. She had a beautiful voice, and she raised her son on her lullabies and songs and her prayers. She loved animals, pets, "God's creatures," always had a cat that she would not forget to feed even on Yom Kippur because "a cat is not obligated to fast." She was all spirituality, living by her faith and her prayers. The only picture of her that exists shows her with high cheekbones, long, almond-shaped eyes—Grade said they were sparkling green, like his—with a tall forehead, wearing a kerchief over her matron's wig, a severe expression on her face. She must have been very young in that picture. The Vella of *My Mother's Sabbath Days* is different. "Why," her son asks despairingly, "is she so humble, so meek toward everyone? Why does she always feel that she has sinned before God?" In his portrayal, she is the very image of De Quincey's "Our Lady of Sighs":

> Hers is the meekness that belongs to the hopeless. Murmur she may, but it is in her sleep. Whisper she may, but it is to herself in the twilight. . . . Mutter she does at times, but it is in solitary places that are desolate as she is desolate, in ruined cities, and when the sun has gone down to his rest. . . .

It had been Chaim Grade's dream to rescue his mother from her hard fate, from her unremitting toil, to give her hope, to give her joy. What he gave her instead was utmost despair, the despair of losing him to "the path of wanderings," and she was to die, to be killed, not knowing whether her only son would survive. Vella Grade's fate was that of ultimate sacrifice and self-sacrifice. Her son knew it, and this knowledge became a terrible lifelong burden. And yet, if he was able to survive, and more, to create, it was because his mother became the guiding star of his life.

Inna Hecker Grade

To the memory of my mother,
daughter of Rabbi Rafael Blumenthal,

VELLA GRADE

Martyred in Vilna on Yom Kippur
5702—1941

To the memory of her neighbors,
the mothers of our Jewish street,
who lived together in holy poverty
and together went to their deaths

My Mother's Sabbath Days

The Garden

Reb Boruḥel and Blumele's children live in Argentina. Their photographs hang on the wall in a semicircle, and beneath them, like a star in the crescent of the moon, hangs the picture of the Ḥofetz-Ḥaim, the Sage of Radun. He is a tiny Jew with great eyes full of sadness and kindness, wearing a tall winter hat. Whenever the two old people look at the pictures of their children, and their gaze falls upon the Sage of Radun, Blumele straightens her kerchief so that not a wisp of hair may be seen, and Reb Boruḥel imagines he can hear the Ḥofetz-Ḥaim sigh:

"Ah, my children, my dear children, the Messiah is coming any day, and you are not ready."

Reb Boruḥel's ashen-gray beard quivers. He looks at his sons' pictures and murmurs:

"Who knows whether over there they are still good Jews? Who knows whether they even keep the Sabbath . . .?"

All his life Reb Boruḥel has been a member of the Artisans' Synagogue, where the pious craftsmen worship. Now, in his old age, when his children are supporting him, he has ceased working. And yet, one day every year he becomes a craftsman once again: on the morning after the Day of Atonement, when he helps to erect the sukkah for the festival of Sukkoth. True, he does not himself hammer the nails into the boards, nor does he put up the roof of branches and twigs; but he hands to the builders the rusty old nails, which he keeps from year to year in a tin box. When the neighbors make their reckoning of the sukkah's cost, and how much each must pay as his share, they forget to acknowledge Reb Boruḥel's contribution. His feelings are hurt, and he never fails to remind them:

"And what about my nails?"

The neighbors laugh and express the wish that he might live to hand them his rusty nails yet again the following year.

One year, shortly before Passover, Reb Boruḥel fell very ill. His withered body became so hot and feverish that the neighbors thought: "Soon Blumele will be a widow." And they were mocked by Alterka the goose-dealer, a coarse fellow:

"This year you'll have to glue the sukkah together with spittle, unless Reb Boruḥel leaves you his rusty nails in his will."

God, however, performed a miracle, and Reb Boruḥel survived to totter off his sickbed. Yet, instead of rejoicing, he was downcast. The neighbors, he was sure, would now look upon him as some unholy freak of nature.

OVER THE CROOKED COBBLESTONES Reb Boruḥel makes his way with tiny steps, his arms hanging at his sides like the drooping chains of the wall-clock in his small dwelling. Soon the clock will wind down, and the pendulum come to a standstill. He is approached by Alterka the goose-dealer, who has just had a drink and is in a good mood:

"Nu, Reb Boruḥel, squirmed away from the Angel of Death this time, did you? You might yet hang on for another year—maybe even two."

Reb Boruḥel hangs his head like a convicted criminal, and pleads in self-defense:

"Layb the innkeeper is older than I—a lot older."

"What a comparison!" Alterka bursts into laughter. "Layb the inn-keeper pours half a quart of whiskey down his gullet every day—and when you pour in oil, the lamp keeps burning. But you—you mumble the 'asher yotzer' when you leave the outhouse and then wipe your fingers as though you're milking them. So I ask you—how long will you be able to go on fooling the Angel of Death?"

Crestfallen, Reb Boruḥel walks away. How can he be angry at the goose-dealer who insults him to his face when even in his own Artisans' Synagogue he is no longer called to the bima to lead the prayers on holidays? The old rabbi, Reb Hirshele, peace be upon him, would never have allowed them to take this longstanding right away from their fellow workingman just because his voice had grown weak. He, Boruḥel, has never failed to pay his dues, nor did he permit his children, long ago, to rebel against the authorities. Many years earlier, at a time when all the youngsters were running through the streets shouting *"Doloi Nikolai!"*— "Down with Czar Nicholas!"—he had dragged his sons to the synagogue. Every Sabbath morning he forced them, eyelids still heavy with sleep, to come with him to services; on the way he held their hands tightly in his own, to keep them from running away. After the services, he would take from his pockets cakes and sweets, stuff buckwheat cookies into their mouths, and make them sit next to him at the table where the rabbi was giving a lesson in the *Ḥayei Adam*. Now his children are scattered far and wide, the old householders have all passed on, and the right of leading the prayers on festivals has been taken from him, just because his voice has grown weak.

It is with these gloomy thoughts that the old man crosses the courtyard and turns slowly toward the gate.

At one side of the gate sits his wife, Blumele; on the other side, my
mother. Each is surrounded by large baskets full of fruit and smaller
ones filled with green vegetables, and they compete fiercely for customers.
People wonder: The two women are partners in the business, so what
does it matter which one a customer buys from? But it seems that it does
matter. Neither woman is willing to lose one of her steady customers—
just in case, as happens every Monday and Thursday, they break up the
partnership yet again, neither wants her housewives to get accustomed
to buying from the former partner. And besides, neither of them likes
to stand idle, hands in apron pockets, while brisk business is going on
across the way. So the two women start to bicker, they recall and relive
old wrongs, and finally they begin attacking each other's family.

"Why do you carry on so?" my mother asks. "After all, your children—praised be the Lord—send you enough to live on."

Mention of her children instantly inflames Blumele's walleye; jumping from her stool, she runs up to my mother:

"Why do you begrudge me my children? If your son, your Kaddish,
went to work, you wouldn't need to drag my customers away from me.
I've news for you: Your Chaimka will become a rabbi like I am a
rebbetzin."

"Salt in your eyes, pepper in your nose!" My mother springs up
from her stool, almond-shaped eyes green with anger. "The nerve of the
woman! You dare to attack my Chaimka! Tfoo, tfoo, tfoo . . ." And she
spits three times to ward off the Evil Eye.

Just then Reb Boruḥel, with his mincing little steps, reaches the gate.
Catching sight of her little old man, Blumele runs toward him:

"Boruḥ, I don't know what Vella wants from my life! We're partners,
everything goes into one pocket, yet when I'm doing some business, she
flares up."

Ever since leaving his sickbed, the old man has been fearful of a
curse, and he does not want to get involved. So he looks into his wife's
baskets, where the apples are beginning to rot, and into the baskets filled
with bunches of last year's onions, potatoes that are already sprouting
beards, cabbages, carrots, and, the most prized of all, the latest crop of
this season—fresh red radishes. My mother's stand contains exactly the
same wares. Reb Boruḥel grasps his sparse ashen-gray beard, as though
comparing it to the potatoes' sprouting beards, and concludes that he has
no reason to envy these growing things: they have no souls. After long
deliberation, he stammers out his verdict:

"Divine Providence apportions to each of us exactly what and how much is his due. So why quarrel? Let one sell the fruit and the other the vegetables."

Toothless as he is, one can hardly make out what he says; he smacks his lips—a sign that he is angry—and speaks sharply to his wife:

"And don't start up with Vella. She is a widow and her boy is an orphan."

" 'Don't start up with Grandfather—he is an orphan!' " Blumele mimics. "You always stand up for my enemies. Vella's son isn't a little boy any more—he's stronger than you and me together. Her Chaimka will become a rabbi like I am a rebbetzin."

"Whether my Chaimka will ever become a rabbi, I don't know," says my mother. "But I do know that he never walks around without a cap on his head."

Blumele understands: her partner is taunting her over the photographs her sons have sent home, in which they are bareheaded and the daughters-in-law have their hair uncovered; her walleye turns still redder, and she bursts into raucous laughter.

"Well, now you're making a proper fool of yourself! The whole world knows that your brat collects discarded wooden boxes and fills them with soil from 'Old Barefoot' Park. You yourself gave him money to buy all sorts of seeds to plant in those boxes. And your son, the would-be rabbi, works on that garden of his like a regular peasant."

"What could I do? He kept nagging and pestering me until I finally gave in and let him have the money for his seeds." Confused and embarrassed, my mother tries to justify herself. "And I can't see what kind of terrible sin he's committing. The courtyard is like a wooden box—the only bit of green is the mildew on the roofs—so he planted a few flower-pots. You yourself, I'm sure, also enjoy looking at the blossoms."

"According to you, then, I'm just a gossip-monger. But everybody knows that your gardener even waters his flowers on the Sabbath. Ask my Boruḥ, if you don't believe me."

"It's true, it's true—" Reb Boruḥel nods his head in agreement— "I saw it with my own eyes. And watering plants is one of the prohibited kinds of work—a real desecration of the Sabbath."

My mother is stunned—never had she expected something like this. Without another word, she leaves her stall unattended and goes to look for me to vent her bitterness upon me.

"It's easy for Blumele to talk," she mutters to herself. "She has the heart of a cutthroat. She wasn't even ashamed to tell me recently that once, when her oldest son didn't want to get up in time for morning prayers, she herself put a pillow over his head and Reb Boruḥel beat him until the boy fainted. She knows I have only this one child, so she wants me to make him live in terror. 'On a tree that's bent low all the goats jump.' Blumele has a husband to stand up for her. But who will speak for me—my only son, who, for the sake of flowers, desecrates the Sabbath?"

Just at this time I am standing over my boxes, watering the plants. I am surrounded by neighbors poking fun at me.

"He'll make us proud of him yet," says Alterka the goose-dealer. "He'll stand at street corners and sell bouquets grown in his own garden to all the fine ladies, like the bath-goy who sells fresh besoms in the Synagogue Courtyard next to the public baths."

"What do you want of him?" protests another neighbor, pretending to defend me. "He doesn't want his mother to have to deal with the wholesalers—so he'll supply her with vegetables himself, grown in his own flowerpots."

I do not answer them, but continue working with stubborn determination. To me it is a matter of life and death that my planting succeed.

There is only one man who does not ridicule me—Sneszko, the janitor of our courtyard, a Gentile and a drunkard. When he is drunk, he shouts: "Better to be a hired hand in a village than a governor for the yids!" But when he is sober, he teaches me how to care for my plants:

"Dummy! You put too many seeds into one box. These aren't your mother's baskets, where plums and cabbages rot together. When the sun is hot, the young sprouts have to be covered. Cover them better. This isn't a yid's skullcap on the point of the head . . ."

"What the boy doesn't come up with! A dybbuk has got into him!" is the neighbors' verdict as they disperse. Sneszko, too, leaves. Now my mother arrives, stands before me, and begins counting off my sins on her fingers:

"Mischief-maker! Look at what I must endure because of you. When you were little, you fought with all the children in the street. The fathers of the boys you beat up would come running to me and shout, 'I'll tear your brat to pieces!' And I had to hide you under my apron. Then you got the crazy idea of raising birds, just like little barefoot gentile boys who carry pigeons around in their shirts. Later you picked up somewhere a big, shaggy black dog that you dragged around with you day and night. Now you've become a peasant with a garden. And as if that weren't enough, you water your flowers on the Sabbath. Don't you know that's forbidden? My great scholar . . .!"

DAY AND NIGHT I stayed in the courtyard guarding my garden, lest other boys carry it off, or the wagon drivers entering the courtyard crush my boxes under their wheels. But in the end I could not save my garden.

One morning I found all the soil scattered and the plants trampled.

The janitor Sneszko, who had been teaching me how to care for the plants, had come home dead drunk the night before and destroyed everything. Now the neighbors no longer mocked me. They, too, were sorry to see the courtyard barren once again, without a hint of greenery. Alterka the goose-dealer cursed the janitor:

"The anti-Semite begrudges Jewish children a bit of grass. May grass grow from his head!"

My mother did not know whether to mourn or rejoice:

"Perhaps now he'll return to the beth midrash to study? . . ."

The Treasure

THE QUARREL of the two partners lasts all that week. Whenever a customer approaches my mother, she responds only grudgingly and in monosyllables, as if to say, "Go over to Blumele." Blumele, for her part, treats the customer even more coldly, so that, by now justifiably angry, he leaves without buying anything: May he, he says to himself, never lack for coins in his pocket as surely as there will be no lack of sellers of rotting apples.

On Friday, shortly before sunset and the onset of the Sabbath, each partner takes her own baskets home; each feels burdened as if she bore a large hump on her back: the following night, after Havdalah, they will have to settle their weekly accounts—and here they're not even speaking to each other.

On the Sabbath, at the time of the Afternoon Service, the two neighbors seat themselves at the entrances of their tiny dwellings, each with her book of Hebrew-Yiddish devotions. Both read aloud with a chanting melody, so as to drown out the drunken screaming and laughter emanating from the janitor's apartment. Sneszko has invited his village relatives over, and their Sunday celebration has gotten off to an early start.

We live in the back room of a blacksmith's shop. The room has no windows, and is lighted all week long by a smoky kerosene lamp, even during the day. On the Sabbath, however, when the smithy stands empty, Mother and I stay in the front room, in the workshop itself. I am gloomy and dejected, thinking about my ruined garden, while Mother, at the doorway, reads aloud from the *Lev Tov*:

"It is the custom to delay the recital of the evening prayers at the close of the Sabbath, because the souls of sinners do not return to the punishments of Gehenna until after the congregations on earth have concluded the final prayers, 'May the graciousness of the Lord . . .' and 'But Thou art holy. . . .' For on Friday night, when the congregation chants the opening blessings of the Sabbath, the Angel of the Realm of the Dead calls out: 'Sinners, leave Gehenna!' When Israel begins the Sabbath, the sinners may leave the fire and cool themselves in a stream of water. From this arises the custom that one whose father and mother have died may not drink water on the Sabbath between the afternoon and evening prayers, for they may at that very time be cooling themselves in the water . . .

"Do you hear, Chaimka?" Mother turns to face the room, speaking softly so that Blumele will not overhear. "Do you hear what is written? And you, woe is me, you have watered your flowers on the Sabbath."

She heaves a sigh and resumes reading:

"At the conclusion of the Sabbath we sing of 'The Prophet Elijah' for two reasons. First, neither the Messiah nor the Prophet Elijah will appear on the Sabbath; therefore, as soon as the Sabbath ends, we sing once more to the Prophet Elijah that he should come and bring us the tidings of salvation. The second reason is that the Prophet Elijah, together with thousands of angels, sits down at the conclusion of the Sabbath and records the names of all those who observed the Sabbath properly, and also the names of those who, God forbid, have desecrated the Sabbath . . . do you hear, Chaimka?"

Blumele sits on her doorstep with her own book, the *Menorath HaM'or*. Her brass spectacles, held by strings, keep sliding down to the tip of her nose. Her small wizened head is buried deep in the large, yellowing pages, each of which is divided by a black line, with the text in Hebrew above and the Yiddish translation below.

This arrangement reminds Blumele of the brick house of the rich produce dealer from whom she buys her wares. On the upper floors he lives with his family in a lavishly furnished apartment. Whenever she goes up there, she has to wait in the foyer like a beggar; and she is frightened by the incomprehensible foreign language that the wholesaler's educated daughters and daughters-in-law speak among themselves. But downstairs, in the vegetable cellar together with the other market women, her spirit revives and she feels at home. Here one may haggle with the wholesaler to one's heart's content, and any reminder he attempts concerning payment of the past year's debts earns him a retort that effectively silences him. Just so, not to make a comparison, appears to her the *Menorath HaM'or* with the thick line in the middle of each page, the sacred tongue above the line and plain Yiddish below:

"We find in the *Midrash Tanḥuma* a story about Rabbi Akiba. It happened once that he visited a cemetery, and there met a man whose face was as black as coal, carrying a load of wood on his shoulders and running with this load as swiftly as a horse. Rabbi Akiba commanded the man to stop and spoke to him: 'My son, why are you doing such hard work? If you are a slave, I will buy you your freedom; if you do it because of poverty, I will give you wealth. Are you a living man or an evil spirit?' And the man answered: 'I am a dead man, and every day I must chop wood and then I am burned on that wood.' Then Rabbi Akiba asked him: 'What was your occupation in life?' And the dead man answered: 'I was a debt collector, and I fawned upon the rich, but the poor I hounded to their deaths' . . . do you hear, Boruhel?" asks Blumele, turning around to the room behind her.

Reb Boruhel is lying on his bed and a shiver passes through his withered frame, even on this warm summer afternoon. He moans and stammers:

"I was never a collector of debts, I've never killed anyone, and I've been poor all my life. Oh, Father in Heaven!"

Reb Boruhel—by nature somewhat ill-tempered, and now trembling as well, as though in a high fever—sits up suddenly on his bed, flails about with his bony arms, and smacks his loose lips:

"It's your fault! It's all your fault! For every little thing you swear, 'May I live to see my children in Argentina!' I plead with you as a man pleads with a cutthroat for his life: 'Don't make me go across the ocean to a goyish land. My bones shouldn't have to roll underground when the Messiah comes, let us go straight to the Land of Israel.' But you insist on going to Argentina, and I will just have to roll."

Blumele does not answer—she doesn't want my mother to hear her arguing with her husband. It is enough that she has already endured Mother's reproaches for the hatless state of her sons in their photographs. And so Blumele pushes her brass spectacles higher up the bridge of her nose and, losing part of the story, resumes her reading with the account of Rabbi Akiba's wanderings from city to city, until he came to Alduka, the town where lived Shushmira, widow of that dead man. There he found also the dead man's son, who had not yet been circumcised. So he performed the circumcision and sat down with the boy to teach him Torah. That very hour the sinner was released from his sufferings. Afterward he appeared to Rabbi Akiba in a dream and said to him: "Your soul shall rest in Paradise, for you have delivered me from Gehenna. . . ."

"Do you hear, Boruhel?"

"I don't have the strength to go listen to a proper preacher," groans Reb Boruhel, "so I have to listen to my wife's preaching." He stares at the wall clock, whose face bears Hebrew letters instead of numerals. The pendulum swings back and forth sedately, as though it too wishes to avoid haste on the Sabbath. The rusty chain with the weight sinks down slowly lower and lower. "Tonight, after Havdalah—God willing—I shall rewind the clock," thinks the old man. "Oy, if only one could rewind a man like a clock, so that he too could go on and continue to tick . . ." Gathering all his strength, Reb Boruhel climbs off the bed, which is piled high with pillows and quilts, and pours water from a pitcher over his fingers to purify them. It is time to go to the synagogue for the Afternoon Service.

I, too, determine to overcome my grief, and go out into the courtyard and look around. Of my garden not a trace remains. The broken wooden boxes with the crushed plants have been removed, the scattered soil has been swept away.

Blumele sees me and closes her book.

"Chaimka, won't you come in and taste a little of my prune compote? My Boruḥ didn't even touch it. It's true your mother is angry at me, but I've done you no harm. You can listen to me—I already have grandchildren older than you."

At that moment Reb Boruḥel shuffles out into the courtyard. My mother calls out to him:

"Reb Boruḥ—may you live and be well—I have a kettle full of hot tea waiting for you on my stove. Don't shame me by refusing. What I wish you is what I wish for myself. So, why does your Blumele have to be angry at me?"

" 'Whatever is decreed by Fate, comes surely soon or late,' " Blumele blurts out.

"And he who does not stint in honoring the Sabbath is repaid by the Sabbath," adds my mother. "As we find in the story of Joseph Lover-of-the-Sabbath—so, I think, he was called—he bought a very costly fish, and when he opened it he found inside a pearl worth thirteen chests of gold. So, Blumele, tell me, why should we fight with one another?"

"True, what reason do we have to quarrel?" Blumele, overjoyed, rises. "Vellenka, come in to eat some prune compote."

"No, Blumele, first you come to me to drink a glass of tea. It's a pity, Reb Boruḥ, that you're in such a hurry to get to services. You go along with him"—Mother signals to me that I should not let the weak old man walk alone. Her face is radiant with the joy of having made peace with her partner—a stone has been lifted from her heart.

"Oy, women, women!" Reb Boruḥel shakes his head as he starts off with his tiny mincing steps.

We pass the janitor's apartment, within which I can see peasants with thick mustaches and flushed faces. Sneszko, gazing out the window, gnashes his teeth at me; he is still reveling in his destruction of my plants.

"That murderer is laughing at me yet," I cry out to Reb Boruḥel. "I'll throw a stone at his head!"

"Heaven forbid! The janitor and his gang will start a pogrom." The old man is trembling. "How do you even dare to talk about throwing a stone at him? Whoever heard of a Jewish boy having such goyish violence in him? Besides, I can understand that a doctor might deal with plants and herbs to find medicines to cure people, but who ever heard of a young Jewish scholar putting aside his Gemara to occupy himself with flowers? Better, Chaimel, you should think how good it is to be a Jew. They carry on, get drunk, and devour the flesh of pigs, while we go to the synagogue for afternoon prayers. Come now, let's hurry! Let's hurry!"

It is really himself the old man is trying to move along. He barely has the strength to set one foot in front of the other, holding onto my shoulder all the while so as not to fall. The narrow street, with its shuttered shops, seems frozen in the blue stillness, like a worshipper silently absorbed, with closed eyes, in the recitation of the Eighteen Benedictions. The moss-covered, hunchbacked roofs resemble the bent shoulders of bearded Jews jostling forward, the better to hear the words of a wandering preacher; even the cobblestones seem to stare heavenward with pious, sharp-featured faces. A triangular garret-window raises its head toward the blue heights, like an old man with a peaked skullcap looking to see whether any star is yet visible in the sky, the signal for beginning the evening prayers and the Counting of the Omer. But it is still too early— within the tiny whitewashed beth midrash they are still chanting the Afternoon Service. From outside we can already hear the sleepy voice of the cantor. Reb Boruḥel, his hand leaning on my shoulder, bends over me; his sparse beard trembles against my cheek as he sings softly along with the cantor: "Thou art One and Thy Name is One. . . ."

RETURNING HOME after the evening service, I find two policemen at our gate, and an uproar within the courtyard. The wife of Sneszko the janitor stands wringing her hands and bewailing her fate before her Jewish neighbors:

"I pleaded with him: 'Stefan, forget the village!' But he told me: 'No, I want to be my own master, not a janitor for the yids. I am a Pole and a Catholic,' he said. So he sent word for his brother to come see him, and his brother came with his sons. And my Stefan says to him: 'Give me half of the house, of the land and of the livestock.' So his brother answers: 'Why should I give you half? You wanted to be a town dandy. But I,' he says, 'rebuilt the house, worked the fields, and fattened the hogs with my own bread. Why should I now give you half?' So they kept downing glasses of our home brew, gobbled up my sausages, sweated, and swore at each other. Finally my brother-in-law stabbed Stefan with his knife. And his two sons screamed, 'Push the knife in deeper!' Stefan's clothes were covered with blood, and he vomited up all the whiskey. So they took him away to the hospital. And that murderer and his bastards ran off. My misfortune! Now who will sweep the courtyard and open the gate? Every night someone comes home after midnight. Then you have to get out of bed undressed, and look for the key in the dark—and no one even gives you ten groschen for your trouble. And to stab his own brother! Dear Lord Jesus! May he be smashed to bits, that brother-in-law of mine!"

When my mother catches sight of me in the crowd around the janitor's wife, she falls upon me and hugs and kisses me, as though I have just arisen from the dead. Barely able to catch her breath, she drags me into the house.

"God in Heaven, how much I have to suffer because of you! When I heard the uproar in the courtyard, my heart stood still with fear. I thought you were in the middle of the fight, and they were attacking you with the knife."

"But I was away at services with Reb Boruḥel."

"If I hadn't known you were in the synagogue, my soul would have departed by now. But who can ever be sure what you're up to? Now do you see what can happen because of gardening? The janitor also wanted to have his own garden and orchards and fields. I feel very sorry for the man. But now, my son, go back to studying the holy Torah. Your father's books are collecting dust in boxes under your bed. Ah, how terrible it is, to be so cramped the way we are, suffocating together in one small room behind a smithy!"

My mother burst into tears. "Ever since the day you were born, your father's affairs, peace be upon him, went steadily from bad to worse—as though that were the ransom the Almighty accepted for your life. First we had to move from our light and airy rooms to a basement in Zawalna Street, and from there we came here, to the rear room of the blacksmith's workshop."

I am choking on my mother's tears. In order to keep from crying myself, I become impatient, angry.

"What are you crying for? It's only early summer, not yet Shavuoth. Father's yohrzeit isn't until the 25th of Elul, just before Rosh Hashanah. Then I'll stand at the lectern to lead the prayers, I'll recite the Kaddish, and I'll go with you to the cemetery."

"And does that mean you don't have to study the rest of the year? Of all your father's wealth, of all the cupboards full of silverware, all that remains are his books. And those you leave under your bed together with your old shoes."

I bend down under the bed and pull out, not a box full of books, but a small box with flowers growing in it—nasturtiums.

At the time I was planting my flowers, I hadn't had enough space in the courtyard for all my wooden boxes, and had put one of them under my bed. At first, I took it out from time to time to water it, but then I became so engrossed in my garden blooming in the courtyard that I forgot about the plants under my bed. Now I stare in amazement at the blooming nasturtiums. Their stems are thin, tall, and soft, the calyxes a consumptive yellow in hue, the leaves watery-looking, with no succulent greenness.

"How can flowers grow under a bed, without sun or rain?" I cry out in astonishment.

"Because you didn't water them on the Sabbath, they grew even in the darkness." Mother once again finds a reason for rebuking me. "In this, too, you can see the miracles of the Almighty."

"But they look dead," I say, and crawl back under my bed. This time I pull out a box full of thin pamphlets, covered with a layer of dust.

"Haggadahs for Passover! Why did Father need so many Haggadahs?"

"For his pupils," Mother answers. "What a man your father was in those days! He wore a top hat and a full, well-combed black beard. The finest families considered it an honor when he accepted their children into his ḥeder."

"Mama, here are more books. Grammar books that teach you how to speak Hebrew correctly."

"I'm not surprised. Your father knew all of the Bible by heart. It's not my fault that you know so little about him. Once a Russian government minister came to visit your father, to observe how children are taught in a Jewish school. The boys were just then studying the Bible portion that tells how the angels visited Abraham to announce that his wife would bear him a son. So your father said to the minister, in Russian, that just as the angels were gracious to Abraham and appeared to him in human form, he hoped that the minister would be similarly gracious to Jewish teachers. Your father had to speak that way, but it must have been quite painful for him to have to compare an angel with a fonya. . . . And what sort of book is that?"

"It's by Maimonides. He was a philosopher and a great doctor in Egypt."

"So you see, one can be both an educated person and a pious Jew. Now do you understand what kind of father you had? And such a man, in his old age, had to become a night watchman!" Mother bursts into tears once more as she recalls how Father would go out every evening to make his rounds as a guard, girded with a rope, and with a heavy staff would knock on the doors of stores to make sure they were closed, and check the locks. But no matter how bitter his life became, he would still study his books. Why, then, shouldn't I study? After all, I had inherited a treasure trove of books from my father, a real treasure!

Blumele

THE SUMMER PASSED, and after the festival of Sukkoth, I left for a yeshiva. Before my departure Mother took me to see her partner and her husband, to bid them farewell. Reb Boruhel gave me his blessing; swaying to and fro, he stretched his hands above my head and murmured:

"Lord of the Universe! I know that I have won no great merit in Your eyes. But I do have this one merit—that all my life I have been a workingman, one who earned his daily bread by the labor of his hands. On this account I ask You, help the son of this poor widow to succeed in the study of Your Torah."

Mother wept bitterly and was at once comforted and scolded by Blumele:

"He's only going to a yeshiva barely three paces away from you, and you're wailing as though they were taking him away into the army. Don't worry, nothing will happen to him. There are Jews everywhere, and when a youngster studies the Torah, he finds favor with people. What should I say? I sent away my children, not to a neighboring town to study Torah but to the other side of the ocean, to a country where there are still savages."

I RETURNED HOME from the yeshiva a week before Passover, appearing suddenly, unannounced, at the gate where Mother sat next to her fruit baskets. The other side of the gate, Blumele's accustomed place, was empty.

Mother does not notice me. She sits stock still, her hands clasped in despair, and does not call out to customers. Her face seems to have become more taut; the wisps of hair that creep out from under her wig are grayer, and her entire body more bent.

"Mama!"

She opens her almond-shaped green eyes wide and gives me a bewildered look, as though unable to recognize me. Suddenly she comes to with a start and, weeping, clasps me around the neck.

"Reb Boruhel and Blumele have died!"

"When?" Frightened, I am barely able to utter the question.

"In the winter, within just three months of each other. Blumele died just three weeks ago."

Though it is still broad daylight, Mother takes her baskets from the gate and goes back to our dwelling with me. She sits down, facing me. She sways to and fro, like a mourner sitting on a low mourning-stool, and, weeping, tells the story of the old couple's deaths.

"One Sabbath morning Blumele got up as usual, took the teakettle from the oven, and waited for Reb Boruhel to come out from the alcove where he slept, to drink his glass of tea and go to services. She waits and waits, but he doesn't come. Then she begins to listen carefully; but he isn't moaning or tossing about on the bed. Those last few months, poor man, he was always shivering and shaking with cold. . . . I, too, am always cold now. I feel a frost in my very bones. I don't know whether it's from overwork and lack of sleep, or because I'm always alone at night, and deafened by the silence. Or maybe it's age—I'm no longer young, my son. . . . Blumele rushed into the alcove and found her dear old man sleeping the eternal sleep. Reb Boruhel died on the Sabbath, truly like a saint.

"That evening, after the Sabbath had ended, when they came to lift the body off the bed onto the floor, Blumele wanted to put a pillow under her Boruhel's head so that he would lie more comfortably. Her sorrow seemed to have confused her thoughts. All night long she sat next to the corpse, talking endlessly—to me, to the other neighbors who came by, to the Psalm-sayers:

" 'I'll never argue again with my Boruhel about where we should go. I won't cry out anymore: "Let's go to Argentina, to our children!" And he won't contradict me anymore and say: "No, let's go to the Land of Israel, to our forefathers." He's gone on a different journey now, an eternal journey.'

"I begged her: 'Blumele, go lie down for a while.' But she answered me with a chant:

" 'What I would wish is to lie down next to my dear old man, but the Almighty did not want to take both our souls at once. Vellenka,' she turned to me, 'a young man prepares for his wedding all his bachelor days, yet the marriage ceremony lasts only a few minutes. Every human being fears death all his life, and yet from the moment of death to the burial no more than one day may pass. Why does the burial have to be rushed so? Why must the funeral be tomorrow? Let my dear old one stay with me at least one more day!'

"I wanted to answer that many portions of our Torah are devoted to the life and good deeds of our Father Abraham, but his death and burial are related in just a few scant verses. But I said nothing, because one may not attempt to comfort a mourner whose dead is still lying before him. She was speaking like someone bereft of her senses. She said to me:

" 'Look, Vellenka, the clock has stopped. No master craftsman knew how to fix it as well as my Boruḥel. Now the pendulum has stopped moving and the Hebrew letters on the face have closed their eyes.'

"When the first seven days of mourning had passed, she seemed suddenly to grow calm once again, but she no longer wished to go on selling fruit.

" 'Vella, let us dissolve our partnership,' she said to me.

"So we each made our reckoning, and asked each other's forgiveness for our foolish quarrels. She went off to the wholesaler and paid off all her debts—many so old that he had long since given up all hope of being paid. She took care of all my debts to him as well.

"Then she sat at her window, put on her brass spectacles, and with a blue pencil wrote a long letter to her children. She instructed them to be meticulous in reciting the Kaddish for their father, and ordered them to send money immediately so that she might be able to buy a burial plot for herself next to his grave, and also to order a gravestone for both of them.

"At the end of the thirty-day period of mourning, Blumele began to sell off all her belongings, leaving herself only the barest necessities. She went to the Artisans' Synagogue, where Reb Boruḥel had been a member all his life, and paid a fee to have a portion of Mishnah studied in his honor every day after the Morning Service. In addition, she paid the beadle to recite the Kaddish for her husband and also, when her time came, for her. She did not want to rely on her children.

" 'I do not want to come before God barefoot,' she said.

"The neighbors were surprised. 'Blumele, why are you selling everything? You'll be left with nothing but the four bare walls!' Then it turned out that she had made up her mind to move out of her home and into a little room that she had rented from strangers in another neighborhood.

" 'I have very little time left,' she said. 'I must prepare for a long journey, so I want to be alone with my holy books.'

"Everyone understood that she wasn't thinking of going to her children in Argentina—that it was preparations for an eternal journey of which she spoke. She bade her neighbors farewell and hired a porter with a wheelbarrow for her bedding. She herself carried her books in one hand, and in the other the old wall-clock—though she had never wound it again, she did not want to part with it. She stood for a few moments in the courtyard and we all heard her lament:

" 'Never again will I be able to watch my dear old man hand his nails to the builders of the sukkah. He guarded those nails from year to year, and kept them in a special box. Never again will I stand by the door of the sukkah to hear him recite the Kiddush. Never again will I carry his meals for him into the sukkah.'

"Thus did Blumele's lament continue on and on, and all the court-yard wept along with her. . . ."

Mother sits facing me, wringing her hands, painfully drawing out each anguished word. I look about me at our smithy-home. In my absence the walls have grown still blacker. The wooden beams of the ceiling creak and crack. Chunks of plaster are falling down, and the smoke of the bellows hangs in the air like a cloud. How dark and dreary it is! I feel a longing to return to the small town of my yeshiva. There, when one looks out through the windows of the beth midrash in the winter, one sees a high-domed sky, glistening snow-covered fields, a dark blue forest, and a frozen, silvery river that surrounds the town on all sides.

As though guessing my thoughts, Mother smiles at me through the mist of tears that hovers over her face.

"I know, my son, I know you are upset with me for greeting you with such news. I should be asking you about your studies, and how you are. But my heart is so full I don't know what to say first. Even a stone has little stones to keep it company—and I've been alone all winter. . . .

"Blumele moved in with strangers, into a tiny room with 'one step between the walls.' Every Sabbath I went over to see how she was. She lived quite far from here, next to the fish market near the Wilja. Blumele would serve me something, and ask about the neighbors, how my business was doing, and what you were writing from the yeshiva. Lately you wrote very seldom, and your handwriting was like chicken scratches, so that I could barely make it out. . . . After we talked awhile, I would take one of Blumele's books, and we would both sit down to recite prayers. Before I left, she would always say to me: 'Not everyone is like Moses Our Teacher, who himself wrote down the day of his death. None of us knows when our time will come. Should anything happen to me, ask your son to think of me during his holy studies. Remember, Vellenka—we used to be partners.'

"It was as though her heart had told her just how it would be. Then there came a week of extreme cold, of blizzards and knee-deep snow. I was frozen through and through, my feet were swollen from running around the markets, and that Sabbath I was so tired I didn't go to see Blumele. All week long my heart was uneasy—but how could I neglect my livelihood? I'm a slave to my baskets, and the wholesaler is always adding on to the account. The following Sabbath was even colder and windier, but this time I let nothing stop me. I put on my felt boots, wrapped myself up in shawls, and dragged myself all the way across to the Wilja. It took all my strength to get there—but I no longer found Blumele.

"She had fallen asleep forever, just like Reb Boruḥel. Her landlords, who were strangers, notified the cemetery committee, and also the beadle of the Artisans' Synagogue. The beadle came with some of the old men who had prayed together with Reb Boruḥel all those years, and they quickly took Blumele away and buried her in the 'good place,' next to her husband, in the plot she'd prepared for herself.

"What shall I tell you? I can't even begin to describe my pain, my sorrow, my bitterness. With her landlords I had no quarrel—how could they have known what a saintly woman had been living with them? An old woman paid them rent, so they gave her a room. It was upon the beadle's head that I poured out all my sorrow and anger. 'You,' I said to him, 'have the heart of a Tartar. How could you not notify our courtyard that Blumele had died?' He answers that with all the frost and snow, it had been at the peril of his own life that he attended the funeral; surely the neighbors wouldn't be willing to risk their lives to come in such weather. That's what he said—go argue with him! It was just fortunate that he at least thought to look in the closet and there found the clothes she'd prepared for her eternal journey. What a disgrace, if Blumele had been buried in shrouds sewn by strangers! The beadle wrote immediately to her children to notify them, and he is reciting the Kaddish, as she had arranged.

"Listen to me, my son—Blumele is already in the True World, and it no longer matters to her, but I tell you that she was determined to have a solitary funeral. She was seeking atonement. She was—may she forgive me—a woman who was hard on herself and on others. Because her children didn't follow in their father's footsteps, she took it as a penance upon herself that no one should accompany her to her final rest. I knew her well, my partner and my neighbor, may she keep away from the living.

"But there is still a hard lump pressing on my heart, and all my tears can't wash it away. If I had been at her funeral, I would have cried and mourned for her, and so found relief. As it is, I simply cannot believe she is no more.

"My son, my Kaddish—may you survive me and flourish—do think of her when you pray and when you study the Torah. I sinned against her many times. I envied her because her children helped her, while my life is so miserable. But if you keep her in mind in your studies and in your prayers, she will forgive me, and will be a righteous intercessor for you in Heaven."

Mother stands up and walks to a corner of the room, where she picks up several books and the clock that used to hang on the old couple's wall.

"Blumele's landlords gave me these. They told me the old woman had asked them many times that, when the time came, they should give her books to me, her former partner. For you she left the clock with the Hebrew letters.

"And it seems to me that you mustn't shame Blumele: you must wind the clock and hang it on the wall so it may keep the right time again. It's very old, of course, and a little rusty and tarnished, but once you clean it, it will tell you exactly the correct time for everything you have to do. Just be careful not to break it when you clean it."

I gaze in silent dejection at the clock face with its Hebrew letters. All the way home from the yeshiva I had been thinking with boyish pride of how my mother would glory in me, and what joy my homecoming would bring to Reb Boruhel and Blumele, who had sent me off with blessings and tears.

Once again there comes before my eyes the small town with the great forest that rustles mysteriously at the edge of the heavens.

How sad is the sunset in a forest that has been cut down! Only yesterday the setting sun hid behind its dense branches, but today the sunbeams seek in vain for the treetops. Of century-old trees all that remains is the roots, rotting in the earth. . . .

New Neighbors

ALTERKA THE GOOSE-DEALER has a stall in the poultry market in our courtyard. So as to be closer to his workplace, he finds it only sensible to move into the vacant apartment that had once been the home of Reb Boruhel and Blumele. In the mornings he used to have to come running from his home, ten blocks away, to open the shop; besides, if you live next door, it is easier to guard against thieves trying to make off with the stock in the night. So says Alterka the goose-dealer.

The neighbors, however, know the truth: Alterka has lost most of his money and daily curses the fate that has compelled him to move into this courtyard of riffraff. The courtyard residents, for their part, are by no means pleased with their new neighbor. Only my mother is happy—no longer will she feel so eerily lonely. Ever since the deaths of Reb Boruhel and Blumele, their home has filled her with dread, as though it were the ablution chamber at the cemetery.

Alterka is short, stocky, and round, like a barrel of sauerkraut; his feet are crooked, as if inhabited by a dybbuk with a duck's webbed feet. His wife is a tall, heavy woman with goggle eyes that bulge out like fists. The third member of the family is a black tomcat, overfed and lazy. He lies always stretched out on the tin countertop, next to the blood-stained cleaver, near the plump, plucked geese, yet he touches nothing, not so much as a gizzard, a wing, or even a chicken's neck. He paces about the courtyard with slow, measured steps, and is so fat that, like his mistress, he can barely breathe.

Lisa, Alterka's wife, is known as "the Madame." She speaks very politely to customers, but keeps her distance from the ordinary women of the neighborhood. Her most important customers she addresses only in Russian. But there came one occasion when she gave her neighbors cause to gape in astonishment at the slop-tub of profanities she proved capable of spewing forth.

It happened when wholesalers from Warsaw brought wagonloads of frozen geese into the city. "We do honest business!" proclaimed the Warsovians in their own dialect. But the Lithuanian women did not trust the Polish Jews, and all the goose-dealers banded together: no one would pay a higher price—let the Polish good-for-nothings choke on their merchandise. Then, suddenly, word spread that Lisa had secretly bought the

Polish geese at a very good price. That was when the great battle broke out. The other goose-dealers screamed:

"We—honest fools that we are—trust her. We hold together like steel and iron, while she goes behind our backs and gets cozy with the Warsaw wholesalers. Now how do you like our Madame, who is so well-bred and speaks only pure Russian?"

The icy-sweet smile left Lisa's face and she burst out: "You pocky sluts." Her loud-mouthed colleagues, women of valor though they were, retreated as though drops of dirty rainwater had trickled under their shawls and onto their hair and necks.

An even fiercer fight broke out between Lisa's husband and the slaughterhouse. The slaughterers complained that the imported poultry was slaughtering them: no one would now come to them to have a fowl killed, everyone would run to buy the cheap Polish geese. Alterka sprang at one of the slaughterers and attacked him. For this his poultry was very nearly placed under a rabbinic ban. He had breathed fire and brimstone against the slaughterers ever since, and was convinced that they had placed a curse upon him—as witness the fact that he has had to leave his airy, pleasant chambers to move into a courtyard of paupers.

He has not, however, lost his spirit. On the very first Sabbath he shows his mettle.

Every Sabbath at the time of the Afternoon Service, my mother would take her sacred books and sit outside, beside her door, to read them. Our cat, with the white spot on her nose, sits next to my mother, her tail curled under her. She yawns deeply, taking care, however, not to swallow any flies on this the Sabbath day. Through the open door directly across the way, Mother observes Lisa placing a basin full of boiling hot water on a stool.

A question arises: Where has the Madame obtained hot water? Still, since there is no smoke coming from the chimney, Mother does not wish to commit the grievous sin of suspecting a daughter of Israel of having secretly lit a fire on the Sabbath.

Then, however, she sees Lisa let down her hair, shampoo it like a young girl, and tear at it with a comb, not in the least embarrassed to be standing half-naked right in front of her husband. Such a desecration of the Sabbath! Mother is greatly upset. But she remains silent, for Lisa might well say: "What right do you have to stick your nose into what goes on in someone else's house?"

Mother is pained to see what sort of people have moved into the home of the pious Reb Boruhel and Blumele. She wants to go back in, so as not to be forced to witness such goings-on. But it is dark inside the smithy; one could ruin one's eyes by trying to read there. Besides, on the Sabbath she did not like to sit in the workshop, next to the bellows, amidst boxes of coal, massive hammers, vises with gaping, lethal-looking mouths, steel saws with fanglike teeth. So she remains seated at her threshold and tries to immerse herself once again in her Yiddish Pentateuch.

Alterka, dressed like a dandy, comes out of his house, examines his fat fingers awhile, then takes a knife from his pocket and begins to trim his fingernails. While doing this he calls out in a pleasant voice: "Lisa, are you ready?"

Now Mother does speak up, gently, almost apologetically:

"Reb Alter, today is the Sabbath."

"So what?" He pretends not to understand.

"Don't you know that on the Sabbath one may not cut one's nails?"

"What business is it of yours?"

Mother throws caution to the winds: "But you sell kosher poultry to Jewish families."

That is all he needs to hear. Enraged, he begins to scream:

"So don't buy any more derma for stuffing from me, my fine lady! Go report me to the slaughterers, report me to your son, the bookworm. Lisa, how do you like this new Devorah-Esther, the saint?"

"Why do you bother talking to the old frump?" answers Lisa from inside the house.

My mother rises, takes up her books, and retires into the smithy. She is not about to profane the sacred day by getting into an argument with such a lout. Alterka calls out after her:

"Just wait, I'm going to smoke a cigar, too!"

"Your mouth may yet come out on the back of your head!" is my mother's parting blessing as she slams the door shut. Our cat barely manages to jump back in time to keep her tail from getting caught; she remains sitting alone outside the door.

Through the window, Mother sees "Madame" emerge from her house dressed in the height of fashion. Above her large head, topped by a small hat, there hovers a large, flowery parasol. Although it is not raining, and the sun isn't very hot, Lisa carries this bright silken parasol on the Sabbath just to show it off on Broad Street. She resembles a large wooden barrel topped by an overturned bowl, with a flat plate suspended above the bowl. Her short, stout husband, striding lightly along beside her, slides his left hand under her arm. In his right hand he carries a walking-stick, while his potbelly bobs before him.

The pair are followed by their fat tomcat, who pads along quietly and stealthily, so his master and mistress will not notice him. But clever as the cat is, Lisa is cleverer yet. She stops, turns her entire body around very slowly, and her husband turns with her. She says nothing, but he understands what she wants and goes for the cat with his stick. The cat, too, understands her intention and slowly and deliberately walks back into the courtyard as though nothing had happened.

Alterka stops, his brow furrowed, and within those furrows a deep and weighty thought lies soaking, like kernels of barley in a chicken's craw. At length the hard thought softens, and the goose-dealer is able to swallow it down.

"Do you know, Lisa, why the whole world hates cats and loves dogs? They both have claws, but a cat hides them in the velvety pads of its paws, while a dog shows his openly. Everyone hates such hypocrites as the slaughterers."

At this display of her husband's wisdom, Lisa beams from ear to ear. Soon, however, the coldness settles once again over her puffy features. She has to bend her heavy body, her large head, and the bright parasol in order to pass through the courtyard's narrow wicket, because the gate is closed for the Sabbath. The couple scramble through, straighten up, and start off on their Broad Street promenade.

Meanwhile, the tomcat is gazing about the courtyard and discovers, on our doorstep, the cat that takes care when yawning not to catch flies on the Sabbath. The tomcat walks by, seemingly lost in thought; then, without warning, he jumps and bites our cat on her back. Mother, sitting inside near the dark window immersed in her women's Bible, suddenly hears a screech. She rushes to the door and lets in the cat, which looks around, more dead than alive, and begins to lick her wounded back.

Never again does Mother go outside to read her books on Sabbath afternoons.

The White Kerchief

FOR OTHER WOMEN, the coming of the High Holidays is marked by the wearing of fur collars, velvet dresses, brooches set with seed pearls, golden bracelets—heirlooms from their grandmothers. Mother, for her part, has a black shawl and a jacket with mother-of-pearl buttons. But for her the most important sign of the festival is her white kerchief. It is in this that she wraps her Roedelheimer maḥzor with its glossy brown binding. The gleaming kerchief is to her like the white curtain hung before the Holy Ark during the Days of Awe—a reminder that on the Day of Judgment, God is a pardoner of sins.

For my mother the very essence of the holiday lies in that white kerchief, whereas I find my joy of the season in a small bunch of grapes, like a cluster of frozen dewdrops, and a slice of red, juicy watermelon studded with black seeds. Mother buys these delicacies in honor of the New Year, so that I might recite the Sheheḥeyonu, the blessing for new occasions. She herself also eats a little of these costly fruits. In the course of the two days of Rosh Hashanah, she also eats a plum and a pear—fruits she has not tasted earlier in the season. As a child I always marveled: where did she find the strength and patience to keep herself all summer long from sampling the fresh fruits in her own baskets, so as to be eligible to recite the Sheheḥeyonu over them on the New Year?

On Rosh Hashanah, sitting in the women's section of the synagogue, she looked more joyous and radiant than any of the rich matrons with their fur collars. She is not a zogerke, a "spokeswoman"—no one has engaged her to pray for a good year for All-Israel—but the poor, unlearned women crowd around her to listen as she translates aloud into Yiddish the story that is being read from the Torah scroll:

"Sarah, the mistress, drove out the maidservant Hagar, with her child, into the desert. And Hagar wandered aimlessly until all the water in her goatskin bottle was gone. Then she placed the child under one of the trees and she herself sat down at a distance, as far as an arrow could fly, so that she would not see the death agony of the child. And she lifted her voice and wept. Then an angel of the Lord called out to Hagar and said to her that her son would become the father of a mighty nation. And God opened the eyes of Hagar, and she saw a well of water, and gave her child to drink."

Even the women who cannot read are familiar with this tale, and they sigh: Life has always been bitter for the lowly. In their hearts they feel resentment against Sarah for her ill-treatment of the servant-girl. Yet the poor women also realize that God is a merciful Father Who can help them as He helped the maidservant Hagar. The moral of the tale is sweet, as sweet as the ḥallah dipped in honey that is eaten at the evening meal on Rosh Hashanah. But they cannot take much time to ponder this, for they are anxious to listen as my mother continues reading.

She reads how the ministering angels came before God and spoke to Him: "Lord of the Universe, do not take pity on Hagar's son, Ishmael. When the Children of Israel will be driven from their land, the children of Ishmael will meet them in the desert and give the exhausted Jews salty fish to eat and, instead of water, they will give the exiles skin-bottles filled with wind. It were better that Ishmael die of thirst now, while he is yet a child, than that such evildoers, the Arabs of the desert, should be his descendants." But God, blessed be He, answered the angels and said that each person may only be judged for that which he has already done, not for what he, or his children, may do in the future.

The women, peddlers and stall-keepers in the marketplace, have never heard this story before, and they are greatly moved and comforted by it. For who nowadays can vouch for his children, especially someone who is poor? One must indeed give thanks and praise unto Him Whose Name one may not utter unwashed, that He does not make a reckoning now for what will happen later.

The wealthy matrons hold maḥzorim whose covers have corners edged in silver. But they cannot keep up with the cantor and frequently lose the place. From time to time a broad-beamed matron makes her way from the East Wall corner to the fruit-peddler sitting in the westernmost nook, almost at the outer door:

"Vellenka, a good year to you. What are they up to?"

Quickly and familiarly, Mother turns the gilt-edged pages of the rich woman's maḥzor as she thinks to herself: "If only I knew how I stood with the Lord of the Universe as well as I know where the cantor and the congregation are up to in the prayers . . ."

Lisa the goose-dealer's wife stands at her place and stares in confusion into her prayerbook; she has lost the place and has no idea what is being said. But she refuses to ask Mother's help—she will not give the fruit-seller that satisfaction. For ever-present to her mind is the recent occasion when she, Lisa, had openly combed and washed her hair on the Sabbath and Mother, so as not to have to witness such a desecration, had fled the courtyard with her Bible and gone back indoors.

When the cantor reaches the climactic *U'nessa'neh Tokef* prayer, there is such a crush of rich matrons and their prayerbooks about my mother

that, if only she had as many customers pressing about her baskets, she
herself would become a wealthy woman. Her hollow cheeks are aglow
with a subdued yet sweet excitement. Till now she has been ashamed to
weep aloud, lest she seem to be lamenting more than others her bitter
lot of widowhood. Only when the cantor reaches the phrase "Who shall
live and who shall die," at which everyone weeps, will she too permit
the wellspring of tears to flow freely from her eyes. Just then, however,
she begins to look about uneasily, and the women near her, who have
today crowned her with honor and respect, ask with much concern:

"Vellenka, what are you looking for?"

"For my kerchief."

Mother, just about to weep, suddenly notices that her white kerchief
is missing. She feels a throb in her heart: such a loss—may it not turn
out to be an evil omen for the New Year! Lisa, noticing that Mother is
looking in her direction, also begins to search, and finds a white kerchief
on the window-sill near her. Overjoyed, she picks it up and hurries over
to my mother, carrying it like a white flag of peace:

"Is this what you're looking for?"

"Yes, Lisa. Early this morning, before the other women came, I sat
near your window to say the first part of the prayers. Here, near the wall,
it's dark, and my eyesight is already weak."

"Vellenka," says Lisa, trembling on this Day of Judgment, "may
you have great joy from your son. What are they up to now? You are
learned in the 'black vowel signs'—and on a day such as this no other
learning is worthwhile."

Lisa is here hinting at her own knowledge of Russian.

Mother quickly turns the pages of Lisa's prayerbook, reflecting as
she does so that to observe the Sabbath is more important for true repentance. One cannot, with mere pious babbling on Rosh Hashanah, buy
absolution for the sins of an entire year . . .

The women's section has become still, like a cooing dovecote where
silence falls just before a storm. A cloud of long-pent-up bitterness seems
to hang in the air; a sobbing arises from heavy-laden hearts. A clap of
thunder resounds through the synagogue. The cantor begins to chant:
"U'nessa'neh tokef kedushas ha-yom . . . ," and before he has reached the
words "who shall live and who shall die," the women's section is already
drowning in a flood of tears.

ON YOM KIPPUR, before the Afternoon Service begins, the beadle pounds
on the cantor's table: there is to be a half-hour intermission.

The younger women, who have their little ones to feed, rush out
from behind the partition of the women's section. The older matrons stay

in their seats, resting or chatting about daughters-in-law and grandchildren. Also remaining in the synagogue are the poor market-women: All year long they are too harried and preoccupied to enter the beth midrash; at least, then, this one full day, the Day of Atonement, they wish to spend wholly within the sacred walls. Thus it is with astonishment that they see Vella the fruit-seller wrap up her books in her white kerchief, place the bundle on her "pew," and leave the synagogue.

Mother is going home to feed our cat: animals are not obligated to fast.

As soon as she reaches the wicket of the main gate, she can already hear the cat's cry. The animal senses her mistress's steps from afar and is scratching at the locked door. At this, Mother smiles—her only smile on this Day of Atonement. It warms her heart to know that at least one living creature is so closely tied to her. Lonely as she is, in whom else can she confide? Her only son has lately become increasingly moody, and sunk in melancholy. He sits in the smithy all day, reading, always reading. She has long understood that he would never be overly pious; now she pleads with him: "Why do you bury yourself in this hole-in-the-wall? At least go out for a walk sometimes. Other young fellows find joy in living." His only response is to grow still moodier.

She opens the door and the cat jumps up at her. From the cupboard Mother takes the saucer filled with bread soaked in milk which she had prepared the day before, places it before the cat, and speaks to her:

"Lazybones, why do you always stay in this hole-in-the-wall? Go on out for a walk."

She realizes with a start that she is speaking to the cat exactly as she has often (not to compare the two) spoken to her son. "I must be growing senile," she thinks. But just then she hears another cat mewing: Lisa has locked her cat up in the house, and he is wailing with hunger.

Wasting no time, Mother hurries back to the synagogue. Lisa is chatting with her "fine ladies" about clothes, and about all the work she will have, on the eve of the festival of Sukkoth, preparing the geese for her customers. When she sees my mother, stern-faced, heading toward her, she becomes uneasy—this time, for the life of her, she cannot think of any offense she might have committed against tradition. On the Sabbath of Penitence, between the New Year and the Day of Atonement, she had not gone out walking with her umbrella, and even her husband had taken his prayer shawl and gone to the synagogue. . . . Mother called her aside:

"Lisa, you locked up your cat. Go, give him some food—he's not obligated to fast."

"But I'll miss the Afternoon Service," objects Lisa, fearful of losing her chance to plead for and win a favorable decree for the coming year.

"That doesn't matter." Mother renders judgment with the assurance of a rebbetzin: "The Almighty will wait for you. Your prayers will ascend to Heaven together with all the others."

Lisa obeys and goes to feed the cat. She walks with her head held so straight and stiff that, had a lamp filled with kerosene been placed upon it, not a drop would have spilled.

The congregation prepares to begin the Afternoon Service. But my mother, instead of reading in her Teḥinah, as she usually does before the start of the congregational prayers, peers through the curtain into the men's section of the synagogue. The older men, wrapped in white linen kittels, are leaning against their oaken lecterns and resting. Others are making use of the intermission to study a paragraph or two of Mishnah. The young fellows stand in a huddle and talk. Only her son stands alone, in back of the cantor's pulpit, and speaks to no one. He looks pale, lost in his thoughts, and unkempt. She is saddened, and with a heavy heart she murmurs:

"Lord of the Universe! All the world says that a mother's heart feels her child's pain. I, however, do not know what it is that weighs so heavily upon my son. Is your Torah so difficult that it robs a young man of all joy? I know I am not worthy of having a son who is a great scholar. Then let him at least be an honest Jew, a craftsman like Reb Boruḥel, may he rest in peace."

OF ALL THE VOICES raised in either the men's or the women's section, I hear only my mother's plaintive cry. The fine threads of her weeping stretch toward me, entwine themselves about me, as spider-webs in autumn entwine themselves about the gnarled branches of trees. I stand behind the bima, unable to pray. Why is she so meek and humble toward everyone? Why does she always feel that she has sinned before God? Why can't I rescue her from her exhausting toil, so that she will not waste away in the heat of summer and in the frosts of winter, sitting beside her baskets? She feeds me and believes in my piety, and here I am deceiving her. . . .

WHEN, at nightfall, Yom Kippur ends and everyone leaves the synagogue, sons stand waiting for their fast-weakened mothers, to take them by the arm and lead them home. Only my mother always rushes home alone, to prepare sweetened tea—so that I may have something over which to pronounce the Havdalah blessings—as well as to warm my food for breaking the fast. She never thinks of herself.

This time, however, as she leaves the women's section, she abruptly stops, confused and surprised: I am waiting for her. I take from her the maḥzor wrapped in the white kerchief, give her my arm, and lead her home. The narrow synagogue street is filled with Jews reciting the blessing for the crescent of the New Moon. I do not stop. Mother utters a weak, frightened laugh:

"Honoring your mother is an important commandment, but it would be better, at the beginning of a new year, if you too recited the blessing for the New Moon."

"I am not that great rabbi of the Talmud whose mother washed his feet and then drank the water. I can't forgive myself for letting you sacrifice yourself as you have so that I might study the Torah."

Mother is silent. She feels a wetness in her eyes, as though the dried-up fountain of her tears is about to flow again. She has a premonition of some impending ill. On Rosh Hashanah she had lost her white kerchief, and Lisa had found it and returned it to her. That was a rebuke from Heaven, for she had chastised Lisa, while her own son . . . She is afraid to think further, and takes the prayerbook from my hand, as though fearing that I might lose her last comfort—the white kerchief.

A Sleepless Night

IT IS FRIDAY NIGHT. In the little copper candlesticks, with their patina of green, the candles have burned down. The flame in the kerosene lamp flickers and twitches. Reddish bands of light envelop the little room in a stillness heavy with mystery. Great shadows overlap and intertwine upon the ceiling and walls, where they seem to have hovered since the Creation.

During the entire night from Thursday to Friday, Mother had not closed her eyes; she had been busy preparing for the Sabbath. On Friday she had stood at her stand by the gate till candle-lighting time, just before sunset, not daring to sit down even for a moment, lest she lose a customer. After Kiddush, she began to speak of my two little sisters who had died long ago. During the meal she collapsed from utter exhaustion. I pulled off her heavy boots and the cloths wrapped around her frozen feet. She removed her matron's wig and the white strands of her hair glistened in the dimly lit room. Feeling her way as though blind, she crept into bed, huddled under the covers, and fell asleep in her clothes.

I sit hunched over a book, trying to immerse myself in my reading, but cannot connect one line to another. The memories my mother has aroused begin steadily to unfold in my mind.

I BARELY REMEMBER my younger sister. She had left us as an infant in the cradle, before she could even utter a word. My other sister was six years old when she died. In my mind's eye I can still see Mother and myself, a boy of nine, holding her little hands and screaming:

"Ettele!"

The child did not answer. Her curly black hair was spread over the pillow, and her large black pupils stared blankly as though made of glass. She no longer cried, no longer asked for a piece of bread.

It was just after the war. My father lay ill in the hospital. Mother, swollen with hunger, could barely lift one foot in front of the other. Typhus raged throughout the city, felling entire families. None of the neighbors responded to our cries. Mother, close to fainting, summoned her last strength to stammer:

"Go to your aunt—ask her to come . . ."

Mother felt reproachful toward her sister, who had failed to help us. Yet it was to this aunt I now ran, weeping loudly all the way, as though she could still save Ettele. As I reached the Ostra Brama Gate, a Polish woman and her small son were kneeling before the image of the Holy Mother suspended over the gate. When the Polish boy saw me, he stood up and mimicked my crying. His mother turned her sanctimonious face toward me—and burst into laughter. Dejected, I grew silent and began to walk more slowly, until I found the narrow street where my aunt and uncle had their shop.

My uncle, a man so tall he reached almost to the ceiling, was standing wrapped in his prayer shawl, reciting the morning prayers. I rushed up to him and sobbed:

"Ettele died."

He bent over me, laid his heavy, hairy hands on my head, and stifled a groan. I knew that he was good-natured and I clasped his knee, clinging to him and crying. He gently picked me up and embraced me, set me down again, and then walked quickly through the rear door into the shop, where my aunt was standing. I could hear him scolding her, and her grumbling response. At last he shouted:

"Go, give your sister's boy something to eat. And don't be stingy! You hear?"

My aunt came into the room where I was waiting. She said nothing, but the eye-slits in her creased and wrinkled face became still narrower. She moved lazily about the room as she prepared my food. My tall uncle, still wrapped in his prayer shawl, swayed silently to and fro, extending his heavy, hairy hands toward the ceiling, demanding something of Heaven. He watched me obliquely while I ate. When he saw I was leaving a piece of bread and butter untouched, he moved his broad palm toward his mouth, mumbling, "Nu-oh!"—his wordless admonition to me to eat it all.

In the meantime my aunt was dressing, pulling on her heavy galoshes and her fur jacket, looking again and again into the shop to see whether any customers had come in—she was clearly reluctant to leave. My uncle was still praying, but he turned repeatedly, with impatience and anger, to look at her. Finally he pointed a long, stiff finger toward the door and muttered angrily, "Nu-oh!"—meaning she should go at once.

Outside, I raced ahead like the wind, but my aunt could barely make her way through the deep snowdrifts. She groaned and moaned and sobbed continually, rehearsing the grief she would show when she reached our house. Then a peasant with a wagonload of wood came toward us. My aunt stopped, touched the wood on all sides to make sure it wasn't wet, and began in a leisurely way to bargain with the peasant. When they had agreed on a price, she called out to me:

"Go on home and tell your mother I'll be there right away. I'm just going to take this fellow back to the store. We make our living from these bundles of firewood—we don't want to die of hunger, either."

When I returned home, my sister's face was already covered with Mother's black shawl. It seemed to me that she had simply covered her eyes and wanted to play hide-and-seek with me. But the stiffness of her pale little fingers frightened me. Mother sat in the middle of the room, rigid, frozen. When she saw me, she roused herself with a shudder and asked me: "Did you eat something?"

Then, in a lifeless voice, without weeping or screaming, she spoke to me as though I were an adult:

"Your father had five sons by his first wife and you, my son, are the sixth, the child of his old age. But your father always yearned for a daughter. And the Almighty blessed me with two little daughters, so that I might find favor in your father's eyes. But one little bird died in the cradle and today Ettele, too, was taken from me. How can I go to your father in the hospital and give him this news? How will I be able to face him? God in Heaven, why have you shamed me so?"

When my aunt came at last, my mother's fountain of tears finally burst open. She wrung her hands and wept:

"A little swallow flew into a cellar. Ettele was my little swallow. Now she has flown away again. Look, Sister—" Mother took the black shawl from Ettele's small face. "My little girl doesn't want to close her bright eyes. She wants her brightness to remain in my house."

My aunt's eye-slits now closed completely. Tears rolled down the rivulets of her creased and wrinkled face. She began to scream, in a voice like her husband's:

"Come to me! You'll help me out in the shop. If you don't listen to me, you'll lose your boy too. These are bitter times."

Mother did not answer. She only sighed deeply, as if to say: I had to lose a child before you could feel pity for me . . .

THE FLAME IN THE LAMP trembles, as if it were reliving my unhappy memories with me. The greenish little copper candlesticks on the table, engulfed by the room's gigantic shadows, look to me like my two little sisters, holding each other by the hand and wandering lost in a darkening forest. In her sleep my mother lets out a stifled scream that tears me from my memories. I jump up and awaken her. For a moment she remains rigid and staring, as though listening to some distant secret sound. Suddenly she sits up and murmurs:

"I didn't find them."

"Whom? Whom didn't you find?"

"My little ones. I looked for them among the paupers' graves. How could I find them? The rains wash away the graves, and I don't even know where they were buried. The gravedigger took the infant away in a little box, and when Ettele was buried my sister wouldn't let me go to the funeral. 'How can you go when you yourself are swollen with hunger?' she said. Just now I dreamt that I was wandering through the graveyard among the tall trees, and the wind was covering me with dry leaves. The leaves whirl about me in circles, like large birds, they enfold me and will not let me go on."

"You were talking about Ettele tonight, Mother, and then you dreamt about her. What made you suddenly think about her now?"

"I've never forgotten her. The older you get, my son, the more I think about your little sister. You're almost twenty—may you have long life—and Ettele would have been seventeen now, old enough to become a bride."

"And where would she have lived? Here with us, in the smithy? And how would she have dressed? A girl ready for marriage needs to have pretty clothes—and I wear a coat even in summer so people won't see the patches on my suit. Just think, Mama, how much she would have suffered because of our poverty."

"Perhaps on her account we might have had a better life. She would have been a capable girl and would have helped me earn our living. And on her account you might not have strayed from the path of Torah. You would have brought her a bridegroom from the yeshiva—one of your friends."

Mother began to shiver:

"Cover me, my son—I'm chilled. When you used to sit and study on Friday nights, it was like medicine for my heart. But since you left the path of Torah, I feel as though I'm living in a house with no mezuzah—a house without God's protection—and that is why such fearful dreams plague me. Go, take a prayerbook, recite The Song of Solomon, and translate it for me. I remember how your father used to teach it to his pupils, and how the sweetness of the melody melted into my very bones. If you would only study Torah, I would feel warm and my thoughts would not torment me so."

I take a Bible from the shelf and begin to chant softly, gloomily:

"The Song of Songs, which is Solomon's . . ."

I chant and translate the verses. It seems to me that Mother has fallen asleep. Her breathing grows softer, and so does my voice. I look about me. A grayish light is beginning to enter through the window of the smithy. Dawn is wrestling with the darkness, like my mother with her dreams. In the glass lamp the kerosene is running dry. The little flame is smoking and writhing in its agony. The shadows on the walls move, awakening from their sleep, and Mother also begins once more to toss about uneasily. I resume my chanting and conclude the first chapter of The Song of Songs:

"Behold, thou art fair, my beloved, yea pleasant; also our bed is green. The beams of our house are cedars, and our rafters of fir . . ."

Mother sits up. Her sunken cheeks glow feverishly: beads of sweat cover her forehead. The frost and ice that had dug into her limbs all winter long now burst forth upon her face. Swollen veins stand out like uncovered roots on her work-worn hands. Her eyes wander about the small room, and she murmurs:

"I stole . . . Why do you give me such a terrified look? I'm not mad and I'm not talking in my sleep. When my sister took me in to help her in the shop, it was agreed that I would eat in her house. 'When I can, I'll also give you some food for the boy,' she said. But I couldn't wait for her to give me something for you, and so I would quietly take a piece of herring, a bagel. I didn't want you too to die of hunger, like Ettele. Your uncle knew what I was doing—I didn't try to hide it from him. Sometimes he'd even give me a wink to take something, without my sister's knowledge. It was from her that I stole."

"Mama, what's the matter with you tonight? You're burning with fever. You yourself say that my uncle knew it all the time and he was the master in his house. You had honorably earned the extra piece of bread that you took for me."

"I myself don't know what's troubling me so tonight. I'm so exhausted that I can't fall asleep. Chant a little more of The Song of Songs. Do it for me, my son."

I read again, no longer in sequence, but wherever my befogged gaze falls:

"By night on my bed I sought him whom my soul loveth; I sought him but I found him not . . .

"Behold, thou art fair, my love; behold, thou art fair; thou hast doves' eyes within thy locks, thy hair is as a flock of goats . . .

"Thy lips are like a thread of scarlet . . ."

Mother looks about her in the small room, and the words she draws out are deeply tinged with gloom:

"Shulamith, the queen of The Song of Songs, seeks her bridegroom, and I seek the little graves of my children. Ettele, too, had black hair and black eyes. When I covered her with my shawl, her dead face still shone through. But her lips were not like a thread of scarlet. Her little lips were parched and burnt."

She gazes at me for a long time and then asks:

"You don't bear a hidden grudge against me in your heart?"

"What for?"

"For your father, my son."

She draws my head to her, and her tears wash my cheeks.

"When your sick father came home from the hospital, there should have been someone constantly at his bedside to take care of him. But at that time I was working day and night for my sister. You bear me no grudge?"

I can stand it no longer and begin to scream:

"You're driving me crazy! You're a pious woman—don't you know that on the Sabbath one is not permitted to mourn, even if someone very close has just died and is not yet buried? Father used to tell me that in all his life he had never seen a woman as devout as you. And yet you're always looking to find fault with yourself. You're ill—I'm going out to find a doctor. I'll wake our neighbors. I'll put up a kettle of water to boil so I can give you a hot glass of tea."

Abruptly Mother grows calm and says sternly:

"Don't call anyone. I don't want anyone to desecrate the Sabbath on my account. The Almighty is the best doctor."

Then she strokes my head and smiles:

"I heard how sweetly you chanted. In the *Tzena Ur'ena* it is explained that the queen of The Song of Songs is the Holy Torah. But even just in themselves the words are beautiful and fine. Do you think I don't understand anything anymore? It's time, my son, for you to give your mother some joy and find a bride for yourself. It's already time. . . ."

The Family

WHEN I WAS A CHILD, my mother would take me every Sabbath day to her sister's house for cholent. This was part of her wages for wearing herself out working in that sister's store all week. Each time, after the meal, the same conversation would be repeated. My aunt would turn to my mother:

"Some husband you've got! An older man, a widower, with such an unholy appetite he marries a girl less than half his age. And you raised his sons by his first wife, you even washed their heads for them, and because they were big boys already and you didn't want to embarrass them before the neighbors, you used to lock the door. Now that they're grown, they've left the country, while here your breadwinner, the husband who's supposed to take care of you, is letting you struggle alone with your boy."

My aunt always began this conversation while her husband was engaged in reciting the Grace After Meals, and so unable to intervene. My uncle, however, would interrupt his devout swaying long enough to shake his heavy, hairy hand at his wife, and mutter, "Nu-oh!," giving her an angry look for seeking—and even worse, on the Sabbath—to kindle the flames of discord between man and wife.

Mother, who had already said grace, could no longer contain herself. She defended my father:

"But what can he do, ill as he is, and confined to his bed, unable to budge? When I entered his household, he had the best heder in the city. It's my bitter fate! His children in America stopped writing because of the war. His oldest son, who lives here, begs him to come live with him, but I won't let him go—I don't want to remain alone."

" 'When I entered his household'!" mimicked my aunt. "A servant 'enters a household,' and you, you think of yourself as his servant. 'When I married him' is what you should say."

On the way home Mother cautioned me:

"You mustn't, God forbid, repeat to your father what your aunt said."

Eventually, my aunt and uncle left Vilna to join their children abroad, and Mother no longer had anyone to give her employment. Only then did she consent to Father's going to live with his son, in the Snipiszek section of Vilna.

My half-brother, Moïsey, was a tall young man with a pointed black beard. "That's just how your father used to look, only his beard was even blacker and fuller," said Mother. But I found this hard to believe, since for as long as I could remember, Father's hair and beard had been white as milk. Moïsey had married into a wealthy family. Taybel, his wife, had a stutter of which she was deeply ashamed. She was a quiet woman, gentle and sweet, and always welcomed my mother with great kindness.

Mother, however, never felt at ease in my brother's lavishly furnished home. Every Sabbath, when the two of us went for our weekly visit, she would instruct me how to behave: I was not to run around; I was not to break anything; I was not to speak in a loud voice; and, in general, I was to sit quietly with my father in his room, which was one of the finest in the house.

"It's hard and bitter enough for me that I have to leave you alone all week without supervision."

To get from our little street to Snipiszek, we had to walk halfway across the city. On the way, Mother would hold me by the hand and talk to me:

"We have to thank and praise God that your father is now able to get up from his bed and stretch his limbs. It all happened during the war, after he lost the ḥeder. Who in those days could afford to send his sons to school? Even the wealthiest people were starving. So your father tried peddling in the streets, carrying his merchandise around in a box. One day he collapsed and they brought him home in an ambulance, half paralyzed. But you couldn't remember that, you were still very young."

Mother does not know that that midsummer evening has remained deeply engraven in my memory. I had come running in from the street, still absorbed in play. A crowd had gathered in front of our door. People looked at me and whispered. I pushed my way in and saw my father propped up on the sofa, his head tilted back, his beard and his legs hanging down, heavy and stiff. Two men in white coats were fussing over him, while my mother wrung her hands. At last, the house and courtyard emptied. Mother rushed off somewhere to get medicines, and I remained alone with Father in the deserted half-dark room. The eerie stillness made me tremble. I gazed fearfully at my father's motionless eyes while at the same time staring in fascination at his peddler's box on the table—never before had I seen such shiny scissors, leather purses, watch-chains, knives, razors. I could not tear my gaze from these things, until I heard my father groan:

"Take off my boots."

All this happened when I was very young, as my mother said. But even now, when I am older, I still look about me in all directions with the amazement of a small child, and Mother has to prod me along:

"Why are you stopping? Every Sabbath you stare at this same window and can't tear yourself away."

The window is of a shop where birds are sold, and where I halt abruptly as though riveted to the ground. There, by the open door, is the owner. He has lost both his legs, yet does not use crutches—his rectangular torso stands on the threshold like a box. His face is handsome, and he is clean-shaven and smiling, with a full head of hair. As we pass by, he deftly hoists his truncated body onto a chair that stands beside him, as if wishing to show me the tricks he can perform even without his legs.

In the beginning I was afraid of the cripple, but he recognized me from week to week and would wave to me. Eventually I grew used to him and began to trust his round, fresh face with its childlike smile.

Through the open door I behold many marvels. Three-fourths of the shop is taken up by a huge wire cage, filled with all manner of doves and pigeons. In the corners hang small wooden cages occupied by colorful parrots and canaries. The room resounds with cooing and warbling, as well as with the shrill cries of several ragged gentile boys who are gaping at the birds.

I continue to dawdle at the shop window. In one cage sits a squirrel on a wire to which a wheel is attached. The squirrel pedals rapidly with its tiny feet; the wheel turns, and behind the squirrel's long, bushy tail the miles slip by—inside the cage. "Silly creature," I say to myself. "She thinks she's climbing trees." Also displayed in the window are glass cases filled with water, in which small golden fish swim about. In one strange potbellied vessel, several long gray watersnakes roll and slither and twist.

"Come on now." Mother tugs at me. "May my words be proven false—you'll yet turn out to be a bird-catcher or pigeon-keeper. The pigeons attract you just too much. I shudder when I look at their owner, who has no legs. Here he owns hundreds of birds that can fly, and he himself can't even walk. As for you, better you should look at the big Choir Synagogue. Above the entrance, do you see, there's a stone tablet with the Ten Commandments. And one of the Commandments is 'Honor thy father and mother.' If only your father were well, he'd apprentice you to the cantor of that synagogue, and you'd sing in the choir. You have a voice that's clear as a bell . . . Why have you stopped again?"

Because I have espied fresh marvels. On one side of the street there is a fenced-in field with ploughshares, scythes, and harvesting machines standing about. To me they are like the extracted teeth of gigantic beasts. On the other side lives a Christian tombstone carver. Chunks of marble and granite are piled in a corner. An angel with widespread wings stands poised for flight from a white stone. A winding marble pillar spirals heavenward like blue smoke. A woman with eyes piously turned upward and hands devoutly clasped sleeps within a slab of granite. A cross and some gilt letters are engraved on a smoothly polished tablet.

"Come, let's go!" Mother pulls me along. "The boy wants to be everything: a bird-catcher, a tombstone carver, a peasant in his field—the only thing he doesn't want to do is to study."

When we cross the bridge over the Wilja, I cannot tear myself away from watching the swimmers, who are jumping into the river from the high banks, treading water or doing the crawl. Mother holds me fast by the hand and looks about her uneasily, as though I too might take it into my head to jump into the water.

"Only God in His Heaven knows how often my heart stands still with fear when you disappear for hours on end. I'm always afraid that you've run off to go swimming . . . To tell the truth, it really shouldn't surprise me that you yearn so for the river, or for the life of a peasant working his fields. At one time your father, too, wanted to give up the heder and buy a farm. He borrowed money to buy land. The farm also had a brickyard. In the end . . . about the end it's better not to ask. In the days of the Czar, Jews weren't allowed to buy land, so your father had to buy it in the name of a Gentile, a so-called 'partner.' Well, the 'partner' took everything—the money as well as the land."

When we finally reach my brother's home, Mother and I go straight to my father's room. Aronchik, my brother's son and my nephew—a skinny boy about my own age—comes running immediately. The two of us begin to chase each other from room to room—and suddenly I find myself in the parlor.

Confounded, I halt in my tracks. At the table sits my brother Moïsey; opposite him, his wife, Taybel; and at the head of the table, her brother, Issak the pharmacist. They are all at their ease, drinking tea, eating fruit, and chatting.

Issak the pharmacist has a pair of cold fish-eyes, a red face, and a long, pointy mustache, like the pincers of a crab. He sits there motionless, like some life-size clay figure, but his mustache lives a life of its own. One moment it is standing stiff and still, the next it is dancing all over his red face. He visits my brother every Sabbath. Now his fish-eyes gaze at me astonished, as though seeing me for the very first time. His mustache twists itself into the shape of two question-marks, and he asks my brother:

"Who's this?"

"You ought to know him by now, Issak. This is my father's son by his second wife."

So speaks my brother Moïsey to his brother-in-law, and smiles at me, as though he too is astonished to find himself with a brother of the same age as his own son.

"Moïsey," says the pharmacist, "your father is, I believe, an educated man—a modern Hebrew teacher, not some greasy old-fashioned me-lamed. Why, then, does he permit the boy to roam about the streets? He ought to be placed in a children's home, where he would receive firm discipline."

My brother stops smiling. His black-bearded face, reflecting his annoyance, seems to grow longer, but he controls himself and makes no retort to his brother-in-law's taunts.

"His mother is a very fine woman," Taybel interjects. It takes her a long time to get the words out and, as though to cover up for this, she quickly takes an apple from the fruit bowl and gives it to me:

"Eat."

She manages the single word without a stammer. Now Issak the pharmacist, too, seems to want to smooth things over, and declares:

"When he grows up, he should go to Palestine. There we need young fellows like him, to drain the swamps."

After which he does not deign to look at me again. As I leave the parlor, my nephew, Aronchik, attempts to comfort me:

"Don't pay any attention to my uncle. Let him go and drain the swamps himself. None of us like him. He smells of medicine, and he's always testing me. Papa can't stand him either."

"You know," I say to my nephew, "on the way here I saw a shop full of birds in cages."

"All birds should be let out of their cages," he replies.

"And what would you do with the snakes?" I ask him. "In that same shop, in a glass case, I saw snakes—as long and as twisted as your Uncle Issak's mustache."

"Snakes should be crushed," answers Aronchik with firm assur-ance.

"Do you know—" I attempt to impress my nephew—"my mother wants me to become a singer in the Choir Synagogue? The men there wear tophats, and at the gate there's a doorman, a Gentile, in a long jacket with silver buttons. But the peculiar thing is that whenever we pass by there, the gates are closed. When do they pray?"

"Praying doesn't do any good," says Aronchik. "Come, let's go to Grandfather. He has hairs growing on his nose, and I pluck them out for him."

By this time, Father is able to get out of bed for a while. He is sitting on a chair and asking my mother how things have gone during the week. When Aronchik and I enter his room, he begins to question both of us:

"I left a glass of milk to clabber between the double windows in the kitchen. Which of you skimmed off the cream?"

"I did," says Aronchik defiantly. "If you want to, you can tell Mama."

Mother calls me over to her and speaks to me very softly, so as not to be heard in the other rooms:

"Woe is me! You went into the parlor looking like that, and in those clothes? I'll have to bury myself alive for shame!"

Taybel now enters the room to make up Father's bed and to change the bandages on his legs. She works quickly and deftly, like a real doctor. Mother stands by helplessly, astonished at Taybel's skill and shattered by my father's moans, so that she even forgets to wish "All good fortune" to "our daughter-in-law."

Then the haggling begins. Taybel wants Mother to go into the parlor, because Moïsey wants to see her but cannot leave Issak alone. But when Mother learns who the guest is, she absolutely refuses to go in. She can clearly sense the pharmacist's annoyance whenever he sees her, as though it were beneath him to have such poor relations. Besides, she does not quite know how to speak to my brother. She had raised her husband's other children, those who now live in America, but Moïsey, the eldest, had been away pursuing his studies abroad. She finds it difficult to address him with the familiar *du*, and he would always ask her with a smile, "Why do you speak to me so formally?" The haggling with Taybel goes on a long time, until at last Father tells Mother to go—if not into the parlor, then into the dining room. His real intention is that Mother and I should at least eat something.

When we go home, shortly before nightfall, I am carrying, as usual, a package of food that Taybel has thrust into my hands. Mother, who had sat in the dining room like a poor stranger, recovers her self-possession only when we are outside once more. Then she begins to speak:

"I'll tell you the truth. My sister, my own flesh and blood—may she swallow without hiccups—never did half as much for me as Taybel does. Taybel, poor soul, bears a burden. It's hard for her to get a word out— I can imagine how many tears that must have cost her when she was a young girl. That is why she now has sympathy and understanding for others. She must have earned great merit in Heaven for the Almighty to have granted her a husband like Moïsey and blessed her with a child like Aronchik. Though, to tell the truth, Aronchik is even more of a mischief-maker than you are. How impertinently he speaks to everyone! But you shouldn't imitate him—your way must be different."

ONE DAY, an ordinary weekday, Mother rushed into the house, seized me by the hand, and cried out:

"Come, we must go to Father, quickly!"

The streets which, when we went to visit Father on the Sabbath, always seemed deserted, broad, and sparkling, were now crowded with people and wagons and filled with noise. Mother seemed to be stumbling over her own feet, and mumbled incessantly to herself:

"Lord of the Universe, how can he bear this? How will he live through it? You have taken from him the son who was the support of his old age . . . Chaimka, for your father, from now on, you will have to take the place of your older brother. Moïsey is dead . . . He left for Berlin in such good spirits. He even calmed Taybel and your father: 'Just a minor operation,' he said, 'some fluid in the chest' . . . And he died under the surgeon's knife."

All the way, Mother wrung her hands and rushed ahead. I ran after her, out of breath and dreading the moment when we would enter my brother's home.

We found it empty. A dead silence pervaded the dark rooms. The window-shades had been pulled down, the tablecloths removed from the tables, the mirrors covered with white bedsheets. We rushed to my father's room. He was sitting on the bed, his bandaged feet on the floor, groaning:

"*Nofloh ateres rosheinu*—'The crown is fallen from our head. Woe unto us, that we have sinned.' . . ."

Mother pushed me toward my father, as though to comfort him by reminding him that I still lived. He grasped my hand, like a blind man seizing his cane. His milk-white beard quivered and he kept repeating:

"Vella, the crown is fallen from our head. Woe unto us, that I have sinned."

We learned that Taybel's brother, the pharmacist, had come and taken his sister and Aronchik with him to his house. Mother and I stayed on in the deserted apartment until after the week of mourning had passed. Only then did the pharmacist come and tell us his plans for the family: Taybel would rent out rooms to students. She would earn additional money by cooking for the boarders, and he, for his part, would also help his sister. But she would not have enough to support her former father-in-law.

When, after the seven days of mourning, Taybel and Aronchik returned home, Mother and I put my father in a hired wagon and took him back to our house.

On the way home, Mother finally revealed the secret she had kept from Father all this time: Our landlord had originally rented us our rooms on the condition that Father would serve as night watchman for the shops in the courtyard. When Father fell ill, Mother had tried to take his place, but the merchants did not want a woman as a guard. So, since we paid no rent, the landlord had installed a smith in our lodgings—

that is, the smith used the front room, leaving to us the back room and the kitchen.

So Father returned with us to the smithy and to the windowless back room. He lay ill in the darkness, choking on the smoke that rose from the bellows and on the rust particles that filled the air. His body swelled up and fluid oozed from the blisters on his legs. He ate nothing and fell completely silent. But just before he died—on a Thursday—he turned his head and said to Mother:

"You must have me buried tomorrow, on Friday, so that you can rest on the Sabbath."

Mother often recalled Father's last words, and she would add with a sigh:

"His wish for me was not fulfilled. I have no rest, not even on the Sabbath."

Aronchik

MOTHER IS CRADLING in her arms a pale little boy with round cheeks and big black eyes. Her face is suffused with a tear-stained radiance. Her lips draw closer and closer to the child's face, but she does not permit herself the joy of a kiss. She leaves me to guard her baskets at the gate, and carries the child into the courtyard to show him off to the neighbors.

Alterka the goose-dealer has gone off to tipple with his boon companions, and Lisa, his wife, is sitting immobile as a golem at the tin counter. She is inwardly cursing her husband, who is always on pins and needles and cannot stay still for a moment. Lying amidst the plucked, partially frozen chickens and geese is the black tomcat, his angular, sated chin snuggled between his outstretched front paws. Like his mistress, he is dozing. Suddenly Lisa comes awake with a start, thinking some fine lady has walked in—and sees my mother with the child in her arms.

"Our great-grandchild, our treasure . . ." Mother beams with joy.

Lisa's frigid face softens with surprise and even the cat raises his square chin in astonishment.

"To the best of my knowledge," says Lisa, yawning, "you're not old enough to have great-grandchildren. How old are you really—sixty-five, or are you seventy already?"

"About that," answers Mother.

Actually, Mother is only fifty-five, but she looks much older. She does not want people to pity her, and so is glad when they overestimate her age.

Lisa is well versed in the family affairs of her wealthy customers, but does not think it worth her while to know in detail the private lives of the poor women who are her courtyard neighbors. Smiling benignly, she responds:

"Even if you've actually reached seventy, you couldn't have any great-grandchildren yet—nor even grandchildren, for that matter. As far as I know, your son is still a bachelor."

But in fact these observations are beside the point, since my mother has not said "my great-grandchild" but "our great-grandchild," indicating thereby that this is her husband's great-grandchild. Since, however, Lisa seems so interested, Mother goes on to explain that the little boy, Moshele, is the son of Aronchik and that Aronchik is the son of Moïsey, Moïsey being her late husband's son and therefore my real brother, for children are reckoned according to their father.

Lisa's bulging eyes now begin to close and the cat, too, lets his chin sink down once more between his paws. Both want to go back to sleep—my mother's account is too long, too involved, and what ancestral pride can there be anyway in the family history of poor people? When, however, Lisa, who speaks only Russian with her "socialite" customers, hears the Russified name "Moïsey," her drowsiness is momentarily dispelled:

"What does your husband's son, this Moïsey, do?"

Mother's face clouds over with grief. She replies in a broken voice:

"Moïsey does nothing anymore. He died while my husband was still alive. They're both in Paradise already. Woe to the father who must recite Kaddish for his son."

MOTHER RETURNS with Moshele. Above her high cheekbones her green, oblong eyes shine now like two radiant suns. She selects the prettiest apple from her baskets and puts it into one of Moshele's little hands, while into his other hand she puts a large silver coin. Then she stuffs as much fruit as will fit into the pockets of his knitted jacket. She dances with the child and bounces him up and down.

"Moshele, may no harm ever come to you—let it fall upon me instead! May your cheeks become as rosy as this apple. I thank you, Lord of the Universe, for this joy that I have lived to see."

Just then Yudes, Aronchik's wife, comes to the gate to take Moshele back. Yudes is a young woman with short, bobbed hair and low-heeled shoes who addresses everyone with the unceremonious directness befitting a loyal member of the Party.

"I was wondering," she says excitedly, "why all of a sudden Aronchik's uncle asked me to come to the pharmacy at lunchtime, when Aronchik wouldn't be there. It turns out he wanted to tell me that, if Aronchik continues to be the leader of the workers, then he, the loving uncle, will have to fire him. So I told him I'm not afraid of his threats. Aronchik didn't ask him whether he should marry me, and Aronchik won't ask him whether he should be active in the union. That bourgeois trembles at the very thought of a strike. My mother-in-law is also angry at me, because she agrees with her brother. And you, Vella, you say Taybel is right."

"Yudes dear," says Mother, "your mother-in-law is only thinking of what's best for you. Taybel herself was widowed very young, and for Aronchik's sake she never remarried. So now she wants you to hold Aronchik back from walking into the fire. And his uncle really might dismiss him."

"Hold him back?" shouts Yudes. "I will not hold him back! Aron-chik says that he's hated his uncle ever since he was a boy. My mother-in-law should also hate her brother. What did he do for her? He let her become a cook for her boarders."

My mother hands the child to Yudes, as though it were a magic charm for calming her down so she won't shout so loudly.

"Listen, Yudes dear!" Mother is beaming with happiness. "What a child you have—may I suffer the aches of his little bones! Smart, smart as a whip, and with those sweet, sticky little fingers. Oh, Moshele, Moshele, my treasure!"

Yudes leaves with the child, and with her going Mother's joy evaporates. She turns to me despondently:

"You see, my son, what happens when a boy grows up without a father. You've become a writer, and Aronchik is this great leader of the workers. But you, after all, are a thinker, you really should have a talk with him. Tell him who his grandfather was, and what sort of father he had. Moïsey, you know, was a Zionist. When the English promised the Land of Israel to the Jews, there was such joy and celebration in Vilna! And I went with all the neighbors of our courtyard to Krengel's Hall. I'm sitting upstairs with the other women, when suddenly I look and there, seated on the stage, is Moïsey together with all the leading men of the city. He is wearing a dress-coat, with a flower in his lapel, and his beauty lights up the entire hall. But I don't tell anyone that he's our son. Then a woman cries: 'Look how handsome he is.' And I forget myself and blurt out: 'Don't bring an evil eye upon him!' . . . You really can't blame Taybel and her brother for being unhappy about Aronchik's involvement with the Communists."

Slowly Mother's downcast face brightens again, as though her great-grandchild Moshele were the sun, whose rays linger behind even after it has set.

"Listen, my son," she says with a smile, "it's time now for you to follow your nephew's example. Oh, how happily I'll carry your son in my arms. Oh, how I'll dance in the streets! . . . Why are you laughing?"

"I BESEECH THEE, O God, that Thou send me my sustenance, and that Thou feed me and my household and all Israel, in honor and tranquility and not in sorrow, in dignity and not in shame. Deliver me from all terrors and disturbances, and save me from slanders and all afflictions. I beseech Thee, grant me good fortune this year, and every new month, and every week, well-being and blessing and success, and grant me grace and favor in Thine eyes and in the eyes of others, so that none may have cause to speak evil of me. Now I raise up my eyes to Heaven, and my broken heart I reveal unto Thee. In the words of King David, peace be upon him: 'A broken and a contrite heart, O God, Thou wilt not despise.' Amen, and may this be Thy will."

Mother recited this prayer of supplication on every Sabbath preceding a New Moon. I know the words and I know the melodious, plaintive chant. From the front room, where she stands near the workbench and recites the blessing for the month of Kislev, cold rays of light penetrate into the dark back room of the smithy where I sleep. Sleep wells up from my young limbs like beads of pitch from a tree sweltering in the heat of the sun. I hear my mother reciting her prayer and, with my eyes still glued shut, I feel that I am smiling, as though I am dozing somewhere in a summery meadow and listening to the buzzing of a swarm of golden bees.

The buzzing of the golden bees is coming closer, closer; it changes into a prickly, angry whine—and a stream of light stabs abruptly into my eyes. I force my pupils wide open and make out the figures of two men. Then a rough voice speaks in Polish:

"Get up!"

The cold air that has entered from outside brings me fully awake. Behind the two strangers I see my mother, mute with fear.

"Please excuse us, we're from the security police," says one of the men, sweetly and politely. "I'm sorry we had to wake you."

"We have orders to make a search here," says the second man, the one with the rough voice. "Blood of a dog, it's dark as a dungeon in here. Light a lamp!"

"It's our Sabbath today—we're not permitted to light any flame," says my mother, softly and submissively.

"We'll have to put in electricity just to clear out the secret meetings," jokes the first man. "Where's a lamp?"

He lights the small lamp that stands on the table. The kerosene has burnt out during the long Sabbath night, and the wick is smoking. In the oppressive darkness the two policemen look about them with suspicion and distaste. They turn on their electric flashlights, and the dark is crisscrossed by two beams of light that form a golden crucifix.

The first agent pulls several dusty volumes from my father's bookcase, turns them upside down, and asks me:

"What sort of books are these?"

"Hebrew books."

"I can't read Hebrew," he says. "I can read Yiddish—'tatelaḥ, mamelaḥ' . . ."

Affecting an air of deep interest, he leafs through the books, until suddenly he asks with assumed naïveté:

"And where do you keep the secret Party literature?"

"I don't belong to any party."

"I found something!" The second man pulls a bundle of letters and several handwritten notebooks out of the table-drawer. "What are these?"

"Letters and poems. I'm a writer."

"That we know," says the first man, sharply and venomously. "You're one of those writers who incite the people against the Polish state. Adam Mickiewicz was the greatest poet in the world, and he wrote: 'Litwo! Ojczyzno moja! . . .'* But you—you want to give our fatherland to the Bolsheviks. We'll look into your letters at Headquarters. Come into the other room—it's lighter in there. We'll make out a report. Jan—" he turns to his companion—"take a good look around. I'm sure you'll find some proclamations, a red flag, and a gun among Mr. Writer's belongings."

This, as I know, is how the security police talk in order to confuse those they're investigating. The thought occurs that they're not taking me seriously: they've come in the morning, not the dead of night, their search of the room is superficial, they're trading jokes as they look around.

In the workshop, in the light of the snowy Kislev day, I look closely at the agent who has come with me to fill out the report. He is short, with narrow gray eyes and short-cropped hair like the bristles of a hedgehog. His attire is neat and clean. Irritated, he takes a long time to wipe his hands, which are dusty from handling the Hebrew books; after cautiously inspecting the chair to make sure it is clean, he sits down to write.

The second agent enters, followed by my mother. This one is tall, with a broad and shiny face. He has full lips that jut out like a pair of wooden boards, large teeth, and bushy, blond, villainous eyebrows. He examines the tools in the workshop, seizes with his iron hands a huge, heavy hammer and swings it down full-force upon the anvil that stands on a wooden block in the middle of the room. The anvil responds with such a ringing sound that the whole dwelling is set atremble. The hedgehog, absorbed in his writing, jumps up; his beady eyes sweep over the room, as though a hidden bomb had suddenly exploded here. He catches sight of his comrade holding the hammer and shouts:

"Jan, stop that!"

Jan bursts into laughter. He picks up a large pair of pliers, places himself directly in front of me, his legs spread apart, and ever so slowly opens the pliers; then abruptly forces the handles together. The sharp blades snap shut like the cruel jaws of a ferocious animal. Next he takes up a steel saw and, with a crooked smile, examines its fine, tightly spaced

*"Lithuania! My fatherland!": the opening words of Mickiewicz's epic poem *Pan Tadeusz*, a Polish classic.

teeth. Finally he unscrews the vise and then rescrews it with such force that his face turns blue from the exertion.

I look at the agent and feel an ache in my throat, in my fingers, as though he had held my limbs wedged in the pliers, in the vise. It seems to me that he has played this entire scene for my benefit, just so I might see what he is capable of. The workshop now assumes the aspect of a torture chamber; I am the condemned victim and he the executioner. He turns to me and says, with a larcenous wink:

"With files and saws like these you could break into the strongest cashbox."

"Jan," the hedgehog calls out, "didn't you find any proclamations, or a red flag, or a gun?"

"The writer's hidden them well."

"Finished," says the hedgehog to me. "Sign it."

I glance at the sheet of paper covered with writing and pick up the pen.

"Don't write on the Sabbath!" My mother seizes my hand. Her face is hard and tense. Her high cheekbones stand out even more sharply.

I explain to the agent that my mother will not permit me to write on the Sabbath.

The hedgehog laughs. "What next? Here you are, stirring up the workers, calling for a revolution—and you don't write on the yid Sabbath. You have to sign—the law is the law."

"We understand your tricks," thunders Jan the executioner. "Later you want to be able to deny that these papers are yours."

Mother stands between me and the executioner like a mother-sparrow whose still-featherless chicks have fallen from the nest and whom she hides with her wings from a large, fierce, shaggy dog.

"My husband was a rabbi, and I will not let my son sign anything on the Sabbath day."

Turning to me, she speaks with a dry fire:

"What my eyes don't see—they don't see. But I would rather be blind than witness you desecrating the Sabbath. And today is the Sabbath before the New Moon."

"Then I'll have to hold him," says the hedgehog.

"Arrest him!" shouts the executioner.

My mother sits down and begins to weep.

"My son helps me with my fruit baskets. Kind gentlemen, let him be, he's my only child."

The hedgehog begins to bustle about. He wants to win my mother's confidence so as to get something out of her:

"Your son doesn't have to sign, he doesn't have to sign. I'm very pleased to see that you're a pious woman—someone who believes in God is not a rebel. We're not arresting your son, we're just holding him. We have no charges against him. We only want to ask him some questions. . . . Just tell me: what connection is there between your son and this fellow Aronchik?"

Mother sits frozen, staring at him. This last question frightens her more than my arrest. She stands up very slowly, as though his sharp, narrow eyes have turned her to stone, and asks:

"What? What Aronchik?"

"You're a wise grandmother." The hedgehog displays a crafty smile and then turns cheerfully to me. "Are you ready?"

"I'm ready. Leave my mother alone—she doesn't even understand what you're talking about."

"Silence!" The executioner stamps his feet.

Mother stretches out her hands in supplication to the two agents:

"Our nephew Aronchik comes from a very fine family. His father died and his mother is a highly educated woman. He has an uncle who's a pharmacist."

"We know, we know," retorts the hedgehog, bustling about. "This Aronchik is a well-known rebel. He called a strike in his uncle's shop, the very pharmacist you mentioned. We're not going to beat your son, just question him. Let's go."

"I'm going too!" my mother cries out and begins looking for her shawl. But her beclouded eyes cannot find it.

"Stay here!" bellows the executioner.

"My son!" Mother clings to me. "Don't sign on the Sabbath. How many times did they issue summonses against me and my partner Blumele, for keeping a stand without a license or for standing beyond the gate. So we went to jail for a few days and didn't pay the fine. Don't be afraid. If you don't desecrate the Sabbath, no harm will come to you."

"No talking between you two." The "executioner" pushes her away, and I leave the house with the agents.

I SPENT ONLY ONE NIGHT in the "Center," the jail in the courtyard of the secret-police headquarters. The next day, after an interrogation, they let me go. I hurried happily home, eager to reassure my mother as quickly as possible.

When I reached our courtyard, I found the gate empty. Mother was not standing there with her merchandise. I raced through the courtyard and tore open the door of our apartment.

Mother was sitting in a chair, cradling Moshele, Aronchik's son, in her arms. But her eyes were brimming with tears and she seemed not even to see that she was holding her treasure, her great-grandchild. She didn't even rejoice at seeing me free once again.

"They've taken Aronchik away." Her chin trembled with barely stifled sobs. "Taybel and Yudes left Moshele with me and rushed off to the prison."

Ramayles' Courtyard

MOTHER HAS MADE UP HER MIND: she won't meddle. In the first place, what does she know? She is, after all, just an old-fashioned woman. Nowadays the eggs consider themselves wiser than the hens. In the second place, would he even listen to her? And what would she gain if her son, by disobeying his mother and doing exactly the opposite of what she said, became guilty thereby of a grievous sin? No, let him marry whomever he wants. Only let him have good fortune, dear God!

And she can surely see that things are going well enough with him. In the evenings he comes home, God be thanked, quite late. And whenever he stands by her side at the gate, he is always nodding greetings—here to a young woman passing by with an intently serious expression as though she were painting a portrait, and there to another, who gives him a friendly smile. It's truly amazing: how long has it been since he was only a youngster studying in a yeshiva? When did he get to know so many young ladies?

She knows all too well that a wedding is still a long way off. Young people nowadays stand about at the gates half the night, they talk, they giggle . . . and at last they get married—he to a different girl, she to another young man.

One girl, she can see, is truly attached to her son: Baylka the linen-seamstress. She is really a fine young girl, tall and slim, and her good breeding would be apparent to a blind man. Still, a strange sadness weighs upon her; and there is, besides, the fact that she comes from Glebokie, right on the border with Bolshevik Russia—one may easily guess what sort of ideas the girls of the town are exposed to.

My mother trembles at the thought of Baylka's turning out to be a committed Party member, like Aronchik's wife, Yudes. If Yudes herself had not, as a young girl, scampered about the streets with a red banner, surely after the wedding she would have restrained Aronchik, and he would not be in prison today. Now that's all she needs, that her own son should bring home such a wife. But that she should let drop a single word of her concern, let alone come between them in any way . . . no, God forbid!

. . .

BAYLKA LIVES in an attic in Ramayles' Courtyard. From her window she can touch the wall opposite with her hand, so narrow is the passageway between them. The facing wall is that of Dvorah-Esther's Synagogue, through whose window Baylka can see an aged woman in a large matron's wig that sprouts upon her shriveled head like dry moss on a roof. She holds in her hand a broken pair of brass spectacles and prays endlessly aloud out of a thick Korban Minḥa prayerbook. At the next window stands an old man wrapped in a prayer-shawl. His small face is wizened and furrowed, but on his forehead he wears a large, square phylactery whose polished box gleams through the windowpane. His withered lips maintain a continuous mumbling.

No matter how early Baylka rises, the first thing she sees is the old man and the old woman, the beadle and his wife, who remain all week long the sole worshippers in their small and empty prayer-house.

Baylka leans her head out of the window and looks down into the courtyard. The pavement's sharp, uneven cobblestones glisten, black and slippery from all the coal crushed underfoot. No matter how much snow has fallen, the crushed coal unfailingly creeps out from under it, just as in damp cellars the green stains of mildew always burst out again on the walls, no matter how many times they have been whitewashed. Women wrapped in shawls sit among sacks of coal and thin bundles of wood bound with straw. The women lean over their braziers, blowing with all their might; but instead of rekindling their fires, they succeed only in making the cold ashes fly up into their faces and eyes. On the other side of the courtyard, men squat in tiny shops amid massive heaps of rusty locks, chains, and hinges. Hunched over, hands thrust into sleeves, they sit with gaunt knees and shoulders shivering as though the scrap-iron's rust has already devoured their bones . . .

Looking up, Baylka beholds a gray strip of sky, like a dripping-wet sheet from which yellowish soap bubbles are trickling down. This sight makes her heart still heavier, and she turns instead to contemplate the surrounding houses.

She cannot help marveling: what is it that keeps this intricate maze of stairs, balconies, pillars, and roofs from collapsing? They crawl one over another, as if there were a fire below. They seem like clumps of smoke that have just for a moment assumed the shape of garrets and have lifted her, Baylka, up high, ever so high. Soon the clumps of smoke would dissolve and she would tumble down into an abyss, as in a dream.

An iron ladder clambers up a windowless wall, but cannot quite reach a small door directly under the roof. Perhaps, Baylka muses, some hairy hermit lives there who has cut himself off from the world—or could it be that this is where, at night, Party cells hold their meetings? In one corner the plaster has fallen off the wall, leaving bare bricks that look like slabs of frozen red meat. Tin waterpipes wind themselves about the walls and hang down like snakes dangling from the branches of trees, with their mouths open. A chimney stretches forth its long, soot-blackened neck and peers enviously out upon the glistening, opulent roofs in the distance, with their whitewashed, potbellied chimneys. Baylka cannot tear her gaze away from one heavily barred window whose broken panes have been stuffed up with rags. Why, she wonders, does that window need bars? What could anyone find to steal there—poverty?

Now she looks out over the arched gates of the ghetto: The winding streets teem and swarm with throngs of people; peddlers and street vendors run to and fro like black cockroaches. It's a pity, she muses, that her window doesn't overlook Butchers Lane. From there one can see both the Mountain of the Cross, near the Wilja River, and Castle Mountain. In the summertime the entire countryside is immersed in a sea of green, while now, in the winter, fresh-fallen snow glistens in the distance. At night the mountain's three crosses are ablaze with electric lights. But here, near her window, there is only a broken, unlit street-lantern that rattles and clanks so in the wind that on some nights she can't fall asleep at all.

Baylka bends over her sewing machine, thinking about her hometown, Glebokie. Her mother's thatch-roofed cottage is small and cramped, her little sisters run about barefoot until late in autumn, and there is never enough bread or potatoes for all. But the countryside is filled with forests and lakes, and a soaring sky. . . . With a start Baylka realizes that the time is slipping away; she cannot seem to get any work done today. Leaning her head against the "pony" of the sewing machine, she abandons herself to her daydreams of Soviet Russia.

From all corners of Poland young lads and girls have streamed toward Vilna. From Vilna they make their way to the Soviet border and then slip across into Communist White Russia. The Soviet Union has opened wide its gates to the unemployed youth of Poland. On the first of May and on the anniversary of the October Revolution she, together with her comrades, listens secretly to the Soviet radio. She hears the happy songs, the Red Army marches, and sees in her mind's eye the demonstrations with banners and the flushed, happy faces of the citizens who march and sing, march and dance. She knows that a Soviet worker, even from the remotest hamlet, can get an official permit to go to Moscow. There people attend the great theaters, walk about Red Square, and visit Comrade Lenin's mausoleum. In the Soviet Union, everyone can realize his ambitions. If you want to become an engineer, you become an engineer; if you want to be a doctor, you become a doctor. She would work in a factory during the day and study at night.

It isn't easy to get across the border. Over there, on the other side, the Soviets let everyone enter, but on this side stand the Poles, and the secret police catch many of the emigrants and beat them, screaming, "You sons of dogs, so you want to go to the Bolsheviks? Just wait, you'll be croaking yet, in your Red paradise, with longing for a Polish prison!" But the young people refuse to be deterred. Couples get married in Poland and then smuggle themselves across the border together: a girl cannot undertake such a journey alone, she dare not entrust herself to the peasants who serve as guides, and even there, in the Soviet Union, it is better to arrive with a comrade.

Baylka raises her head. The cold steel "pony" of the sewing machine has not cooled her feverish thoughts. Her fantasies flow as quickly as the white sheeting under the needle, and she begins to sing, in time with the rhythm of her foot pressing on the treadle, the song of the new happy life of the Soviet proletariat:

> *"See the fine house that stands nearby—*
> *Who built it, who created these riches?*
> *Who finished it with lime and with clay?*
> *A naked young lad from the ditches."*

EVERY EVENING, after Baylka has delivered her piecework, she lingers near our gate until I arrive. Everyone seems to be watching as I walk off with her; only my mother stands facing her merchandise and her scales, as though she hasn't noticed us at all. In a booming voice Alterka the goose-dealer gives expression to his thoughts:

"The former yeshiva student isn't doing any fasting now."

In the moonlight the narrow lanes of the ghetto are an interwoven network of light beams and shadow. The tiny houses seem to have moved even closer to one another, huddling together as if to protect Baylka's secret and mine from alien and envious eyes. We stand on the winding staircase that leads to a second story, sunk in a silent embrace.

Above us, in the dark corridor of the third floor, stand another couple: Layala and her young man, Paysaḥka the leather-stitcher. Baylka and Layala love each other like sisters, and share the same bed. Layala is a thin girl with transparent skin and weak, pale hands—a plant that has grown between the cobblestones of Ramayles' Courtyard. Her eyes are large and dark, and brim with a bluish moisture. Quiet and timid in bearing, she has a perpetually preoccupied air, as if her late mother had left her a house full of younger sisters to care for. But in fact she is her father's only child.

Paysaḥka the stitcher looks even more despondent than Layala—he is ashamed of his inadequacy as a man. These two have known each other a long time, longer than I know Baylka; as she and I stand quietly, intoxicated with our love, the voices of the now-solemn couple on the floor above drift down to us, echoing in the silence.

Layala:

"My father says he won't let me keep company with you anymore. If you don't marry me, he'll turn you out of the house."

Paysahka:

"I know we ought to get married. After all, we love each other. But tell me: what will we live on? I work only a few months a year, and you—not even that much. Where would we live?"

Layala:

"I managed to save a hundred and fifty zlotys when I was working, and my father will add to that—he'll borrow from the Free Loan Society. There'll be enough to buy warm clothes for both of us and to pay off the guides who'll smuggle us into Russia. There we'll easily find work and a place to live. Isn't that right, Paysahel?"

Paysahka:

"That's right, Layala. That's what all the Party instructors from Minsk say. I've never met them myself, but that's what I've been told in their name."

Layala:

"Don't you have to get permission from the Party to leave?"

Paysahka:

"I don't need anyone's permission. I'm not an official Party member, only a sympathizer."

Baylka moves away from me: she wants me to give heed to these dedicated, loyal comrades. Paysahka truly means to build a free life with Layala in the Soviet Union. Paysahka, unlike others, has no wish to remain in a dark Poland, freezing in some dark corridor together with his comrade.

"What was it Paysahka just said?" I ask Baylka softly. "He doesn't have to get the Party's permission to leave? And who does have to get permission?"

"Comrades of the Party cells, the ones who carry on its work," answers Baylka, still more softly. "Such members aren't allowed to leave without the permission of the Central Committee, unless they're in danger of being caught by the police—then they may flee and save themselves in the Soviet Union."

Baylka snuggles up against me, trembling with joy.

"Oh, life there is so good! Those who cross the border are sent to different places, some to the coal mines in the Donbas, and some to the factories in the Urals."

"Why don't they just let everyone go where he wants to?"

"Because for stealing over the Soviet border there has to be a punishment."

"But you only steal over the border on the Polish side, the Soviets invite you to come in."

"But there still has to be some punishment for crossing the border illegally—so you have to work it off for a few years in the Donbas or the Urals," replies Baylka with a tone of great authority and conviction.

"But why does there have to be any punishment, if they themselves ask you to come?" I persist, irritated by her sheeplike devotion. "Don't you understand that the instructors are fooling you and that this is all just pretense? They let people in in the first place only because they want unpaid laborers for the coal shafts of the Donbas and the Urals."

Baylka, as though fearing that the couple above might hear us, tries to calm me down:

"Siberia isn't the same now as when the Czar used to exile the revolutionaries there. Now Siberia is just like the Crimea—people from all over Russia go there for their vacations. All the workers in Russia have the right to paid vacations."

And, to pacify me further, she again begins to sing:

> *"Take a look at the bread, freshly baked, not a fable,*
> *Who sowed the seeds, who created these riches?*
> *Who put the bread on our table?*
> *A naked young lad from the ditches."*

"Listen, Baylka, the whole effect of that song is in the rhyme 'created the riches/ ditches.' It's a made-to-order bit of entertainment, just like a badhen's verse-making. The pious believe in God—and you believe in the demons of the ditches, of the Glebokie swamps. . . . I feel cold. Good night."

"Don't leave!" cries Baylka, terrified. "I'm cold, too. Warm my hands."

A frosty, silvery moon peeks in through the window at the narrow, winding stairs and winks at me:

"How much longer can you stand on the stairs, quarreling and making up? Be sensible, young man, be sensible. It's time to set up the wedding canopy. . . ."

"Demons of the Glebokie swamps, you say," Baylka whispers, tears trembling in her voice. "If only there had been swamps in Glebokie all year round, my father would be alive today. It was on a moonlit winter's night just like this that he went off to peddle in the villages. He drove his horse and sleigh across the frozen river, but the ice broke and he drowned. When I see how brightly the moon is shining and how peaceful everything is, I realize that in such brightness and peacefulness my father didn't suspect how thin the sparkling ice was, and that it would break just when he was in the middle of the river."

"That's true, Baylka, true. When the moon shines so bright and everything is so peaceful, no one would suspect that the sparkling ice could be so thin and break just when he is in the middle of the river." I breathe on her frost-numbed fingers to warm them.

When I get home, after midnight, our back room is dark. I do not see my mother's face, but in the mysterious stillness I sense that she is not asleep.

The moon appears in the window of our front room, as though she has stealthily followed me from Ramayles' Courtyard. Her face, even fuller than before, smiles the unctuous smile of a pious beadle's wife, a collector of good deeds:

"It's time to set up the wedding canopy. Be sensible, young man, be sensible . . ."

But my mother says not a word.

Friday Afternoon

ON FRIDAY AFTERNOONS Alterka's shop is as busy as a country fair. The work is enough to exhaust a lumberjack, but Alterka shows no sign of fatigue. With his blood-stained cleaver he cuts the geese up, while his wife, Lisa, speaks Russian with her more fashionable customers.

My mother sits beside her baskets and wonders: How is it that all these fine ladies need chickens, turkeys, and geese, but no fruit or vegetables?

"Malaga wine grapes, bottles of wine—who will buy? Who will buy?" Mother cries herself hoarse.

The ladies become curious—they know that the woman at the gate sells onions, raw horseradish, and overripe fruit. They walk over to look into her baskets, and burst into laughter: "She calls those frozen apples of hers 'Malaga wine grapes, bottles of wine' . . ."

Mother grows silent, scolding herself inwardly for envying the goose-dealer's wife. She lowers her eyes, as though she has decided to stop watching the goings-on in Lisa's shop, and forces herself to think of other matters:

She really cannot complain about her son. Every Friday, before sunset, he helps her bring her merchandise into the house and then recites the Kiddush for her. Often, when she is returning from the wholesale market, he waits for her and helps her carry her baskets to her stand at the gate. Yet she would have been a thousand times happier if he had remained a yeshiva student, and didn't help her carry her heavy loads. Such work was unworthy of a scholar.

Mother had not gone to bed at all the previous night; she had been busy preparing for the Sabbath. Now she begins to feel drowsy and dozes off—but almost immediately senses that someone has stopped beside her. Softly as a dove, she opens her eyes, to behold Reb Mayer, the egg-peddler.

Reb Mayer delivers fresh eggs to the homes of the wealthy. By Friday afternoon his work is done and, being a widower, he has no reason to rush home. He sees my mother sitting at the gate and, God be thanked, with no customers besieging her. He stops, takes the woven basket off his arm, and sets it down off to the side, so that no one will crush the remaining eggs, those rejected by his customers.

Reb Mayer is a fine, upright man, and Mother rises for him as though he were a scholar.

"What do you charge for this fruit?" he asks, and with two fingers, as carefully as though selecting an esrog for the Sukkoth festival, he takes from one of the baskets a wintry apple with a yellow-wrinkled skin.

Mother says that for this apple there is no charge.

Reb Mayer answers that he won't take it without paying for it, for it is written that "He that hateth gifts shall live." But if she were to accept an egg from him in exchange, then he would be willing to take the apple he is holding in his hand.

Mother peers into the woven egg-basket and tells Reb Mayer that he would be making a poor bargain to take such a wrinkled, last-year's apple in exchange for a fresh egg, radiant as the sun.

Reb Mayer answers that the two cannot be compared: they're entirely different kinds of food. To the All-Highest all things are possible, and He has created in His world a full and varied table, so as to give Jews the opportunity to pronounce many different blessings.

Reb Mayer wipes the apple with care, and with a glazed look pronounces the blessing ". . . Creator of the fruit of the tree." Mother, her hands folded under her apron, devoutly responds "Amen"—and blushes to the roots of her hair under her wig: Alterka's small eyes, she sees, have become moist and shiny, and over Lisa's round plump face has spread a smile. One might think that the goose-dealer and his wife are too busy with customers even to blow their noses, yet somehow they find the time to wink at each other about the widow and widower who stand chatting amicably at the gate.

Reb Mayer brings her luck; three housewives stop at her stand. But Mother—who, with her hand propped under her chin and a pious expression on her face, is now ready to listen to words of Torah, though it is still only mid-afternoon this Friday—is thrown into confusion by these newly arrived customers. How can she so abruptly turn away from Reb Mayer just as he is speaking of Torah? Reb Mayer, however, is not at all offended; on the contrary, he addresses one of the women, an inveterate haggler:

"If Vella asks for ten groschen for a bunch of onions, you must not argue with her. Vella will not cheat you."

The woman seems awed by this man and pays the full ten groschen. Now Reb Mayer, more sure of himself, turns to the second customer:

"How many Antonowkas do you want, a kilo?"

Deftly, like an experienced shopkeeper, he piles the apples into a paper bag and gives the bag to my mother to be weighed. In her confusion, Mother gives the woman too much, which upsets Reb Mayer:

"You're not obligated to do that, neither according to the law nor for the sake of justice."

Mother does not even hear what the third housewife wants. She stands aside, as though she is the stranger, and watches Reb Mayer attend to the customer.

AT THAT VERY MOMENT there appears at the other end of the street Reb Nossen-Nota, the synagogue Gabbai. He has just emerged, freshly bathed and combed, from the mikvah, and is thinking to himself how little pleasure there was in dealing with the shopkeepers just before candle-lighting time: if they have no fear of the sin of desecrating the Sabbath, will they be awed by a gabbai? But there was no help for it, one had to be ready to sacrifice himself, if need be, to make them close their shops.

Passing by a grocery, Reb Nossen-Nota observes that the window is shuttered and the door three-quarters closed. "Ḥatzkel the grocer attends my beth midrash," muses the Gabbai. "On Festivals, he's more eager than anyone to be called up to the Torah. On the High Holidays he purchases the honor of opening the Holy Ark. And yet, with all this piety, he still keeps his store just a little bit open." Reb Nossen-Nota pokes his head through the door—and stands frozen with shock and amazement.

The shop is packed with customers, yet such quiet reigns within that one might hear a feather drop. Evidently the customers know that they must be careful not to attract the attention of the "Sabbath Guardians." Ḥatzkel himself is so absorbed in weighing and measuring and counting money that he does not notice the Gabbai's long curled beard protruding into the open crack of the shop-door. Reb Nossen-Nota, seething inwardly, waits to observe the grocer's expression once he sees him, the Gabbai, standing there.

And at last the long curled beard in the doorway does catch the shopkeeper's eye.

"Reb Ḥatzkel," roars the Gabbai, "what is the meaning of this?"

The preoccupied shopkeeper, showing no sign of embarrassment, says simply, "I'll be closing up right away."

"Turn the customers out!" orders Reb Nossen-Nota.

"This very minute," agrees Ḥatzkel. He runs out from behind the counter, and sees women standing outside who want to enter the store but cannot—the Sabbath Guardian bars their way. The shopkeeper hastily flings the door open, and the Gabbai all but tumbles head over heels as the throng behind him surges in.

"And you," rants Reb Nossen-Nota, beside himself with rage, "you shut your eyes so piously and sway so fervently when you pray!"

Hatzkel closes his eyes, as though indeed in prayer, and leans angrily forward toward the Gabbai.

"Do you pay my debts? Do you pay my taxes?"

"You pay your debts, you pay your taxes," comes the acid retort, "but you don't pay the pledges for charity you announce in the synagogue."

A charge that he used false weights and cheated his customers would not outrage Hatzkel so much as this accusation of failing to pay the pledge he had made for the honor of opening the Ark. He shakes his hands as though scalded and screeches, his eyes still closed:

"Get out of my shop!"

In the face of such impudence Reb Nossen-Nota is left speechless. He does not even try to resist when the shopkeeper, without further ado, shoves him out of the store and slams the door behind him.

"It's easy for him to talk," Hatzkel harangues the housewives before him. "He's got a hardware store, so he can afford to close early. Who needs locks or bars on Friday afternoon just before candle-lighting? But let him just try to keep a grocery and sell retail. Here it is, almost Sukkoth. The shop has to be closed for the first two days of the holiday, the day after that is the Sabbath, and then comes Sunday—not to mention all the gentile holidays. Where is the Gabbai's sense of justice, I ask you? Where is his human decency, will you tell me?"

"Reb Hatzkel," interrupts one of the women, "I have no time. My fish will be burnt."

Once more the grocer begins to weigh, measure, and take money— hurriedly, since, after all, he does not want to be late to the synagogue for the Welcoming of the Sabbath.

"What can one think, what can one say?" reflects the Gabbai. If Hatzkel speaks to him in such a fashion, how will others speak? He passes by several shops without even deigning to look inside. "May my sins too fall on their heads," he thinks. But as he approaches our courtyard, his self-confidence returns: this is his courtyard; he is the landlord, and his tenants will not dare to defy him.

All this boldness vanishes, however, when he sees the horde of customers in Alterka's shop. Every time he, Reb Nossen-Nota, asks Alterka for the rent, the goose-dealer tells him: "Come back tomorrow." Reb Nossen-Nota is afraid to insist too strongly, for Alterka, a man who has shown himself capable of beating up a slaughterer, would be all the less likely to stand on ceremony with him. So now he, the landlord and Gabbai, speaks softly:

"It's time to close up shop."

Alterka does not answer; he pretends not to have heard.

The Gabbai speaks again: "Time to begin the Sabbath."

Lisa, chatting away in Russian with her better-heeled customers, stops just long enough to give her husband a look. Alterka's face turns blue, like a plucked, half-frozen turkey, and he emits a murderous growl:

"Come back tomorrow."

The Gabbai does not dare say another word. "I'd be risking my life," he thinks, and walks away. He is about to head straight for the beth midrash, when he catches sight of the fruit-seller still standing at the gate, deep in conversation with the egg-peddler.

"My son has strayed into other paths," Mother is complaining to Reb Mayer, "but he does keep the commandment 'Honor thy mother.'"

"Honoring one's mother is a very great merit," pronounces Reb Mayer. "My daughters have all married very well. They plead with me: 'Father, why should you keep on peddling? Come stay with us.' But I don't want to have to inspect their pots and pans to see whether they observe kashruth."

"It's best to visit children just on holidays," says Mother. "'Better a straw husband than golden children.'"

"So this is the kind of pious woman you are?" an angry voice breaks in. It is on Mother that the Gabbai now vents all his pent-up rage. "And here I've been charging her next to nothing for her space at the gate. I said to myself, 'She's a poor widow, a religious woman, she'll observe the Sabbath.' On people like you, it's forbidden to take pity!"

"But there's still ten minutes to candle-lighting time," protests Mother, bewildered.

She does not know where to hide for shame—that she should need to be reminded of the Sabbath's beginning! And even worse, in Reb Mayer's hearing. It is just at this moment that I appear on the scene. She gives me a deeply forlorn and guilty look, as though I have caught her committing the most heinous transgression. Reb Mayer, for his part, does not find it to his taste to stand and listen to the Gabbai's accusations, and he likes even less my staring at him. . . . He vanishes in the wink of an eye. Mother hurriedly takes her stand apart.

"Carry the baskets into the house," she tells me.

The Gabbai now draws himself up, hands behind his back, like a general surveying troops who have been derelict in their duty, and shouts at the top of his voice:

"I closed my hardware store two hours ago, and you can't tear yourself away from your rotten apples. No wonder your son grew up to be such a brazen libertine. I see you wear both a wig and a kerchief—that's probably your way of atoning before the Almighty because this jewel of yours walks around bareheaded, without a hat."

"Get out of here!" I fall upon him. "Your so-called piety is worthless before God! You flay the skin off your poor tenants' backs!"

"I'll hack off your hands and feet and put you in chains!" screams Reb Nossen-Nota. "You think I don't know you write articles in the newspapers against the landlords? You rabble-rouser! I'll see you rot in jail yet!"

"Bloodsucker!" I fire back.

The Gabbai stands open-mouthed: This ill-begotten brat of this beggar-woman who sits at his gate, lives in one of his apartments—this scum dares to speak this way to him, the landlord of the entire courtyard? No, he simply cannot believe his ears.

By now a crowd of passers-by has collected around us. Alterka deserts his turkeys and all his fashionable customers and comes running, breathless. He swells with delight to hear me berate the landlord, the Sabbath Guardian—the ally of his, Alterka's, enemies, the ritual slaughterers. But my mother clasps me to her with trembling hands; I can hear the feverish beating of her heart. Overcome with grief and agitation, she can barely speak:

"My child, don't shorten your life with such a sin—after all, he is an old man."

"I a bloodsucker?" The Gabbai in high dudgeon harangues the staring passers-by around him. "These people live in my house for years without paying a penny. If I say a word, they threaten to have the newspaper write about me. If I weren't a Sabbath observer, they'd obey me like puppy dogs. But they know that, out of fear of desecrating the Name of God, I don't want people wagging their tongues against pious Jews—so they take a ride on my back."

Alterka the goose-dealer, rubbing his hands with glee, baits the Gabbai:

"You'd better get away. He might really beat you up. You're playing with fire!"

"With such an atheist," the Gabbai says fearfully to himself, "who can tell! And to think this is someone I used to allow through the door of my beth midrash! One ought to scorch with fire the place where he used to sit."

But Reb Nossen-Nota is destined to face terror yet again this day. As he turns to walk down the street, he suddenly sees women lugging baskets in their hands and running in panic, like chickens with outspread wings. The Gabbai, more dead than alive, looks around desperately.

The peddlers who have no permanent stands are unable to obtain legal permits to do business. They stand in the streets with their wares, always keeping an eye out for policemen. But the police, in their dark-blue uniforms, have a way of coming upon them stealthily. Abruptly, with no warning, one woman catches sight of a gleaming black boot kicking her basket. The merchandise scatters into the gutter, and the policeman hisses:

"Patent masz?"—"Do you have a permit?"

The other peddlers begin to run. But rows of policemen close off the street on all sides and the women fall into their clutches.

The street is filled with tumult and weeping. The peddlers' wares are scattered and roll on the pavement, and the women are taken to the station-house.

The Gabbai, recovering from his needless fright, draws his own moral from the incident:

"Had the women gone home at the right time, well before sunset, they would have avoided this punishment from Heaven and wouldn't be in jail at candle-lighting time."

And Reb Nossen-Nota enters the well-lit beth midrash for the Welcoming of the Sabbath.

Mother is one of the lucky ones: she does business at the gate of the courtyard, and therefore has a permit. As the arrested women are led past her, her heart is torn with pain. She has not yet recovered from her earlier humiliation, and her face burns with shame. She looks down at the ground and her tears flow as though the cobblestones were her Sabbath candles.

Velvel the Tailor

"**B**AYLKA WAS ASKING about you," my mother tells me. "It's just as people say: 'The daughter-in-law has been living in the house for seven years and still doesn't know that the cat has no tail.' Day in, day out, you've been going for walks with Baylka, and I never knew till now that she's boarding at Velvel the tailor's."

Though Mother long ago made up her mind not to meddle in my relationship with Baylka, she has lately been forgetting that resolve. From day to day her face assumes a steadily more festive look—the look of a bridegroom's mother, pondering what dress to wear to the wedding.

"Why does it make you so happy to know that Baylka is living at Velvel the tailor's?" I ask.

"I don't mean anything at all," says my mother, "but Velvel the tailor—though I don't wish to speak ill of him—is such an angry and a gloomy man. His wife, Roha, has suffered quite enough on that account. I don't say anything—just that, if Baylka can get along with him, she must be a very fine and gentle girl."

At once Mother realizes that she has said too much. Oh, the tongue, the tongue! It is soft and moves as if on its own, like a windmill. A few words let loose, and what terrible destruction it has wrought! For a single careless word, one may lose both this world and the World-to-Come. . . .

"On the other hand," Mother continues, "one can't really blame Velvel. Although he's been poor all his life, he's a very decent person, and a fine baal-tefilah besides, leading services in the synagogue. And his daughter Layala is as good as gold, and has suffered a great deal in silence. She's a friend of Baylka's, and one may well say: Show me who your friend is and I'll tell you who you are."

VELVEL THE TAILOR has a reputation for ill temper and bitterness. I have known him since I was a child. He attended the Artisans' Synagogue together with our neighbor Reb Boruhel. Once on Simhat Torah my mother and I were visiting our neighbor Blumele, who had invited us over for tea and cake. The door opened and in tottered Reb Boruhel, her dear old man. Blumele smacked her hands together:

"Boruḥel, you're not alone!"

She realized immediately that he had taken a few drinks with the workingmen at the synagogue in honor of the festival. His head was spinning and a dozen Boruḥels swam before his eyes—Blumele had good reason to say, "You're not alone!"

From behind him an angry voice called out:

"Indeed, he's not alone!"

Velvel the tailor, a slight and bony man with a small beard and a large hump on his back, was supporting Reb Boruḥel to keep him from falling.

Blumele was vexed by Velvel's tone of voice and by his grimaces, which suggested a certain mockery of her dear old man's difficulty in staying on his feet. With obvious chagrin, she responded:

"Nu, and you drank nothing in honor of Simḥat Torah?"

"I drank and remained sober," answered Velvel gloomily. "It's my misfortune that I just can't get drunk."

"You, Velvel, are never satisfied. Even on a holiday you're grouchy," said Blumele.

"And what do I have to rejoice for?" retorted Velvel more gloomily still. "All the Torah I've managed to study during the year?"

"How is your Roḥa?"

"How should she be, with a husband who's a ne'er-do-well, a buttonhole sewer?" Velvel tugged at his beard; it was clear that his ill humor was gnawing the life out of him. He left without so much as looking at the refreshments that Blumele had placed before him.

Blumele put her husband to bed and then turned to my mother:

"People might think my Boruḥel is a tippler. The truth is that he gets dizzy if he just sips a little soda-water. . . . I've seen many poor people in my life, but I've never known anyone as bitter as Velvel. Yet his wife is truly a saint. Indeed, the Almighty sits up high in the Heavens, and arranges marriages down here on earth. Only a woman like Roḥa could get along with such a kill-joy."

Roḥa was a tall, plump woman, short of breath, who always wore an apologetic smile, as if she felt indebted to everyone. Actually, her only debt was to Blumele. It was from her that Roḥa borrowed money from time to time, in secret, so that her husband, Velvel, might know nothing about it. Blumele, for her part, felt that, with her children in Argentina sending money regularly, she could afford to give charity—though under the pretext of a loan so as not to put Roḥa to shame.

Work was something Velvel had never had too much of. Every Sunday morning he would go down to the Synagogue Courtyard to look for the posted announcements of recent deaths. In the matter of funerals he was so efficient that he would sometimes manage to attend several burials in one day. When he was seen hurrying through the streets with his little cane, people asked one another: "Who died?"

In these funerals Velvel played a prominent role. From the moment the corpse was carried out of the house to the final closing of the grave, he issued a steady stream of commands: "Set the coffin down! . . . Pull out the bier!" And since everyone knew he had great experience in these matters, all the mourners obeyed. During the eulogy he would sigh and moan no less than the closest relations of the deceased. Afterwards he would say:

"Ah, that was a fine eulogy. I had a really good cry."

People wondered about Velvel: He's small as a fig, yet has the voice of a lion. Why didn't he become a cemetery-cantor, or at least a grave-digger, or one of those who help prepare the corpse for burial? Then he, the patcher of old clothes, would at least make a living.

"But you know what he says," a neighbor pointed out in answer to this question. "He attends funerals in order to enjoy a good cry. At his sewing machine he sits as glum as if all his ships had gone down at sea. But if the cemetery becomes his livelihood, it won't be a holiday, won't be a pleasure to him any more. Don't forget, this is a hunchback you're dealing with!"

After Reb Boruhel and Blumele died, Roha no longer had anyone to turn to for succor. Her breath became even shorter and more labored. Then, one day, just as she had dragged herself up the narrow winding steps that led to the attic where they lived, she slipped and fell back down the steps—and never rose from her sickbed again.

On those same garret steps down which Roha had fallen, her only daughter, now a young woman, often stood with her fiancé, Paysahka the stitcher, and there on moonlit nights they dreamed of going together to the Soviet Union. Velvel, however, insisted that they get married first. Layala sided with her father, and Paysahka gave in.

WHEN MY MOTHER told me that Baylka had asked for me, I went to see her. She was not at home. The only one I found in was Velvel, bent over his sewing machine.

"They've all gone off to set things up with a band of musicians," he said morosely. "Our bridegroom suddenly decided that he has to have fiddles and drums. 'You'—he says to me—'don't want to let your daughter leave until she's stood under the marriage canopy, and I don't want to get married without music.'"

Velvel proceeded to repeat to me his entire conversation with his son-in-law-to-be, Paysaḥka the stitcher:

" 'A marriage canopy'—I tell him—'you can have in the rabbi's home, but once you call in the musicians, it has to be a big wedding. You have to hire a hall, invite guests, and feed a lot of freeloading gluttons, not to mention paying the musicians. Layala's savings will barely be enough to buy the two of you warm clothes for your journey. As for the loan I'll get from the Free-Loan Society, all of it will go for your travel expenses: the border guides, those bloodsuckers, demand a fortune.'

" 'No,' says he, 'I want a wedding with music.'

" 'You're always telling us'—I say to him—'that in Russia, ever since they got rid of the Czar, there's nothing but singing and dancing in the streets. That's where you're going now, so you'll have plenty of music and merry-making.'

"But the bridegroom digs in his heels: music!

"And I understand him! He has no father, he has no mother, he's marrying a poor girl who lives in an attic in Ramayles' Courtyard, and for a dowry he's getting a shroud sewn with kosher threads. So he's rebelling against God and wants to have at least one day in his life when he won't feel like a pauper.

"Well, he's getting his way. But still, being merciful, he's willing to compromise a little—he didn't insist that I hire a regular hall. So I ran around like a lunatic until I found a man who's willing to let us use his home for the wedding. Then your Baylka came up with the good news that she's heard of a band I won't have to pay for: they're paid by the couples who dance at the wedding. And Baylka is really looking forward to dancing with you. . . . 'And you, Father'—says my Layala to me—'you'll sing; you have a good voice.' 'Of course I'll sing'—I say to her. 'I'll sing the Purim song "The Rose of Jacob," because for me you are a rose—a rose that grew in Ramayles' Courtyard.'

" 'In the Soviet Union'—pipes up our bridegroom—'there are no stinking courtyards, all the houses are made of glass.' Russia, he tells me, is so big that the sun never sets there. When it sets for the Bolsheviks in the west, it rises for the Bolsheviks in the east. A country, he says, that's one-sixth of the whole world.

"I look at him and say to myself: Paysaḥka the stitcher needs a country that's one-sixth of the entire world? He expects, it seems, to become King Solomon there, riding on the clouds, having breakfast in Jerusalem and dinner with the Queen of Sheba. . . .

"Paysaḥka sees that to me the length and breadth of his kingdom don't amount to much, so for me he finds a different consolation. 'In the Soviet Union,' he tells me, 'you wouldn't have to stand in the rear of the synagogue. You'd be an honored member of the congregation, like every-one else, and you could lead the services every day.'

"How do you like that? He thinks it bothers me that I don't get to lead the services in our beth midrash. . . ."

And Velvel breaks into mordant laughter.

For as long as I remember Velvel, he has never changed: his small beard has not become grayer, his face has not aged—only the hump on his bony back seems to have grown. Whenever Velvel coughs his dry cough, his bent back bends still lower and his hump leaps up, leaps up like some living creature sitting on his back—a giant toad relentlessly driving him on, to sew, to cough, to speak:

"I've never tried to push my way up to the cantor's pulpit. At a funeral, if the deceased is an ordinary, poor man, I help with the ar-rangements, but at the funeral of a rabbi or a scholar, where it is an honor to be a pall-bearer, I stand at a distance and listen to the eulogies. As for leading the services on a festival, I know there are others more worthy than I. People do say I have a powerful voice, but it has no soft tones of supplication, only those of anger, of complaint. It's true that when I listen to a good eulogist, I can be moved to tears, but when I myself pray, I snarl like a cutthroat. So I stand buried in my corner, and it doesn't even occur to me to glance up at the cantor's pulpit, I know that on Yom Kippur Reb Kalmonka leads Ne'ilah, Reb Zalmanka chants the Additional Service, the Morning Service is led by Reb Zoraḥel, and the early prayers at daybreak by Reb Boruḥel.

"Once it happened that Reb Boruḥel was unable to lead the prayers—this was about a year before he died. Actually, he was as good as dead already, but Blumele with her prayers had 'shrieked away' the Angel of Death. If anyone ever tried to 'shriek death away' like that for me, I'd kill him: haven't I suffered enough in this rotten world already? But then, Reb Boruḥel wasn't a ruffian like me; he was like an unblemished lamb—so good, so quiet, so humble. And who can say, it may be that leading the prayers on a holiday earns you great merit in the sight of Heaven, and so lets you draw out another year. Still, say what you will, Reb Boruḥel is so weak that no one can make out what he is babbling, and the Gabbai says to me: 'Velvel, you go up to the lectern.' And it so happens that on this day there is no one more to the congregation's liking than Velvel. I say to myself: 'Am I really the man to stand at the lectern—I? With my appearance, my clothes, my respectability?' But then the Gabbai tells me again: 'Velvel, go!' I say to myself: 'Who can really refuse—I? Rich man that I am, with all the contributions I make to the beth midrash? So let me at least contribute one prayer service.' And so I did. And how did I lead the service? I led it—nothing to make a fuss over! To chant the opening prayers is like—you should pardon the comparison—like making a buttonhole. When I finished, I went back to my place in the rear of the beth midrash.

"At the end of the service, I see Reb Boruḥel coming toward me with his doddering little steps. I'm thinking he must be feeling weak, and wants me to walk him home. Who else would he ask, some rich craftsman who's in a hurry to get home to make Kiddush? But what I get from Reb Boruḥel instead is accusations and complaints. 'There's a beth midrash right near my house,' he said, 'but I drag myself all the way here because in this beth midrash for years I've had the privilege of leading the early morning prayers on holidays. You, Velvel, have robbed me of this privilege,' says he. 'You've shamed an old friend,' says he. You hear? That's how he abuses me.

"So, I ask you—" in his anger Velvel starts to rip out with his teeth the threads of a poorly made buttonhole—"would Reb Boruḥel have spoken that way to any more upstanding member of the congregation? Looking at him, you'd think, such a weak old man, bent over almost to the ground, his soul barely clinging to his body—and still he is stronger and superior to me. He would never talk like that to a proper tailor— not even to a patch-sewer in Laybe-Layzar's Courtyard. But to me, the town goat, the official funeral attendant, the fifth wheel on the cart, the artist who sews buttonholes in cheap garments from wholesale tailors— to me, everyone can say whatever his spittle brings to his lips."

As Velvel talks on, I feel as though I myself have grown a gray beard and am sitting in an old-age home, amid old men who continue to keep alive ancient quarrels from the distant past. I look out upon the snow that is falling on the slanted garret window, and I think of how the wind must be sweeping the snow from the graves of Reb Boruḥel and Blumele. Their two gravestones huddle against each other just as the two old people had clung to one another in life.

"I think you exaggerate," I say to Velvel. "You yourself said that Reb Boruḥel was like an innocent lamb and only wanted to earn merit in Heaven. That's why he was upset when he was denied the right to lead the service. And he certainly didn't mean to humiliate you, and the trustees of the beth midrash didn't show you any contempt. You're imagining it all."

"Of course they don't show me their contempt"—Velvel jumps up— "or I'd scratch their eyes out! But I know what they think of me in their hearts. And even if they don't think it, I think myself that I don't deserve respect. And furthermore I don't deserve a share in the World-to-Come. What my lot is in this world, you can see for yourself; but I don't have any part in the next world either, not a crumb of it. How little I study Torah, how little I give to charity—that can be excused: I'm poor and I'm ignorant. But who stops me from being gentle and good-hearted, like Reb Boruḥel? Now take my Roḥa, peace be upon her. She earned the next world, she earned Paradise. She suffered, and she accepted her suffering: she smiled. And it wasn't only from our poverty that she suffered, but from me, her crazy husband, wicked of the wicked. And it was just because of the way she accepted our sorrows, because of her constant smile, that I made her suffer. I used to scream at her: 'What are you smiling for? My wise one, what is it you understand that I don't understand? Go to the doctor in the charity hospital—maybe he'll cure you of that foolish smile. It's an illness—a kind of paralysis of the mouth . . .' That was how I screamed at her. And I would see her lips begin to quiver: now, I thought, she'll cry at last—but no, then again would come that smile.

"Only at Blumele's funeral did she weep, weep as though it were her own mother who had died. It was a day of bitter frost, and the wind was so icy it would have sent wolves howling. Even I, the 'official' funeral attendant, didn't stick my nose out the door. And sure enough, it's on just such a day that our synagogue beadle comes to give me the news of Blumele's death. So I say to myself: In such a fierce frost, who will attend the funeral? In this case, it's a 'mitzvah for the dead' to go. So I go, and Roḥa with me. There was almost no one else at the cemetery: after Reb Boruḥel's death, Blumele moved away from your courtyard and hid herself somewhere on Poplawska Street; and the beadle, with the day as cold as it was, didn't make the rounds as he should have to inform people—he didn't even tell your mother.

"Out there in the graveyard, the blizzard and the cold are even worse. So the burial is rushed, there are no words of eulogy, no tears shed. Blumele, after all, had lived out her allotted days. Only my Roḥa weeps and weeps. She bends over the open grave and speaks into it: 'Blumele, may God reward and repay you!' To repay what, and why, I didn't know. But when we return home, Roḥa tells me how Blumele had often lent her money secretly, so that I shouldn't find out about it. 'You would only have screamed that we couldn't repay it,' Roḥa says. Once again I, with my pride, am the villain.

"Only after Roḥa died did the smile at last leave her face. In death, she looked so pale and worn out, as though all her life she'd been wearing heavy chains which only now had been removed. When a person fixes a smile upon her face, fixes it as if it were set with putty and plaster, to keep herself from crying out in pain, is it any wonder that she becomes short of breath? My one fear now is that my Layala might begin to smile like her mother. . . .

"Since Roḥa's death I no longer attend funerals. I'm no longer trying to gain merit by escorting the dead to their graves. I don't deserve to share in the World-to-Come. I can't even shed tears any more over a eulogy, I'm dried out like an old tub. And even if I could still manage to squeeze out a tear, I wouldn't permit myself the pleasure of a good cry.

"Paysaḥka, now, is an atheist—so be it. He's rebelled against God, against the whole world, and is going over to the Bolsheviks. I, Velvel, don't have the gall to become an atheist. But there is one question I want to ask you: When the Messiah comes—so it says in the holy books—he will ride on a donkey and will spend the Sabbath in the home of a poor man. Could it really happen, then, that the Messiah would find his way to a Jew who lives in an attic, a pauper whom no one calls 'Reb Ze'ev'* or even 'Reb Velvel,' but just plain 'Velvel'? Could the Messiah really come to someone like that? It's hard to believe. . . .

"But I see you can't sit still any more; listening to me talk is to you like eating a bitter onion. You're right, I'm a regular chatterbox. It's only that so often my thoughts are too much for me; I get cramps in my belly, and I just have to ease my heartache by talking to someone. And yet, do you really think that talking or spitting green bile as I laugh makes it any easier to bear? Not by so much as a hair!"

Velvel bites his lips with such force that the hairs of his scraggly little beard stand out stiffly, as though a handful of needles have become embedded in his chin. For a long time he sits motionless, lost in thought. At last he says:

"The girls should have been back by now. It's not so easy, it seems, to find musicians who don't have to be paid. . . . And when will you and Baylka be celebrating your wedding? When you get married, you'll be making things easier for your mother, too. You and Baylka will go to the Bolsheviks together with my Layala and her Paysaḥka, and your mother will marry Reb Mayer, the egg-dealer."

I myself can't say whether the chagrin I now feel is due to Velvel's getting me married to Baylka and sending us off to Russia without further ado, or to the idea that my mother is planning to marry the egg-dealer.

"How do you know my mother is going to marry the egg-dealer?" I ask, stunned.

"How do I know?" says Velvel. "Everybody knows. Reb Mayer is a fine man, respected by everyone, your mother will have in him a man who pleases both God and his fellow men. Who else, then, should your mother marry—me? . . ."

*"Ze'ev" ("Wolf") is the formal Hebrew name of which "Velvel" is the informal Yiddish version.—Trans.

The Temptation

THAT SABBATH MORNING, my mother returns from services with face drawn and eyes downcast. She enters the room in silence, sets her prayerbook down on the workbench, and murmurs in a strained voice, more to the walls than to me:

"Good Sabbath."

I can see that she is deeply distressed. Without removing the frayed fur jacket that has been her "Sabbath best" ever since her wedding, she sits down dejectedly.

"It would have been," she says, after long deliberation, "more fitting for you to speak to me directly, instead of sending a messenger."

"What sort of messenger did I send you?"

"You sent Velvel the tailor to speak to me."

I look at her in surprise, and my expression tells her I have no idea what she is talking about. Then she explains that Velvel, who usually attends the Artisans' Synagogue, had prayed this week in our beth midrash. When she emerged from the women's section, he was waiting for her, and at once gave her to understand—in characteristically angry and resentful tones—that she must not interfere with my marrying Baylka or our going to Russia. "I have only one daughter," he said, "yet I'm letting her go to the Bolsheviks with her husband. Just because Baylka has no dowry, does that mean she must remain an old maid?" Thus Velvel.

"And now I ask you—" my mother turns to me with great emotion—"have I ever said a word against your marrying Baylka? Velvel, of course, is quite right: what if Baylka is poor, does that mean she should never marry? To tell the truth, I've never been able to condemn poor girls who get involved in love affairs. How else can they get married if not through affairs—can they send a matchmaker? It's the young men of today who are no good. They take up with a young girl, break her heart, and then cast her aside, leaving her to cry the years away, just as the songs say. By all means, marry Baylka. I like her very much. She's a pretty, gentle, hard-working girl, not one of those painted dolls you see nowadays. But why do you have to go away and leave me all alone?"

"Mother, I never asked Velvel to speak to you, and neither did

Baylka. He would like us to go together with his children so that things will be happier for them."

"I'll treat Baylka like my own daughter," says Mother happily, and she draws a deep breath—a heavy stone has been lifted from her heart. "I will yet live to have joy from you and to carry a grandchild in my arms. Blumele, peace be upon her, used to find cake-crumbs stuck onto her children's letters. 'We had a party,' the children would write, 'so we're sending you some of our cake.' And my partner, may she keep away from the living, would cry both for sorrow and for joy. Often the letters were also covered with such squiggles and curlicues that even a scholar who knows all the seventy languages of the world couldn't have figured them out. That was because her daughters-in-law would put a pen into a child's fingers and guide the little hand across the sheets of paper—a greeting for Grandmother. You can imagine how Blumele felt, knowing that she couldn't cover her grandchildren with kisses. So I wasn't a bit surprised that she wanted to join her children in Argentina, or that she argued with her Boruhel, who only wanted to go to the Land of Israel.

"But as for me, my son, I don't want to go to the Bolsheviks in Russia, not for all the gold in the world! I've heard that they've closed all the synagogues there, and I've heard also that they don't let in old people—they only want those who are fit for labor. So, my son, wouldn't it be better for you and Baylka to remain here, so I may live to have joy from you? The Almighty can help you here, too—He is everywhere. . . . And no matter what, here you'll remain closer to true Jewishness than if you go there." These last words Mother utters softly and pleadingly.

"Baylka will never marry me unless I go to Russia with her."

"Oh—but why?"

"Baylka says that here she'll always remain a slave to her sewing machine, while in Russia she'll find happiness. That's why she absolutely will not stay here."

Mother remains sitting quietly, her head bowed. Her hands lie limply in her lap; she stares at her work-worn fingers, cracked by frost and gnarled by years of toil.

"Then Velvel the tailor is right after all," she says at last, in great agitation. "It's because you don't want to leave me alone that you don't want to marry Baylka and go away with her. So it seems that I'm responsible, and for my sake you're giving up your bride, an orphan."

"She's not my bride yet!"

"What do you mean, she's not your bride? Haven't you been keeping company with her and turning her head? Well—I mean . . . haven't you ever kissed her, or stroked her cheek?"

"Yes," I say, "I have."

Mother's face lights up. She looks at me as though in wonder: just when did her little boy turn into a grown man? But at once she becomes serious again. What does she have to be so proud of, that her son, for the sake of some fun and good times, doesn't hesitate to turn a girl's head? She takes off her fur jacket, wraps herself in a shawl, and starts to leave to fetch the cholent.

"Mother—" I call her back—"I still need to talk to you about another matter. All your life you've thought only about me, and forgotten about yourself. As long as I was a child, you never wanted me to have a stepfather. Since I grew up, you've been waiting for me to get married. Now that nothing's happening between Baylka and me, I don't want you to wait any longer. Do you want to marry Reb Mayer?"

Mother takes her hand off the doorknob and remains standing with her back toward me.

"You wouldn't be angry at me if I were to marry Reb Mayer?"

"Of course not! Reb Mayer is a very fine man and I know he'll be good to you."

Mother walks back from the door with slow, unsteady steps, like an invalid just risen from a sickbed.

"Reb Mayer," she says softly, "is a fine man. When he delivers his eggs to the housewives, they always ask him to sit down for a while and have a glass of tea, and they enjoy chatting with him."

"You see, Mother, just what I said. When you marry Reb Mayer, you'll begin to live for yourself too, not just for me."

"I'd have someone to say Kiddush for me," she continues, even more softly. "You, my son, say Kiddush only to please me, not because it's God's commandment. And you no longer recite the Grace After Meals."

"And Reb Mayer will help you in your business, too."

"And Reb Mayer," she echoes my words, "will help me in my business, too. He, may no evil eye befall him, brings luck. Whenever he stops at my fruit stand for a little while, customers begin flocking to me from all sides. And when he tells the women the price of the fruit, they don't try to bargain with him. People respect him."

"And he himself earns a living, too," I add.

"He earns much more than I do," agrees my mother with satisfaction. "Although he carries his wares from house to house in a basket, he earns more than I do at my stand."

"And you won't have to take care of any small children. His daughters are all married."

"And very handsomely married!" she exclaims with pride, as though Reb Mayer's daughters were her own nieces. "I wouldn't need to be a stepmother."

In her heart, Mother has to this day never been sure she did enough for her stepsons. She had always imagined that they looked askance at her for having taken their mother's place. So she never touched the dresses that had been left by the dead woman, and she had been more devoted to her husband's sons by his first marriage than to me, her own and only son. No matter how one treats her own flesh and blood, nobody will say anything, but whenever a woman joins herself to a widower with children and the slightest thing goes wrong, people say, "That's a stepmother for you."

Mother speaks her final thought out loud:

"I will never again marry a man who still has children to be cared for."

"So what is your decision, Mother—are you going to marry Reb Mayer?"

She looks at me in confusion, as though she has completely forgotten how our conversation began.

"And what about you?"

"I'll move into a furnished room."

"No," she sighs. "I shall not remarry until you've celebrated your own wedding."

"But why? I can go and live by myself. Or, if you absolutely insist on it, I'll stay and live with you. I'll get along well with Reb Mayer, I promise you."

"No." Mother shakes her head. "I shall not remarry as long as you're not married. I don't want people to talk about me and say that I couldn't wait until my son found his own happiness. And for the sake of your father's memory also, peace be upon him, I don't want to do it. Besides, I don't know whether Reb Mayer would want to live together with you. I've just said that I don't want to marry a man who has children living with him, so why should he want a widow with a son? And, on top of that, you've cast off the yoke of tradition, while Reb Mayer is a very pious Jew. I'm your mother, so I endure it, but he's not your father. . . . Yet it's true, I've been thinking that once you found your proper wife, I could then make life easier for myself."

"Well, then, do you want me to marry Baylka and go to Russia with her? She won't have me otherwise."

"What are you saying?" Her lips tremble. "That I want my only son to leave me just so I can get married? Is that what you think, you, my only child?"

"And I also know that I have only one mother." I gently pat her wig and kiss her face.

"Don't kiss me—I'm not a Torah scroll," she says sternly. Her cheeks tremble and her chin quivers, as if she is exerting all her strength to keep from bursting into tears. "You might have found a girl who isn't drawn, as if by tongs, to the Bolsheviks. Then I wouldn't have to choose between you and Reb Mayer. But such is always my bitter fate—may my words not be reckoned against me in Heaven."

And Mother went out to get the cholent.

When she returns, her face is dry and red, as though she has been crying. She puts down the pot, takes off her shawl, and begins to set the table.

"The cholent has gotten cold, and the baker complained because I kept him waiting so long. You've addled my wits with all your nonsense," she says angrily. Her jaw is firmly set, her forehead wrinkled, as though with determination to expel all dreams from her head.

Bit by bit, however, the rigid lines of her face soften. Slowly she lowers her long eyelashes and begins to smile.

"A peculiar man, this Velvel the tailor. He came to me, or so it seemed, to talk about you and Baylka, but it turned out he had something to say about Reb Mayer as well. 'When your son leaves, you'll marry the egg-peddler,' he tells me with this strange excitement. 'Mayer has a very dignified appearance, tall and straight, and his beard isn't plucked out.' And at the very moment he said this, he was plucking at his own beard. Anyone else would avoid dwelling on his own affliction, but Velvel was clearly referring to his crooked back. 'For all the housewives,' he says to me angrily, 'Reb Mayer is the best of the best—not a mere buttonhole-sewer from the attic in Ramayles' Courtyard.' He, Velvel, was eating himself alive with anger. And here I always thought that such envy existed only among us women, the stall-keepers. But then, you can't really blame him. He's letting his daughter go far away and he'll be left all alone."

She sits awhile lost in thought, her head bowed.

"Mother, why aren't you eating?"

"I don't feel like eating, my heart is heavy. But you go ahead and eat. The cholent is already a little too cool, but it turned out well, fit for a very honored guest."

She turns away from the table and, with a sad smile, addresses her work-gnarled hands which are lying in her lap:

"Reb Mayer could take a young wife—even a rich one—so he wouldn't have to peddle his eggs from a basket any longer. I don't begin to understand why he wants only me. It would be ridiculous for me to ask him to wait until my son gets married. He'd just find himself a wife who is richer than I and younger than I."

The Parting

L AYALA'S WEDDING ENDED in a quarrel between the bride's father and
the musicians. The flutist, a tall fellow with a hungry look, screamed
at Velvel:

"You beggar! That's all you're used to, flutes and violins? You told
us the dancers would pay—so where are they, your dancers and your
son-in-law's family? This was a funeral, not a wedding."

"Cutthroats!"—Velvel did not suffer this in silence—"You make
accusations? And just because no in-laws showed up, did you have to
devour the whole supper by yourselves? Here I had a single bottle of
Carmel wine, and you guzzled it down and didn't leave me even a drop
to wet my dry throat."

The musicians departed, slamming the door so hard the windowpanes rattled. This set the apartment tenant to trembling. Blinking his
eyes, he wailed:

"What are you doing to me? I wanted to earn a good deed, so I let
you use my home and my dishes—whatever you needed. Do you have
to break my windows, too?"

"If you want to earn a good deed," retorted Velvel curtly, "you have
to pay the price." He turned to his son-in-law, Paysaḥka the leather-
stitcher.

"All this from your head! You had to have a wedding with musicians.
May my words prove false: watch out that all the joy and music that are
waiting for you in Russia don't turn out like this wedding."

In the now-empty rooms, the electric lamps shone dully with a damp
and yellowish glow. The host rushed about, turning the lights off.

"My life's blood is burning up. It's midnight already, the wedding's
over."

But the bride's father, still seeking victims on whom to vent his
bitterness, now began to rant at Baylka:

"You, it's your fault! You were jumping around like a she-goat:
'The couples will be dancing.' As it turns out, you yourself didn't dance,
not even with him"—pointing at me.

The only one who answered Velvel was his humiliated and disappointed daughter. Layala reproached her father:

"You promised me you would sing. You sing at the lectern in the synagogue, and you sing while you work. But at your only daughter's wedding you just sat looking miserable and sighed."

When I left with Baylka, she would not let me take her arm.

"You don't love me. You sat there angry all evening because people were looking at us as an engaged couple. Next Saturday night Layala and Paysaḥka are leaving for Russia. They'll be passing through Glebokie, and I'm going with them—I'm returning home to my mother."

Baylka broke away from me and went home alone.

THAT WEEK I spent every evening at home. My mother gave me sidelong glances from time to time, seemed to want to ask something—and held back. On Saturday night, at the conclusion of the Sabbath, I said sullenly:

"Layala and her husband are leaving tonight."

"And Baylka?"

"Baylka is going with them as far as Glebokie, where she'll stay with her mother."

"Baylka isn't going to Russia?" exclaims my mother, astonished. "Didn't you say that she refused to marry you unless you went to Russia with her?"

"That's right," I answer impatiently. "But without me she doesn't want to go to Russia, and she doesn't want to stay in Vilna either. So she's going home to her village, Glebokie."

"I can't believe my ears!" cries Mother. "Surely she'd have been willing to stay here with you. Do you really not understand—or are you just pretending not to understand? If you had been willing to go with her, she would have taken that as a sign of your love. But she sees you've grown cool to her, and she'd be miserable staying here alone with Velvel— that's why she's going back to her village."

Mother shakes her head sadly:

"Yes, the cat's out of the bag now—she realizes you're not in love with her anymore. Oh my son, my son! If I suffer because of you, so be it, I'm your mother. I've already told Reb Mayer that I can't think of remarrying as long as you're not married. But my heart breaks for Baylka. . . . Wait"—Mother gives a start—"didn't you tell me that she's also leaving tonight, together with Velvel's daughter and her husband? Aren't you even going to say good-bye to her?"

"Baylka is angry with me."

Mother abruptly gets up and goes over to her market baskets. She selects the choicest of her fruits and makes up a package.

"Where are you going?" I ask.

"I'm going to say good-bye to Velvel's children and to ask Baylka's forgiveness. If you still have God in your heart, you'll come with me."

For a moment she pauses, her face long and grave, as though she is pondering a fateful decision. Then suddenly she goes into the other room. I can hear her opening and shutting the old and battered linen chest. She returns carrying a neatly folded tablecloth.

"I've been keeping this for years and years—" She spreads the crocheted cloth over her arms. "During the war, a bitter time, I had to start unraveling it at the edges, for thread to mend your clothes—to sew on a button, to patch a hole or a tear. You were a mischief-maker, and your clothes were always in tatters. Every time I unraveled a section of the design, I promised myself I wouldn't touch it anymore—but a week later I'd be doing it again. Once, I remember, you called out to me: 'Mama, don't unravel the tablecloth—keep it for my bride.' You were just a little boy, but your words upset me so, I began to cry. After that I never touched the tablecloth again. It's narrower and shorter now than it once was, but it's still lovely. The design is beautiful. Now I think I ought to give it to Baylka. She's not your bride—but you have shamed her. When, my son, will you grow up and think beforehand about what you're doing? Let's go now."

We walk through the dark snow-covered streets, my mother sighing all the way. The nearer we come to Velvel's garret, the deeper become her sighs as she continues to complain:

"I don't understand what's become of you. You used to study the holy books—where is your Torah now, where is your sense of decency? If you're not willing to go to Russia, you must know that the situation there is bad. Then why don't you at least try to talk Layala and her husband out of going?"

"Stop torturing me!" I cry out. "Isn't it enough that you hold me responsible for Baylka—am I to be responsible for Velvel's family, too? I don't want to go to Russia because I feel it's not good for me. I haven't been there. Everyone else says it's wonderful, so how can I give advice to Velvel's daughter? Paysaḥka, her husband, is a worker and he believes in the Soviet Union as deeply as you believe in the coming of the Messiah. And if he were to suddenly change his mind, that would be a real calamity. Here they have no place to live and no work. They got married in order to be able to leave together. Don't you say anything to them—you'd only be causing trouble."

"God forbid!" My mother claps her hand over her mouth. "But it grieves me that Velvel may envy me because you're staying here, while he has to send his only daughter so far away."

At Velvel's, we find everybody busy packing. Baylka gives my mother a friendly smile and then, in confusion, begins to throw her things into her small valise. She seems strangely preoccupied, and keeps looking anxiously about her, as though she has just lost a great treasure. Paysaḥka has wrapped his feet in leggings and is pulling on a tall new pair of boots—his dowry. Spread out on the bed are his coat, with its full-length quilted cotton lining, and also his fur hat with long earflaps. The slender Layala is unrecognizable: Wearing half-a-dozen underdresses and petticoats, she is puffed up like a pregnant woman. She can barely lift her feet, now encased in felt boots and glossy black galoshes. Her father has taken out every shawl that belonged to his wife, Roḥa, and insistently urges Layala to wrap herself in all of them.

"You're going to Siberia," he says, while dashing back and forth across the dimly lit garret as though a fire were raging on the floor below. He stops beside my mother and shouts, as if trying to be heard above the din of hoses gushing forth water to quench the flames:

"See what I've got to show for my life, ha? Send away your only daughter, and remain alone in your old age, because if she and her husband stay here, they'll starve to death. And over there? All I know is that the youngsters say it's the Garden of Eden. That's what I've got to show for my life, and the world can just as well burn to ashes!"

My mother tries to say something. She coughs as though to summon her courage—and remains silent. She stands in a corner, dejected and guilty, and Velvel screams still louder:

"Oy, how I envy my old neighbor, Reb Boruḥel. If only I too had died ten years ago, how well off I'd be now. My hump would already have rotted away, and my soul would be purified. By now Reb Boruḥel has atoned for all his sins. And what luck he had—a world of luck! He died before his Blumele, while I—first I had to send my Roḥa off to the cemetery, and now I'm sending my daughter off to the Garden of Eden."

Layala bursts into tears, my mother wipes her eyes, and Baylka buries her head deeper into her little valise. But just then Paysaḥka, his baggy trousers tucked into his new tall boots, decides to assert his masculine authority, warning Layala sternly:

"Stop crying! You might be heard."

Layala falls silent. The Polish secret police know that the underground route to Russia passes through Vilna. There are spies everywhere. One must be careful—the walls have ears. Paysaḥka continues to argue softly with his wife and her father. My mother tugs at my sleeve.

"Go over to Baylka."

I walk toward Baylka and feel my lips becoming dry. I am sorry she is leaving.

"Baylka," I mumble, "if you're not going to Russia after all, you can stay here. I'll help you find a better place to live, so you won't have to stay in Velvel's attic."

Baylka smiles sadly. "No, I'd better go back to Glebokie. You do not love me. When you first got to know me, you had just left the yeshiva—I was probably the first girl you ever met. But you're changing, day by day. I understand. You're an intellectual and I'm just a simple girl, a seamstress."

She notices my mother approaching us. Her face assumes a friendly expression and her voice a more cheerful tone, as though to comfort my mother, who looks so downcast.

"Glebokie is surrounded by open fields, by forests and rivers. Soon it will be summer. Here, when I look out through the window, I see only dirty yellow walls, garrets, and black chimneys. No sun and no sky. That's why I want to go home. Besides, my mother misses me, and I also miss my little sisters."

"Baylka, I've brought you a present—a tablecloth. Someday, with God's help, you'll spread it over your own table. Don't refuse it, I beg of you—do me this favor. I give it to you gladly with all my heart, just as if you were my daughter-in-law. Don't think, Baylka dear, that I'm trying to make up for any wrong I've done you: As God is my witness, I did not meddle. I love you as though you were my own daughter. If only you were indeed my daughter-in-law! But that, I see, was not meant to be. Please give my best wishes to all your family and, for the love of God, ask your mother not to curse me and my son."

Baylka, holding the folded cloth in her hands, looks first at me, then at my mother. The smile on her face sinks into the trembling corners of her mouth.

"And this, Baylka dear"—my mother pushes the parcel of fruit into her hands—"is for you and Layala to eat on the way."

Before Baylka has a chance to answer, everyone in the room is stunned into terrified silence. Velvel has thrown back his head, spread out his hands, and uttered a wail of anguish, as if he were chanting the penitential prayer at the lectern, at daybreak in the month of Elul.

"*Ahl tashliheinu l'eys ziknoh* . . . Lord of the Universe, forsake me not in my old age, when I will no longer have the strength to sew buttonholes in peasants' shirts. Lord of the Universe, no one believes that I'm already an old man—people think I'm still a young buck. My bitterness eats me up and will not let me grow old. My bitterness keeps me bony and lean. Who will take pity on an ill-tempered old man? *Ahl tashliheinu l'eys ziknoh*—Forsake me not in my old age . . ."

"Father-in-law, they'll hear you!" Paysahka is quaking with fear.

"Father, I'm not leaving!" Layala again bursts into tears.

"Indeed, why should you leave?" The distracted Velvel sits down on a stool. "Here, look at Vella. She too is poor, yet she's not letting her only son go. At least wait another week."

The usually placid Paysaḥka is suddenly unrecognizable. He appears to have lost all semblance of self-control, to address Velvel as he now does, with such disrespect:

"Father-in-law, you're acting like an old woman. What do you mean, we should wait another week? The money we've already paid for the border crossing will be lost, and the guides will never take us on again, no matter how much we offer them. Besides, the border will soon be sealed off entirely—the Soviet Union doesn't want to let any more in. The last groups are leaving now."

"Then go! Go!" Velvel jumps up. "How can you live here? . . . Stop crying this minute!" he shouts at Layala.

"Father, you promised me you'd have your picture taken for me to take along." Layala sobs still louder.

"I'll send it to you! I'll send it!" Velvel begins to scurry about. "Hurry! Hurry! You'll miss the train!"

Layala's and Paysaḥka's parcels are small—one cannot take much when stealing across the border. I carry Baylka's little valise. One by one we cautiously descend the winding staircase.

With all her wraps, Layala can barely move. She is virtually shackled by a huge woolen shawl that is tied in a knot on her back. Of her small face, only her pointy little nose is visible. She stops in the middle of the staircase and stares out through the window, as though looking for the moon that used to peek in when she and Paysaḥka embraced on the steps. But the moon does not appear. The sky is overcast and outside it's dark. From a window in Ramayles' Courtyard comes a murky, watery glow that illumines patches of the peeling walls.

Layala frees her lips of the woolen wrap and whispers:

"Good people, how I'll miss Ramayles' Courtyard!"

Velvel, stumbling behind me, moans into my ear—softly, so his daughter cannot overhear:

"How I envy Reb Boruḥel!" he says again. "If only I had died ten years ago, how well off I'd be now. My hump would already have rotted and my soul would be purified . . ."

In the courtyard, Baylka turns to my mother:

"Thank you for coming, and thank you for the gifts. Let's embrace."

"We'll go to the train with you," says my mother.

"No, that won't do," Paysaḥka cuts in. "That would be too large a crowd. There are police spies all over the station."

We say our good-byes, we kiss—and the small group steals silently out of the courtyard. Baylka walks with Paysaḥka, and Layala with her father. Velvel wobbles and stumbles, then makes a jump and begins to run ahead, so that Layala can barely keep up with him. They turn a corner and disappear.

Mother and I stand in silence in the dingy snow of Ramayles' Courtyard. Across the way looms the deep darkness of the Synagogue Courtyard, and all around us it is deadly still. Only a broken lantern sways back and forth, emitting rusty, otherworldly sounds.

A Letter

MOTHER HAS AGREED with Velvel that as soon as the first letter from his daughter and son-in-law arrives, he will come with it to our house. But when a month has passed and Velvel has not yet appeared, Mother says to me:

"Go over to the tailor's and find out what's happening. It would be a kindness in any case to pay him a visit. You know Velvel: he'd rather stay alone in his attic like a werewolf than go out among people."

I went over and found the door of his garret locked. I went a second time, and again the door was locked. When I told Mother this, she became frightened:

"Who knows what might have happened to him? He's all alone . . ."

As things turned out, nothing had happened to Velvel. It was just that he had been running about for days on end to inquire of those who might know, why he had received no mail from his children. But he had learned nothing. He began to make daily visits to Mother's stand at the gate. Walking up to her without so much as a "Good day," he would utter a single word:

"Nothing."

Having said what he had come to say, he would leave without saying good-bye.

Once, however, he came with a secretive smile on his face. As she waited to hear his melancholy "Nothing," Mother felt a numbing ache in her ears. But this time he said something different:

"You may congratulate me."

"Congratulations!" Mother cried, tears gushing from her eyes. "Mazel tov! What do your children write?"

Velvel, still smiling his ambiguous smile, said calmly:

"You may indeed congratulate me. My children are . . . spies."

And he burst into such an eerily piercing laughter that Mother began to shudder.

"I searched and searched, until I finally managed to get to one of 'their' bigwigs. He told me that their comrades in Russia are afraid there may have been spies among those crossing the border. So they don't let anyone write home, lest they betray the secrets of Paradise."

"But that doesn't mean your children are spies—" Mother barely found the strength to utter the words.

"No, it doesn't mean that my children are spies. For the time being, they're only under suspicion. But maybe their bigwig wasn't telling me the whole truth—maybe he knows that they've already arrested Layala and Paysaḥka."

Velvel spoke calmly, as though of a sorrow long past, and with the same calm he walked away, his body bent almost to the ground.

ONE FRIDAY EVENING, just as Mother and I are sitting down to the table, the door opens and a shadow slinks in—Velvel:

"I have a letter."

The little smile that twitches about his lips bodes no good. Velvel seems to take pleasure in torturing himself and others. When he sees that we remain silent, he softly begins to laugh his sharp, demented laugh:

"I have a letter from Baylka. She sends her warm regards to you, Vella—and to you, too. But she reproaches me: Layala and Paysaḥka promised her faithfully that they would write to her, and they haven't kept their word. Things must be going very well there with Layala, Baylka writes, if she has forgotten her friend so quickly."

Velvel stops his snickering, is silent for a moment, and then, in a tone of icy anguish, continues:

"God is playing a game with me. I sit there at my machine, I sew and I talk to myself: 'Don't expect anything—there'll be no letter—it's as though you've never had a daughter.' Suddenly I hear footsteps. By their sound I can tell that it's someone who isn't used to our winding stairs. He's looking for something—he knocks on closed doors and curses in Polish. My heart jumps and I feel dizzy—it's the letter carrier. And I think: Don't ask questions. Our Patriarch Jacob grieved and mourned for his son Joseph for many years, and in the end he heard '*Ohd Yosef hai*'—'Joseph yet lives.' I open the door—Thank you, God in Heaven— there is a letter! My hands tremble; I can't open the envelope; all is black before my eyes. The letter carrier has left—it's only when he's already reached the bottom of the stairs that I come to with a start: What am I doing? When a man brings me such joy, he must be thanked. So I run after him and give him a zloty. He looks at me as though I were mad, and leaves. I run back upstairs to my room—now I can't find the letter. I search for it on the table, on the sewing machine, near the door—it's gone. I break out in a cold sweat—it was all my imagination, the work of a demon. Then I see that I'm holding the letter in my hand. I tear it open, but can't grasp the meaning of what I read. Now I look at the signature—it's from Baylka . . ."

Velvel draws a packet of folded sheets of paper from his inner coat-pocket, carefully pulls out an envelope, and hands it to my mother with such gravity one might think it contained the Divine Writ of Judgment for the New Year: "Who shall live and who shall die." Mother looks at the tailor, afraid to open the envelope. Thinking that this is surely Baylka's letter, I stretch my hand across the table and take the envelope from my mother. I am surprised to see that it is pure white, with no address, no stamps affixed. From it I pull out—pictures of Velvel.

Again Velvel begins to snicker like one possessed:

"Before she left, my Layala asked me for a picture of myself. So I went and let them 'make my double.' Now that my children have forgotten to write to tell me where they observe the Sabbath, I'll take these half-dozen pictures, hang them on the walls of my attic, and take pleasure in looking at my own beautiful face."

Velvel stretches his hand out to me, snapping his fingers gaily as though expecting me to give him a bundle of banknotes to count. I hand him the pictures. He shuffles them and reshuffles, his eyes squinting, and passes one picture to my mother:

"See, Vella, in the picture I have no hump on my shoulders. I went to a photographer who's a real artist and I said to him: 'I'll give you as much as you sing for—just make sure the pictures show a Velvel without a hump.' So he kept ordering me around, moving me from one position to another, and I obeyed him like a schoolboy. He, the artist, pulled a cloth over his head, just like a true magician, buried his face in a box with a big glass eye, and issued orders to his assistant: 'Turn on the light! Turn it off!' There was thunder and lightning as in hell—until at last out came a Velvel without a hump. Over there in Russia, I thought, my Layala will want to show people that she wasn't born of a stone, that she has a real father of flesh and blood—so let her not be shamed by a father who's a hunchback.

"But don't worry—the Almighty hasn't forsaken me entirely. True, I don't hear anything from my only daughter (and that's as it should be—she had no business becoming a spy!), but I have an only son to comfort me in my old age: my hump. And even though you can't see him in the picture, he's growing over my head. My hump, with the help of the Almighty, will yet succeed in bending me down to the ground, and burying me in it—and then, at last, the way will be clear for him. He'll jump off my shoulders and hop out into the street, like a bullfrog that's jumped out of the swamp and merrily leaped all the way to the marketplace under a horse's hooves. He can hardly wait till I come to a bad end, this only son of mine. At night, when I'm tossing in my torment, he rehearses; I can feel in my back—a hole. That's because he's torn himself off my shoulder and is dancing around the attic. He's having a wonderful time, that hump of mine."

"Reb Velvel, stop eating your heart out!" Mother can no longer contain herself. "I have a wonderful dinner tonight—a royal banquet. Gefilte fish fit for the Emperor himself. Which do you prefer, Reb Velvel, a slice from the middle or the head portion? I also have chicken soup with a golden bubble of fat, and a nice piece of chicken. Today I cooked some extra—just as if my heart told me that you would come to grace my Sabbath. Go wash your hands, Reb Velvel, and I'll put out two nice little ḥallahs for the Kiddush."

"Good," he says, but remains motionless as a stone, lost in thought.

Mother starts to rise to serve her guest. But Velvel begins once again to torment himself, and she remains seated:

"When the Bolsheviks were fighting the Poles, they came here to Vilna barefoot and in tatters, swollen with hunger. So there remains the question—" Velvel begins to chant softly and gloomily, like a bereaved widower singing to welcome the Sabbath on Friday night in his empty house—"When did the Bolsheviks become so rich that they can take care of others, including young people in Poland who don't have work? All told, it was only fifteen years ago that they themselves walked barefoot. And, what is even more astonishing—why didn't I ever ask that question before my children left to go there? That's why I deserve to have my children suspected of being spies!" he cries, and he jumps up and runs toward the door.

"Reb Velvel—" Mother runs after him—"at least recite the Kiddush!"

"You forgot your photographs!" I call out to him. But he is already gone.

Dejectedly, Mother sits down and stares at the cold bluish flames of the Sabbath candles. Suddenly a thought strikes her:

"One shouldn't speak of it now, during the Sabbath, but tomorrow night after sundown you must, in God's name, immediately write a letter to Baylka and warn her not to go there. You must take pity on a poor orphan and her widowed mother."

"You needn't worry about Baylka, Mother. She couldn't get across the border even if she wanted to—the Russians aren't letting anyone else in."

"Then, as it turns out," Mother sighs, "instead of cursing you, Baylka's mother should bless you for not marrying her daughter, so that the two of you didn't go to Russia . . . Ah, the wisdom of our Sages is limitless! Once in a holy book I read a story about two friends who were supposed to set out on a journey on the same ship. But one injured his foot on a thorn and couldn't go. He complained to God and cursed his cruel fate. Later he heard that the ship, with his friend on it, had sunk. Then he thanked the Most High for having caused him to injure his foot."

Mother pulls the corners of her kerchief tighter round her throat, as if wishing to stiffen her chin, which has begun to quiver with agitation and grief.

"A 'disturbed Sabbath,' " she murmurs. "May God not hold it against me. The man who was unable to make the journey indeed had cause to thank and praise the Holy One, blessed be He, because he himself was saved. But how terribly sad for his friend who was drowned, and all the more so for the wife and children who were awaiting his return. And how can one even begin to speak of an old father who has been left behind? Only God in Heaven can comfort him. My heart is torn to shreds for Velvel . . ."

King Solomon and the Commissar

BY THE SABBATH after Purim, Mother is "in debt over her head." Who knows whether she will manage to look over the weekly Torah portion; part of the Scroll of Esther, begun on Purim, still remains to be read, and she hasn't so much as glanced at the *Targum Shayni*—so overwhelming is Mother's temptation to immerse herself in this volume, with its marvelous tales of King Solomon and his golden rooster, of Solomon and the Queen of Sheba, that she turns down the corner of the page in her Bible to mark her place, and plunges directly into the *Targum Shayni*:

"And it came to pass in the days of Ahasuerus, who reigned from India even unto Ethiopia, over one hundred and twenty-seven provinces. Ahasuerus is one of the ten Kings who have reigned over the entire world and will one day reign again. The first is the King of Kings, the Holy One, blessed be He—may His Kingdom be speedily established over us. The second is Nimrod. The third is Pharaoh, King of Egypt. The fourth is King Solomon. The fifth is Nebuchadnezzar, King of Babylon. The sixth is Ahasuerus. The seventh is Alexander, King of Greece. The eighth is the Emperor of Rome. The ninth is the Messiah, the Anointed King. The tenth will be the King of Kings, the Holy One, blessed be He . . ."

She gazes through the smithy window at the sodden day outside. In the balmy days of early spring, when the ice begins to melt in our courtyard, the little houses, gradually emerging from beneath their blanket of cottony disintegrating snow, look like paupers in tattered clothes. She feels a chill in her bones, as if the melting snow were seeping into her own body. Since Velvel's visit on the preceding Friday evening, a stone has rested on her heart. She sits lost in thought, yet keeping her hands on the pages before her, lest the letters fly away, and with them the wondrous tales.

Yet it is precisely the beautiful stories of the *Targum Shayni* that have stirred up melancholy thoughts in Mother. She feels the need to unburden herself, and glances over at me. I, however, am sitting with my back to her, shoulders squared, head buried in a book of my own. Seeing thus clearly that her son has no time for her, even on the Sabbath, she speaks to herself, to her hands resting on her Bible, and let listen who would:

"It seems it has ever been the way of the world for kings and kingdoms to be continually changing. First Nimrod, then Pharaoh, and the wheel keeps turning. He who is at the bottom today, will be tomorrow on top. In Vilna itself, after the war between the Russians and the Germans, we had six different governments in two years. First we had to welcome the Polish Legionnaires, those Hamans, may their name be blotted out. Next came the Great Ones, as the Bolsheviks were called. Then the Poles again. And then again the Great Ones, leading by the hand their heirs—the Lithuanians in their wooden clogs. And then, like the potato pudding that follows the cholent on the Sabbath, the Poles were back again.

"What's true is true: the Great Ones did not start any pogroms. On the contrary, each time they came they saved the city from a pogrom. The local Poles had already begun to plunder the shops, and if the Great Ones had arrived just one hour later, Jewish blood would have been flowing like water. So it was no wonder that the entire city, kith and kin, went out to welcome them. Not only the workers, but also the shopkeepers sang their praises, especially because of one incident . . ."

Mother, her book still on her lap, turns toward me. Her voice grows louder, and she no longer cares that she is disturbing my absorption in the "deep mysteries" of wanton, worldly novels.

"One day a Russian soldier stopped a Jew in the street and took his watch right off his arm. Just then a commissar was riding by on his horse. So the Jew runs over to the commissar, tells him what happened, and points out the soldier. The commissar gets off his horse, takes out his pistol, and orders the soldier to get down on his knees, right there in the middle of the street. The soldier began to cry, pleading for mercy for the sake of his wife and children, but it did him no good. The commissar put a bullet in his head and then kicked him with his boot. Those who saw it happen said afterwards that when the soldier's body was carted away an hour later, a rattle could still be heard coming from his throat."

My mother's voice has grown shrill, her face is taut, her eyes burn with a green fire, and she keeps straightening her wig—even in the grip of her excitement and indignation, she takes care not to uncover her hair, especially not on the Sabbath and with the Bible in her hands.

"I don't know whether or not the Jew who denounced the soldier later regretted it—if the informer felt no remorse and he has since died, let the earth spew him forth! But that the shopkeepers were pleased, this I saw for myself. 'We don't approve of the Reds' plan to confiscate the shops, but that the Bolsheviks treat Jew and Gentile alike, and that they don't permit their soldiers to loot and plunder, that we like very much.

As for the fonya, serves him right—he shouldn't have tried to steal, he deserved to die!' That's exactly the way the shopkeepers talked, those fine Jews.

"I stood there beside my fruit basket and kept quiet. Did I have a choice? The Almighty in His mercy had kept me alive during the war, and now I had a sick husband and young children to care for—did I have the right to risk my life to speak out? Yet what shall I tell you? I could have spat in the faces of those Jews. My hands trembled, I wanted to cry out, to tear my hair . . . 'Lord of the Universe,' I prayed soundlessly, 'give me the strength to remain silent.'

"Oh Lord, what has become of Jews? That Jews should stand by and not turn a hair when a human being is shot because of a watch! 'The commissar is an honest judge,' they said. But I felt that a judge who could kill a man for stealing a watch was a thousand times worse than the thief himself. And Jews who can take pleasure in such a 'judgment,' such an outrage," she shrieks, "they themselves have the hearts of murderers!" She is beside herself, foam covering her lips.

"Don't excite yourself!" I cry out. "Why all of a sudden are you thinking about something that happened fifteen years ago?"

"Don't you dare tell me not to get excited!" She stands up and snaps her book shut. "How dare you call this just 'something that happened fifteen years ago'? My Wise Man of the Four Questions, it's that same commissar who's now accusing Layala and Paysaḥka of being spies."

A seething anger distorts Mother's face. She wipes the foam from the corners of her mouth and continues speaking, rapidly:

"I've never been short of worries of my own, so over the years I'd forgotten about that soldier with the watch. But since Velvel brought us the dark news about his children in Russia, that they're suspected of being spies, the story has come back to me in full detail.

"At the time, I walked about in a daze and kept asking people what the soldier had looked like. They stared at me and shrugged their shoulders: 'Why do you need to know? Was he a relative of yours?' Go tell them that a dybbuk—may God preserve and protect us—had taken possession of me. I thought about him day and night, as though I didn't have enough to worry about. I imagined him as a cheerful little fellow, a peasant. He comes to Vilna and walks about the streets. He sees everyone busy, everyone wheeling and dealing, and all the shop windows full of merchandise—while he walks about in bast shoes, or maybe even barefoot. So he thinks to himself: 'They made me come running to Vilna with my gun to save the Jews from a pogrom—now I'll take something from these Jews so I can buy myself a bottle of whiskey.' Or perhaps he just wants to take the watch back to his village, to show his wife and children, so they'd see he really had been to the far corners of the world. Or maybe he didn't think anything at all—maybe it was just the war, the violence, bursting out of him. Probably he had once served in the Czar's army, and there he'd never seen or heard anything against robbing the people in a conquered city. In short, he wanted a watch. Did he deserve to die for that?"

"But, Mother, why have you forgotten the slaughter that the Poles started as soon as they entered the city? They shot ten Jews right there in the street, and arrested and tortured many others. Seventy Jews lost their lives then. You seem to have forgotten all about them, and remember only the commissar who shot one soldier as a warning to others not to loot and steal."

"My great sage!" Mother snaps back at me. "How can you compare those Poles, those pogromchiks, with a man who's put on a high hat with a red star and become a 'judge'? The butcher makes a virtue of his butchery! After it was over, the commissar got back on his horse, proudly raised his head with the high hat and red star, and rode off like a hero. As for his warning other soldiers—that makes me laugh, though I feel like crying. When the other soldiers heard in their barracks that one of their comrades was shot because a Jew informed on him, they all became our sworn enemies, of that I am sure! Besides, someone who can kill a man over a watch can kill for other reasons, too—as we were to learn only too soon. All this had a bitter ending. . . .

"As the governments continued to change, with a new one taking over every Monday and Thursday, there also came to be a great confusion of currencies. I, for my part, had no problem—the Czar's rubles didn't stay in my pockets any longer than the German marks. But when all the tumult of kerenkas, zlotys, and litai began, you could really go mad. A merchant might earn tens of thousands of kerenkas one day, go to sleep a millionaire—and find himself a beggar the next morning: the Poles had arrived during the night, and Russian money was as worthless as the dust of the street. So later, when the Great Ones returned, the towns-people didn't want to accept their money.

"One day I was standing beside my baskets and a Cossack rode by, black and tall, a giant. And to top things off, he wears a tall, white fur Cossack hat, carries a lance in one hand, and rides on a white horse. I tell you—Og himself, King of Bashan. He leans down from his horse and very politely asks me for a pound of apples. I weigh the apples and give them to him. I have to stand on tiptoe, tilt my head backwards, and extend my arms in order to reach him. He asks me what they cost, and pays me with Soviet money. I think to myself: 'A Cossack in a tall fur hat, with a lance, and riding on a horse, yet he asks politely for his merchandise and pays the price that's asked—fine, indeed! And at least some Soviet money may stay in my pocket.'

"But the owners of the big stores don't want to accept this new currency. Russian soldiers roam about, their pockets full of money, but nobody will sell them anything. The storekeepers keep their merchandise hidden and admit customers only through back doors. And then one day two customers enter a yard-goods shop. They are not in uniform like the Great Ones, but dressed like everyone else, and they ask to see the merchandise. The shopkeeper, having no idea with whom he is dealing, shows them his goods. They make their selections in a leisurely manner, don't argue about the price, and tell the merchant to cut off the amount of cloth they want. When it comes time to pay, they offer him Soviet money. But the shopkeeper demands either Polish zlotys or 'noodles,' as dollars used to be called in Vilna. To make a long story short, the two men took the shopkeeper away and he was shot.

"Now terror and dread descended upon the merchants. The very same merchants who were once so delighted with the commissar, that bandit, and his 'heroic' deed, now trembled with fear. How was it possible, how could anyone take a man and shoot him for something so trivial? What these good people didn't understand was that the commissars who had no pity for one of their own would surely have no pity for them.

"I'm only a simple woman, but I know that when the ten sons of our forefather Jacob came to Egypt during the famine to buy wheat, and the Viceroy said that they were spies, the brothers said to one another: 'We are guilty! We had no pity for our brother Joseph, when he begged us not to throw him into the pit.' But those merchants of Vilna, terrified when a Jew, one of their own, was shot, never gave a thought to that little soldier, poor soul, who was rotting in his grave because of a trinket, a watch—although it was as plain as day that there was a thread running directly from that first bandit of a commissar to the two disguised commissars who had the shopkeeper executed. And you too, my son, fail to see that that very same thread continues right to this day, right to Velvel's children, whom the commissars in Russia won't even permit to write a letter to their old father. And maybe they've already put them in prison, as Velvel fears. What more is there to say? It's a fine world we live in!"

Her tale at an end, my mother, without stopping to catch her breath, opens her Yiddish Bible and begins to read—with agitation, as though the words of the *Targum Shayni* were the continuation of her own:

"Consider Ahasuerus, that same Ahasuerus in whose day the countenance of Israel was blackened like the sooty bottom of a pot. He is that same evildoer and fool Ahasuerus who first killed his wife Vashti upon the advice of his favorite, Haman, and who later killed his favorite, Haman, for the sake of his wife, Esther . . ."

Slowly my mother grows calmer, and when she reaches those passages that speak of the splendor and greatness of King Solomon, her face clears like the sky after a thunderstorm. She reads aloud the description of the throne upon which Solomon sat and rendered righteous judgment:

"The throne was fashioned with great skill and mastery, and no craftsman in the world could fashion another like it. And there were steps leading up to the throne.

"On the first step there lay a golden ox, and facing it, a golden lion. On the second step there lay a golden wolf, and facing it, a golden lamb. On the third step there lay a golden leopard, and facing it, a golden camel. On the fourth step there lay a golden eagle, and facing it, a golden peacock. On the fifth step there lay a golden hawk, and facing it, a golden dove.

"And all this signifies that, at the seat of justice, the weak need not fear the strong."

The Day
of the Beggars

I

ON A MONDAY MORNING in the month of Nisan, a sudden gust of wind fills the air with the chill scent of Elul, with threatening clouds and the odor of the graveyard.

It is the day of the beggars.

Alterka the goose-dealer is already seething. As soon as he catches sight of the first beggar coming down Jatkowa Street, he stations himself at the courtyard gate to watch the "merrymaking."

"Here they come—our in-laws, the shnorrers," he says to my mother. "As if we didn't have enough of them at Zarecze Cemetery on the Fast of Gedaliah and the eve of Yom Kippur, now they're coming here, too. And when? Just before Passover, when everyone counts on doing business."

"But they can't live all year long off the alms they get before Yom Kippur," answers my mother, who is busy putting out her wares. She at once regrets getting involved in a conversation with the goose-dealer— even at dawn, on an empty stomach, Alterka is ready to start an argument:

"Hear, hear, how she pities them! Every one of these tramps has a bundle—they all have fortunes stashed away."

The first one to stop at my mother's stand is the local idiot, who hangs about the Synagogue Courtyard by day and spends his nights, wrapped in lice-ridden rags, in some building vestibule. He laughs with his toothless mouth wide open, the spittle running from his fleshy lips. Had he been of sound mind, Mother might have been angry at him for rushing in so early, before she's even had her first sale for the day—"for good luck"—but since he is a poor imbecile, she gives him a coin and sends him off, with a sigh:

"May our enemies be blessed with such wits as his."

"I have nothing against this simpleton." Alterka, too, gives him something. "You can tell just by looking at him that he's not even fit to be a slaughterer."

The poultry-man never misses an opportunity to needle my mother.

The shaytl she wears, the wig of a pious woman, is in his eyes proof positive that she sides with his enemies, the ritual slaughterers.

THAT ALTERKA has the heart of a Tartar, everyone knows. Ḥatzkel the grocer, in contrast, is a good-natured soul. He has placed a small pile of copper coins within easy reach on the counter, so as to be able to distribute alms without wasting time. He casts a contented glance at the goodly cluster of shoppers waiting impatiently for him to start weighing and measuring—and then another glance at the beggar's hand stretching out to him for alms.

Ḥatzkel is dumfounded.

The palm being thrust at him is hard and broad as a shovel. At the same instant he notices a second hand with fingers that are pointed and spread wide, like a pitchfork. A third hand, with a cluster of twisted yellow fingers, twitches, whines, and demands its just portion. Before Ḥatzkel can recover himself, he is approached by a lump of solid, hardened flesh attached to a withered bone. The fingerless stump of a wrist thrusts itself at the grocer: Here, look your fill, enjoy.

Ḥatzkel feels a stabbing pain in his heart, a tightness in his chest, a choking in his throat, as though all these invalids and cripples were tearing him apart, piece by piece. He hurls coins into open palms and steps backward, as if he were throwing food to ferocious beasts. The beggars utter not a word; they turn back to the door in such unyielding silence they might be the dead, risen from their graves to demand their just share of earthly pleasures.

A pall of dread descends upon the grocer; he does not dare lift his eyes to look into the beggars' faces. Speechless, immobilized, he watches as they leave his store.

One man strides seemingly without moving, as if he were not actually walking but simply letting the floor slide away from under him. Another, who is lame, is so twisted over his crippled leg that he almost touches the floor; he waves his hands about, winglike, as though seeking something to hold onto so as not to sink into the ground. The body of a third is totally rigid, while his head and neck writhe in convulsions. A fourth . . . a fifth . . .

Ḥatzkel sees his customers grimacing with disgust; they are nauseated, ready to vomit; they begin to back out of the shop, holding their noses. A stench of urine, of the odors of back alleys and outhouses, of mildew damp and stale, emanates from the beggars, as though barrels of rotting garbage were standing about in the shop.

Ḥatzkel can stand it no longer. He begins to scream with his eyes closed, a sign that he is very angry:

"Why don't you go to the bathhouse? Why don't you use the public bath?"

And there is yet one more thing he wants to know:

"Tell me, which is your day, Monday or Thursday? Let's hear it, once and for all—when do you go from house to house?"

"Monday!" A score of faces twist into grimaces of misery: "Monday is our day!"

"That's a lie!" Ḥatzkel stamps his foot. "Today happens to be Monday, so you say Monday is your day. On Thursday you'll say your day is Thursday. And what is my day? When will you let me earn a groschen in peace?"

The grocer is beside himself. It seems to him that the paupers want to carry off everything he owns. Trembling with fury, he points his finger at two of the beggars:

"You were already here earlier today. And you, too. I'm wise to your tricks. You go out and then get back on line again."

"We swear we haven't been here since Monday a week ago," avow the mendicants. "May our collection be as good today as that's the truth."

Ḥatzkel looks forlornly about him. Not one customer remains in his shop—there is only the line of paupers twisting and turning like a snake, with no beginning or end. It is no longer just a single line; now the beggars come in pairs . . . three abreast . . . four abreast. The ice has melted and the Wilja is overflowing its banks! A swarm of locusts has descended upon him! Woe, woe—all the beggars of the Synagogue Courtyard are coming, all the inmates of the poorhouses, all the wretched hostels of the poor, all the decaying back alleys are on the march . . .

"Help!" Ḥatzkel tears at his hair. "Help me, good people! They'll ruin me. I myself will have to throw a sack over my shoulders and go begging from door to door."

In despair, he seizes the pile of copper coins and runs out to stand at the entrance of his shop.

"Quickly! Quickly!" Hurrying the far-stretching line of beggars along, he distributes his coins. "I see you have plenty of time, just as if this were afternoon Sabbath after the cholent. Father in Heaven, the line is as long as our Jewish Exile. Exile, when will you end?"

WHAT IS TAKING PLACE in Ḥatzkel's shop is child's play compared to what is happening near the gate where my mother has her stand—though here the situation is altogether different.

Here the passers-by are besieging a little blind old man and showering alms upon him. The little old man has found favor in their eyes, because, to begin with, he is not part of the horde of shnorrers, but is on his own; clearly, he was once a respectable householder himself and used to give charity to others. In contrast to a born beggar, moreover, he does not demand his alms brazenly, as his due, but pleads for them in tones of supplication:

"Please give alms for a blind man, please give alms for a blind man!"

And Jews, "merciful children of merciful fathers," give. There is such a throng surrounding the old man that one might think the greatest bargains were being offered here, that Paradise itself was being sold for next to nothing. Some in the crowd, curious about the old man's history, begin to interrogate him:

"Did your house burn down, my good man?"

"Do you have grandchildren who are completely orphaned?"

"Are you from out of town, Grandfather? Where are you staying?"

But to all questions the little old man makes just one reply:

"Give alms for a blind man, please give alms for a blind man!"

Suddenly a newcomer starts to push his way into the crowd, using his fists vigorously and stepping on people's toes. Turning about, the crowd discovers another little old man wailing:

"What's going on here? What's going on here? Who says that he's blind? I am blind!"

The first beggar is, it turns out, also somewhat deaf. He plucks at the newcomer's sleeve and cries:

"Give alms for a blind man! Do give alms for a blind man!"

"You—give me! You—give me! I'm a pauper, too," screams the second man. "I'm from this city and you're a stranger. I'm the true blind seer and you're a fake. You're a liar—I can tell by your voice that you're not really blind."

In the face of these accusations, the first beggar starts to tremble. He sobs and pleads with the crowd that surrounds them both:

"Ay, what a cutthroat he is! Ay, what a cutthroat he is! Why should it bother him that people want to help an old man?"

He begins to back hastily out of the circle of onlookers. The second beggar runs after him, banging his stick on the pavement:

"Catch him! He's not blind. Hold him! He's a pickpocket!"

"The devil with both of them!" hisses one man in the crowd. "The scoundrels—they mock the whole town, while they're sweeping up gold from the streets. I wish I had what they've got."

"Just what I say." Alterka slaps his belly. Standing at the gate, he laughs derisively at the bleeding hearts who let themselves be taken in by every swindler. "They won't lead me around by the nose," he thinks to himself as he turns back into the courtyard, back to the poultry shop where his wife, Lisa, sits behind the tin counter, waiting for her "fine ladies."

Into the courtyard there now walk two men, all in black, like the Angels of Destruction. They stop near the goose-dealer, mumbling something into their mustaches. Alterka looks at them suspiciously and cries out:

"You're psalm-sayers, aren't you? Go sit in the Synagogue Courtyard, or on the steps of the Gravediggers' Chapel, and wait for your 'celebration,' for someone to die."

"And if the rich don't want to die," asks one of the men, softly and submissively, "should we, God forbid, pray for funerals?"

"You'd better give," the other says harshly, "so that you won't be needing our services too soon. 'Charity delivereth from death.'"

Alterka is genuinely frightened, and gives each of them five groschen. As for Lisa—who has been sitting all this time with her arms folded across her chest, a yawn frozen in the plump corners of her mouth—the psalm-sayers' veiled warnings make her feel as though ants are crawling over her heavy, swollen body. "Recite psalms for us," she pleads with the two black-robed Jews, "for our good health, and that we may earn a decent living."

When the pair have left, Lisa falls upon her husband:

"You think everybody is just like the slaughterers. Who are you starting up with—the Angel of Death?"

Now a tall young fellow in a leather jacket, his potato-shaped face full of pimples and with one blank, cataract-covered eye, enters the courtyard. His good eye, glistening like a knife blade, cuts into Alterka. Even as he extends his hand in seeming supplication, his face is hard and cold.

"Go to work," says Alterka.

A network of fine wrinkles forms around the youth's beclouded eye, as though it is giving him much pain, while his clear eye grows still larger and brighter. He moves a step closer to the short and stocky goose-dealer, seizes the belt of his trousers, and tugs at it so hard that Alterka feels his stomach quaking. The fellow bursts into laughter, as if this were just a joke, and says calmly:

"Keep your advice to yourself. Give me money for a shot of whiskey, if you know what's good for you."

Alterka takes the measure of the fellow, and his shoulders of iron, and realizes that this hoodlum is spoiling for a fight. "Against him I'd be no more than a capon," he reflects. "I'll end up having my feathers plucked, and handing everyone a good laugh"—and, biting his lips, he gives the man several coins.

The hoodlum stares at the coins in his broad palm for a long time, as though he is thinking of swallowing them; at last he says coldly:

"Too little."

The goose-dealer's blood begins to boil. He eyes the tin counter, on

which the cleaver is lying: at this moment he would gladly shake it right
in this impudent fellow's face. The latter, as though understanding Alterka's thoughts, moves still closer to him and hisses:

"You heard me—it's too little."

Lisa appears to see nothing; she seems to be sleeping with eyes open,
like an owl. But suddenly she cries out to her husband:

"Give him more and let him get out!"

Alterka gives the young tough another ten-groschen piece and decides to put up a good front, so as not to appear to have come out of the
affair the loser:

"When I'm dealing with a decent sort, I can be a good fellow, too."

When the hoodlum has left, Lisa proceeds to pour salt on her husband's wounds:

"Do you think everyone's like our landlord—somebody you can
frighten just by yelling at him when he comes for the rent? You wanted
to play games with that gangster? He might have put a knife in your
ribs."

Now, a woman with a high, furrowed forehead and a back bent by
years of pious prayer, enters the courtyard. With her large, veined hands
she grasps the tin counter as though she were clutching the Holy Ark
in the synagogue, and begins to sway to and fro:

"Jewish children, give alms. It is written in our holy books that one
must give charity to the poor. Anyone who doesn't want to believe that
should take a look at a book of Mussar and he'll see it for himself, black
on white. The beggar who accepts charity does the giver a greater favor
than the giver does for the beggar."

"Don't do me any favors!" roars the goose-dealer. "Go out and
work. It's almost Passover—you can knead and roll out the dough in a
matzoh-bakery. Or you can pluck chickens in the slaughterhouse. Why
are you after me? I've given enough today already."

"Our Sages say"—the woman answers in the sing-song chant of a
prayer-leader in the women's section—"that when a poor man comes to
ask for charity, you shall not turn him away by saying: 'I've given already
today—come back another time.' You must not let him leave empty-
handed. God, blessed be He, sends an angel to see whether the rich man
gives the beggar his alms in a friendly manner and with joy, or with a
bitter mien. On this subject there are many verses in the Scripture. . . ."

The bags under Alterka's eyes swell with rage. He is within a hair
of grabbing the woman by the nape of the neck and flinging her out of
the courtyard "on two splinters"—when to his astonishment he sees a
broad smile spreading over Lisa's face, while her mouth overflows with
sweet milk and honey, with kind words:

"What do you want, my good woman? A donation? There's no

need to plead so much." Lisa reaches into the pocket of her apron and jingles the coins within.

No one could accuse Alterka of a "lean head"; he looks around—aha, now he understands! A well-dressed matron in a plumed hat is approaching the counter, followed by a maidservant carrying a basket. Lisa, seeking to make a good impression on this grand lady, begins to count out loud as she drops coins into the beggar's outstretched palm:

"Not one, not two, not three, not four."

The beggar woman nods her head approvingly as she accepts each coin—yet continues all the while to drone on as in a graveyard monologue:

"When counting human beings, one must say: 'Not one, not two,' so that no evil eye may befall them. But one must not be stingy with money. The charity given by women is more highly valued in Heaven than the charity given by men. When we give to the poor, it is as though we have given to the Almighty Himself. No one ever became poor because he gave too much charity. We find it written in the Gemara . . ."

Hands over his ears, Alterka runs out of his shop like a man escaping gunfire. He knows that if not for the fine lady's arrival, his wife would have given this pious shnorrer "the change of a golden ducat." But when necessary, his Lisa can put on an expression as sweet as sugar. He, however, can stand it no longer. He stops near the gate and pours out his heart to my mother:

"Listen, Vella, you're always talking like a rebbetzin yourself, but compared to that preacher in skirts, you're—small potatoes. Go and listen to how she pours on the oil, how she shnorrs with Bible verses. It's enough, I tell you, to give anyone a stroke!"

II

SITTING AT HER STAND, Mother is growing increasingly worried. The more she has to dig into her pocket and give away the groschen she has earned with her sweat and blood, the more troubled she becomes. At first there had come a line of ordinary beggars. But now a new procession has begun, accompanied by a great clangor and loud cries, like a band of musicians marching ahead of a regiment of soldiers.

Alterka stands at the gate and calls out, like a badhen announcing the wedding presents:

"The alms-boxes are coming, the alms-boxes!"

A Jew with thick gray earlocks and a broad, unkempt beard approaches. His face is all but drowned in hair; the sole visible feature is a pair of large, protuberant ears. He shakes and rattles his box:

"Give to the Torah-Study Society. For the neglect of Torah, the world is being destroyed."

Mother throws a few coins into the box.

The man thanks her:

"May you live and be well to be able to give again next year."

"Amen," responds my mother. "And may you live to hear the trumpet of the Messiah. Give me a blessing for my son, too."

"May you live to see your son become a great scholar in Torah."

Mother is confused: That much she does not expect; she would be happy enough if her son at least prayed the required three times a day. But her thoughts are interrupted by a second Jew, who makes his appearance as soon as the first one has left.

This new alms-collector is a rather short and thin man wearing a heavy, round lambskin hat. The wind is pulling wads of cotton from the torn lining of his long and tattered coat, which has become entangled between his legs. A rope is tied around his waist, and the open upper half of his coat is stuffed with bits of the food apportioned to him for his sustenance.

"Give to the Society of Supporters of Torah." He rattles his alms-box. "For the sin of contempt for the Torah, little children die. . . ."

He sings out these words, and all but dances to them. But the dire warning makes my mother shiver, and she gives him an apple, throws coins into his box, and adds her good wishes:

"May you never need to ask for charity again."

"I don't complain—I make my living honorably," answers the ragged man. "I'm no scholar, but I heard the rabbi say while teaching Torah at the Sabbath table, that poverty is as becoming to a Jew as red flowers adorning a white horse." With this the cheerful mendicant is already calling out to someone else: "Give for the Supporters of Torah! Give for the Supporters of Torah!"

Now a third Jew approaches the gate, wearing a stiff hat, a stiff rubber collar, gold-rimmed spectacles, and a coat with a fur collar. He does not shout, nor does he rattle his alms-box. Instead he bears it carefully before him with both arms outstretched, as though he were carrying an esrog and lulav for the Festival of Sukkoth.

This time, Mother sees, she is dealing with a person of refinement. Still, she would like to know where her hard-earned groschen are going.

"For whom, Rabbi?"

"For the Dissemination of Torah," the man answers. "During the war years, together with all the other refugees from Lithuania, many rabbis came to Vilna and established houses of study here."

"Who, then, are the Torah-Study Society and the Society of Supporters of Torah?" Mother asks.

The man straightens the gold-rimmed spectacles on his nose; smooths his mustache with his fingers, one stroke this way, another stroke the other way; and after due and lengthy deliberation comes to a decision— to speak no evil:

"During the war there also came to Vilna, together with the other refugees from Lithuania, the Mussarists of Slobodka, the brilliant scholars of Telz, and the zealous scholars of Poniewicz. These young scholars are maintained in their studies by the Torah-Study Society and the Society of Supporters of Torah."

Having said his piece and received his donation, the man departs slowly and sedately, as befits a Torah scholar from Zamut.

My mother, nonetheless, is still troubled in her mind and speaks aloud:

"It's fifteen years since those refugees he spoke of came here; after the war the rabbis returned to the towns they came from. Who, then, remained here?"

"The alms-box remained here," Alterka interjects.

Mother had merely been thinking aloud. But to the goose-dealer it seemed that, just because she had contributed a groschen (not to speak of it), she was capable of suspecting a pious man of who-knows-what! Exasperated by Alterka's clever sally, she answers him crossly:

"Not all the rabbis went back to their towns. Maybe other men took over their pulpits, or maybe they themselves just didn't want to be rabbis anymore. Some men have such a strict sense of honor that they're unwilling to render judgment on matters of law. And besides, right here in Vilna we have Ramayles' Yeshiva, as well as the recluse scholars of the Gaon's Synagogue and of Reb Shaulka's Synagogue, and also the Council of the Yeshivoth."

"And for each one there's a separate collection," says Alterka. "There's never any shortage of pests."

Now there approaches a Jew with a yellowish beard and yellow tufts of hair on his fingers. In a small basket he carries bundles of yellowed eightfold ritual fringes as well as "arba kanfoth," tallith-katan's, and religious books.

"Buy 'arba kanfoth' for your grandchildren!"

"I don't have any grandchildren yet." Mother smiles. "My son isn't married."

"Well, then, buy a tallith-katan for your son." The peddler becomes animated: "Take a look at this merchandise! Pure wool and an ell in length, just as the Vilna Gaon required."

Like someone guiltily hiding stolen goods, Mother glances furtively at Alterka, to see whether or not he is laughing at the peddler's offering her an ell-long tallith-katan—clearly, none shorter would suffice for her pious son. . . . But even in ill luck one must have luck: Alterka has just walked away, and has heard nothing. Quickly she offers the man a small donation, to get him to leave. He, however, refuses to be put off:

"I don't take charity. Add a few groschen and buy a Teḥinah. It's a new one, by a modern writer, and it's printed in big square letters—not in wooden type as in the old days."

"No," answers my mother impatiently. "I have my prayerbooks that were written by the Jews of olden times, and I don't need any new-fangled ones."

The peddler of religious objects is now elbowed aside by a lively young fellow who has no beard or earlocks but does have an alms-box.

"Give for the sunset clocks."

"What is that?" asks my mother, puzzled.

"I'll tell you what it is!" the young man exclaims, greatly pleased at this opportunity to advertise his cause. He slides the collection box under his arm and begins to count off on his fingers:

"That money is needed for the public bath and for the poorhouse—that you understand. For women in childbirth, for poor brides, for orphans and widows—that you understand. For the hungry man and the charity kitchens—that, too, you understand. But that there have to be three clocks in the Synagogue Courtyard—one to show the time for the shops to close on Fridays, the second to indicate the time for lighting the Sabbath candles, and the third to show the time when the evening service may begin at the end of the Sabbath, and that there has to be a person who sets all these clocks, and that this person has to be paid—that you don't understand."

But Mother is no longer listening to the lively young man. Instead, she is gazing intently and fearfully at someone now walking down the middle of the street.

WALKING DOWN THE STREET is Ḥayka the Maiden. Her wooden face is painted red, paper flowers are stuck into her hair, her dress—short and tight—is pulled up high over her swollen, pointy belly so that the calves of her legs, with ribbons tied around her knitted woolen socks, are visible. Her skinny knees seem almost to have grown together, so that she points her feet sideways and sways from side to side.

Mother blushes red with shame and turns her head away, so as not to witness the degradation of a daughter of Israel. Let it not be so, she thinks, the Maiden is pregnant again. . . . Year after year Ḥayka bore a child in the charity hospital. The infants were always taken from her and placed in an orphanage. Had they been left with her, she might easily have smothered them; she is, after all, a lunatic. Still, there are those who lust after her. Dogs—that's what they are, not men.

The merchants, gloomy all day from being under siege by the paupers, now become cheerful and even ribald. They gape after the girl and exchange leering winks. One begins to hum a merry tune, another heaves a meaningful sigh, as though remembering the great lover he himself had been once upon a time. A shopkeeper with a goatee whistles lewdly—and is frightened: against his will, the rowdy of yore has popped up from beneath the dignity of the goatee.

Fat belly jutting prominently forward, hands dug deep into his pants pockets, Alterka stands in the middle of the street and observes the Maiden with eyes half closed, as befits a great connoisseur:

"To want that one," he spits out, "you have to have a brass stomach."

Ḥayka neither sees nor hears anything happening around her. She heads straight for our gate and halts at my mother's baskets:

"What do you want?" asks my mother, harshly and reluctantly.

Ḥayka, along with all her other "virtues," also has a speech defect. Slowly she stammers out:

"An a . . . ap . . . apple."

Suddenly she bends down and takes from the basket the largest cider apple—the one whose beauty is displayed to attract customers.

"Th . . . this . . . this one," she stutters.

Mother snatches the apple out of Ḥayka's hand with a scream:

"Your betters don't dare to treat themselves to apples like that!"

The Maiden stands still, her mouth gaping wide, her eyes flashing angrily. She makes a fist and threatens:

"Just wait!"

"She'll sic her lovers on you!" Alterka roars with laughter.

The Maiden staggers away. My mother's anger abates and she is overcome with compassion: a poor innocent creature—may God have mercy upon us! She selects several small, wintry apples and runs after the girl:

"Here, take these."

Ḥayka takes the apples, examines them a long time with a look of disappointment on her face, and slowly drags out the words:

"Look . . . at . . . what . . . she's . . . giv . . . ing . . . me."

She flings the apples to the ground.

My mother watches her merchandise roll into the gutter and swim away together with the dirty melting snow.

"Lunatic!" she cries out.

"A lunatic she may be, but only for hitting someone else's head, not her own." Alterka holds his sides with laughter.

Mother sits down on her stool, dejected. She does not regret her refusal to let Hayka take the largest cider apple: God Himself would not demand that she be such a generous donor, especially since the merchandise has been taken on credit from the wholesaler. Even so, she is angry at herself for having lost her temper. There were times when she would insult some "fine lady" who insisted, in the midst of a busy market-day, on haggling over a groschen off the price of a bunch of onions, and for this she feels no qualms, not even during the Ten Days of Penitence. But that she should have fallen with such an outcry upon a poor, half-dumb creature—that was a grievous sin. Weren't there plenty of less-than-perfect children born into substantial, respectable families? But where there are parents who take proper care of them, such backward children are not exposed to mockery or derision. Hayka, however, in addition to her defects, is also an orphan and comes from a background of such poverty as most people could not even imagine. Not without reason is it written in the sacred books that, if one were to take all the miseries of the world and place them on one side of a scale, and the miseries of poverty on the other side, those of poverty would outweigh all the others.

III

ALTERKA THE GOOSE-DEALER shades his eyes with his hand, so as to see better; he gazes into the distance like a ship's captain observing the sky, where a small cloud has appeared, the first harbinger of a devastating storm.

"Hell is on the march!" he cries out. "It's 'Rasputin' and his seven wives."

Hatzkel the grocer, who has with great difficulty rid himself at last of the caravans of beggars, is just opening the door of his shop wide to air out the paupers' odors, so that customers can enter once more. When he hears Alterka sound the alarm, he is terrified:

"Jews, close your shops! It's a pogrom!"

Like the obscure Siberian peasant Rasputin who rose to such great heights at the Czar's court and there turned the heads of the prettiest princesses, so has one of the Vilna shnorrers won the hearts of seven women-beggars. And "Rasputin," accordingly, is the name bestowed upon him by the townspeople; some have even dubbed him "the Emperor."

Rasputin's strategy is to station his seven wives at the corners of the most fashionable streets, where they let no one get past them. Just one look at a passer-by tells them exactly how much money he has in his pockets, even if he looks like a nobody and is dressed in rags. As for any pillar of the community who comes their way—some leading official, say, or charity fund trustee—he never escapes their clutches until he is stripped bare. Should he prove a difficult quarry and remain unmoved by their pleas, the women fall upon him like she-wolves:

"Blood-sucker, give us the millions that America sends for us!"

The worthy gentleman sees everyone eyeing him like some just-exposed swindler or dealer in fake diamonds, and he seeks to ransom himself:

"Take everything I have—just let me get out of here alive."

"Rasputin" and his women seldom make an appearance in the narrow streets near the butcher shops—how much, at best, could they hope to collect there? Most likely, then, Alterka's conjecture is correct:

"They must have had a miserable day today, if they've wandered way out here."

Already a tumult has arisen on Rudnicka Street: Three of the beggar-women are plundering a store. Two others are dancing around a passer-by wearing a soft-brimmed velvet hat and carrying an umbrella. The two remaining ones surround a matron laden with parcels:

"Little mistress, make a gift," sobs one.

"Little madam, deliver us!" groans the second.

"Will you give alms or not?" screams a third one in the murderous voice of a highway robber seizing a merchant and holding a knife to his throat.

"No one answers us!" wails the fourth, like a condemned felon with the gallows before his very eyes.

The passer-by opens his umbrella to protect himself against the storm and flees, the lady with the parcels breaks breathlessly into a run—both pursued by the beggar-women's blessings:

"Look at him tossing his arms—may he toss about in a fever and be thrown nine ells high."

"Look at the parcels she's carrying—may she be carried to her grave piece by piece."

The wealthy matrons who lounge idly about their homes all morning and go out to shop only when the day is half over, are unaware of the tempest now raging in the street. They stand calmly in Alterka's shop, chatting cozily away with Lisa. Alterka himself stands at the gate, feet spread apart, firm as a rock: These beggar-women will not get inside his poultry shop. If they even manage to break into our courtyard, the matrons will run off like so many frightened geese. So he remains on guard, his short pleated neck red and swollen with rage, and to calm his fury he starts to badger my mother:

"Never fear, Vella—it'll get worse yet. Today, Monday, it's the beggars' manifesto—but God has also given us Friday, and Friday is the day of our 'nobility'—the worthy householders down on their luck, and the pious ones with backs bent from sitting over their books. Vilna is world-famous for her Gaon and for her shnorrers."

Abruptly, Alterka breaks off, and moves hastily toward the open wicket of the gate to block the way of someone who is trying to steal unnoticed into the courtyard.

Before the goose-dealer stands . . . Rasputin himself.

Rasputin has sniffed out the juicy pickings awaiting him among the wealthy housewives standing about the poultry shop. But he had also at once noted the goose-dealer on guard at the entrance, and so attempted to enter the courtyard with the stealth of an enemy soldier infiltrating a besieged fortress while the guards are asleep. Alterka, however, has spied him in time and spoiled his plan.

Although inwardly seething, Alterka addresses the beggar very politely—with the politeness of his wife, Lisa, when she is speaking in Russian with her favorite customers:

"I see that you're lost. May I ask whom you are looking for?"

No one since the world began has ever denied Rasputin alms. If all else fails, he wrinkles his forehead so that his eyelids, blood-red from a trachoma inflammation, roll up of their own accord. His victim, overcome with repugnance and disgust, empties his pockets to the last groschen.

Now, realizing that he cannot avoid the goose-dealer, Rasputin looks him over with his slit-narrow eyes, and makes his decision: War!

The entire street holds its breath. Everyone is intensely curious about the outcome of this contest.

Rasputin straightens his muffler, which is knotted many times, as though each of his wives has tied one knot to ensure that he won't catch cold. Then he coughs once and springs toward Alterka on tiptoe, as nimbly and softly as a demon leaping on his rooster feet. He bends his knees so that the short goose-dealer can look down like a lord upon him, the beggar—and stretches out his hand:

"Give alms!"

Alterka looks down at the outstretched palm, examines the lines of the beggar's hand, yawns, and, as though he has not heard, asks:

"What do you* want me to do—spit in it?"

The beggar, who has already made a pathetic face and rolled up his trachoma-inflamed eyelids to arouse the goose-dealer's disgust, abruptly steps back and, as though greatly puzzled, asks:

"Who are you talking to?"

"Who else am I talking to, the Chief Rabbi of Vilna?" says the goose-dealer, shrugging his shoulders. "What do you* want?"

---

* Alterka is here using the "familiar" second person singular *du* instead of the "polite" second person plural *ir*—an insult when used with someone other than a friend or relative.—Trans.

"Scum!" The beggar's outcry echoes through the street. "Lout! Who are you calling *du*?"

Alterka is dumfounded; this was not at all what he'd expected. Usually you could spit in Rasputin's face and he would say it was raining— and here he is, thumping his chest with his fist:

"Do you know who you're speaking to? Do you know who I am?"

Alterka feels an urge to seize Rasputin and fling him away as he would a chicken's guts; but he doesn't want to give that satisfaction to his neighbors, the other storekeepers, who are standing about the gate, breathlessly eager for a scandal. "It won't bring me any honor to get involved in a fight with a beggar," he tells himself. He decides to make light of the whole affair, and gently mocks Rasputin:

"How should I know who I'm talking to? Tell me, who are you, then?"

"Who am I?" Rasputin repeats the question and falls silent for a moment, as though actually unable to remember who he is. "Who am I? You're a lout! Whoever I may be, I won't let you speak to me with disrespect."

When roused to anger, Alterka is capable of tearing someone limb from limb, but now he is afraid of becoming a laughingstock. It occurs to him that Rasputin might be playing out this little scene precisely in order to get his alms. He draws a coin from his pocket and says contemptuously:

"Enough of your currish tricks. Take what's given you and get out of here!"

"Sink into your grave and take your money with you!" screams Rasputin, even louder.

Just at that moment all seven beggar-women—sweating, hair disheveled, eyes hungry—come running from the nearby alleys. Seeing the goose-dealer with the coin in his outstretched hand, they fall upon him like a flock of black ravens, like frenzied witches:

"Give alms!"

"Take nothing!" Rasputin screams imperiously.

The women look about, alarmed and surprised. They see a crowd of people on one side, the goose-dealer at the gate on the other, and in the middle, proud and upright, their husband and emperor. The beggar-women open their mouths and a flood of curses pours forth.

"Silence!" orders Rasputin. "Don't beg in this stinking street. Go!"

The women become quiet as lambs, straighten their hair and their kerchiefs, and meekly turn away, walking in single file. The last to leave is Rasputin himself—head held high, not deigning to cast a glance at the assembled curiosity-seekers.

The goose-dealer stands rooted to the spot, totally humiliated. He cannot very well chase after the beggar with clenched fists, but neither will his pride permit him to leave the gate vanquished. Fortunately, his wife now comes to his aid. She has been busy all this time with her customers in the shop, and has heard nothing of what has been happening outside.

"Alter!"—her voice carries from inside the courtyard—"Alter, where are you?"

"What do you want me for, Lisa?" he calls out in an intentionally loud voice, so that everyone may hear that he is being summoned. He gazes at his neighbors contemptuously and points a finger in the direction of the departing beggars:

"You deserve each other," he laughs spitefully, and reenters the courtyard.

The other shopkeepers, who have till now kept quiet out of fear of incurring Alterka's wrath, gloat with unconcealed satisfaction as soon as he has left.

"He's always sticking his nose into everything, but nobody wants to get into an argument with him and his big mouth. But this time he started up with an even bigger mouth. Ay, did Rasputin ever give it to him! Serves him right!"

"Usually you can throw a dead cat at Rasputin's face and it won't bother him—why did he get so upset this time?"

"Rasputin is used to being shaken off like a pesky fly by people who don't want to give him anything. But here he saw that Alterka was baiting him, and his sense of honor was aroused. After all, he's king of the beggars."

Hatzkel the grocer sighs deeply, his eyes turned heavenward:

"I only wish Rasputin would forbid all the beggars to come to our street, as he forbade his wives. . . ."

My mother does not enter into the conversation. She sits beside her baskets and thinks: A beggar, too, is a human being. When someone shames him, he, too, will stand up to fight for his dignity. . . .

Suddenly she realizes that the day is nearly past and she has earned next to nothing. She begins to call out for customers:

"Cider apples! Cider apples! Pure bottles of wine, bottles of wine. . . ."

Women at the Cholent Oven

I

ALL WEEK LONG, while tending her baskets at the courtyard gate, Mother pays no heed to the other women's gossip. But I know that on the Sabbath, when she returns from the bakery with our cholent, she will bring a mountain of news.

Although she does not rush to the bakery as she rushes to the synagogue for morning prayers, she nonetheless always arrives in time to find a bevy of gossip-mongers still holding forth.

The "prayer-leader" in this congregation is Mariasha, a busybody and a slattern. No one has ever seen her with her hair combed, or properly dressed; feathers invariably cling to the kerchief thrown hastily over her tousled hair, and objects are forever slipping out of her hands. She has a house full of little ones, and the courtyard resounds day and night with their clamor. From her home, late in the evening, the din of a noisy argument is often heard, with the clatter of broken glass, and the neighbors nod their heads knowingly: Mazel tov! Once again Mariasha's husband is smashing dishes and throwing everything on the floor.

Mariasha's husband would come home from work exhausted, only to find the house in complete disarray. The dirty dishes from the day before are still unwashed, the beds have not been made, the children are untended and hungry, and Mariasha is nowhere in sight: she is running from one neighbor's house to the other, busily washing everyone's dirty linen. Only late at night does she finally return home, bustling and excited, and seek to appease her husband's ravenous appetite with a herring roasted on coals, which she serves him together with the ashes. And so he breaks the dishes.

Mariasha's big day is the Sabbath, at the bakery, when the women come to get their cholent pots. There she reigns supreme, her face radiant.

"A good Sabbath to you, Vella—Hatzkel the grocer went bankrupt."

Mother looks at her suspiciously. The other housewives, their cholent pots in their hands, silently poke each other with their elbows. They enjoy Vella's naïveté.

"Vella, you're like a new-born babe," says Mariasha. "You sit beside your baskets and don't see what's going on right under your nose."

This is Mariasha's way of taunting my mother for dozing off while sitting with her wares at the gate, at times nearly falling off her stool.

"Everybody knows—" Mariasha resumes her moral discourse—"that Ḥatzkel doesn't want to pay. He says, 'Prices are soaring. My customers bought on credit and now they owe me a fortune. Taxes and fines have pushed me up against the wall,' he says, 'and the hoodlums who won't let the peasants enter any Jewish shops have completely wiped me out.'"

"So why does it give you so much joy to see a Jewish shopkeeper go bankrupt?" asks my mother.

"Indeed, it's no cause for rejoicing," says Mariasha, piously pursing her lips. "But still, you could die laughing. His creditors, the wholesalers, wanted to tear him apart like a herring. 'What are these stories you're telling us about Polish gangs?' they screamed at him. 'When has any of the uncircumcised so much as stuck his nose into your shop?' And he answered them with a sob: 'It isn't only the goyim—it's the Jewish paupers, the beggars who make their rounds on Mondays collecting alms: they've carried away everything I own.'"

Mariasha's imitation of Ḥatzkel is deft and skillful, and her Sabbath audience, holding their cholent pots, greatly relish her mimicry. She concludes her performance with an observation to her light-headed housewives:

"You have to be on your guard against these 'pious' ones as you do against fire. Ḥatzkel, you know, always prays with his eyes devoutly shut."

This is a gibe at my mother's piety as well. Mother, however, doesn't wish to start up with such a scandal-monger. She takes her cholent and quickly departs.

She comes home greatly upset, puts down the pot, and says angrily:

"She has the tongue of a scorpion, that Mariasha. As soon as something goes wrong, it's always the fault of the Torah. What a slanderer!"

Mother unwinds the wrappings around the pot, takes off the lid, and receives an unpleasant surprise:

"I took the wrong cholent," she says with annoyance. "And guess whose? None other than Mariasha's. Look at the size of this iron cauldron— even you can see that it must be hers. No one else around here has such a large family. We were standing right next to each other, and I was so upset by her needling I couldn't see straight."

Mother replaces the lid, but just before she does so takes a look inside:

"Well, this is definitely Mariasha's cholent! Her gluttons, as she calls her children, like only big beans and tiny potatoes. Yesterday she turned my sack of potatoes upside down and took out only the very smallest. And this is her noodle pudding—probably made with eggs and chicken fat, cinnamon and raisins. Her husband's a good breadwinner, so she can afford it."

"Listen to me, Mother. Let's eat her noodle pudding. By now she's surely taken a pot even bigger than hers and left."

"Believe me," says my mother, "Mariasha is still at the bakery gossiping. Every week she's the first to come and the last to leave."

As Mother walks toward the door, she speaks with still greater annoyance:

"I'm up all night every Thursday preparing our Sabbath meal, so to me what I've cooked myself is better than the finest dish from the Emperor's table."

And, already outside the door, she adds:

"I know, my son, that you don't care at which butcher shop the meat is bought, and you don't worry about whether it's been properly soaked and salted—I know . . ."

AT THE BAKERY, Mother finds two women still there: Mariasha, and the candy-seller who has only recently opened her shop on the corner of our street, where three lanes intersect. All the neighborhood shopkeepers and merchants visit her sweets shop to treat themselves to candy, soda, and lemonade, and while there take the opportunity to have a chat. Mariasha soon became friendly with the new neighbor, for it is only logical that, just as all the nearby streets converge at her shop, so must all the bits of local gossip come to the candy-seller's ears.

The baker, tired of waiting for the chatterboxes to leave, had flung down his long-handled paddle and told them, with a shrug:

"Hang yourselves or drown yourselves! If my wife were like you, I'd poison her. It's stones your husbands will be eating, not puddings." He went through the back door into his own house and left the two women in the now-empty bakery, with the oven that had grown cold and the bare, flour-dusted shelves.

"No offense," my mother says to Mariasha, "but we've mixed up our pots."

"Really?" Mariasha's eyes open wide. "And I never even noticed. Ha-ha-ha! Ḥena the rag-picker once let slip that she eats her cholent until Wednesday. Ḥena," explains Mariasha to the new neighbor, the candy-seller, "is the woman who buys and sells old clothes in the courtyard walkway. 'Why until Wednesday?' I asked her. So she told me that on the Sabbath she eats only the 'scab' of the cholent. 'What do you call the "scab"?' I asked. 'Don't you know,' she answered, 'that the pudding that's stuck on top of the pot is called the scab? Even my grandmother called it that,' she said. She's an old-fashioned yenta herself. Ha-ha-ha!"

Mother takes her own pot from the table and turns to leave. Mariasha grasps the big iron pot my mother has brought back and looks it over suspiciously.

"But, Vella—" Mariasha purses her lips and wrinkles up her nose disdainfully—"you've torn the string and the paper off the pot."

"I didn't notice at first that it wasn't my pot," explains Mother.

"Oh well, it doesn't matter." Mariasha smiles her friendliest smile, and wraps a cloth around the cholent, as one might protect a baby against the frost. "Why are you in such a rush, Vella? Listen to me—it's better not to be born at all than to be born a woman. And when I say that, I mean in particular Lisa, the goose-dealer's wife."

"Why—what's happened to her?" asks Mother in surprise. "Yesterday she was in the poultry shop all day and today I saw her at her window."

"But, Vella, you live in a dream world." Mariasha's sharp, pointed chin becomes still sharper. "Didn't you hear anything yesterday of the hullabaloo that Lisa raised against me—and all just over a chicken neck, a little piece of giblet?"

"Well, what of it?" Mother asks impatiently.

"I have nothing against Lisa," sighs Mariasha, full of sympathy. "Lisa, poor thing, has a very heavy, bitter heart."

Mother perceives that, although Mariasha is doing her best to try her patience, the whole story amounts to nothing: a platter of fish without the fish.

"Well, come to the point then, what did happen?" Mother asks drily. "I don't have the time to stand here all day. My son is waiting for me to sit down to eat."

"Your son won't die of starvation," laughs Mariasha caustically. But when she sees my mother actually start to leave, she bars her way.

"Do you know Ḥasska the butcher girl?"

"So?"

Mariasha leans over and whispers something in my mother's ear. Mother turns all colors. Her face expresses first disbelief, then astonishment, the next moment fear, and finally she is totally enveloped by a flush of embarrassment.

Mariasha catches her breath, points at the candy-seller, and says loudly:

"Let her tell you."

The candy-seller is a quite attractive brunette. The thick curls piled up on her head emphasize her high, white forehead. But there is a gleam of anger in her large, motionless eyes, and on her neck one can see the scars of many surgically stitched cuts. Till now she has maintained a trancelike silence, but suddenly she speaks in a deep, masculine voice, as if she were possessed by a dybbuk:

"Ḥasska the butcher girl is Alterka's paramour."

"The way he's carrying on, he's really lost his head," says Mariasha, rocking to and fro. "Lisa, his wife, is a true lady, while Ḥasska the butcher girl is an abomination."

"What can Alterka see in her?" Mother muses aloud to herself.

"Exactly what I ask myself," says Mariasha in a singsong chant. "Lisa is gentility itself—poised, educated—her fancy customers go to her as they would to a learned rabbi. And it's always looked as though she had Alterka well under her thumb. But now it turns out that all his devotion isn't worth a pinch of snuff. He's traded in such a jewel of a wife for a hunk of flesh with two eyes."

"Well, Alterka is Alterka," says my mother with a shrug. "But Ḥasska—how can she do such a thing, to take a man away from his wife? She must be only half his age."

"How can you even ask?" says Mariasha, encouraged now, and tears of joy well up in her eyes at this opportunity to tell her tale over again. "Don't you know that that's what Ḥasska lives for—the pleasure of taking husbands away from their wives? She unscrews a man's head with just one turn. What does she care if Alterka is twice her age, as long as he buys her presents. She hasn't had a lover for a long time, and she was going around like a bitch during the nine days before Tishah B'Av, with her tongue hanging out. But since she's turned Alterka's head, she's walking around again with hands on hips, swaying from side to side, and looking right and left with those slanted eyes. Her face is red as a beet, her behind is like a copper kettle, on her head she wears a little hat like a chamberpot, and in her hand she carries a handbag—probably a present from Alterka, bought with money earned by Lisa's labor. She looks everyone straight in the eye, with a laugh, as if to say: 'Go on, burst with envy!' It's she who should burst, Good Father in Heaven!"

Mother feels that she is desecrating the Sabbath by listening to such talk, yet she cannot move from the spot. Lisa, now that she thinks of it, has indeed seemed depressed lately—her customary smile had faded from her lips. "One can never truly know," Mother muses, "what is in another's heart."

"Let her tell you." Mariasha points at the candy-seller. "Hasn't Ḥasska been spending half of every day in your store, drinking whole syphons of seltzer with all sorts of flavored syrups, lemon, cherry, and raspberry?"

"That's true!" cries the candy-seller in her low, masculine, dybbuk's voice. Her face, nonetheless, remains rigid, as though she is indeed a witness summoned from the Next World.

At long last, Mariasha takes her cholent from the table and speaks to the candy-seller in tones of great devotion and deep affection:

"A good Sabbath to you, Madame Lapkin. It's time to go."

Mother is the first to rush to the door. The cholent in her hands is cold, but her head is hot. Mariasha calls her back:

"Vellenka, I have something very important to tell you."

She utters these words with such a secretive air that they bring a pang to Mother's heart: this, she feels, must be some matter that concerns her directly. She stops and waits.

Madame Lapkin, however, sees clearly that Mariasha wants her out of the way and walks out, visibly distressed.

II

A s soon as Madame Lapkin has left the bakery, Mariasha looks about her with her swiftly darting eyes and then says to my mother, her voice full of compassion:

"The candy-seller's lot is not to be envied either. You, Vella, never see anything but the birds in the sky. You haven't the slightest idea how she got those stitches on her neck. Compared to her husband, the goose-dealer is Moses the Lawgiver. The goose-dealer has only one mistress, but her husband changes his paramours the way he changes gloves. One time he drove her so far that she lay down in her bathtub and slashed her throat. They were barely able to save her life. Now do you understand why she has the voice of a dybbuk and the eyes of the Angel of Death? She's terrified that now her husband will lose his head over Ḥasska. She used to own a shop on Broad Street, where she raked in the money hand over fist. But then she became a tasty dish of gossip served up to the whole neighborhood, and that's why she's moved here, to us—she thought that here no one would know about her trying to take her own life. But the world does not sleep."

"Upon the heads and limbs of my enemies!" Mother hisses. "To think that in times like these, when Polish hoodlums won't let the peasants enter a Jewish shop and there are pogroms in the small towns, there are still Jews who are such sinners."

Mother is so upset that she turns on the talebearer in whose mouth a fire burns on the Sabbath itself, when even the souls of the wicked in Hell are permitted to rest:

"I just don't understand the pleasure some people get out of sticking their noses into other people's pots."

"My, what a saint you are!" Mariasha grimaces and her nose puckers as though she needs to sneeze but cannot. "It was you who looked into my pot, not I into yours. And when the time comes to wish you Mazel tov, make sure to invite me, too, for some cake and whiskey. She's a really fine girl."

"Who?"

"Vella, are you just pretending to be so naïve, or do you really not know that your son is once again keeping company with a young lady?"

"And what harm is there in that?" asks my mother quickly, so as not to reveal how totally surprised she is by this news. "All the other young fellows may, and he may not? I shouldn't think you really have anything to say against my son."

"May anyone who speaks ill of your son sicken and wither," coos Mariasha, as daintily as a turtledove. "And if your son didn't marry Baylka—the girl from Glebokie—is it any business of mine?"

But this time Mariasha is not destined to get off unscathed. Her venomous tongue is about to earn her unforeseen trouble.

Every Sabbath morning the baker opens the door and the shutter of one window to give himself just enough light to take the pots out of the oven. The other window remains closed. Who could know that the candy-seller has been standing outside, behind the closed shutter, listening to everything being said about her? As soon as Mariasha begins to speak about something else, Madame Lapkin, having no reason to listen further, rushes back into the bakery:

"I knew this slattern would blacken my face like burned kasha. How do you like this one?" she screams at my mother. "She herself can't tie a ribbon to a cat's tail, and yet she laughs at other people. Just recently she cooked some fish, and to cool them off she put them outside, on the grating over the sewer that drains off the filth of the whole city. When her husband found that the fish stank, he threw them right back in her face."

"Angel of Death!" screeches Mariasha.

Who knows how the quarrel might have ended had not at that moment one of Mariasha's children—a little boy with a dirty, tear-stained face and tattered clothes—run into the bakery.

"Mama, why are you talking so much?" he sobs. "We're hungry, and Papa is breaking the dishes again."

"What did I tell you?" cries the candy-seller triumphantly, sated with sweet revenge.

Just then the baker appears at the back door. He has heard the shouting even in his house and, furious, has risen from the table in the midst of his Sabbath meal.

"Out!" he bellows, still chewing the food in his mouth. "If I had a wife like you, I'd give her poison."

Mariasha, though now in mortal dread of the scene her husband will soon be enacting for her, still finds the strength to answer the baker in kind:

"You sell bread with nails in it. This Sabbath I found a piece of string in your ḥallah."

And she gets back at the candy-seller as well:

"Just wait, you trollop, I'll see to it that you have to run away from our street just like you ran away from Broad Street."

"Hussy!" shrieks the candy-seller. "Before you drive me away from this street, I'll drive you into your grave. Your husband will soon be throwing that pudding in your ugly face."

"But your husband doesn't send anyone looking for you," is Mariasha's parting taunt as she makes her escape, followed by the ragged, sobbing child.

MOTHER RETURNS HOME, pale and distressed, and sets the now-cold cholent down on the workbench, but makes no move to untie the rag wrapped around it.

"You're bringing great honor upon me," she says with tears in her eyes as she sits down. "You're keeping company with a girl and my neighbors throw it up to me."

"What of it—is it forbidden?"

"If you're planning just to carry on with the girl and then throw her over, like Baylka, at least don't let yourself be seen with her here, on our street."

"I'm planning to marry her."

Mother stares at me a long time: am I speaking in jest or not? When she sees that I am in earnest, her face clears and is lighted by a smile. She gets up and begins to unwrap the pot. But gradually her mood of dejection returns; a shadow drives the smile of happiness from her face:

"It seems you don't think your mother deserves to have you tell her the news yourself. I had to find out about it from others, from the gossip-mongers."

"Of course I intended to tell you, and I want to invite her here. But it's a long way off still. I don't even know whether she wants me."

"A bright girl," Mother decides. "She realizes there's no depending on you. . . . In the meantime, the cholent has turned into a lump of clay."

She puts some of the rocklike cholent on my plate and also forces herself to eat it. She does not appear inclined to resume the conversation about the girl; the wedding day, after all, still seems a long way off. Saddened, she stares out through the pane at Lisa's window, directly across the way. She cannot get Mariasha's story about Lisa's husband out of her mind.

"It doesn't bear thinking about." She shrugs her shoulders. "People have entirely cast off the yoke of law and tradition."

When I fail even to ask what it is that has so upset her, she adds, hurt, that there is no one to whom she can say a word. She cannot understand these modern girls: What do they see in the pleasure-seeking young fellows of today? The young men of former times, say the girls, were savages, with their beards and earlocks. It used to be that bride and groom didn't even look at each other until after the wedding. But what's the use of the modern young men's playing at love, kissing and caressing their fiancées before the wedding, if afterwards they look for other women? For a pious young man his wife is and remains—his wife; and his home— his home. And a man without a beard isn't a proper man at all, to her way of thinking.

"What's happened?" I ask.

Mother, who has devised this long introduction only to set the stage for her story, suddenly takes fright:

"I've become a talebearer just like the others. . . . Still, since everyone else already knows the story, I suppose you might as well know it, too. But don't write about this, as you wrote about me sitting with my baskets at the gate. That's all you need—for Alterka to find out you're making poems of him."

"You want to tell me about Alterka's affair with the butcher girl? That's old news already."

"And what do you say about it?" she asks, sorely disappointed by my evident indifference. But before I can answer, she looks through the window and hastily begins to clear the dishes from the table, as though in expectation of an important guest.

Pausing hesitantly outside our house is Lisa.

"You mustn't, God forbid, let slip a word about what you know," whispers Mother before Lisa opens the door.

"A good Sabbath," says Lisa, flustered. She had lingered outside a long time before concocting a proper excuse for her visit. "I've heard, Vella, that you're to be congratulated—on your son's engagement."

"May you have only good things in life," responds Mother. "Sit down, Lisa."

The lines show on Lisa's face; she has obviously not been sleeping well. The bags under her eyes are puffy, as if she were suffering from dropsy, and she gazes continually out the window.

"My husband seems to be delayed somewhere gabbing with his pals. . . ." She turns to me. "Is she really the daughter of a rabbi—your fiancée?"

"Yes," I answer reluctantly. "She's a rabbi's daughter."

Mother starts to rise from her chair, but then sits down again. She wants to cry out: "A rabbi's daughter?!" But she keeps an iron grip on herself: There is no need for Lisa to learn that she, his own mother, didn't know this. She lowers her head so that her neighbor cannot see her eyes.

"So you did, after all, seek out a distinguished family—even though you're a writer and side with the workers," Lisa says with a smile.

"Family distinction is no defect," I answer sharply. "At the wedding one of the fathers, a simple coachman, say, may behave with more refinement than a father who is a rabbi. Of course, if it should later come to a divorce, then it makes a big difference whether you have to argue with a rabbi or with a coachman."

"You're talking foolishness!" Mother cries out, upset at me for thus pouring salt on Lisa's wounds. "At the time of the betrothal, who, God forbid, is thinking of a divorce? He's just annoyed because he had to wait so long for the cholent—he's in a hurry to leave." Mother is at once excusing me and hinting to me to leave the two of them alone.

"That's right, I did see you go by twice with the cholent," says Lisa hastily. "I realized that you must have taken the wrong pot. And I wondered what was taking you so long—Mariasha must have been delivering a proper sermon."

"She wants to find out from me what Mariasha's been saying," Mother thinks to herself. "That's why she came here. Then again, she may simply feel sad over being left at home all alone. Maybe she needs to talk to someone, to get things off her chest?" Mother winks at me to leave.

"What, you don't want to talk to me at all? You think I'm just an old-fashioned woman?" Lisa says to me as I am putting on my coat. But the forced playfulness of her tone cannot conceal how glad she is at my departure.

III

MOTHER SITS FACING LISA, at a loss as to how to begin. She dares not give her visitor any hint that she knows about her husband and his paramour. But neither does it do any good to pretend total ignorance; Lisa could easily sense any attempt to avoid causing her distress, and that might distress her even more. Mother finds it best, therefore, to say nothing at all.

Lisa takes heart and speaks first, with a forced laugh:

"Your son said: 'Family distinction is no defect. If it comes to a divorce, it's best to know in advance whom you're dealing with, with a rabbi or with a coachman.' "

"Does he really know what he's saying? After all, he's still only a youngster." Mother seeks to nullify the impression my words have made on Lisa.

"Don't make him out to be such a ninny," says the goose-dealer sharply. "But, really, tell me—what should a woman do if her husband no longer cares for her? You, after all, are a woman of learning, familiar with sacred writ—what do the holy books say about that?"

"My knowledge of sacred writ actually comes to very little, and in worldly matters I'm a very simple woman," says my mother. "But it seems to me that women today spoil things for themselves with their husbands. They dress up, paint themselves, make themselves attractive— all for others. But inside the house they go about with their hair uncombed and half-naked, in their underclothes."

"Forgive me, Vella, but you talk like an old-fashioned woman. Is it really possible always to be on your guard with your own husband? And if a man loves his wife, he loves her even when she's not dressed up."

"That's true," says my mother meekly. "But if a woman is as shame-less before her husband as if he were just a house pet, she ceases to be his special joy, and loses her charm for him."

"A woman is already in a bad way," Lisa sighs, "if she has to think of tricks in order to hold on to her husband." Little by little she sheds her affected dignity, her air of the *grande dame*, until at last there sits before Mother only a broken old woman.

"Tricks are no use," answers Mother. "One must not try to outwit a husband as though he were a peasant in the marketplace. But to be clever, that doesn't hurt. And even if the woman is the smarter of the two, she should let him feel that he's the wise one."

"Is that too written in your books?" asks Lisa.

"I don't remember precisely whether it's written in any of the holy books," says my mother, annoyed by Lisa's assumption that a fruit-vendor could understand nothing on her own. "In a family," she continues, "where the wife is constantly showing her husband that things always work out as she predicts rather than as he does—in such a family peace and harmony are destroyed. There are women who keep their husbands under their thumbs. Such a 'woman of valor' may think, 'I've nothing to worry about, he never says a word to contradict me.' True, he never says a word, but he gets his own back quietly. And if he ever comes home after he's had a glass too many, and she reminds him later of every foolish thing he said while he was tipsy, then he really begins to hate her."

"And what if he doesn't stop at a glass or two, but downs vodka by the bottle, and spends his time in the company of loafers and drunks? What is the law of the Torah then?"

"I don't decide Torah law like a rabbi—" Mother strokes her knees, as though to steady them and keep them from trembling. It seems to her, she says, that a wife must not let her husband get into the habit of seeking his entertainment elsewhere. And even if he consorts with undesirable friends, she ought to invite them to her home. If she is there with them in the house, even his cronies will be ashamed to talk him into doing anything really bad, and certainly they will not be able to taunt him with being a henpecked husband.

"Do you really mean that?" Lisa is beside herself. "And what if he plays cards with a bunch of good-for-nothings—should one invite those to one's home as well?"

"Anything is better than for him to go elsewhere to carry on—" Mother presses her knees harder. "In his own home he won't gamble away as much. But if he does lose money, the wife must not say: 'Serves you right!' If he gets into debt, she shouldn't try to talk him into not paying up. But there's one time when she must not give in: when he wants to get into a fight. Then she must dare to put her foot down and keep him from fighting. No need to worry—later he'll realize that she was right. That's how it seems to me, according to my simple common sense. But I'm no rebbetzin."

Mother falls silent. Her careworn face is illumined with the stillness of dusk and on the table her books lie disconsolate. A shadow envelops them, as though they feel a chill because she has not opened them all day. Lisa, too, sits engulfed by shadows and thinks: "The fruit-seller speaks as though she were reading from a book, but she really means— me and my conduct towards Alterka."

As the twilight deepens, Lisa's sorrow weighs more and more heavily upon her. She moves closer to my mother and begins to speak confidentially: She realizes that Vella wants to avoid causing her any anguish. But why should they play games or try to dissemble? When there are children in a home, the husband is a husband; but when the house is empty, one cannot hold on to him even with pliers. Alterka would be happy if it were always daytime and the shops always open. But when the poultry shop is closed, he cannot bear to stay at home; he gets depressed. It is well known that his sharp tongue spares no one, yet toward her he has always behaved with the greatest courtesy. He has never treated her coarsely, never pressured her to go to doctors. She herself, of her own free will, has gone to every specialist and even to quacks—but if it is not God's will, even a Tartar sorcerer cannot help.

"Is he truly such a fine person, this goose-dealer," Mother wonders, "or is Lisa simply trying to cover up her misfortune before the world? And yet it's true that no one has ever heard him talk about his wife's childlessness. After all is said and done, one must never underestimate the heart of a Jew. . . ."

It is growing darker. Lisa keeps glancing through the window out of the corner of her eyes, but Alterka does not appear. She grows more and more melancholy and fretful. Mother seeks to comfort her: If all this misfortune is due to Alterka's feeling sad, he will eventually come to see that he can find no real happiness with Ḥasska. She will only bankrupt him and then throw him over, as she has done with others. But Mother does not dare to say all this openly. Instead, she intimates it to Lisa indirectly:

"There are all sorts of manias—some that pass by themselves and others that no doctor can cure. Take my son, for example. When he gave up his studies, he told me that he could no longer bear my having to support him. So he became a writer. I ask him: 'What do you get out of writing poems to be sung?' So he laughs and tells me that when one sings, one becomes happier at heart. But I can't see that he's any happier— he goes about as sulky and angry as ever. Now tell me, what good did it do him to give up the study of the Torah for the sake of writing?"

Lisa understands the implication in her neighbor's reference to "manias that pass." She grasps eagerly at this comforting thought, and seeks to repay my mother in kind:

"How can you say that the writing doesn't do your son any good? Is fame nothing? You yourself haven't lost by it, either. I see people stopping at your stall and asking whether you're Chaim's mother."

"That's something I don't like at all. In the eyes of God I've done nothing to deserve such attention. What good is it to me that people stare at me, and what do I need it for?"

"It's sinful to talk that way, Vella. Many poor youngsters grew up on our street. But your son is known throughout Vilna, and so are you. They say that he wrote about you sitting at the gate with your baskets."

"I'd rather he hadn't." Now Mother becomes agitated. "What happiness—he wrote about me! Today at the cholent oven Mariasha taunted me because I sit at my baskets and sleep, fall on my nose—and he, my genius, did the same thing. I know he meant no harm, but I don't want people to pity me. It's small wonder I doze off: At daybreak I'm already at the wholesale market, and late at night, after I've closed up, I still have to reckon up my accounts, to see what I've earned. Thursday nights I don't so much as close my eyes—I'm preparing for the Sabbath. Then he goes and describes how I fall asleep while I'm weighing out the merchandise for a customer. I've already told him, in no uncertain terms, that he must never do that again. But he says he'll keep on doing it."

"Why?"

"Do I know why? He says that he doesn't mean only me; he means all the mothers like me, all the women of my kind. I ask him: 'Why did you have to choose me?' So he answers that he chose me because he feels guilty toward me. 'I gave you a lot of trouble when I was little. And even now I can't make your life any easier,' he says. I ask you, Lisa—does that make any sense? God is my witness that I'm not angry at him for not helping me with my livelihood. May I only have the strength to keep on working! 'You don't owe me anything,' I say to him. 'It's the Almighty to Whom you're in debt. Don't sit down to eat without first washing your hands and pronouncing the blessing.'"

But Lisa is no longer listening. She sits hunched over, staring into the darkness outside the window, like a lost wanderer who spends all night long on a rock waiting for the dawn to find his way.

"But you shouldn't be calling him 'Chaimka' up and down the street anymore—he's an adult now." Lisa rose, her back stiff with pain. "I think you may light your lamp, the Sabbath has ended—I can see several stars. A good week to you, Vella."

"I hope she won't regret having unburdened herself a little—she's such a proud woman," thinks my mother, when she is alone. Through the window she sees that Lisa has not lit any light. Any other woman in her position would have created a scandal that would have resounded throughout the city, but she is probably lying there in the darkness and crying. Her fine husband is still not home.

Mother moistens her fingers with the bluish dew on the window-pane and, with a heavy heart, begins to whisper the Sabbath-closing prayer: "He Who separateth . . ."

The Betrothed

I

THE SABBATH CANDLES in their polished candlesticks are twice as large as usual this week, in honor of our guest. Out of their own radiance the bright flames weave a white bridal veil. The shadows move closer together, concealing the chinks in the cracked, wooden beams of the ceiling and in the blackened walls, and wink at each other: Oh, what a guest we have! A guest indeed! Even the books with their leather spines gaze out from the glass-paned bookcase, as a scholar engrossed in his studies might look crossly through his spectacles at a pretty girl who distracts him.

The guest is a young woman with fresh, full lips and longish, narrow eyes. When she smiles, her eyes become narrower yet, sweetly half closed, and she reveals gleaming white teeth; but the smile hints at a streak of stubbornness. Her full-bodied, perfectly chiseled figure seems as if poured from a mold. She moves her head restlessly, as if attempting to free her small, transparent pink ears from the waves of black hair that cover them. Her face glows with shyness—even the Sabbath candlesticks and the shadows, she feels, are inspecting her knowingly; she, for her part, is astonished by the smithy-chamber.

At the time I invited her to our Friday night meal, I had taken great pains to alert her to our living conditions in the back room of a smithy. I had talked about this so long, in fact, that she had lost patience and said it was unworthy of me to apologize so profusely, like a petty bourgeois, for inviting her to something less than a palace. Nevertheless, she had not expected to see walls whose paint has peeled so badly, or a ceiling so darkened by smoke. Now she is looking about her with barely concealed curiosity, and almost a touch of fear.

Mother sits at the table, her Sabbath shawl covering her head, and recites the Friday evening prayers from her large prayerbook. As long as her lips continue to mumble, she does not need to speak to the guest, does not have to be fearful of uttering an inappropriate word, and can let herself indulge freely in her thoughts:

When her son had told her that he wished to invite his sweetheart for Friday evening, he had told her her name, Frumme-Liebche, and had spoken of her as though she were already in fact his bride. She had immediately thought: "What's interesting is that he never once invited his former girlfriend, Baylka, to the smithy. With this girl, then, he must really be serious about getting married." And she had begun to scurry about the room to set it in order. Her son had laughed and teased her, saying that she was acting just as she did on the day after Hanukah: when the wealthy housewives begin to buy geese and render the fat in anticipation of Passover, she climbs up on a stool, broom in hand, and sets about sweeping away the spider webs that hang from the rafters, though the webs will surely grow again before Passover. But now, with their guest seated at the table, one look at her son tells her that his self-confidence has vanished into thin air and that it is he, not she, who is plainly ashamed of their home.

Vexed, Mother thinks:

Cleaning and straightening the house in honor of an expected guest is surely no sin. But as for being ashamed of my poverty—not for one moment! No one gives me charity. I work hard, with the help of the Almighty, to earn my daily bread. If my son is serious about getting married, he himself should want his bride to know his background, his present situation, and his faults—more even than his virtues. It's also quite possible that the girl wants to find out about her future mother-in-law; she herself, after all, comes of a distinguished family. I won't be grateful to my son for not being ashamed of me, though I'm only a simple woman. Well, whoever I may be, I shall not become any more beautiful than I am now, nor will I pretend to be wiser than I am. And if I'm not a suitable mother-in-law—well then, as the saying goes, they can take out the cow and burn the barn.

Soon, however, Mother realizes that she is getting angry and upset for no reason at all. The girl appears to be very sweet and refined. She has been silent all this time, so as not to disturb her hostess's prayers. It's not proper, Mother says to herself, to keep a guest waiting such a long time; she finishes the prayers quickly, gently kisses the cover of the prayerbook after closing it, and says softly, "Good Sabbath."

"Good Sabbath," answers Frumme-Liebche cheerfully, freed at last from her prolonged silence. "Do you never skip saying the evening prayers?"

"It depends," answers my mother. She cannot, after all, explain that last night she had snatched a couple of hours of sleep so as not to fall asleep during the meal this evening, and that today she had closed her stand a full hour before candle-lighting in order to have enough time to wash up and change her clothes.

Under the freshly laundered napkin on the table I espy two crisply browned hallahs, larger than we normally have. I begin to recite the

Kiddush hurriedly, but gradually slow down in response to a grave look from Frumme-Liebche and her warning signs not to rush so. Mother, standing to one side with hands folded and looking down at the table, does not fail to note the girl's signal to me to behave properly. She observes as well how patiently her guest listens to the Kiddush—not out of piety, but for her, the hostess's, sake.

Mother recites the blessing over bread, but says nothing else until she has swallowed the required olive-size morsel of ḥallah.

Frumme-Liebche hesitates a long time, as though debating with herself: should she recite the blessing over the bread or not? At last, she reluctantly begins to chew. She doesn't want to upset me, Mother reflects, yet she doesn't want to appear more pious than she is—and, to help her guest past this embarrassment, she says aloud:

"We buy our ḥallah from the baker, his shop is full of all good things. He bakes braided festival loaves and Purim cakes all year round, as well as honey cake and all sorts of sweet pastries that are a delight just to look at. We in the big cities have no time to do our own baking. In the small towns, I know, the women bake at home. That's probably how it's done in your family."

"Yes, in our town the women do their own baking. On Fridays our house is a regular marketplace, they all come to my mother to buy yeast. Rabbis in small towns make their living by selling yeast," says Frumme-Liebche, with evident resentment.

"When you bake your own ḥallahs for the Sabbath, they have a different taste entirely. Your heart rises as you watch the loaves rise in the pan." Mother stands up. "Well, I'll go bring the fish."

"I'll help you," says Frumme-Liebche, familiarly and gaily.

"There's really nothing to do—" Mother's eyes light up. "Please sit down. You might catch your dress on one of the pieces of iron or a box of tools. We're already used to moving around in this tight space."

MOTHER RETURNS from the kitchen laden with plates of fish, and coughs discreetly to make sure the "children" hear her coming. When she opens the door, they have barely managed to tear their lips apart in time.

The tiny room is filled with a warm coziness and Mother herself is growing calmer. Her apprehensions concerning her guest, she now realizes, had been quite unnecessary. Joy suffuses all her weary limbs, but her expression remains impassive as she doles out the portions of fish.

"It's very tasty, very well prepared." Frumme-Liebche begins to eat with evident appetite.

"Thank you. I'm really not a great cook and, besides, I can't take the time to watch the cooking as carefully as I should. How do they make gefilte fish in your family—like ours, or differently?"

"We make fish as you do in Vilna, but Polish Jews add sugar to it." Frumme-Liebche's face turns crimson, as though my mother were trying to cross-examine her.

"Sugar?" Mother is astonished. She knows it is customary to cook sweet-and-sour fish for the holidays: one uses raisins, lemon or vinegar for tartness, some bay leaves and other spices, and a piece of cake for browning. But to add sugar to gefilte fish—that seems very strange to her. "What else do Polish Jews put into their gefilte fish?"

"The other ingredients are the same as in Lithuania," answers Frumme-Liebche, and the blush on her face deepens. "You mix in an egg, salt, pepper, a chopped onion. The finer you chop the fish, and the longer you cook it, the better it is."

"We also put in saffron, to make the fish yellow," adds my mother, her heart now overflowing with joy: a good housewife—she's already a really good housewife!

"In Vilna," says Frumme-Liebche with a laugh, "I've seen women carrying ground chickpeas in hot, covered pots, which they sell in small paper bags."

"Why, yes." Mother cannot understand what is so surprising about this. "The other vendors buy the little bags and spread the ground chickpeas on slices of bread. Other women sell oatmeal with milk. In the winter, when they sit freezing by their baskets, the women warm themselves with a bowlful of porridge. There's a saying, you know: 'Some cry because they have so few pearls; others because they have so little soup.'"

Mother goes into the nearly dark workshop and takes down, from atop the coal chest, a well-laden tray that has all this time been standing there mysteriously under a cover. She returns, her face radiant.

"After the fish it's good to take something to drink." From the tray she takes a bottle of wine and several small silver goblets.

"You're using the Passover goblets now, when we're eating ḥometz?" I exclaim.

"I'll tell you the truth—" Mother pretends not to understand me— "why do we need a full dozen Passover goblets when there's only the two of us? One needs nice things during the rest of the year, too. My husband, peace be upon him, had a large family," she explains to the guest. "He used to sit down to the Seder table with six children, a few guests, and several poor relatives—so he had a large household. But now . . ."

Mother does not complete her thought; her head sinks down. Frumme-Liebche, deeply moved, remains silent. In her eyes glisten the flames of the Sabbath candles, the wine—and tears. She slowly picks up the goblet, and says consolingly:

"May your son bring you much joy."

"And may your parents have great happiness through you," Mother responds.

What she really wants to say is: "May Heaven bless the two of you." But since she has not yet been informed explicitly of our engagement, she does not wish to rush in prematurely with her blessing. They probably, she reflects, don't even discuss that among themselves—both of them, after all, are modern young people. If she has a right to complain of anyone, it's of her son, not his fiancée. The girl is well educated, proud, demanding. She hasn't let a match be arranged for her—not even by her father the Rabbi.

"And you—won't you drink anything?" asks Frumme-Liebche.

"I'll take a drop, too," answers my mother.

"L'chaim," says Frumme-Liebche to me, with a peal of diamond-clear laughter, and drinks a little from the goblet. Mother, too, takes a sip.

I, however, indulge myself. I empty my goblet and refill it immediately. My tongue loosens and I begin to talk. I tell how my mother keeps a treasure chest full of Passover dishes packed away atop the oven—everything from a tiny goblet no bigger than a thimble to the large "Cup of Elijah." An ornate Seder dish for the matzohs and wide-bellied carafes with thin, braided necks for the wine. Saucers with red-and-blue-striped borders and polished, sparkling tea glasses of crystal. Mounds of plates and bowls, for salt water and eggs, for borscht and chicken soup. Deep bowls for matzoh-balls, platters for fish and cups for compote. Heavy-handled forks and knives, stirring spoons and skimming spoons. Not to mention pots, mixing bowls, and deep vessels for soaking meat, a copper pestle, a sieve and a wooden mortar. When I was a boy, I would dream all year of the Passover nutcracker and sugar tongs, while my mother watched me as she would a thief, lest I take anything from atop the oven. "'The Passover dishes and the books are all that remain of your father's possessions,'" she would say to me. "But today," I conclude my recital, "Mother herself took down the silver goblets in honor of our guest."

What a chatter-box he is, my son. Mother is inwardly annoyed. She notices my betrothed signaling me to be still. She has more sense than he has, and knows what's what, Mother thinks to herself, as she sets about smoothing things over:

"I've been planning for a long time to take down some of those dishes. My husband, peace be upon him, had an entire cupboard full of enameled saucepans, as well as nine samovars."

"Nine samovars?" echoes Frumme-Liebche, astonished.

"Made of copper," adds Mother modestly. "Old ones and new ones. During the war the Germans took away the copper and melted it down to make cannon. We weren't always so poor, and we didn't always live in a place like this."

She gets up and goes into the kitchen to bring the second course. She feels dizzy, but does not know whether this is due to the sip of wine she has taken or to her fatigue. Usually on Friday nights at this time she would already have been asleep. But she manages to hear Frumme-Liebche saying to me:

"I didn't imagine you'd have such a quiet mother—you're so boisterous."

Already she knows him inside and out, nods Mother to herself. On her way to the kitchen she remains standing for a moment in the nearly dark workshop, where no one can see her, and whispers:

"She must truly be his bride. She doesn't look the sort of girl who'd speak so familiarly with a young man if she didn't mean to marry him."

II

WHEN MOTHER RETURNS from the kitchen with heaping platters, she is at a loss:

"We eat the meat first, and the soup afterwards, but I hear that other people have the soup first and then the meat."

"I'll do as you do," answers Frumme-Liebche. She catches me looking at her and blushes crimson. "Would you like me to help you?"

"If you like, it would please me," answers my mother. She looks on as Frumme-Liebche quickly and deftly cuts the meat into portions, and thinks: May I have a year as blessed as she is capable!

But she becomes utterly confused when she sees that Frumme-Liebche has served her first, and with the largest portion of meat. All through the years she has been used to serving her son first, while she herself ate what was left over.

"No, I don't want so much meat." She pushes her plate over to the guest, who has taken too little for herself.

"Not unless you just don't want me to eat." Frumme-Liebche's forehead is furrowed with annoyance, but suddenly she bursts into laughter so loud, cheerful, and childlike that even Mother begins to smile. To her it seems that no such innocent laughter has been heard in her sad home since her little daughter, her Ettele, died, may her son's betrothed be blessed with a long and happy life. . . . If I am only privileged to have her for my daughter-in-law, she will be like my own daughter to me, sighs Mother inwardly, as she turns her attention to what Frumme-Liebche is saying:

"When my uncle died, the town wanted his son to take over his father's pulpit, but my cousin is lazy, too lazy to be a rabbi. He's even too lazy to get married. So now there he sits in his father's synagogue day and night, gets stouter from day to day, and when he needs to wash for the blessing before a meal, his old mother brings a basin and a towel to him at the table. When he's ready to pronounce the blessing over bread, and the salt isn't within his reach, he snaps his fingers like this, and mumbles in Hebrew: *'Nu-a . . . melaḥ.'* And my old aunt has to get up from her chair and move the salt shaker closer to her son, that 'great scholar.' But when I visit my aunt, I don't let her cater to her son. The old bachelor can very well get up from the table and help himself."

Frumme-Liebche gives me a pointed smile, as though to mock me: You're another one of that ilk, but with me you won't be such a privileged character. I respond with a knowing look: You'll become softer, in time. . . . Under my gaze, she feels a flush of warmth suffuse her throat and, as she always does when ill at ease, she begins to fuss with the curls on the nape of her neck, as if to free it of the waves of hair.

After all, she's still a child, Mother muses. She's a rabbi's daughter and you would think she'd know better, yet she doesn't understand that her aunt, the old rebbetzin—though it must surely grieve her that her son hasn't married—finds some comfort in the fact that he has at least remained a faithful Jew. Children don't understand how happy mothers are to take care of them. . . .

But now, weariness at last overcomes her; her head sinks down . . . until it strikes the hard edge of the table. She rubs her eyes; she has been dozing. The thought runs through her mind that the young people will laugh at her. She glances quickly at them—and finds them both staring, with looks of astonishment, at the door. She turns her head, to behold Mariasha and the candy-seller.

So very recently, at the baker's cholent oven, these two had been ready to tear each other's hair out, and now, thinks Mother, greatly puzzled, here they are, cooing at each other like two lovebirds. But she does not have long to ponder; Mariasha is already in full swing:

"Good Sabbath to you, Vellenka. The delicious aroma of your cooking fills the whole courtyard. But you should install electricity—one could break one's neck in the dark on your crooked stairs. I see you have wine on the table, Vellenka. We didn't even know that congratulations are in order."

"What do you want?" I ask angrily.

"What do I want?" Mariasha never takes her moist, appraising eyes off Frumme-Liebche. "I need a few carrots, a few onions, some dill and parsley."

"Are you really just going to cook your fish now?" asks Mother, greatly surprised.

"May my enemies be so crazy! I don't know what I'm saying—" Mariasha shrugs her shoulders. "My husband and children, those bottomless pits, finished the fish off long ago. I came to get a kilo of Antonowka apples. I'm expecting a guest today, some distant relation of my husband's—some 'grandchild of a horse's hoof's shoe.'"

"But, Mariasha, you know I don't weigh merchandise or take money on the Sabbath."

"May you be as sure of your son's good fortune as you can be sure I'll pay you for the apples. You don't have to weigh them, you can count them by the piece."

"And what do you want?" asks my mother drily, turning to the candy-seller.

The candy-seller is in a very awkward position. She herself, in her candy shop, sells sugar-sweet pears, oranges, and even bananas. Each individual fruit, wrapped in tissue paper, costs more than a full pound of the apples that my mother sells at her stand near the gate. She finds it difficult, therefore, to think up a reasonable pretext.

"I came in to ask how Alterka the goose-dealer is feeling," she says at last, her Angel-of-Death eyes bulging.

"Go and ask him!" I snap angrily at her again.

Mother looks at me fearfully: Oh, that temper of his! He's ready to start a fight with these gossip-mongers, who came just to see what they could sniff out, lick up, and then serve up to the whole neighborhood. Frumme-Liebche, for her part, regards the two women with evident curiosity. She's wondering who my neighbors are, thinks Mother, and gets up.

"Alter the goose-dealer, poor soul, is very ill." As she answers the candy-seller's question, she virtually pushes the two women out of the room and goes out with them, closing the door behind her. In the workshop she bends over her basket and begins to search for apples.

"Don't bother!" says Mariasha, grinding away like a mill. "My husband's relative, that horse's hoof's shoe's grandchild, will have to get along without any treats. May she spend on doctor's bills what she costs us—and it's like throwing it all in front of pigs. I'd kick her out head first if it weren't for my husband. If you dare say a word against his piggish family, you put your life in danger . . . Listen, Vella, that's some daughter-in-law you're going to have—your enemies will burst with envy."

"Why should anybody burst with envy?" Mother is annoyed. "May all Jews have cause for rejoicing. The girl isn't just anybody, she's very selective. More than one great scholar was anxious to marry her, to become the son-in-law of her father the Rabbi. And she herself—may all Jewish daughters be like her! And she's of such distinguished ancestry, besides."

"Distinguished ancestry is good for the cemetery!" shrieks the candy-seller in her deep dybbuk's voice.

"Don't say that, Madame Lapkin," says Mariasha, trying to mollify her. "For someone of fine ancestry even the evil spirits have respect. A rabbi's daughter is still a rabbi's daughter, even if she did run away from home and her parents are up in arms about her way of life. And don't let it worry you that her mother the Rebbetzin is against the match, she'll come around later."

I knew they couldn't bear to see my happiness, Mother thinks. How could I ever have let myself get into a discussion of family lineage with them? Unable to forgive herself for her earlier boasting, Mother now begins her defense:

"Of course a mother gets upset when a daughter acts without asking her advice. But why should the Rebbetzin be against the match? My son wasn't born next to a fence. His father was a very fine man."

"Well, I'm not God's prosecutor, but you, you're such a pious woman. Just now, for example, you were afraid I was about to cook fish on the Sabbath, yet your future daughter-in-law doesn't observe the Sabbath, so I've heard," sings Mariasha into Mother's ear.

"She's a nurse, a sister of mercy," Mother stammers in confusion. "To save a sick person's life, it's actually a duty to violate the Sabbath."

"Someone can look like a sister of mercy and still be a nasty creature," rages the dybbuk's voice out of the candy-seller's throat.

"Please don't shout so," Mother pleads.

"He's already broken the heart of one girl, your righteous son—" The candy-seller is seething. "You'd better see to it that all his promises don't fizzle out this time too. What was the name of the girl he threw over?" she screams to Mariasha.

Mother begins to tremble, as if before her stood two Destroying Angels who have descended at precisely the moment when her son is sitting with his betrothed, and who wish to drag him down to Gehenna for his old transgressions.

"Baylka, that was the name of the girl her son threw over," Mariasha sings out melodiously. "Madame Lapkin, why do you bring up these old tales?"

"The bride and groom I snap my fingers at, never mind them. I just want to know how Alterka is doing," persists the candy-seller. "How is he, the goose-dealer, that overstuffed craw? He had a yen for Ḥasska the butcher girl. Now he's flat on his back, his soul barely clinging to his body, and Ḥasska doesn't give a damn about him. She's already busy turning another man's head."

"I'm telling you, Vellenka, it's no wonder Alterka is so deathly ill." Mariasha wrings her hands. "Every time Ḥasska came into the candy shop she gorged herself on whole pounds of candies, pistachio nuts, and grapes, and paid for it all in cash. Alterka would stand there looking unconcerned, but he was turning hot and cold together; he was shaking with fever. He knew that later he'd have to refill Ḥasska's purse with his money. Am I telling the truth or a lie?" Mariasha, stern as a judge, turns to the candy-seller for confirmation.

"The truth!" shrieks the latter in the murderous tones of a brigand.

I ought to take a broom, Mother thinks, and sweep these two idle troublemakers out of the house. She knows, however, that she cannot do that, especially not in the presence of a guest. She is also afraid that her son may hear what is going on and come running. So she has recourse to a stratagem:

"You really should go over to visit Lisa—let her see that her neighbors are not her enemies."

"Go see that snob?" rages Mariasha. "She doesn't want to talk to us even now, when her husband is on his last legs and the earth is already beginning to cover him. She still walks around putting on airs."

At that moment the door opens and—may the Messiah come as quickly—Lisa enters, clearly in distress. As soon, however, as she notices the two gossips, she straightens herself haughtily, gets a grip on herself, and addresses my mother:

"My husband finished eating and was feeling fine. But suddenly he began to have cramps. I'd like to ask your son's fiancée to go in to see him. The doctor gave him a prescription for an injection if he feels any pain. I have the medicine. He gave me the name of a nurse on Broad Street, but since your son's fiancée is a nurse and she's visiting you . . ."

Without a word, Mother returns at once to the room where we are sitting. She is careful to close the door behind her, as though in fear of some evil eye that might, God forbid, do us harm. The two talebearers remain standing where they are, as frustrated as witches who are denied even a glimpse of Paradise. They seethe with anger, especially at Lisa, who does not address so much as a word to them.

A few moments later, Frumme-Liebche, Mother, and I emerge. The women move aside as respectfully as for a doctor.

"Do you have a syringe?" asks Frumme-Liebche.

"You can get one in the pharmacy at the corner of Rudnicka Street, just a few steps from here," answers Lisa. "I'd run over there myself, but there's no one to stay with my husband."

"Go to the pharmacy," Frumme-Liebche says to me. "Get a syringe, cotton, alcohol, and iodine." She goes out, followed by Lisa. In the half-dark workshop there remain the two other women and my mother, who is debating with herself: Should I go too? No, she decides, I won't—if the goose-dealer sees a lot of people coming in at once, he'll be frightened.

The candy-seller, however, runs after them at full speed:

"I want to know once and for all whether his fiancée really is a nurse or just pretending."

Mariasha remembers only too well how the candy-seller had stood behind the door of the bakery and listened to what was being said about her. Now, very much on guard, she looks out through the window and remains as silent as a fish until she sees the candy-seller station herself at Lisa's window. Only then does she burst forth like fire and flood:

"Madame Lapkin's in a bad mood today and biting like a fly just before it dies, because her husband is on the prowl again, looking for a new paramour. Trying to slit her own throat in the bathtub didn't do her any good at all. Ever since Ḥasska the butcher girl broke off with Alterka, the candy-seller has been trembling with fear that her husband might get involved with that girl. Building on Madame Lapkin's friendship is like trying to build on a church steeple. She rushed into my house almost ready to faint. 'Mariashele,' she says to me, 'you've got a head like a prime minister's, think up a good excuse and let's go over to Vella's—her son's fiancée is visiting there now.' Did you see how your son followed her? His girl, I mean. He follows her about like a kitten."

Mariasha cannot decide what to talk about first. In the end she, too, can no longer restrain herself and runs outside. Mother remains alone, gazing out through the glass pane; but the two women in the courtyard hide Lisa's window from view.

It's not merely a job for her, muses my mother. She really is a sister of mercy and wants to help the sick. There she was, sitting radiantly happy, deep in conversation with my son. But as soon as she was told about the sick man she got up at once, thinking only of her duty. My son grimaced because they were interrupted, but she looked at him and her face turned red, not from shyness now but from anger. She can, it seems, be very severe.

"Let me tell you, Vella—" Mariasha bursts into the room—"she's not only beautiful but capable as well. She made a bed for Alterka, helped him get undressed, and wasn't the least bit embarrassed that he's a man. Lisa is just standing there, unable to move. The candy-seller can't say another word—she might burst a blood vessel yet. Your son's fiancée has golden hands."

And Mariasha disappears.

"And a golden heart." Mother raises her eyes to the ceiling.

"Did Mariasha say anything about me?" The candy-seller rushes in, out of breath. "Mariasha can cook up a lie with the most brazen straight face. She hasn't even put up her supper, that slattern, but she told you her family'd already finished eating. Great-lady Lisa is kissing your daughter-in-law's hands like a servant girl, and Alterka, that whipped cur, looks up at her as if she were an angel."

With this, the candy-seller runs back out into the courtyard.

Mother does not wish to look out the window any longer; she goes back into our tiny room, sinks down on a chair, and begins to murmur:

"Who am I and what am I? Only a poor fruit-seller. It is not for my merit's sake that my son is getting such a bride. Lord of the Universe, You are not mocking me? It is not just a dream?"

A film begins to cover her eyes. From joy, she tells herself, one may weep perhaps even on the Sabbath, and she fixes her gaze on her husband's bookcase, as though asking the books to deliver a message to him in Paradise, to tell him that she has watched over the son born to him in his old age, and that she herself has not remarried before their son found his destined mate.

What a Human Being Being Comes to

I

SINCE THE FRIDAY NIGHT when Frumme-Liebche rushed over to attend to the goose-dealer, his wife, Lisa, has become greatly attached to her.

"First is God and right after Him—your son's betrothed," she tells my mother. "My husband won't let any other nurse come near his bed. No one, he says, is as gentle with her hands as she. Help me, Vellenka, I beg of you . . ."

"Why do you need to beg me, Lisa? Whenever you call her and even, it seems, when you don't, she goes to look after your husband."

"But your son, I can tell, is annoyed."

"You mustn't hold that against him. After all, he's a young man— sometimes he'd like to go for a walk with his fiancée—but she's often at your house day and night."

"I don't ask her to do it for nothing—I want to pay. The trouble is, she won't take any money. 'You'll pay me everything together later,' she says. But my husband insists that I must pay right away. 'Later she won't take it,' he says. So I want to ask you, Vellenka, to save the money I owe your future daughter-in-law for her."

"What am I—a cash box? If she finds out, she'll be very angry at me. You want to turn me into a shrew of a mother-in-law even before the wedding . . ."

God sends the cure before the disease, thinks my mother after Lisa leaves. My son became engaged to a nurse just at the time when my neighbor needs her as much as life itself . . . Here she comes now, blessings upon her dear head!

At first, Mother had found it very difficult to use the familiar mode of address with Frumme-Liebche, but now that she has grown accustomed to doing so, it gives her a special joy.

"Lisa was complaining about you because you won't take any money for attending to her husband."

"I don't feel right about taking money—" Frumme-Liebche's face clouds over—"the goose-dealer has a disease for which there is still no cure."

"Just for that reason, it seems to me, you ought to take the money when Lisa offers it to you, even if you later give it to charity, so she won't guess that you think her husband's case is hopeless."

"You're right." Frumme-Liebche gives her a surprised look, as though she would not have expected such wise words from a woman who was only a simple fruit-seller.

"And you should tell your fiancé to go along with you when you visit the goose-dealer, so his wife won't worry that my Chaimka is angry about your taking care of her husband. Ah, it's a bitter way to earn one's living."

"It's not a bitter way to earn one's living." Frumme-Liebche bursts into laughter and little wrinkles form around her narrow, longish eyes. "When you give the patient his medicines, or administer an injection, and you can see how it helps him get better, you feel a great sense of satisfaction at being able to be useful. When my father tried to talk me out of studying nursing, he said to me, 'You want to be a sister of mercy in order to help people, yet you'll be taking money for your help.' I answered him, 'I'm going to study nursing because I want to be able to support myself, not because I want to be a sister of mercy.' And yet, no matter how much money a nurse takes for her work, there's always an opportunity for her to do something extra for the patient, over and above what the job requires."

Frumme-Liebche goes off to attend the sick man. Her rounded, shapely figure, shod in soft little shoes, barely manages to stay upright as she traverses the crooked cobblestones. She walks, therefore, very quietly and cautiously, as she is used to doing in the hospital so as not to awaken the patients.

My mother—hands in her apron pockets, the woolen kerchief atop her wig pulled down over her forehead, her face perspiring, her lips parched by the midsummer heat, but withal, radiant with happiness—gazes after Frumme-Liebche and rejoices:

She has a lovely full figure. . . . Even though she's left her parents' home and is no longer under their authority, she is still clearly the daughter of a rabbi. She will not tell the sick man exactly how ill he is, as a Gentile doctor would. And how modest she is! After all, she sees naked bodies every day, and isn't embarrassed to attend to the needs of male patients, yet she blushes flame-red at any little thing. I really don't know what she sees in my son. A scholar, like her father the Rabbi, he's not, he earns nothing from his writing, yet she believes in him as a pious Jew believes in the Messiah.

When Mother at last turns back to her baskets, she finds herself surrounded by her neighbors. The entire neighborhood reveres the nurse, and on her account they extend a measure of respect to her future mother-in-law as well:

"Rebbetzin, how is the goose-dealer?"

"I'm not a rebbetzin," protests Mother.

"What do you mean, you're not a rebbetzin? Your son's fiancée's father is a rabbi, you yourself wear a matron's wig, so you're a rebbetzin. And what does she—your future daughter-in-law, that is—say about the goose-dealer? How is he?" The shopkeepers speak softly and with gestures, so that Lisa, in her shop in the courtyard, will not overhear.

"How should he be?" Mother does not raise her eyes from her baskets. She is afraid to reveal the truth, lest Lisa be able to tell, by the expression on her neighbors' faces, how matters stand with her husband.

GRADUALLY, however, Lisa herself came to realize the truth. She closed up her stand in the poultry market and spent all her time at her husband's bedside. The neighbors, no longer guarding their every word, gathered near the gate and discussed the situation openly.

"She bears a heavy burden indeed—Lisa the goose-dealer, I mean." Mariasha, the gossip-monger-in-chief, sniffs as if about to weep. "Before, her husband didn't even bother to look at her—all because of Ḥasska the butcher girl. Only when he collapsed more dead than alive, that was when he remembered he had a wife. Why should it bother you, good people? Things have turned out badly for him and his wicked lust. I always predicted that Ḥasska would suck him dry and then cast him aside. But that this would just about finish him off, that I didn't expect."

"It's all because of the fight," interjects the candy-seller. "Big Ellinka once gave the goose-dealer such a thrashing that he collapsed. 'You miserable little worm, where do you get the nerve?' says Big Ellinka to him. 'Where are you trying to sneak your way in? Don't you know Ḥasska is my bitch?' And then he hit him again, which really put the goose-dealer in a daze. If only God set such Ellinkas upon all unfaithful husbands!" the candy-seller cries out in savage tones, and it isn't hard to understand her bitterness. But her husband, who, in Mariasha's words, changes his mistresses as often as his gloves, has the good luck of a goy; he has never come up against someone like Ellinka.

"Go on," laughs Mariasha at the candy-seller. "Alterka cared as much about Ellinka's slap as about a fly on his nose. It was Ḥasska's laughter that did him in. While Ellinka was thrashing him, she stood by and laughed at the silly ass who had let himself be taken in by her. Being made a fool of, that was what really made him sick—for, as the saying goes, 'A slap fades away, but an insult will stay.'"

"A plague upon you, you vicious tongues!" Ḥatzkel the grocer spits out. "You won't even let a man die."

"You—we'll let!" Mariasha plants her hands on her hips. "For you we'll have even higher praise than for the goose-dealer. 'Ḥatzkel,' we'll say, 'with his eyes piously closed, declared bankruptcy so as not to pay his debts. And he blamed it on the beggars who collect alms every Monday and Thursday—they made him a pauper.'"

Ḥatzkel can only stand silent, overcome with confusion, as the crowd laughs. My mother, however, can endure this no longer:

"Mariasha, you haven't danced your last dance yet, either. Don't forget that you have little children. Instead of spreading slander about a sick man, you ought to pray to God that you yourself won't come to need a doctor . . . And you, too," she admonishes the candy-seller, "would do better not to drag a hopelessly ill man through the mud."

The two gossips are frightened by these warnings and take their leave, grumbling that the fruit-seller has lately become too proud: Her son's father-in-law-to-be is a rabbi, so she has begun to reprimand and moralize like a rebbetzin. Besides, the son's fiancée is herself half a doctor, may one never need her help. Yet one cannot know what the future may hold, and it is best not to start up with Vella.

THUS FAR, the neighbors have been unable to bring themselves to pay a proper visit to the sick goose-dealer. For years an open war has raged between him and all of them; now they are afraid lest he see them as coming to gloat over his misfortune. Had Lisa given the least hint that she would welcome their visits, no one would have shirked his duty. She, however, avoids them all as though they were enemies. "The only one Lisa really trusts," the neighbors tell one another, "is Vella's future daughter-in-law—since she's a stranger here, Lisa has no old accounts to settle with her."

One time I went along to the sick man's house and stood by while Frumme-Liebche changed his bed and administered his medications. He was moaning all the while and did not speak to me. But just as I was about to leave, he turned his bloodshot eyes toward me and spoke with a wan, pathetic smile:

"Forgive me for tiring out your fiancée and for disturbing you in your time of joy. I still remember you from the days when you were a small boy, so you should be able to have compassion for me. You won't have to suffer much longer on my account—" he opened his eyes wide, and I could not tell whether he was speaking to me or to Lisa, his wife—"perhaps God will take pity on me and soon gather in my soul."

Mariasha, who never missed an opportunity to station herself at the goose-dealer's window, overheard these words and promptly passed them on to the neighbors. Those who heard this story saw in the goose-dealer's words a deathbed confession. Ḥatzkel the grocer pressed his eyes closed, in the manner of one reciting the Eighteen Benedictions—a sign that he was deeply moved:

"Ay, what a human being comes to! Alterka, who was always rushing to take on the whole world, roaring like a lion; Alterka, who stood up against everyone and didn't even spare the slaughterers; Alterka, who rebelled against the Torah and did anything his heart desired—that Alterka should speak so submissively, that he should ask a youngster for forgiveness and wait for God to take his soul. Ay, what a human being comes to!"

A second man—Shaya the grain-dealer—tugged thoughtfully at his goatee and chanted, in a slow, mournful melody:

"Alterka the goose-dealer is done for."

II

PEOPLE BEGIN TO FORGET about the goose-dealer, almost as though he were already dead and buried. Once, however, it happens that Shaya the grain-dealer comes rushing by, distracted and sweating, all but boiling in the heat. He has come, his soles scorched, from distant streets where one's feet sink into molten asphalt as into hot pitch. He is on his way to streets even more distant where the tall windows of buildings are reflected in the windows of automobiles, where everything glitters, bathed in dazzling light—streets filled with continual hustle and bustle. Abruptly he halts in his tracks: passing by him is Lisa, on her way back from the pharmacy, carrying labeled bottles of medicine. She glides past in silence, like an apparition, seeing no one, hearing nothing of the hubbub that surrounds her, only nodding her head to Vella, the fruit-seller at the gate, who looks at her with an unspoken question . . . then Lisa passes into the courtyard, a mournful stiffness in her bearing, as though she were entering a cemetery. Shaya looks right and left, and catches sight of Ḥatzkel the grocer.

"How is he doing?" Shaya points toward the gate Lisa has just entered.

"He's already done for," sighs Ḥatzkel, and rushes back into his shop—customers are waiting for him, he needs to weigh and to measure, time does not stand still.

"Vanity of vanities—that's all the world amounts to." The grain merchant scratches his goatee and hurries off to attend to his affairs. . . .

But once something happened that reminded everyone that the goose-dealer was still alive and still suffering.

One hot afternoon, as the damp heat settled lower and lower over the street, putting to sleep the women vendors sitting next to the dried-out gutters, and driving the storekeepers into the furthermost shaded nooks of their stores, Ḥasska the butcher girl came walking down the street.

Just out of bed, and having taken her fill of yawning and stretching herself, she rocks her full hips to and fro, clearly taking enormous pleasure in the solid fleshiness of her body. One shoulder is jauntily raised, the other droops slightly. She walks slowly and lazily, with the calm self-assurance of a strong woman of pleasure who knows her power; but the slanted eyes in her beet-red, heat-steamed face burn with belligerence. The handbag Alterka had given her swings from her arm and a stylish little hat, another of Alterka's presents, sits coquettishly on the very tip of her head. She stops beside my mother:

"How is he—Alterka?"

Mother lowers her eyes and does not answer.

"It doesn't suit you to speak to me?" screams Ḥasska. "If anyone says I'm to blame for Alterka's illness, I'll tear his eyes out. He himself told me once, when he was drunk, that he had kicked a cat with his boot and it croaked. That's why God is punishing him."

"Ḥasska," my mother pleads, "let God be in your heart, and go away. You're a Jewish daughter, you must understand what Lisa is suffering. You've seen other men like him, but for her, it's her husband who's dying. Go away!"

"Don't worry! I may not be a sister of mercy like your son's betrothed, but I have a heart too. I'd like to have things out with Alterka, so that he won't leave the world with anger against me in his heart, but for the sake of his wife I won't do it. As for the rest of the neighborhood, I laugh at all of you"—her voice rises to a scream, for all to hear—"I couldn't care less about being in people's mouths the way I am. It was Alterka who ran after me, not I after him. And now the candy-seller's husband and Big Ellinka and ten other such curs are running after me. But you're a rebbetzin, so I want you to know: I'm not responsible. Alterka himself is responsible—he kicked a cat with his boot and it croaked, and that's why God is punishing him."

Ḥasska strides away, a defiant smirk on her lips, looking straight into the faces of the men who have oafishly stuck their heads out from their shops, like cattle poking their nuzzles out of a barn. She swings her hips knowingly, and in her slanted eyes Gehenna burns with a light-bluish flame. The she-demon dwelling within those eyes looks out and scoffs: "See what a tempting morsel I am . . . burst just for wanting me."

"Filthy whore." The women curse her under their breaths, afraid to speak aloud. "God protect and shield us from her tongue. Just see how strong and healthy she is, the blood boils in her face, the earth trembles beneath her feet."

HASSKA'S APPEARANCE on the street reminded everyone that the goose-dealer was wrestling still with the Angel of Death. But the reminder, instead of arousing compassion, awakened once more all the old hatred they felt for him.

For years the goose-dealer and his wife had kept a black tomcat that would lie about on the tin counter and never so much as touch the plucked geese. But at long last the cat stretched out his four legs and died, for even an elephant does not live forever. Thereafter a series of cats successively came and went at the goose-dealer's, none of which seemed to last for long. One gobbled down too many leftover poultry scraps, and died. Another one went off for a walk and never returned— one of the housewives must have grabbed her up, or she was nabbed by the dog-catcher. The goose-dealer himself chased away the third one, because she became mangy. So it was quite possible that he had kicked it with his boot, and it was this dead cat, the neighbors decided, that was torturing Alterka and would not let him die. But one merchant, the goateed Shaya, laughed at this tale:

"May the enemies of Israel have on their tongues the sickness that Alterka has in his body. Alterka has a certain hard lump of flesh which, if you cut it out in one place, grows again somewhere else. But he won't let them cut him up, and that's why he can't swallow any food and vomits everything up. So what kind of tales are you telling? All this talk about a cat is just so much noodle pudding."

"Why, then, did this hard lump of flesh, as you say, come upon him, of all people?" the neighbors ask, and answer their own question: "Because of the cat!"

"Just hold on here," Hatzkel the grocer argues reflectively, with eyes pressed closed. "If you're trying to discover the goose-dealer's sins, well, then, it's an established fact that he once threw punches at the slaughterers in the slaughterhouse. Now if you tell me that up in Heaven they're calling him to account because of the slaughterers, that I can understand. But for a cat?"

"That old story!"—the neighbors stick to their guns—"Isn't it just awful about the slaughterers! Don't they charge an arm and a leg? Besides, it's comparing apples and pumpkins—like saying that because the moon is round, a basketful of split wood must have pointed ends. A human being can defend himself, with his hands or with his tongue, but what can a dumb little creature do? That's why its cause is taken up on high."

"Imbeciles!" Ḥatzkel shrugs his shoulders. "Here is a Jew, a goose-dealer, who in his lifetime has killed off a million geese, ducks, turkeys, and chickens, and for that he gets no punishment at all. But if once he kicks a cat that's likely half-dead already, the heavens open up to judge the case?"

"Reb Ḥatzkel, your head isn't screwed on right. The poultry we eat, and from the feathers we make pillows. But to go and kill a dumb little creature, a cat, for no reason at all?!"

Not far from the gate where the crowd has collected stands Reb Nossen-Nota, the Gabbai of the Guardians of the Sabbath Synagogue, and the landlord of the courtyard. He is trying to make up his mind: Perhaps just now, when the goose-dealer is suffering so greatly and stands so in need of divine mercy—perhaps now he'd soften and be willing to pay the rent he owed? On the other hand, the landlord reflects, one could also argue here on the principle of *a fortiori*: if the goose-dealer would not pay before, then now, when his shop is closed and the doctors are costing him a fortune, he is even less likely to pay. In vexation the landlord grasps a few strands of his long, well-groomed beard and winds them about his fingers, as an exorcist might wind about her finger the kerchief over which she has pronounced her invocations.

"Idle chatterboxes!" The Gabbai can no longer keep silent. "I'm not here to discuss Alterka's fight with the slaughterers, but to talk about the rent money. One doesn't need to be devout to pay one's debts, one need only be an honest man. Every time I would come to ask for my money, he'd answer, 'Come back tomorrow.' And on Friday afternoons, when I'd remind him to close his shop and not desecrate the Sabbath, he'd also say, 'Come back tomorrow.' So why do you keep going on about the cat?"

"Some comparison!" the neighbors retort. "In Reb Shaulka's Synagogue they didn't have to wait for Alterka to close his shop before they could begin the Friday evening service—but a cat?!"

"And as for you," shouts one of the neighbors at the landlord, "you obviously don't need any fast-day prayers said for you—as we can see, praised be the Almighty, you haven't died of starvation. But the cat did die."

Discouraged and despondent, the landlord walks away. He has made up his mind: he will not ask for the rent money.

Mother, sitting at the gate, cannot understand what she has just heard: The neighbors, of course, are the neighbors—what else can one say?—but surely the Gabbai must know that when a man's life hangs in the balance, one must not mention his sins, but recount only whatever good deeds he has done, so that he will have as much merit as possible to intercede for him on high.

ONE NIGHT, toward the end of summer, Mother was awakened by a loud knock on the door. I, too, jumped out of bed. Frumme-Liebche, who had been sitting up with the sick man, stumbled into the room, terrified:

"The goose-dealer is dead."

"Boruḥ dayan emes—Blessed be the Righteous Judge." Mother wrings her hands and bows her head.

"Why are you so shaken?" I ask Frumme-Liebche. "It's been expected for a long time, after all."

"He was tossing so dreadfully all night long—" she breathes heavily— "he gnashed his teeth, and kept staring with his wide-open eyes at one corner of the room and clenching his fists, as though someone were standing in that corner. Suddenly he tore off the bedcovers, jumped naked from the bed, and ran over to the corner. There he fell down and began to beat on the floor with his fists. Lisa and I ran over to pick him up, but he wouldn't let himself be lifted. He contorted his fingers into claws and groaned: 'I have to strangle her!' That's what he kept repeating over and over again: 'I have to strangle her!'—until he was dead."

"Woe is me!" Mother's face shows her dismay. "He didn't die in his bed—the Angel of Death dragged him off. May that then be his atonement, the expiation for all his sins, so that he need not undergo the punishment of the grave."

Hurriedly she begins to dress.

"Where are you going?"

"To Lisa. You can hear how quiet it is over there—she hasn't cried out once. She must be lying there in a faint. I have to wake up the neighbors. . . . Cover her, she's cold!" She points at Frumme-Liebche, and rushes out.

Early every morning that summer, when Frumme-Liebche had completed her night's vigil at the bed of the sick man, she would come to us. Each time, it just so happened that Mother had not yet left for the wholesale market. Frumme-Liebche would have a glass of hot tea and then return to her own place to rest after the difficult night. Only after she had gone would Mother rush away, uneasy: In the summer one had to hurry to the market at the crack of dawn to buy the day's merchandise, yet she would always linger at home until the bride-to-be had left. . . . It wasn't that she meant to keep watch over the children—just that she didn't want to give people any chance to gossip about them. But now, in the face of such misfortune in the courtyard, and the girl's trembling, she does not stop to think about what gossip-mongers might say.

"I don't want to work with old people anymore," murmurs Frumme-Liebche. "I want to work with children. I want to be where life begins, not where it ends."

She is lying in my arms. I smooth her hair, push it back behind her small pink ears, and kiss her long eyelashes, which droop wearily over her long narrow eyes like thin branches, wilted by the heat of the day, which droop in the evening over the water that mirrors them. She moves her head, as though weakly trying to ward off my caresses, and her lips mumble:

"Something was troubling the goose-dealer."

"Lying chained to his bed was what was troubling him," I murmur into her half-slumber, trying to lull her asleep.

"No—there was something else—" Suddenly she stretches and sits up. "I'll tell you what it was: all the time I was there, not one of his neighbors ever came to visit him. It was his war against the whole world that tortured him. Even Lisa, I think, never cried or complained all the time he was sick because she sensed that, while some sympathy might be aroused for her, no one would feel any compassion for her husband. . . . I'm cold." Frumme-Liebche begins to tremble again. She nestles against me, sweetly ripe and weary, until her head once more falls back onto the pillow and she smiles with eyes closed. A radiance hovers upon her long lashes, as though the day that was dawning somewhere beyond the horizon was also dawning beneath her skin and melting her fear like ice.

"A nurse in a white uniform is not an angel, but neither is she a machine," she whispers dreamily. "I know it bothers you that I always talk about my patients. . . ."

And she falls asleep.

III

MOTHER RUSHES into Lisa's apartment—and at once retreats to the threshold, terrified. The goose-dealer, covered with his coat, is lying in the same corner where he had fallen, and Lisa is sitting on a chair, bending over him, as though whispering something in his ear.

"Lisa!" calls my mother.

"Sh . . . sh . . . don't wake him," Lisa whispers, as though she were trying to get a sick child to fall asleep. "He's suffered enough, my poor chick."

"We have to call the neighbors, to lay out the body on the floor, and to light candles," says Mother, feeling a shudder pass over her.

"No, don't! Once they begin the burial preparations, he'll no longer be mine. Look how he clings to his corner, he's afraid of the world that talked about him behind his back and dragged his name through the mud. Tell me, Vella, what harm did we do our neighbors that they hate us so bitterly?"

Mother glances out the window and sees the neighbors. They stand in a circle in the courtyard, unwilling to enter. When Mother had gone to rouse them, they had told her immediately that it would be best to wait for morning, when strangers would come to lay out the corpse. Lisa would not want her courtyard neighbors to attend to her husband.

Lisa bends down to the dead man, uncovers him, and kisses his forehead. Then she closes his eyes, covers him once more with the coat, and speaks to him:

"No one knows how considerate you were to me, but I know it. You never reminded me of my childlessness. If, once in your life, you behaved badly toward me, it bothered you till the day you died."

She means Ḥasska, thinks my mother. Maybe the goose-dealer was truly sorry that he had let his head be turned by that lewd woman.

Meanwhile, it is getting lighter and lighter. A bright late-summer morning enters through the window and bathes the room in blue. Bands of light tremble on the walls, on the ceiling. Only in one corner does a small, still mound remain dark, its shadow flowing into the shadow of the woman who sits unmoving on the chair. Lisa sits with her back to the daylight, as her husband lies with his back to the courtyard and to the world.

Mother sits down on a stool near the entrance, lowers her head, and closes her eyes.

When Lisa had uncovered the body, Mother had seen the goose-dealer's twisted mouth and the stiff mustache that stood away from his face. Only the day before, he had summoned the barber and had himself shaved. Now there he lay, the corpse of an elderly Jew with a twirled mustache, looking for all the world like a Gentile freshly shaved and decked out in his best suit before being placed in his coffin.

Mother thinks of Reb Boruḥel, peace be upon him, who had lain years before on the same floor where the goose-dealer is lying now. She remembers how Blumele, peace be upon her, had wept and wailed for her dear old man with such lamentations that the heart of everyone who heard her was torn. And her own son, Chaimka, had once told her that he could not forget Reb Boruḥel and Blumele, just as one cannot forget the two white birch trees standing at the fork of the road that leads to the town in which one was born. Reb Boruḥel had been a white-bearded Jew, pure as an unblemished lamb. He had always lived in dread lest someone have cause to bear any resentment against him. He had died on a Sabbath morning, falling asleep like an innocent child, at peace with all the world. But Reb Alter, may it not go too hard with him, had in his death-agony jumped off his bed while threatening someone with his fists.

"Do you remember, Vella—" the widow breaks off her reverie— "one Sabbath evening we talked about children. Without children, life is no life and death is no death. When there are children to carry on, one has done something for the world, and the world in turn respects you."

She is silent for a moment and then continues, speaking more to the dead man than to my mother:

"If only you could have seen, Vella, the love in my husband's eyes when he looked at your son's betrothed, how he thanked her for everything she did for him, then you would have understood what a fine person he was. Whenever he felt a little better, and the nurse happened not to be present, he would say that if only he had known people like her before, he would have been a different man himself."

Now strangers enter the house; they lay out the body and place candles at the head. Someone has rushed over to the Synagogue Courtyard and brought back a pair of psalm-sayers. The room begins to fill up with curious onlookers, people from distant streets whom no one knows. They inquire of one another about the deceased and about his illness, speaking softly in deference to the mistress of the house, who sits silently, her back to the crowd. From time to time, however, she glances at my mother, as if appealing to her not to go, not to leave her, Lisa, alone with these strangers.

Some of Lisa's wealthier customers now enter, old classmates of hers at the Russian *gymnasium*. When Lisa sees them, she bursts into tears. The crowd of simple people look at one another: In front of us she doesn't find it proper to weep—only in front of her rich ladies.

"Calm yourself, Lisa," bleats one of the ladies out of the depths of her double chins. She wears a flowered hat and carries a massive handbag.

Lisa's heart is racked with pain, and the ears of the assemblage now prick up at the shrill, high-pitched cry that bursts forth from the widow's throat, like dammed-up water that has found a narrow crevice through which to escape.

"Lisa—" the lady bleats once more; her voice trembles. But, apparently determined to avoid a common woman's display of emotion, she turns her head away so that none may see her tear-filled eyes.

Lisa falls silent. The two psalm-sayers, who have been reciting verse after verse aloud, now mumble the words softly into their beards. Even the candles at the dead man's head burn silently, bleak and dim, as though they were in a deep, dank cellar.

With Lisa now surrounded by her ladies, Mother understands that she is no longer needed. Quietly she slips away.

OUTSIDE in the courtyard the neighbors, the local shopkeepers, are standing about in clusters and talking. Mother stops for a moment to listen to a stranger, one of those who had laid out the body:

"I only knew him—the goose-dealer, that is—from a distance. What a strong man he was! You should see what has become of him: Yel'ow as a carrot and as dried out as last year's esrog. A little bag of skin and bones, I tell you, no heavier than a wooden splinter."

"Oi, what a human being comes to!" Hatzkel the grocer sways to and fro, his eyes closed. "Alterka, who used to drain dry an ocean of liquor. Alterka, who played cards all through the night with his cronies. That Alterka should be lying so still, his feet pointing to the door—oi, what a human being comes to!"

Hatzkel is speaking in deadly earnest, but his very seriousness calls forth smiles from the others. One man coughs to clear his throat, as though deliberating: Should he speak or not? But at last the temptation to poke fun proves too strong:

"You forgot, Reb Hatzkel, to mention the cholents the goose-dealer used to devour."

"There won't even be anyone to recite the Kaddish for him," laments Hatzkel again.

"If he had at least, before he died, bought a gravesite and arranged for someone to recite the Kaddish for him," says the grain merchant, plucking at his goatee, unable to contain his anger any longer. "He lived a swinish life, may he forgive me for saying it, fie!"

Reb Nossen-Nota, landlord of the courtyard and Gabbai of the Guardians of the Sabbath Synagogue, is pacing about dejectedly. Now he can light a kopeck's worth of candles in mourning for the rent that Lisa owes him, for the poultry-stall as well as for the apartment. It makes his blood boil to listen to the ignoramuses who are worrying because the goose-dealer has left no one to recite the Kaddish for him.

"Idol-worshippers, all your faith is worth as little as your Kaddish-saying."

"What have you got against our fathers?" The crowd now turns angrily upon him. "They were better Jews than certain Gabbais."

"Who's saying anything against your fathers? May they rest in eternal peace," intones the Sabbath Guardian, suddenly quite frightened of these simpletons with their great pride of ancestry. "I'm talking about those mourners who rattle off their Kaddish in the Sheva K'ru'im Synagogue or in the vestibule of the Grand Synagogue. Saying Kaddish isn't one of the six hundred and thirteen commandments, but praying daily with phylacteries, observing the holy Sabbath—that's what really matters! But what do we see? We see those smart young fellows who never put on phylacteries, who desecrate the Sabbath, running helter-skelter to the synagogue to say the Kaddish. They even draw lots to decide who will stand at the reader's lectern to lead a slapdash service, without proper knowledge of the Holy Tongue, without inner devotion, just to recite the Kaddish."

The neighbors turn away from the landlord and he stands once again alone, like some wandering preacher whose audience has melted away. He looks around angrily and notices that my mother has been listening to his preaching with an expression of intense piety and devotion. Instead of giving him satisfaction, however, this serves only to further inflame his wrath. This woman's son, after all, is a brazen libertine, far worse even than those "smart young fellows" who have cut off their earlocks and draw lots to lead a slapdash service.

Mother returns home. She has many things to attend to. First of all, she wants to see how her future daughter-in-law is feeling after the difficult night she has just endured. Secondly, she must prepare breakfast for her children. Next, she needs to moisten the vegetables in her baskets, to prevent their wilting from the heat, since her merchandise will be staying in the house all day long. Today she will not be setting up her stand at the gate. After the funeral, the "fine ladies" will probably take their leave. It will then be her task to prepare bagels and hard-boiled eggs—the first meal of the mourning period—for Lisa, and to see to it that the widow does not remain alone in the empty house.

Mother opens our door and says, still standing outside:
"Water."

I hand her a dipper filled with water across the threshold. She washes her hands, but does not dry them, and speaks sternly to me:

"In God's name, you must accompany our neighbor at least as far as the Zarecze Bridge."

IV

NEWLY COME TO VILNA is a little Jew, a wandering preacher who styles himself the "Mayssegoler Maggid." Judging by his woeful appearance—he is small, thin, lame, and almost beardless—one might more readily take him for a lowly ḥeder assistant, but he asks for donations with a true maggid's dignity. On Monday and Thursday mornings, after the reading of the Torah in the synagogue, he ascends the bima and commences a sermon. The congregants, anxious to be about their business, surround him shouting:

"On the Great Sabbath you'll get your chance to preach. But today is 'short Friday.' "

"You want a donation? Then say so straight out. Here, take your money and let us finish the service . . ."

The Mayssegoler Maggid is not at all perturbed by this abridgment of his sermon. What matters is that he has won acknowledgment of the principle that charity is the foundation of the world's existence. He moves about amidst the congregants, collecting his donations, and limps out, making his way from the Sheva K'ru'im Synagogue to the service in the vestibule of the Grand Synagogue, thence to the Gravediggers' Chapel, and from there to still other houses of prayer. There was, praised be the Lord, no lack of synagogues and chapels in Vilna, if one could only manage to get to all of them.

This takes up half the day. Then, after the early Afternoon Service, the lame little Jew begins scurrying about the back courtyards in the poor neighborhoods, and finds his way unerringly into those houses where the newly dead are laid out, yellowed and wizened like the grass that grows on the crooked roofs. The Mayssegoler Maggid delivers eulogies for humble tailors, for shoemakers, even for porters. He invariably makes his appearance at just the right moment, just as the coffin is about to arrive and the entire family, weeping and wailing, is gathered around the body. The Maggid pushes his way straight to the head of the bier and, without waiting to be asked, begins the eulogy: "*Oi, rabboyssai, rabboyssai*—my good and learned friends . . ." He finds merit in every deceased. If nothing else, he will exalt his merit of poverty, "May it be reckoned in his favor on the Day of Judgment; may we live to see the coming of the Messiah, and may he 'swallow up death forever,' and let us say, amen."

The mourners accompany his eulogy with tears and lamentations that rend the heavens. Here, in contrast to in the synagogues, no one tries to push him out of the way. On the contrary, they wish him to speak on and on, and they ask him as rabbi to charge the deceased to intercede before the Court on High on behalf of his wife and his children, that they should no longer be dying of hunger.

The mourners empty their pockets and with their whole hearts give the Maggid their last few coins. Even strangers in the assemblage donate to the rabbi, a path is cleared for him (he is already rushing off to another house of mourning), and everyone joins in denouncing the community's official rabbis:

"When it's a rich man they're all there, the rabbis, but at a poor man's funeral they're nowhere to be seen."

At the goose-dealer's funeral, too, the Mayssegoler appears at just the right moment. Disheveled and agitated, he limps into the courtyard—only to find, to his great astonishment, that instead of giving him a warm welcome, the neighbors are actually barring his way:

"Where are you rushing? There's no eulogy to give here."

"There is no Jew who isn't as full of good deeds as a pomegranate is full of seeds," argues the Mayssegoler—though, in case they really refuse to let him approach the corpse, he stretches out his hand, ready and willing to accept donations all the same.

"Don't rend your coat just yet," they tell him soothingly, and his hand is quickly filled with coins. "The goose-dealer's tallith is thirty years old and still brand-new."

The Mayssegoler checks to see whether what he has received is adequate to his dignity, and is satisfied. Nonetheless, he does not wish to leave the impression that it makes no difference to him whether a man does or does not wear his prayer shawl; and so, swaying from side to side, chanting in the melody of the Sabbath of Penitence, he begins a sermon of exhortation:

"The Maggid of Kelm, may his merit defend us, once arrived in a small town. The entire town, men, women and children, came to the synagogue to hear him preach. People were hanging from the rafters. And the Maggid of Kelm arose before the Holy Ark and said:

" 'Oi, rabboyssai, rabboyssai, once I entered a house and found it completely abandoned and empty—not a soul within. So I go out of one room and into another, and then into a third room, and there, what do I see but a tallith lying on a table and weeping. Then I ask the tallith—oi, rabboyssai, rabboyssai—"Little tallith, little tallith, why are you weeping?" And it answered me: "Why shouldn't I weep? My master has gone off to a great fair. He took his wife along and his children along so that they could help him earn money, and he took along merchandise to sell, and he took along all sorts of pots and dishes in which to prepare his food—only me, his tallith, my master forgot to take along." So I said to the tallith—oi, rabboyssai, rabboyssai—"Little tallith, little tallith, do not weep. The time will come when your master will depart on a different journey. And it won't be a fair he will come to, but a place where one must render an accounting for all the fairs of his life. And on that journey there is nothing he will be able to take along with him—no merchandise to sell, no dishes of gold or of silver—no, not even his nearest and dearest can then accompany him. Only you, little tallith, you alone, will he take with him." ' "

Mother, who has just emerged from our house ready for the funeral, hears the sermon, and her heart overflows within her at the Maggid's words. It is as though she is being struck in the face on her son's account;

true, as a bachelor, he is not yet required to wear a regular tallith, but he is obligated to wear a tallith-katan under his shirt. As for the shopkeepers, they give vent to pious sighs and moans, and shake their heads: All one's hustling and bustling isn't worth an empty eggshell. One labors to fill one's belly and one fills one's belly to feed the worms.

Just as the Mayssegoler is about to tell another tale, he sees that the shopkeepers have turned their heads away and are winking slyly at one another.

ENTERING THE COURTYARD is Ḥasska the butcher girl. Usually she walks through the street bedecked with the goose-dealer's gifts, and takes up the whole sidewalk. This time she creeps in stealthily, a kerchief covering her hair, and looks fearfully about her—she does not want to be noticed. But people have already noticed, and a low murmur arises:

"She's come to say good-bye to her lover."

"Rabbi, what did the Maggid of Kelm say concerning a concubine?" Addressing this question to the preacher is a broad-shouldered man whose full, red cheeks burst with desire. "Will a concubine also serve as her man's footstool in Paradise?"

The Maggid blinks his eyes sheepishly, and the broad-shouldered man with lustful cheeks questions him further:

"And at her man's funeral, should a concubine be honored as much as the wife, or a little bit less?"

Till now, the assembled onlookers have restrained themselves somewhat from gossiping about the goose-dealer. But now they give their tongues free rein—it is hardly their fault, after all, that the "pure deceased" has left behind such witnesses to his good deeds. One man tells the Mayssegoler Maggid that the goose-dealer once killed a cat and that, when he was breathing his last, he imagined the dead cat staring at him with its green eyes and gnashing its teeth. The dying man had jumped down from his bed and thrown himself upon this creature of his imagination with clawing fingers, screaming "I have to strangle her!"

"Don't believe a word of it," laughs a second man. "With a cat you may frighten the geese, but not the goose-dealer. Alterka was a tough nut and if he imagined he saw someone in that corner, it's far more likely he was seeing Ḥasska the butcher girl, his former mistress . . . The butcher girl is also a cat, a wild alley-cat." The speaker nudges the Maggid to take a look at Ḥasska, who is standing, lost and ashamed, in a corner near the gate, just as, at the conclusion of the Day of Atonement, she is accustomed to stand near the door of the men's section of the synagogue, waiting for the last long blast of the shofar to tell her it is time to break the fast. To enter the women's section, or even to stand on the far side of its threshold, is something she does not dare to do, for she is well aware that the other women loathe her like a spider, and she is reluctant to get into a fight at the beginning of the new year.

Bewildered, the Mayssegoler Maggid begins to edge his way out of the crowd. This is the first time he has ever heard people maligning the deceased so freely even before the burial. My mother also moves away from the others, passes by the butcher girl and whispers to her softly:

"Ḥasska, go away. Spare Lisa and her husband's honor."

Silently Ḥasska obeys. Covering half her face with the corners of her kerchief so as to avoid the neighbors' baleful looks, and keeping close to the wall, she steals out of the courtyard.

"The coffin is coming!"

People can hardly believe their eyes: even in death the goose-dealer is playing his tricks. Coming to fetch him now is a rich man's hearse, its two horses covered with black blankets to their very eyes. The coffin is decorated with silver-engraved letters that spell out verses from the Book of Psalms, and the driver high up on the coach-box wears a cape. Lisa's rich ladies had sent their husbands to the Burial Society and they have arranged for a rich man's funeral. "All that's missing here," remarks a neighbor, "is the cantor of the Choir Synagogue, wearing his tall skullcap with the fringes, and the choir with their narrow prayer shawls about their throats, all in a procession surrounding the casket and chanting: 'Righteousness shall go before Him . . .'"

"Just wait and see, they'll be putting him in the front row yet," prophesies another neighbor. "Oh, money, money! As the saying goes: 'Silver and gold purify bastards.'"

"But the rent for the shop, not to mention the apartment, that," grumbles the landlord, "the widow won't pay."

Shortly, the crowd receives another surprise. Lisa emerges from her house dressed in mourning, her face covered by a veil. She is surrounded by her lady friends. The dead man is carried in such total silence as has not been witnessed in the back streets of Vilna since the world began. A Gentile funeral.

The body is placed immediately into the coffin, the hearse halts for a moment at the poultry shop where Alterka had sold his geese, and the crowd pours out of the courtyard into the street, which is throbbing with its normal weekday bustle. Even the storekeepers who are accompanying the funeral procession have not closed their shops, but left their wives and daughters in charge. And even before the hearse makes its way out of the narrow streets, the crowd begins to thin out rapidly.

My mother is falling behind. She had been up half the night with Lisa, watching over the body, and has not sat down once all morning.

Now she is dizzy and her feet feel heavy, like blocks of wood. But she intends, God willing, to go to the cemetery. They have been neighbors and sometimes they have argued; now, after the ritual purification of the body, she wants to ask forgiveness of the goose-dealer for herself, for her son, and for her son's betrothed, the nurse—for, no matter how carefully Frumme-Liebche had attended to the deceased, there was always the chance that in some way she had failed to do all that was needed.

Suddenly Lisa stops and the crowd of mourners stops with her. She turns around, lifts her black veil, and reveals her face for all to see, red and swollen with weeping. Her gaze turns here, turns there, and her ladies stare at one another: what is she looking for? Mother senses that it is she herself Lisa is seeking, and quickly comes up to her. And Frumme-Liebche, who has been walking arm-in-arm with me in the last row of the procession, also tears herself away and goes up to the front. Lisa does not move again until both women, my mother and Frumme-Liebche, are beside her, directly behind the coffin.

SOME DAYS LATER, Mariasha swore by her life, by the lives of her children, calling as witnesses the candy-seller as well as the beggars and cemetery cantors, that, on the morning after the funeral, Ḥasska the butcher girl and Big Ellinka stood at the goose-dealer's grave and Ḥasska screamed at Ellinka:

"Ask Alterka's forgiveness for hitting him. If you don't, I never want to see your ugly mug again!"

Ḥasska, Mariasha continues, threw herself upon the freshly heaped mound of earth and shouted into the grave:

"Alterka, plead for me in the Other World! It wasn't my fault that you died, it was your own fault. You kicked the cat and it croaked, that was why God punished you!"

And then Ḥasska had distributed alms like the wealthiest of women, and carried small stones to the goose-dealer's grave as one would to the sepulchre of a holy sage.

People listened to Mariasha's story and laughed cruelly. They laughed, refusing to remember that the goose-dealer had died childless, with no one to recite the Kaddish for him, and that his widow was still observing the Seven Days of Mourning.

"Whatsoever a man's desire is in life," one of them pronounced, "that is what he receives after death." And they all scattered to attend to their affairs.

Later, Mother related this incident to me and asked me why the neighbors had so little compassion for the deceased. I replied that these petty shopkeepers were envious of the goose-dealer because he had enjoyed the pleasures of this life, had drunk whiskey, played cards, and kept mistresses.

Mother remained silent a long time. At last she shook her head and told me I was talking nonsense. I didn't understand, she said, that our neighbors were a great deal more devout than they themselves realized. After all, the goose-dealer had done no one any harm. Even if he had occasionally had an argument with someone, no one would be so relentlessly unforgiving as to remember that now. What, then, did they have against him? Only that he had not been a good Jew, may he forgive her for saying it. "Our neighbors, it's true, don't look with favor on excessive piety, but they do have great respect for the ways of Torah. They themselves don't know how devout they really are."

The In-law

AMIDST A CLEAR AND BUSTLING WEDNESDAY, our street suddenly grows as still as on a Sabbath afternoon, when the householders take a nap before returning to the synagogue. The shopkeepers stand in front of their stores and stare with amazement at the gate, where Vella the fruit-vendor is speaking to a tall Jew with a golden-blond beard who carries a large tallith-bag under his arm.

"The Rabbi is her future in-law—the father of her son's betrothed," explains Shaya the grain merchant to Hatzkel the grocer. "The Rabbi has come to look for his son, who ran away from the yeshiva to become a halutz."

"What a misfortune! What a misfortune!" Hatzkel smacks his lips. "The Rabbi clearly has little joy of his children. His daughter has picked herself a husband who's as fit to be a rabbi's son-in-law as I am to be governor of a province. And as if that weren't enough, his son has become a halutz."

"That's surely no tragedy," says Shaya. "You really think any blessings-mumbler is better than a halutz?"

"It's easy to see you're a Zionist," growls Hatzkel. "You sound just like all the Zionist small-fry around here—'a blessings-mumbler.' When the son of a rabbi joins up with those freethinkers the kibbutzniks, then there's real cause to weep and lament."

"Vilna isn't like your Warsaw, swarming and teeming with Hassidim with their little hats," the grain merchant warns the grocer. "In Vilna we detest the Agudah fanatics like pork. You hear, Reb Hatzkel?"

While the two shopkeepers carry on their quarrel in low voices, my mother is speaking with great deference to my future father-in-law:

"Let the Rabbi not be angry with me; it wasn't my doing. They met and became engaged. And when your daughter left for Warsaw because she wanted to get experience in a hospital there, my son followed her."

The Rabbi does not look directly at the woman, but he listens attentively to what she is saying. His daughter has written him that she did not want to say anything about her fiancé, since whatever she considered to be his virtues her father would regard as faults; but she went on to say that her fiancé's mother was the finest woman she had ever met. Judging by her manner of speaking, the Rabbi thinks to himself, the mother does indeed seem to be a truly fine woman, and he answers with a smile:

"There's no need to justify yourself. As far as the mother is concerned, I have no objections at all to this match. My doubts concern your son: He might have asked me whether I'm willing to have him as a son-in-law. The excuse he might wish to offer, that my daughter herself didn't ask my permission, is no excuse at all. And if your son were really concerned about my family, he would have tried to persuade my boy to return home."

"How could my son have done that, when he himself has abandoned the study of Torah?" asks my mother.

'For these things I weep,' reflects the Rabbi. Whose example could the son of my old age follow—his older brothers'? So I thought to myself: My daughter will marry a Torah scholar who will bring her back to the right path, and perhaps he will even be able to influence his youngest brother-in-law. But instead my daughter has chosen 'one who has fallen away.' And perhaps, indeed, she chose him just because he is a former yeshiva student and she wants his help in tearing herself away from home, from Faith and Tradition.

Nonetheless, feeling that this pious woman at the gate has herself already suffered quite enough on her son's account, he does not wish to cause her further grief.

"You must be lonely since the young couple went away?" he asks with a furrowed brow, and sighs as though he were thinking of his own wife, alone at home.

"A little lonely," admits my mother. "But when your son comes for the Sabbath, then I'm happy. He says the Kiddush for me."

"My son says the Kiddush for you?" The Rabbi is astonished. "When I went to see him in his kibbutz, he said nothing about that. So then, he hasn't yet become a complete unbeliever. Perhaps the Almighty may yet help me persuade him to return to his studies." He confides in the fruit-vendor as he would in his wife. "Well, I'll go back to the inn now to have breakfast. And while I'm here in Vilna, I must pay my respects to the city's rabbis and also buy a book or two."

The future father-in-law is silent a moment, shifts his tallith-bag to his left arm, and, with his right hand, strokes his golden beard. In a tone of thoughtful deliberation he says:

"You say my son comes to you every Friday evening?"

"He stays with me for the entire Sabbath and sleeps in my son's bed."

"It would be better," the Rabbi murmurs, "if I could speak with him privately and not in the kibbutz, where it's so hard for him to tear himself away from his friends." Raising his heavy eyebrows, he looks directly at the fruit-seller. "How would it be, in-law, if I were to come to you this Friday evening?"

"If the Rabbi trusts in my kashruth," replies Mother, disconcerted by his addressing her as "in-law," "it would be an honor I would never have thought myself worthy of receiving from the Almighty."

"Would God I could trust my children's kashruth as much as I can trust yours," says the Rabbi with a smile.

"Regarding your children's piety I cannot speak," replies my mother, plucking up courage. "But as for their goodness and decency, I can vouch for your son and your daughter more than for myself."

"And can you vouch for your son's character as well?" he asks sternly, as though examining a witness in his rabbinical court.

"Concerning my son—let others speak," says my mother, bowing her head.

My daughter is fortunate in her choice of a mother-in-law, reflects the Rabbi as he walks off. God grant she be equally fortunate in her choice of a husband.

Not even for Passover has my mother ever prepared more carefully than for this Sabbath. How it would actually turn out, however, she could never have imagined.

The Rabbi has already been seated at the table for an hour, but his son has yet to arrive. Mother has remembered just in time that a pious Jew must not remain alone in the same room with a woman, especially at night, so she has opened wide the door to the second room and also left open the door to the courtyard. She herself has remained in the front room, the dimly lit workshop, from which she continually peers into the inner room at the Rabbi, sitting in silence. At last he calls to her:

"In-law, please forgive me for spoiling your Sabbath. I'm waiting for my son. He's already established his title to reciting the Kiddush for you—" the Rabbi smiles bitterly—"but it seems he won't be coming tonight."

"I'm really surprised." Mother approaches the doorway to the inner room. "He always comes for the Sabbath. I told the Rabbi the absolute truth."

"Of course, of course," he mumbles, somewhat impatiently. "I've been to see him once more at the kibbutz. Again I tried to argue with him and his only answer was: 'No, I don't want to go back.' Then, when I told him I'd be having dinner here tonight, he said nothing. At the time I didn't realize that that meant he wouldn't come. Now I begin to understand: he doesn't want to listen to any more pleading. Nu, we must go ahead and wash for the meal."

Mother brings in a pitcher of water, a bowl and a towel, and then returns to the dark smithy. "She is a saintly woman," thinks the Rabbi. "She doesn't want to stay in the same room with me because of the prohibition against 'seclusion.' She's overworked and worn out, poor soul, yet she won't sit down to eat with me. But if I should leave, she'd be even more upset. She has prepared everything for me and my son." He rises and, in a quavering voice, chants the Kiddush:

"On the sixth day . . ."

Mother stands on the threshold, her gaze fixed reverently on the Rabbi: The Divine Presence rests upon him; the holiness of the Torah shines from his countenance. Lord of the Universe, how had she ever become worthy of hearing such a great scholar recite the Kiddush in the smithy that was her home? Nonetheless, her joy is incomplete. For herself, nothing would be too hard to do for the Rabbi, yet his own son has refused to give him even the joy and satisfaction of joining him for dinner. The young man is a quiet, gentle soul such as one hardly ever finds among young people today, and still he is causing his father grief. It would seem, then, that this entire rabbinical family is, in its quiet way, stubborn.

Throughout the meal the Rabbi chews on a single mouthful and stares at the bookcase that faces him. He takes out a book, leafs through it, puts it down, and draws out a second one. In this way, a pile of books with worn leather bindings grows steadily beside him. Suddenly remembering that the mistress of the house has gone to great pains to prepare the meal for him, he tastes one dish, then another, but then pushes the plates away. He grows more and more uneasy and agitated, and angry at himself for desecrating the sanctity of the Sabbath with his unhappiness; he begins to drum on the table with his fingers, to bite his lips, to look all about with flashing eyes, as though he were sitting at his own table at home and resting his severely disapproving gaze on his rebellious children.

"At the very moment I told my son I would be here, he made up his mind not to come." His face turned crimson with wrath. "Whose books are these?"

"My husband's, peace be upon him."

"And has your son ever looked into them?"

"When he was younger, he used to study them at night. But now—"

"Now he reads modern novels." Seething with anger, the Rabbi finishes the sentence. "It's no wonder, then. When one starts with books like these, one ends with forbidden books."

"Are these, then, bad books?" asks my mother, astonished and hurt—her late husband, peace be upon him, had treasured them all his life as the apple of his eye.

"They are not bad books," replies the Rabbi, somewhat more calmly. "They are works of speculation, of philosophy. A mature person, one past forty, may look into them, provided he has already studied a great deal of Torah and is an upright Jew. In that case they will do no harm. That is to say, even then they may cause one to stray from the right path, but the danger is not as great. But when a mere youngster tries to ascend to the heavens on them, he will fall as one falls from a crooked staircase, into the deepest abyss. The atheists of our time think they are wiser, not only than pious Jews, but even than the enlightened thinkers of the past. And today's youth have already divested themselves of every trace of Faith and Tradition."

"May the Rabbi forgive me, but my husband used to study these same books even when he was old. He never exchanged them for new ones."

"That's just it," the father-in-law-to-be shouts angrily. "Because your husband was already old and sick, he wasn't able to run as far and as fast as your son!" But then he quickly catches himself. "How can one compare the generations of old to those of today? In any case, what right do I have to complain about your son? Is my son any better? . . . Well," he concludes wearily, his voice drained of life, "it's time to say the Grace After Meals."

Mother does not dare point out that he hasn't eaten anything. She brings in to him the "last water," preliminary to saying Grace. The Rabbi moistens his fingers, strokes his forehead with his wet hand as though trying to calm his turbulent thoughts, closes his eyes, and begins to sway to and fro. He recites Grace very rapidly, virtually swallowing the words; my mother—still standing on the other side of the threshold, and listening for the end of the initial blessing so she might respond "Amen"—strives in vain to hear the concluding words. Suddenly the Rabbi stops dead and, as if lost in thought, begins to stammer, repeats a particular verse with intense concentration, and then starts to sway again, even more fervently. He is seeking to banish the thoughts that have become entangled with the verses of his prayer, but they give him no peace.

"The Merciful One, He shall rule over us forever and ever . . ." And what of Your promise, Master of Creation, that whenever three successive generations of a family devote themselves to the study of Torah, the Torah shall cleave to that family forever and ever? Were not my ancestors truly righteous men and great rabbis? Yet, the question is not really a question. The words of our Sages are holy. For, when a guest returns to his customary inn but is refused admittance, he departs and seeks lodgings elsewhere. The Torah came to my sons, but they would not admit her into their hearts . . .

"The Merciful One, He shall be blessed in the heavens and on earth . . ." My only daughter did not want to marry a scholar from the Mir Yeshiva and has chosen, instead, a writer of heresy and ungodliness. Now she's in Warsaw with him, and my relatives there shrug their shoulders; they read the newspapers, but they say they've never heard of him. Only she believes that one day he will attain fame, in the realm of impurity. Neither Torah nor fame—wherein then is he worthier in her eyes than a young man from the Yeshiva of Lomza or of Mir? Who knows whether he's not, God forbid, one of those whose head never bears tefillin? Perhaps I made a mistake when I didn't go to see him and exact a promise that he would at least observe the Sabbath and pray with tefillin.

"The Merciful One! He shall be praised through all generations . . ." As for my three older sons, no use even thinking about them. One has gone across the ocean, the second across the Mediterranean to the Land of Israel, and the third, still in Warsaw, is also going to the Holy Land. The only one who remained with me was the youngest, and I nurtured him as the apple of my eye. He is the quietest, the finest of all my children—my "child of delights." " 'He shall be our comfort,' " I said to myself. But now the spirit of folly has entered into him as well—he has become a ḥalutz. Oh Master of All Creation, this is not the ḥalutz of whom it is written: "and let the ḥalutz pass on before the Ark of the Lord. . . ." The ḥalutzim of today, in their free-thinking settlements in the Holy Land, do not observe the Sabbath, they eat food that is not kosher, and their young people care nothing at all for the laws of family purity. And it is these whom my youngest son has made his comrades! He even turns to me and says: "I'm surprised, Father, that you should be against the resettling of the Land of Israel. That is, after all, one of the greatest of the commandments of the Torah." He, the righteous one, wants to speed the coming of the Messiah, and of all the six hundred and thirteen precepts of the Law, he accepts only this one—to dwell in the Land of Israel.

"The Merciful One! He shall lead us with dignity to our land." One of my sons is already there, the second one, from Warsaw, is preparing to go, and now the child of my old age is setting out on the same journey. What, then, am I doing here? For whose sake am I maintaining my rabbinate—for my future son-in-law? And how long must I continue to deal with my congregants, exhorting them to be pious, bearing the moral responsibility for them? In the World-to-Come I shall be held to account not only for my own children but for my town, for the entire community. But how can I be a guardian for others when I have been unable to safeguard my own house? And how long shall I continue to make of the Torah "a spade wherewith to dig," to live off my piety? My wife cannot bear having to earn our livelihood from her sale of yeast and my fees for supervising the slaughterers. She dreams of living an independent life in the Holy Land and raising poultry. Perhaps if my children hadn't witnessed how a rabbi is obliged to live off the community, they would not have fled my house. And perhaps, if I live there too, my sons will not cut themselves off entirely from tradition—they will not want to grieve their father. And my youngest won't be able to throw it up to me that he fulfills the commandment of "dwelling in the Land of Israel," while I do not. Immediately after the Sabbath I shall, with God's help, go back home and begin selling off our belongings. I shall go to the Land of Israel and fulfill all those precepts that pertain directly to our Holy Land . . . "The Merciful One! He shall grant us a day which is wholly Sabbath, wholly a day of rest, for life eternal . . ."

A FEW DAYS LATER, the Rabbi stood once again at the gate, his tallith-bag under his arm, and spoke to the fruit-vendor:

"I have decided to leave my pulpit and go to the Holy Land. My rebbetzin has long wanted to give up being a rebbetzin, but I always thought, 'The children . . .' Now Heaven has given me a sign that I have reasoned falsely. May it be the Almighty's will, blessed be He, that with His help—" His voice was choked, and he drew his bushy eyebrows together so that no tears would fall on his golden beard. "May it be His will that my daughter walk in her mother's way, and that your son will turn to his mother's way. I beg you, in-law, keep an eye on my youngest. I see that he is attached to you. And just because you are not a rebbetzin, but simply a hard-working woman who is yet meticulously faithful and devout, just for that reason you may be able to influence him more than I have, with all my illustrious ancestry and all the sacred learning to which I have devoted my life, without hope of reward, as the Creator of the Universe knows."

Had my mother not been standing at the gate, she would have wept aloud; but she did not wish the neighbors to come running. Trembling, she asks:

"Will the Rabbi, then, not wait for his daughter's wedding?"

"My daughter's wedding?" The Rabbi furrows his brow, as though he has totally forgotten this matter. "She never asked me whether I wanted this match, so why would she need me at the wedding? No, I shall not postpone my departure for the Land of Israel for that, and my wife, may she live and be well, will agree with me."

The bride's father coughs hard, as though he were trying to change his voice. Angry red patches appear on his cheeks, and in the stern tones of a presiding judge he cries out:

"Write to your son that you order him, by virtue of the honor and respect he owes you as his mother—and I shall write the same to my daughter—to get married at once. It is already more than a year since their betrothal."

With a silent nod of the head, he walks quickly away. He dares not stay longer, even to say good-bye, lest his anger overwhelm him and he bring still more sorrow to this poor downtrodden woman. Tall and erect of bearing, the large tallith-bag under his arm, the Rabbi strides down the street without noticing the unknown shopkeepers who stand at the entrances of their stores and gaze deferentially after him.

Mother remains standing at the gate, her head bowed low; she does not even feel the tears that are quietly streaming down her face. With a start she comes to herself, and begins to run after the Rabbi. She wants to ask him to give his rebbetzin a message: to plead with her not to resent the fact that she, the rebbetzin, would not be present at her own daughter's wedding, while she, the fruit-seller, would be there at her son's wedding.

But then Mother realizes how foolish it would be to run after him with such a message. And even if she were to ask the rebbetzin's forgiveness, would that ease her pain?

She feels a pang in her heart. A thought begins to take shape in her mind, a thought that frightens her. She bends over her baskets, rearranges her merchandise, calls out to customers; but the thought grows steadily stronger. She turns to the wall and talks to herself:

"That would really be best: let them get married in Warsaw. The girl has many relatives there, and I will give my son my blessing from a distance. Here the whole town would be talking: 'The bride's parents left for the Land of Israel before the wedding. That just goes to show how little this match was to their liking.' And how will I feel when the bride, standing under the canopy, looks at me with eyes filled with tears: her parents aren't there on her day of joy—only I, the mother of the groom. It's possible that my son would not agree to it; he knows, after all, that I've been waiting all my life for his wedding. At the slightest excuse I've always said, over and over, 'May I live to see you under the wedding canopy.' 'And now, Mother,' he'll probably write, 'you're not going to be there?' Then I'll answer him: 'Foolish boy. True, the Almighty has heard my prayers and I've lived to your wedding day. But where could I possibly put up guests? What sort of festive meal could I offer?

What sort of table could I set for the poor? What musicians could I hire? And on the other hand, the trip to Warsaw would be too difficult for me. Trains always make me dizzy. And what kind of impression will I make on my Warsaw in-laws, when I can't even understand the way Polish Jews speak?' . . . It's just my good luck—" Mother laughs to herself as the tears stream from her eyes—"it's just my good luck that the Rebbetzin is going away. How would a simple woman like me even talk to such an in-law? . . ."

The Rabbi's Son

I

"**M**OTHER VELLA."

That is what Moshele, the Rabbi's son, calls her.

"Moshele, don't call me 'Mother,'" she pleads with him. "You have a mother, may she live to a hundred and twenty. Your mother in the Land of Israel will be upset if she hears about it."

He listens with a smile in his soft, dreamy eyes behind their large glasses, and continues to call her "Mother Vella."

Since the departure of his father the Rabbi, Moshele has resumed his weekly Sabbath visits to her smithy. Of the Friday evening when his father had waited for him and he had not come, he never says a word, and so Mother never speaks of it, either.

And what, indeed, is there to ask about? She sees clearly that the Rabbi and his son are as alike as two drops of water. Both are stiffnecked and stubborn. Because his daughter had chosen a mate without asking his consent, the father refused to meet his future son-in-law; Moshele, having made up his mind to become a ḥalutz, had stayed away that Friday evening to avoid a lecture from his father. The same personality, the same build, the same expression. The father is a tall man with a golden beard, and Moshele, may no evil eye fall upon him, is a tree in a forest. His delicate young face sprouts a silky, dark-blond beard; he looks like one of those young Russians of a bygone day who wore peasant shirts, let their hair grow long, and ate no meat.

Moshele arrives before sunset on Fridays and helps her take in her baskets. On the day before the Sabbath, she always sets out a great deal of merchandise, so that when candle-lighting time approaches, she has to make at least ten trips back and forth to put everything away. For some years her Chaimka had helped her, but when he left for Warsaw with his betrothed, she had thought to herself, Well, I'll just have to drag it all in alone, just as she had done when he was still studying at the yeshiva. But she had been younger and stronger then. So now the Almighty has sent her a Moshele. Normally he walks with the slow, measured steps of his father the Rabbi, but when he is carrying the baskets, he races like a storm-wind. He tries to move all the remaining baskets from the gate to the house before she has managed to carry in the first two.

Since he became a truck gardener in Soltaniszki, he has been coming to see her on Thursday evening, right after he finishes work. And on Friday morning, when she returns from the wholesale market, she finds her baskets at the gate, her scale hung in place, and Moshele already selling her wares to the housewives.

The first time this happened she could not believe her eyes. She stood speechless for several minutes, watching the Rabbi's son act the vendor. Only now did she understand why, the evening before, he had been asking about the prices she charged for her fruits and vegetables. At the time she had thought he was simply curious—after all, he himself was a truck gardener; now it was clear that he had carefully planned this out in advance.

"Moshele," she said, "what are you doing? Your parents will be very angry with me when they hear about this."

"On the contrary, they'll be pleased," he answered in his calm and deliberate manner. "Since I'm going to the Land of Israel to live on a kibbutz, it's important for me to know how to sell produce."

"But is this proper for you, a rabbi's son? Even my son never did it while he was a yeshiva student."

"But now your son would be doing it. Or he would go to the market with you, while I would be selling. It wouldn't do to make him the seller—he's too much of a hothead," said Moshele with a smile.

She had to laugh: though her son was older, Moshele was by far the steadier of the two. Which was why, she realized, no matter how hard she tried she could never dissuade him from his intention of becoming her assistant.

As a vendor he presents a curious spectacle. The women all stand gaping around him, unable to make sense of it all. The nobility and goodness shining in his face attest clearly to his fine breeding, to a family background of the highest distinction; and yet, quite puzzlingly at odds with this impression are the simple attire and sun-tanned features that bespeak a life of outdoor labor in the fields. And so the women stand about with open mouths, their gaze fixed more on him than on what they are buying. To any customer who decides to haggle, objecting perhaps that "The vegetables should be cheaper now that it's summer," he answers quite calmly: "That can't be. I work for a truck farmer, and I know that vegetables haven't gone down in price."

Mother asks him whom he works for, since she knows all the farmers. But when he tells her his employer's name, she is dismayed. It is someone she has known for years, a man far removed from any gentleness or refinement, and, indeed, as hard as steel—no one has ever been able to bargain so much as a groschen off his price.

Moshele, she knows, keeps things to himself; he will tell her nothing of his life on the farm. She too, therefore, remains silent—as he has made his plans, so she also now has a plan.

THE FOLLOWING MONDAY MORNING she seeks out the farmer from Soltaniszki at the wholesale market. She finds him standing atop a large wagon laden with open sacks of potatoes, red tomatoes, yellow carrots, young red radishes grown in hothouses, larger white radishes, heads of cabbage, and cauliflower, squash, and other vegetables. He is besieged by fruit-and-vegetable women trying to bargain with him, but, hard and obdurate as ever, he refuses to yield an inch, and at last the women go off in search of more tender-hearted dealers. She, however, does not haggle with him this time; she makes her purchases, sends them off to her gate with a woman-porter, and lingers around the marketplace until the Soltaniszki gardener has sold all his produce. Then she returns and questions him about his worker, Moshele.

He, however, knows nothing of any Moshele. He has, he says, got lots of goyim working for him, both men and girls, and also some Jewish roughnecks and girls; pushing his cap to one side, he moves to start up his already fed horses.

She entreats him to wait just a moment more. She tells him that Moshele is the youngest brother of her son's fiancée, that he comes from a small town and is preparing to go to the Land of Israel.

"Oh, the ḥalutz!" says the farmer, as he seats himself on the coach-box; and he begins to laugh so hard he seems ready to burst.

She interprets this as meaning that Moshele is a poor worker, and pleads with the farmer to take pity on the boy: he is a rabbi's son, and not used to such hard physical labor.

"Not at all, he's a very good worker," says the farmer; if not, he wouldn't have kept him on—he has no use for freeloaders. The fact that the fellow is a rabbi's son isn't worth an onion to him, and he doesn't care either where he's planning to go—to the Arabs in Palestine, or the black Africans, or the "little red Jews" over the border. He's laughing about something else entirely.

And the truck farmer proceeds to tell Mother a tale that makes the day go dark before her eyes.

The crew that works for him are all young, and the hot blood seethes in their veins. Any free moment they get, the goyim take a roll in the tall grass with the sweating shiksas, in the fields, in the forests round about, between the hothouses, or wherever they find a likely spot. There's a saying for it: "Where even swine won't bed down, Love will." And the Jewish louts and their girls don't lag behind the goyim. But this ḥalutz, with his short little beard, never hangs around with the rest. When the sweaty shiksas caught sight of him, handsome lad that he is, they tried to get something going with him. And the Jewish girls didn't keep their distance either. But he escaped from them to where the pepper grows, and that just made them all the crazier about him.

The farmer claps himself resoundingly on the brow:

"You say he's a rabbi's son? That's right—the peasant girls do call him the Rabbi."

Mother wrings her hands: she was used to hearing such stories bandied about concerning ordinary young fellows—but that they should dare to pester Moshele, a rabbi's son?

"Woman, the whole world doesn't spend its time in fasting and prayer!" The truck farmer laughs in her face.

"But you, you yourself are a decent man, after all," says Mother. "You have grown children of your own. See to it that the others don't torment the Rabbi's son so. Try to imagine that it's not I, the fruit-peddler, who plead for him, but his father the Rabbi himself."

"Don't upset yourself so, woman," says the gardener. "The ḥalutz can hold the fort quite well by himself. Bit by bit the whole crew has learned to respect him, and now nobody starts up with him. I'll tell you more: when he walks by, the shiksas stop giggling and move away from their fellows, just as if one of their own priests were passing by. Woman, Soltaniszki has been turned into a synagogue!"

The farmer slaps his forehead again:

"But I really am a pig! When the ḥalutz first came to me, we agreed that, until he knew his work, he wouldn't get a kopeck in wages—only his food and a place to sleep. Now he knows the work better than any ten of the peasants, but he's never said a word about the money. This week I'll pay him his full wages. That's the way I am: If I say I'll take something, I'll take it. But if I say I'll give, then I—just say it." Laughing, he cracks his whip and drives off.

Master of the Universe, what kind of person is he, this Moshele? my mother reflects on her way back from the market. To stay at home in his parents' house—that he doesn't want. To study in a yeshiva—also not. But to be a field hand for a truck farmer—that he wants. Go argue with him, he's got a will of iron! He's been visiting me every Sabbath, yet I've never had the slightest idea of the humiliations he's been suffering in Soltaniszki all week long.

The following Thursday night, when Moshele appears as usual, she scrutinizes him intensely . . . nothing. He is as calm and serene as ever, like a senior yeshiva student come home for a holiday or festival. His expression offers no clue as to whether the farmer has told him of his meeting with her. Well then, she thinks, I'll keep quiet too.

He brings her merchandise into the house, joins her at dinner, begins to leaf through a book, and then, still immersed in reading, says to her, as though speaking of the most ordinary, routine matter:

"Mother Vella, today I got my wages. Here, take this toward your Sabbath expenses." And with that he hands her a roll of bills, wound into a tight ball so as to appear smaller than it actually is.

"Don't be angry, Moshele, but you're acting like a child. How can I take money from you? Aren't your sister and my son engaged to be married? Do you still think of me as a stranger?"

"Very well, then"—he takes back the money—"I just won't come to you for the Sabbath any more."

This really frightens her. Moshele, she knows, is not one to make empty threats; what he says, he means. If even his father the Rabbi couldn't make him change his mind, she certainly won't be able to. Hastily she says:

"All right, Moshele, I'll take two zlotys from you, but keep the rest for yourself. No one should be without money—especially not a young man."

After midnight, when Moshele is already asleep, she is still in the kitchen preparing for the Sabbath. "A son!" she thinks. She had had no labor pains at his birth, nor had she suffered the travails of rearing him— and yet the Almighty has sent her a son. Since her own son went off to Warsaw, his bed has been occupied by a diamond, a heart of light, a golden head. Her only fear is that her great joy might be accounted a sin. Far away in the Land of Israel, his real mother is pining away with longing for her youngest child, while she, a stranger, has been vouchsafed so much joy.

She picks up the kitchen lamp, passes through the workshop, and walks into the back room. She has come to fetch something, but cannot remember what . . . no, she doesn't really need anything—she has come only to take a look at Moshele asleep.

He lies stretched out on his back, his strong arms under his head. His fresh, full lips are partly open and he is breathing quietly. His thick and curly hair merges into the hair of his silky beard, and his tanned neck seems made of bronze. No wonder the girls like him, she thinks, and sighs deeply. Her own son tosses about in his sleep, awakens ten times a night at the merest rustle, and rises in the morning exhausted.

Perhaps because of her deep sigh, or because she has not adequately shaded the light of the lamp with her hand and it has flashed into his face, Moshele opens his eyes—so quietly one might suspect he has all the while only been pretending to be asleep. He looks at her and smiles: "Mother Vella."

"We have a great-grandchild whose name is Moshele, too," she says, overcome by confusion. "My husband's oldest son's name was Moïsey. Sad to say, he died while my husband was still alive. When Moïsey's son, Aronchik, grew up, he married and his son was given the name Moshele. Aronchik himself doesn't give us much joy, he's a Bolshevik, but his little boy is a splendid child. All Mosheles are just splendid," she says with a quiet, bashful laugh, and leaves the room.

"I've really become senile," she murmurs to herself. She cannot forgive herself for having disturbed Moshele's sleep.

II

THE FARMER FROM SOLTANISZKI, in the heat of a vigorous dispute with a group of women, shouted across the length and breadth of the market square:

"Go to the ḥalutz—the brother of Vella's son's fiancée—and he'll tell you I've paid him every groschen that was due him, just as much as I pay the louts who work for me every season. The ḥalutz won't tell you any lies—he's a rabbi's son, and he chased away all the shiksas who were after him. I don't lay claim to anything that belongs to others, but I don't want other people claiming what is mine."

Temporarily, the peddler women left off cursing "the swine" who wouldn't lower his prices by so much as a groschen, in order to question him about the rabbi's son and the shiksas. Laden with this news as with heavy baskets of merchandise, they spread and trumpeted it about among the neighborhood shopkeepers.

"What did I tell you?" cried Ḥatzkel the grocer, resuming his argument with Shaya the grain merchant. "Aren't they real Jeroboams? The ḥalutzim, I mean. To take a rabbi's son, talk him into leaving home, and ship him off, as if to Siberia, to Soltaniszki outside of Vilna, where he has to dig the earth with his nose and cope with shiksas."

"That's true," agrees the grain merchant. "If the ḥalutz runs away from the shiksas, he'll surely run away from the Arabs."

"That's what I've been saying all along," exclaims the grocer triumphantly. "Who is it they're sending off to drain the swamps, who? Who is it they're sending to break up rocks, who? A rabbi's son?"

"Then who will do it, Reb Ḥatzkel? Will you? Will I?"

"Whoever wants to! But not the children of good families. It's a fine state of affairs when the sons and daughters of rabbis, of wealthy families, live twenty to a room in the kibbutz in the charity houses, and roam about the city looking for work in a tannery or a sawmill. Just the other day a couple of youngsters came into my shop, one with a saw and the other an axe over his shoulder, to ask whether I might want a cord of wood sawed and chopped. The kibbutzniks want to become 'hewers of wood and drawers of water,' like the Gibeonites."

I've got better things to do than stand here jabbering away with this simpleton, thinks the grain-dealer to himself. It's all well and good for Ḥatzkel, he's already declared bankruptcy several times, so he's got something put away for a rainy day. But I don't even have anyone to declare bankruptcy against.

The grain merchant sighs, and dashes off in quest of a little business.

A few days later, several young men pass through the neighborhood wearing the blue-and-white student caps of the modern Tarbuth school. Heads held high, ignoring everyone around them, they converse in Hebrew, amid much loud laughter. From these back streets of Vilna they evoke stares of amazement, and the grain-dealer turns to the grocer:

"Well, what do you say now?"

"What I said before! Jews shouldn't be drawing attention to themselves. We Jews like to imitate the Gentiles. They have students, so we also want to have students."

"You're out of your mind, Reb Ḥatzkel. Because the priests at the Bakszt seminary wear long cassocks, should our rabbis stop wearing their kapotes? What a load of noodle pudding! Listen to me!" shouts the grain-dealer, as he grabs Ḥatzkel by the beard. He has thought of an unanswerable argument: "It's wrong, you say, for our children to go to the Land of Israel, but is it better when they make revolutions instead? Have you already forgotten what happened in the streets this year on the first of May—the stones flying, the bloody heads, the 'Angels of Destruction' on their horses, and all the demonstrators who were carted off to jail? According to you, it's pleasanter to be in a Polish prison than to live in a hut on the banks of the Jordan, where Joshua led the Jews across . . . So, Reb Ḥatzkel, you have nothing to say?"

"The best thing is to stay in your own home," sighs the grocer. "This past Lag B'Omer the Jewish schools took all the children, with a band playing music, for an outing to Zakret Forest. Everybody ran to watch them, so I ran too—and got a jab in my side from a Pole who said, 'Zhidi do Madagaskaru!'* That's exactly what he said. And what could I have done if he had yelled, 'Zhidi do Palestiny!'? Nothing at all."

· · ·

*"All Jews to Madagascar!"

It is Friday afternoon and Mother is at her stand, surrounded by customers. She speaks with restraint to even the stubbornest hagglers among them, because Moshele is standing at the gate and about him, as always, is an air of serenity and peace, like the radiance of the Sabbath candles. Mother's face already mirrors her joy at the prospect of spending the entire Sabbath day together with Moshele.

Suddenly a large open wagon, loaded with cartons, appears. Seated on the coach-box is a young giant, who drives the big brown horse directly into the narrow gateway.

"Wait!" shouts my mother as she hastily begins to dismantle her stand. But the teamster does not wait, and urges the horse forward. One wagonwheel catches onto the stand, dragging it along and causing two baskets full of fruit to tumble off and spill their contents. With an anguished cry Mother throws herself under the wagon to pick up her wares. She struggles to pull free the braided baskets now entangled in the wheels. The driver hears her wail and comes to a halt. Moshele, who has also rushed forward to help take the stand apart, now abandons it to pull Mother out from under the wagon.

"It's borrowed goods, it's the wholesaler's money!" she moans, perspiring and disheveled, and feels in her apron for the few apples she has managed to pick up from the cobblestones; but they are crushed, and disintegrate in her hands like gruel. "My blood, my labor, my Sabbath!" she cries out, clapping her hands to her head in despair and letting her rescued goods fall back onto the street.

The teamster climbs down from his seat, grasps the horse's bridle, and starts to pull the wagon into the courtyard.

"Murderer!" Mother throws herself upon him with clenched fists. "Don't move the wagon, let me take my goods away first!"

The tall, broad-shouldered youth looks down at the tiny slip of a woman with green eyes burning with rage and yellowish foam on her lips, threatening him with tightly clenched fists—and he bursts into raucous laughter:

"Oi, I'm done for now." His laughter doubles him up, as though he has been seized by a stomach cramp. "Look who's attacking me!" From his open mouth loud guffaws roll out like claps of thunder, as he turns back to the horse. "You really think I'll waste half a day, and on Friday to boot, waiting for you to take your garbage away?"

But because of the baskets entangled in the wheels, and the narrowness of the gate, the horse cannot move. The overloaded wagon begins to shake and a full, square box falls off, striking Mother on the shoulder.

Mother utters a single scream; then, numb with pain, falls silent. She seems about to collapse, but Moshele catches her and she hangs limply in his arms.

"Vella, Mother Vella, what is it?" he cries out.

"My shoulder," she groans feebly, unable to utter another word.

"She needs cold compresses," calls out Lisa, widow of Alterka the goose-dealer, who has run out from her shop.

Lisa and Moshele take hold of Mother under the arms and lift her. The pain from the sudden twist in her shoulder revives her:

"Don't carry me, I'll walk by myself. Moshele, you stay here with the merchandise, it isn't paid for yet."

Barely able to walk, she is led away by Lisa. There is a buzzing in her brain, an echoing sound in her ears, a dizziness before her eyes.

In the meantime a crowd has gathered at the gate. A shopkeeper takes courage and begins to berate the wagoner:

"You have the heart of a Cossack. Other drivers wait until the woman has had a chance to take away her stand, but you drove straight at her. You nearly killed her. It was just lucky it was only a cardboard box."

"Let her not stand in the gate when she sees that someone is driving in," shouts the teamster. "And as for you, get out of the way, unless you want me to twist your shoulder. I'll do a better job of it than the cardboard box. Giddy-up!"

"You were told to wait, so wait until I've taken away all the baskets!" Moshele rushes at the driver, who is again pulling the horse by its bridle.

By now the driver is exasperated; everyone is telling him what to do. Enraged, he looks up to see before him a pious young bookworm, with spectacles and a beard.

The ḥalutz, tall and slender, looks like a deer whose back this wild ox of a teamster could break with one blow: so the neighbors are thinking as they stand watching with bated breath, afraid to interfere.

The wagon driver senses the fear he is arousing in the onlookers. Leisurely he turns to the young man who is facing him, pale and tense but composed.

"Hey, you there—are you going to hit me?"

He reaches out, grabs Moshele's cap by the brim, and pulls it down over his entire face to the chin.

Moshele pushes the cap back up on his head, slowly takes off his glasses, and furrows his brow exactly like his father the Rabbi when he is deciding which book to consult for the correct solution to some difficult ritual problem. But suddenly he jumps up and pulls the pole from which the scale is suspended out of the ring that holds it.

"Oho!" The wagoner moves further inside the gate and positions himself close to the wall. "Look at the tough guy! He's got an iron pipe, and I've only got my bare hands."

Moshele glares at him darkly and throws away the pole. At almost the same instant he grabs the fellow by his bearlike paws and with his bent head smashes into the wagoner's jaw, like a soccer player leaping into the air to bounce the ball off his skull. The wagoner's teeth are knocked together; he lets out a howl and, leaning back against the wall for support, lifts one knee and rams it into Moshele's stomach. Moshele doubles over, releasing the driver's hands. The driver seizes him by his full, curly hair and pushes his head down, down, like a butcher twisting a steer's head by the horns until the animal falls to the ground with a roar of pain.

Moshele, his lips clenched tight, utters no sound. He cannot free his head, and his neck is strained to the bursting point. Now from below he jabs his fists, like hammers of iron, up into the teamster's bloated face. Then, getting a grip on his beefy neck, he slams the driver's head against the wall, again and again. Only now does the driver let go of Moshele's hair; grunting like a wild boar, he kicks out at his opponent. A leg outstretched like a heavy log sends Moshele sprawling, but he pulls the burly driver down with him as he falls, and the two of them go rolling together over the paving stones.

The bystanders, who have been watching in silence since the fight began, break all at once into passionate yelling and screaming. They rejoice to see the loutish teamster getting his comeuppance. Still afraid to become directly involved themselves, they encourage the Rabbi's son with shouts and cheers:

"Give him a good thrashing!"

"Give him what David gave Goliath. Let him know that God still rules the world."

"Give it to him like a ḥalutz, like a true ḥalutz!"

"Beat him with the strength of the Torah, with the power of your father the Rabbi!"

"Moshele!"

A scream rends the heavens. My mother, inside the house, has heard the uproar and her heart has not misled her. With her last ounce of strength she runs across the courtyard, closely followed by Lisa.

Moshele, as though he was the only one to hear my mother's cry amid all the noise and commotion, jumps nimbly up from the pavement and seizes the iron he has just thrown away. Mother, seeing his swollen face, throws herself upon him and embraces him.

"Moshele, take pity upon your dear parents," she pleads with him, trembling and drawing him close to herself. "Look, my child, calm yourself—" It is as if, in her distraction, she were addressing her own son. "Come inside the house. Never mind about the merchandise and the money. God has punished me for making such a fuss about my spilled apples. It's nearly time to light the Sabbath candles. Moshele . . ."

He is silent. One of his arms enfolds my mother, the other holds the metal pole. His watchful, suspicious gaze closely follows the movements of the driver, now rising slowly and clumsily from the cobbled pavement. Suddenly Mother turns to face the bully, keeping Moshele protectively behind her.

"You don't have God in your heart," she wails. "May you have the kind of Sabbath that I will have because of you."

The shopkeepers surround Moshele and Mother to shield them, and now begin to berate the teamster without fear:

"You boor, don't you dare raise your hand against a rabbi's son. His father will put a curse on you!"

"We'll call the police. There's still justice in this world."

"You'll drop dead before you get another load from us. We'd rather give our business to a goy than a murderer like you."

But the driver has no intention of resuming the fight. He wipes his bleeding face and looks with astonishment at his palms, which are also smeared with blood. Who has given him such a beating—was it really that pious bookworm with the eyeglasses and the beard? He vents his wrath upon the horse, which has all this time been standing in the gate with ears pointed, as though savoring the spectacle of his master, who whipped him regularly, being trounced. The wagoner strikes the animal across the muzzle:

"Carrion, what are you blinking your goggle-eyes for? Giddy-up, you bag of bones, may you drop dead!"

Moshele takes my mother home, and the neighbors bring in what is left of her merchandise. They find the halutz standing in the smithy with sleeves rolled up, soaking pieces of cloth in a pot filled with water. He wrings them out with his strong hands and hands them to Lisa. Lisa places the cloths on Mother's shoulder, which is shivering with successive waves of heat and cold.

The neighbors now gather in a circle in the courtyard to talk. So astonished are they by what has just taken place that they even forget to bemoan my mother's suffering.

"That wagoner must have been drunk, or he would never have let a youngster beat him to a pulp. . . ."

"He's no youngster, that one, he's a regular tough nut. He gave it to the driver with his head coming up from below, like a real underworld thug."

"No, a thug leaves no marks when he beats someone, but he squashed the wagoner's nose."

"A Napoleon!" exclaims Ḥatzkel the grocer.

"Well, what do you say now?" the grain merchant taunts the grocer. "This was a sign to you from the heavens, Reb Ḥatzkel: Don't talk like the Ḥassidim from Warsaw, with their little hats. And don't talk like the Lubavitcher Ḥassidim in Oppatov's Synagogue. The Messiah is indeed the Messiah, but until he comes, you have to know how to fight back."

"That a rabbi's son should have such strength and courage," marvels Ḥatzkel. "That's fine, very fine."

"And you were moaning and groaning over him!" scoffs the grain merchant. "He may have run away from the shiksas, but as for the Arabs, that's different! They'll be running away from him. It's his kind we need in the Land of Israel—just his kind."

III

THURSDAY EVENING. Mother is standing in the kitchen and rushing to finish preparing the Sabbath meals before Moshele arrives.

Two Thursday nights earlier, Moshele had placed the lamp upon the workbench, directly facing the open door of the kitchen, rested his elbows on the screw-vise, and begun to read a book.

She had been puzzled: Moshele always sat in the other room with his head buried in a book, ruining his shining eyes with constant reading, just as his father did studying the holy books; but why, tonight, has he gone into the workshop and started reading standing up? Perhaps so she should not feel lonely while working in the kitchen? She had peeled the potatoes, mixed together all the ingredients of the cholent, and blown up the fire in the oven. And all the while Moshele had kept turning the pages and reading.

One half-hour passed, then another. The summer night is short, and she knew that early in the morning Moshele would set up her baskets at the gate and begin to sell her merchandise, until she herself returned from the market. At last, unable to restrain herself any longer, she asked:

"Moshele, why aren't you going to bed? Usually at this time you're asleep already."

"And why don't you go to bed?" he replied.

"At my age one doesn't sleep so well any more," she said, with a light laugh.

"Then I won't go either," he said.

More time passed, but he did not move from the spot, just as if this were quite customary. She had no wish to scold him as she might have her own son, but his behavior was upsetting her very much. What a youngster will think of! This has been her way for many years, ever since she became a fruit-vendor. Neither her husband, peace be upon him, nor her son, may the Almighty grant him long life, had ever succeeded in persuading her to go to sleep on Thursday night.

"I see, Moshele—" she tried to argue with him—"that you're on strike against me. But I still have to stuff a chicken-neck with flour and fat, to peel the carrots, and to grate the horseradish for the fish."

"It isn't necessary," Moshele said sternly and closed his book, as though he already knew that, whatever her show of resistance, she was about to give in.

"To tell you the truth, Moshele," she said, "I never really know which dishes you like and which you don't. You thank me equally for all of them."

"I like all the dishes, Mother Vella," he answered. "Everything you cook is good and tasty, just like my mother's cooking at home. But if you won't go to bed, then I won't go either, and next week I won't come at all. I know that for yourself alone you wouldn't be staying up all night."

Whereupon, without another word, she quickly moved the pots inside the oven onto the glowing coals, closed the oven door, and immediately went to bed. She understood quite well that if Moshele said something, he meant it.

While she was lying on her bed and Moshele, facing her, was on her son's bed, he told her a story of his student days at the yeshiva:

"Every Thursday night the yeshiva students held a 'mishmor'—that means they stayed up all night to study. But then the rosh yeshiva forbade this practice. 'I realize now,' he said, 'that instead of becoming more diligent students, as you imagine, you are really wasting time and studying less. On Thursday the day is disrupted because you're already preparing for the mishmor. On Friday and on the Sabbath you cannot study because you've been up all night for the mishmor. And on Thursday night itself you do study, but some of the time you're dozing as you stand at your lecterns.'"

This story, she realized, was Moshele's attempt to apologize for having insisted upon having his way. And, after all, he was right: On Thursday nights she could hardly stand on her feet, and tasks that should have required no more than an hour took her three hours. On Fridays she would stand at the gate exhausted and befuddled, not even hearing what her customers were saying, and immediately after the Kiddush Friday evening she would fall asleep with her head resting on the edge of the table. She herself didn't eat and neither did Moshele, for, not wanting to wake her, he would wait for her to rouse herself to serve the second course.

But why hasn't he yet come tonight, when it is already so late? Usually on Thursday evenings, Moshele arrived in time to help her take in her baskets, and his failure to show up must mean that something, God forbid, has happened to him. Ever since the box fell on her shoulder, he has never permitted her to carry the baskets herself. Perhaps he has fallen ill and is running a fever from standing for so many hours with head bent under the sun? A youngster alone, far from home, sleeping in a barn together with the peasants. And here she's been rushing to finish her work before he came. What will she do now for the remainder of the night? She won't be able to close her eyes even for a minute anyway. As soon as dawn begins to break, she'll run to the market to wait for the farmer from Soltaniszki . . . Praised be the Almighty! She hears the door being opened. It's he, it's his walk—but why is he entering so very quietly? She takes the lamp from the kitchen and goes into the workshop to help light his way, so he won't hurt himself stumbling over some piece of iron lying about. She finds him carrying a heavy sack.

"Good evening, Mother Vella. The work at Soltaniszki has come to an end now, so I had to settle accounts with the owner and say goodbye to my friends. That's why I'm so late. I brought along all my things."

"So from now on you'll be staying with me all the time!" she cries out joyfully, but regrets her words immediately. It's ridiculous to ask this of him, she thinks. After all, he owes her nothing.

Moshele gazes at her silently, solemnly, but she is so overjoyed at seeing him safe and unhurt that she doesn't notice this; she does not even realize that her hard, work-worn fingers are stroking his thick, curly hair:

"Oh Moshele, how perspired you are—" She wipes the sweat from his forehead. "I just didn't know what to think, because it was so late and you weren't here yet. I received a letter from my son today, he writes that he and your sister will soon be coming home. Moshele, go and eat."

He sits down at the table to read for himself the letter from Warsaw. Mother brings in her finest delicacies: a portion of fish, a hot meatball, a bowl of soup. For her own son she has never served a Sabbath meal on Thursday nights—he had to wait until after the Kiddush on Friday evening. But Moshele is hardly more than a child! And, to please him still further, she says:

"I've nearly finished all my work, and you won't need to go on strike again. Why don't you eat, Moshele?"

"How is your shoulder?" He rouses himself abruptly from his reverie and begins to eat. But my mother senses that this is not what he meant to say, and he is obviously forcing himself to eat.

"The Almighty be thanked," she answers, "the shoulder is completely healed. But I haven't fully come to myself yet since you had the fight with that wagon driver."

She feels the urge to scold him once more for having started up with that ruffian of a teamster, but she remains silent. From his deeply wrinkled forehead she can tell that he has something important to say to her and is trying to decide how to begin.

"Mother Vella," he says at last, in a strangely altered voice, "I'm leaving for the Land of Israel."

He begins to shift uneasily on his chair, displeased with himself for not having broken this news more gradually and gently to Mother Vella.

She remains seated, her hands stiff in her lap, unable to breathe. Moshele, as though he has expected this, adds hastily:

"You did know, Mother Vella, that I was working in Soltaniszki only in order to prepare myself for joining a kibbutz in the Land of Israel, and I promised my father that I would go there as soon as I finished my training."

"For whom now will I prepare the Sabbath?" she murmurs to herself.

"Your son and my sister will soon be returning home"—Moshele hastens to comfort her—"then you'll have someone to prepare the Sabbath for again, and you won't be lonely."

"But my son and your sister will be living by themselves, somewhere else," she says with a stiff smile, her tears rolling down.

"Oh, Mother Vella—" Moshele shakes his head—"don't you need to live for yourself? You're always looking for someone to love and to sacrifice yourself for."

Mother gazes at his full, warm, half-open lips, now trembling, and regains her composure: Moshele, after all, is going to the sacred Land of the Patriarchs, and his own parents are already there. His mother has surely been yearning for him quite long enough, his father has even given up the rabbinate in order to be together with him, and their only daughter is remaining here, with her, Vella's, own son; how, then, does she dare to ask that Moshele also stay here, to help her carry her baskets?

To make him forget the foolish words she has uttered, she begins, in a cheerful tone, to tell a tale:

"Our eldest son, Moïsey, was also a Zionist. If only Moïsey's son, Aronchik, were like his father and like you, may you be granted long life, his mother wouldn't have to tremble now, day and night, at the thought of his being arrested again. But Aronchik always laughed at his Uncle Issak, the pharmacist, who used to tell my son when he was still a boy to go to the Land of Israel to drain the swamps."

"Aronchik was right to laugh at his uncle," says Moshele with a smile. "One should go oneself, not tell others to go."

"Our neighbor, Reb Boruhel, may he keep away from the living, also wanted to go to the Land of Israel, to die," says Mother, increasingly disturbed by her inability to control her agitation, "but his wife, my partner, Blumele, only wanted to go to her children in Argentina. But in the end both of them, poor souls, remained in Vilna, in the cemetery in Zarecze."

"A pity," says Moshele regretfully. "Of course it's better to go to the Land of Israel to live and to work. But if someone at least wants to go there to die, it's a sign that he would have wanted to live there, too, but didn't have the strength to carry it through."

Mother sees that Moshele is trying to help her distract herself. Anger at herself rises in her, and with trembling hands she takes a small canvas bag from her purse:

"Moshele, every week you gave me two zlotys out of your wages. I didn't want to argue with you because you said that if I didn't take the money, you wouldn't come to me for the Sabbath. So I took the money and put it aside. Now that you're about to leave on such a long and difficult journey, I beg of you: take back your money and use it to help pay for whatever you need."

"Mother Vella—" Moshele pulls a bundle of bills from his pocket— "I, too, didn't want to argue with you. You didn't want to take the money you had coming to you, so I held on to it. But I had no use for it—all week long I ate and slept in Soltaniszki. Now that I'm going away, I want to give it to you. My father is sending me the money I need for the trip."

Mother feels a choking sensation in her throat—if only she could hide away in some corner, where she might weep over her prayerbook.

"Moshele, you shame me."

Moshele gazes at her in astonishment and pushes the coins she has taken from her bag into one heap with his paper zlotys.

"Well, then, Mother Vella," he says calmly, "we'll buy a gift together for your son and my sister."

"Moshele, are you leaving right after the Sabbath?"

"No, Mother Vella. I'll wait until my sister returns from Warsaw."

"Moshele, when you write a letter to us from the Land of Israel, don't address me as 'Mother Vella.' Your mother, the Rebbetzin, might resent it. I beg your mother not to be angry at me because her daughter hasn't married into the sort of comfort and wealth that she deserves. If it were in my power, I would treat your sister like a princess."

She draws a deep breath, as though to fill the emptiness in her heart. Bands of light creep over the walls of the smithy. The dark blue in the window grows lighter and lighter—Moshele has forgotten to remind Mother Vella to go to bed. He sits silent and sad, his head resting on both his hands.

The Stocking-Peddler

I

SOME YEARS EARLIER there had lived in the goose-dealers' courtyard a family named Press. The typesetter Zalman Press—a short, thin man with long hair below his ears, and a tongue forever unbolted—had no other name for his employers than "the exploiters." His relations with his fellow workers, however, were even worse. He suspected them of intentionally slipping him extra boxes full of leaden type to carry, in order to give him a hernia. From time to time he would explode like a match bursting into flame, and scream:

"If the typesetters of Vilna ran a government of their own, they'd be greater cutthroats than the bosses of The Brothers Romm*; they'd be worse even than that exploiter, the printer Matz."

The other printers, for their part, nicknamed Zalman "the hemorrhoidnik": although he jumped about like a flea, he had hemorrhoids, so they claimed, like some benchwarming bookworm. Others called him "Hotzmaḥ"† because once, years before, he had performed with an amateur theatrical group. He had been an amateur on stage and, according to them, remained an amateur at his work, a bungler. Yet others dubbed him "the payet" because he loved to declaim from memory, hand clasped to breast, the poems of Morris Rosenfeld. And there was one final nickname which attached itself to him—one that all but buried him alive. People took to calling him "the Social Democrat."

Once Zalman had taken it into his head to invite a co-worker—one of the few with whom he hadn't yet had a fight—to his home on a Sabbath afternoon. He decided to show his guest how politically aware his children were, and asked the youngest boy:

"Mottele, what will you be when you grow up?"

"A Social Democrat," piped Mottele in nasal tones.

No more was needed. The visitor spread the story far and wide. From then on, the other typesetters tormented Zalman at the slightest provocation:

---

* A Jewish publishing house in Vilna.—Trans.
† A comic character in a play by Abraham Goldfaden.—Trans.

"So you're a Social Democrat, are you? A lazy good-for-nothing is what you are! You'd like others to do your work for you while you march around spouting the party line in hifalutin Sabbath language."

"Having his Mottele join the 'Children's Bund,' that's not good enough for him. No, Mottele has to be a 'Social Democrat.' Such a hemorrhoidnik! Such a Hotzmaḥ! Such a 'payet'!"

Jethro's names.

A polar opposite to the short, puny, talkative Zalman Press was his wife, Fayga. A stout woman, calm and sedate, she held the sceptre in her hands and was the true head of the household. She paid about as much attention to her husband's ideas as to the flies which, having survived the summer, buzzed in winter about the corners of the putty-sealed windows. She used to complain to my mother:

"That little husband of mine has always been a scatterbrain, a loafer and a show-off. Years ago I used to think that an idealist had to be a failure in practical affairs; after all, I myself was once an idealist, a proper mooncalf—I remember it now as if it were yesterday. It was about two years after our happy wedding. Every Sabbath afternoon, after the cholent, my little husband would dress up with his wide flowing bow-tie, spend an hour in front of the mirror, hum to himself, and prance about—the actor's rehearsal. Then he would clasp a book under one arm, take his walking-stick in the other hand, and march off to Teliatnik Park to engage in discussion. I, fool that I was, stayed home to rock Yudka, our eldest child, to sleep. More than once my hero came home from the park beaten and bruised, yet he'd boast to me: 'Did I ever give it to them'— with his mouth, that is."

Fayga spoke slowly, accompanying her words with gestures to demonstrate how her husband tied his bow, primped before the mirror, and went off with his walking-stick. Apparently she too, like her husband, had theatrical blood in her veins.

Their boys attended secularist Yiddish schools and all three of them, from the eldest to the youngest, painted. They had large palettes with paints, thin boar's-hair brushes, stacks of heavy drawing paper, and even canvases. Their house was always a mess: the walls, the chairs, and the table were forever smeared with watercolors and oil paint, and the boys stood glued to their easels. The father would hop from one of his geniuses to the other—here closing one eye, there squinting with the other—then pirouette to the back of the room so as to judge from a distance whether the pictures had proper "perspective," all the while enunciating his expert opinions.

For a short period of time I had attended a secular school together with Zalman's sons. In class, taking after their pugnacious father, they were constant fighters. They would pretend to be watching what the teacher was writing on the blackboard while kicking other boys' shins beneath the desks. During recess their victims would pay them back in kind, and there was always a cluster of hands and feet around them, as though an intertwined band of monkeys were vigorously scratching one another.

I, for my part, got along well with Zalman's sons. I too wanted to become a painter. I managed to acquire paints, brushes, and paper, and implored the born artists to show me how they painted whole stories in their pictures: peasant huts, fences, trees, a path, a wagon pulled by a horse, and flocks of birds flying below the clouds. But Zalman Press trembled lest anyone manage to worm their secret out of his sons, and always chased me from the house:

"I don't run an art academy or a youth club here. Go to the 'Help Through Work' office; there you can learn to become a house-painter."

Now only one hope remained: I had to observe Zalman's sons when they went out into the courtyard to paint from direct observation the Rudnicka Street church-steeple. But Zalman was on guard. He chased me away, and even yelled at the neighbors who were looking on in amazed delight.

"Go away! What are you staring at? It's always the way of the exploiters to copy other people's ideas and make profits off them."

Only when it came to declaiming, hand upon heart, the poems of Morris Rosenfeld or his own compositions, then only did Zalman Press not stint or hold back. It was from him that, for the first time in my life, I heard verse spoken aloud.

Eventually Zalman Press left our courtyard with its goose-dealers' row and moved into a poorer courtyard on Nowogrodzka, and this was followed by still another move. When Yudka, his eldest son, grew up he became, not a Social Democrat like his father, but a Communist; and when the Soviets opened the "Green Border," he escaped into Russia. There, like all the other illegal immigrants, he vanished like a stone thrown into water, and Fayga never ceased to throw it up to her husband that it was his fault Yudka had deserted them.

Zalman could no longer bear the constant quarreling with his Fayga, the ceaseless warfare between him and the other printers. So one day he spat upon all Vilna and went back to his home town—Kreuzburg, or perhaps Jakobstadt on the Dvina. For a number of years he wandered among the Letts, until at last he returned to Vilna, with a long beard and even longer hair.

Zalman Press had become a stocking-peddler.

. . .

MY MOTHER at her gateway stand can no longer see the daylight. On the street, just two paces away, stands her former neighbor, Zalman, now a stocking-peddler. Around him the crowd is as dense as a swarm of locusts. But it is not with his wares—the woolen men's socks and silken women's stockings thrown over his left arm—that he has attracted customers; nor does he ensnare passers-by with the combs, pocket mirrors, hairpins, safety pins, and other knickknacks contained in the basket he holds in his right hand. It is with his rhymes that he attracts them, with his songs that he captivates them. People who couldn't care less about stockings surround him, enthralled and bedazzled by the verses he seems to shake out of his sleeves and pull from his pockets, like a magician flinging out the coins he has drawn from his nose and ears.

A woman carrying a basket over her arm walks by. She is in the late months of pregnancy. Noticing the crowd, she stops, and the hawker quickly asks her:

"What's your name?"

"Fayga," she answers, smiling. From the pleasantly excited faces around her she can tell that the man is a devil-may-care type, a jester.

"Fayga?" In real or pretended terror, the peddler jumps backward; he wrinkles his eyebrows a moment, and out comes a verse:

"My angel of death, my wife, is named Fayga too,
But she's not at all in the same advanced state as you."

The crowd, turning to look at the young woman and her swollen belly, relishes the peddler's double entendre. And now Zalman quickly makes his pitch:

"If you have a son named Avrom,
Buy, to cure his nits, a comb;
And if a girl is added to your kin,
Buy the chaste maiden a safety pin."

The crowd is astounded: what a wickedly clever rogue the fellow is! The pregnant woman, having drawn so much attention, is embarrassed to leave without buying anything—she looks over the contents of his basket and does select a few items.

Of all the onlookers, the most excited is Mariasha the gossip-monger. She had just run out to buy something in the grocery for her husband's meal, to stuff up his hungry mouth, and on her way back from the store caught sight of the crowd. And so there she stands, the herring in her hand, a kerchief over her disheveled hair, her dress rumpled, her stockings falling down. Having entirely forgotten about her husband waiting "on hot coals" for her return, she pleads with the peddler as if with a bandit for her life:

"Make up a rhyme for 'Mariasha.' "

These words are accompanied by a sly wink at the other onlookers, as if to say: "Watch me make a fool of this windblown little Jew, this comedian!"

One glance is all the peddler needs to take the measure of the person before him. Giving his long locks a shake, he begins instantly to chant:

"Be your name Yaḥna-Dvosha or Mariasha,
To be a slattern is appalling;
What then to do? Says our sage Rashi:
Buy garters, woman, to keep your stockings from falling."

The laughter dies in Mariasha's throat. But it finds another outlet in the candy-seller, whose quite lusty roar betrays her vengeful pleasure in her amiable neighbor's downfall. Mariasha, however, quickly recovers from her confusion and displays once again her sugary smile:

"Well, then, make up a rhyme for the candy-seller too."

Whether the peddler is intimidated by the candy-seller's ferociously glaring eyes, which bore right through him—"Say just one word, and I'll kill you!"—or whether he is simply for once at a loss for a rhyme, is difficult to tell. But he turns abruptly toward the gate and points at my mother:

"To get a rhyme for the candy-seller, you'll have to go to Vella's son. He's one of these modern writers who can rhyme . . . everything."

Delighted because Mariasha has failed to make a fool of her, the candy-seller emits a clearly feminine shriek—as if the dybbuk whose deep masculine voice has always issued from her, has burst at that instant into thin air.

"Oh, I'll die laughing! You're good enough to be a badḥen at a wedding."

For a moment the crowd is struck dumb with amazement: Who would have expected the candy-seller to come up with such a brilliant idea, a stroke worthy of a statesman? A general tumult ensues as everyone crowds closer to the peddler to proffer advice:

"Why bother with peddling socks? Become a wedding badḥen, and you'll rake in the gold."

"The Zezemer Badḥen is a puppy dog compared to you."

"Eliakum Zunser just might be good enough to light your oven for you."

"Go visit weddings, rich people's weddings. They'll positively fight over you."

"So what?" The peddler's gaze sweeps over the crowd. "And what's wrong with you as wedding hosts? The whole world is a cozy wedding feast for the big-bellies while we, the paupers, stand outside and gape through the windows. There, in the fancy halls, the Zezemer Badḥen or Reb Eliakum Zunser stands up front, announces the wedding gifts, and doles out the ceremonial honors to the wealthy relatives, and in return they throw donations into his skullcap. But the poor wretches outside also need a master of ceremonies—and that's me. My rhymes cost nothing, I give them away as a bonus with the socks, the pins, and all the other silly junk. So now, listen with both ears to this song I've just composed for such wedding guests as you."

He sets down on the pavement the basket he has been holding in his right hand, straightens the socks draped over his bent left arm, throws back his head, snaps his fingers, and begins to hop about as he sings:

> *"There's a wedding, a great hubbub—*
> *Let us dance also and be hearty!*
> *All we need to make things perfect*
> *Is a blessing for our party!*
>
> *"Through the windows stare, you paupers!*
> *Gape at dainties, fish and meat!*
> *If you'll sing the good host's praises,*
> *He'll throw you, too, some scraps to eat.*
>
> *"For these tidbits, O you shnorrers,*
> *Praise the groom and hail the bride;*
> *For some bones with bitter radish,*
> *Praise relatives on every side.*
>
> *"Dance you cobblers, dance you tailors!*
> *Dance and dance, you working masses!*
> *But watch out that while you're dancing,*
> *You don't show your naked ———."*

Abruptly the peddler stops and waits for his listeners to deduce the last rhyme for themselves. Someone in the crowd utters the word—and everyone bursts out laughing so hard the windows seem about to shatter. It is just this moment that the peddler seizes to take up his basket and disappear into the courtyard of the goose-dealers' row, like an actor who exits the stage while the audience is still applauding.

The listeners look this way and that, their laughter dies down, and their faces cloud over as though reflecting the dull autumn sky above them. They frown and shake their heads:

"Imagine, an old man using such vulgar language . . ."

"Imagine, a bearded Jew jumping around like a billy-goat and making such a fool of himself."

Slowly the crowd melts away. My mother, at the gate, is happy to see the light of day once again. But suddenly she feels someone tugging at her arm: Zalman has leaped back out of the courtyard and is whispering to her furtively, rapidly:

"What do you say, ha? Did you see how they all listened to me? Tell your son about it. He's one of these modern writers, and to him I'm just a rhyme-smith. I haven't even finished all my verses yet. Here—I'll sing another one for you:

> "Come, musicians—bring your fiddles,
> Bring your fifes and drums to play—
> Play and play till all your heartstrings
> Burst! Play all your strength away!
>
> "Badḥen! Waiters! Don't get bored, you—
> Turn handstands, hop and jump and leap!
> Some kind soul may yet reward you
> And leave a kopeck as a tip.

"You see, Vella," he continues without pausing to catch his breath, "I recently read a pamphlet published by your son and some of his friends, in which they said that we need to make new kinds of rhymes. So I'm showing that I can do this too: 'bored, you/ reward you.' "

"I don't understand anything of these matters—" Mother is somewhat frightened by the stocking-peddler, who shakes as he speaks, like someone with a raging fever—"but it seems to me that you're mocking yourself."

"That's it! That's it!" Nearly choking with joy, Zalman thrusts a finger in Mother's face. "You say you don't understand, but the truth is, you understand perfectly. Those donkeys out there in the street shrieked with laughter, but they didn't realize I was making fun of them and of myself, too. As long as someone still believes that this topsy-turvy world can be straightened out, with its feet down and its head up, he cries and he scolds, he curses and demands action, action—like your son, for instance. He, after all, is still a youngster. But once one knows what I know—that this upside-down world can never be set on its feet—then one stands on one's own head. Who, tell me, will straighten out the world? I, whom my own wife, Fayga, calls a 'stinkpot'? You know, don't you, that Fayga goes around from shop to shop, proclaiming 'I hate my husband and I don't hide it.' And she's succeeded in influencing my children so that they, too, laugh at me. Am I, then, the one to set the world to rights? So I laugh at myself, and there's green gall in my laughter. Tell your son about the verses you heard from me."

"What are you saying, Reb Zalman? How can I remember it all, with my weak head? One would need a cast-iron memory for that. You know what? Write it all down on a sheet of paper and give it to me, and I'll show it to my son. Since he returned from Warsaw, he and his wife live in an apartment of their own, but he stops by here at the gate every day."

"So that's what you're after!" Zalman bursts out laughing, as though he has been expecting this suggestion all along. "You want me to write them down on paper so your son can have them printed under his name, as though he were the author."

"My son is not, God forbid, a thief," says my mother, offended. "You, Reb Zalman, have always been suspicious of everyone. Even when you lived in our courtyard and my son was still a child, you were afraid to let him into your house, for fear he'd steal the secret of how to paint from your sons."

"And I was right!" exclaims Zalman, as confidently as if he has just caught hold of a strange hand in his pocket. "I was right. Others did become painters—they study in the academies, their pictures are shown in exhibitions, while my children remain shlemiehls like their father. Fayga goes from store to store and buys up sacks—potato sacks, flour sacks, barley sacks—and my sons help her carry them. As for their painting, that just fizzled out."

Zalman's stocking-bedecked bent arm begins to tremble, like a laundry-laden clothesline shaken by the wind. He snatches up his basket and dashes off.

He's become even more bitter than he used to be, muses my mother. That's what happens to a person who doesn't achieve what he wants in life. Keep me, God, from letting my hardships bring me to such bitterness, and guard my children against it as well. I simply can't understand people whose only desire is to win applause from outsiders and strangers. . . .

SEVERAL DAYS LATER, Fayga stops by at the gate. She sets a bundle of sacks down on the ground, takes a deep breath, and begins to speak, slowly and deliberately:

"I hate my husband and I let the whole world know it. But he tells me your son likes his little verses very much, and—so he says—will be coming to see us any day now. So I want to know whether my husband is just making up stories, as usual, about how the whole world envies him, or whether, this once in fifty years, he's telling the truth. And you yourself, Vella, really ought to pay an old neighbor a visit, too."

Mother can't believe her ears: There seems no end to the stocking-peddler's wild fantasies. But since this is clearly such a matter of life and death for him, she will just have to get her son to visit him.

"All week long I struggle with my baskets," she defends herself to Fayga. "When the Sabbath comes at last, I'm exhausted. And everyone needs time to fill the mouth with a Jewish word, sinners that we all are. But I shall come to see you, with God's help."

"And your son?"

"My son? You know, Fayga, that he was married only recently, so he's quite busy, you know how it is with a young couple. But since he's promised to come, he will surely come."

II

I HADN'T SEEN ZALMAN since his return as a stocking-peddler, and so I agreed to go with my mother to visit our former neighbor on the following Sabbath afternoon. I was curious to see what had become of the enthusiasm with which he once declaimed, hand upon heart, the poems of Morris Rosenfeld. I was not at all eager, however, to meet his sons, who had taken to averting their faces when we happened to meet on the street.

In the courtyard on Szklanna Street where the Press family was now living, there were many oddly shaped roofs, along with countless doors, windows, and wrought-iron staircases. Housewives sitting in their respective doorways chatted amiably, ragged and dirty children played everywhere, and over them all swayed clotheslines full of laundry.

"Compared to this courtyard," Mother said to me, "ours is a real palace." She asked one of the women where the Press family lived.

"Why in the world would you want to enter Gehenna of your own free will?" responded the woman in astonishment. "Do you see the outhouse over there, in the corner? And those pig-filthy steps and the windowpanes stuffed with rags, do you see them? You should be able to figure out for yourself that that's where that family lives, with its demons and crazy husband, the Press family, as you so politely call them."

"Be careful you don't take any bedbugs or lice home with you," calls out another woman.

"You'd better pray to God you get out of there alive," warns a third.

"Fayga doesn't seem to get along well with her neighbors," observes my mother as we walk carefully up the slippery, garbage-strewn stairs. "But don't you get into any fights now with your old friends."

When we enter the apartment, our "Good Sabbath" greeting sticks in our throats. There is nothing of the Sabbath here; the workaday world shrieks at us from every nook and corner. The apartment is even more of a trash heap than their home was years ago, when they lived near us in the goose-dealers' courtyard. Fayga, in a soiled dress and with hair disheveled, stands at the stove, scouring pots. "On the Sabbath?" Mother looks at me in great alarm. Mottele, the youngest son, a tall, strapping fellow, has one foot up on a chair and is polishing his brown shoes—a task he finds so absorbing that he does not even turn to look at the newly arrived guests. To make up for this, the middle son, Aizikel, pierces us with his glittering black eyes. Pitifully short and thin, with a bony chin sparsely covered with wiry wisps of hair, he is sitting at the table, his fingers dipping and scrabbling among bunches of rusty, oddly shaped keys. Around him on the floor stand small wooden boxes filled with all sorts of locks and padlocks. Zalman Press himself—decked out in a broad black bow-tie, his long hair combed smoothly behind his ears, his beard puffed up in frizzy curls—sits at one end of a tattered sofa, one hand on the armrest, the other nonchalantly extended over the sofa back, looking as though he were waiting to have his picture taken. Laid out along the walls are heaps of empty sacks, which exude an odor of damp potatoes and dry flour dust.

"Have a seat," says Fayga in the cold, irritable tone one might use toward poor relations; she thrusts her head into the cooled-off oven.

"Why are you standing with your back to our company? The pants are practically bursting on your broad backside!" Zalman calls out gaily to Mottele. "When you were little, you said you wanted to be a Social Democrat, but you've grown up to be a dancer. Our grand gentleman is dressing up to go to his dancing class," his father confides to us in the tone of someone denouncing an offender to the police; and a malicious smile smolders in his eyes, as if to say: "You'll soon hear how my son answers me."

Mottele takes his foot off the chair. Mockery flashes from his puffy cheeks and light-blue eyes as, brush in hand, he points at his father:

"When I used to say I wanted to be a Social Democrat, I was just babbling your propaganda, but when I grew up, I got more sense than you ever had."

"If we'd listened to our father, we too would have become 'world-liberators,' " says Aizikel, picking at the wiry hairs on his chin as though they were rusty keys.

"You see," says Zalman triumphantly, "Comrade Fayga made fun of my ideals for so long that her children now imitate her."

"His ideals!" Fayga turns green with rage, advances to the middle of the room, and assumes her husband's accustomed pose for declamation.

"Clown! When I hear from you as often as I hear from our Yudka, then I'll be satisfied. You drummed Ess-Dek* ideology into him for so long he became a Bolshevik just to spite you. Do you hear, Vella? I hate my husband."

"That's just it!" Zalman jumps up, delighted that Comrade Fayga herself has brought up her weakest point. "You brought the principle of class war into our home. But instead of the slogan 'Proletarians of the world, unite!' your program became 'Children, hate your father!' And so Yudka led the opposition against me in both theory and tactics, until he got sick of these internal conflicts and went over to the other side. I myself am a bitter foe of both Bolshevik dictatorship and the Bund's nationalistic program."

Nothing upsets Fayga—who was once herself, as she has said, "an idealist"—so much as Zalman's sarcastic manner of speaking. It makes her feel that he is mocking the simple-minded admiration she had for him when she was a young girl and he attracted her like a magnet with his dramatic gifts and his other talents.

"How can one not hate such a good-for-nothing?" she appeals to my mother, and begins counting off his failures on her fingers: "When he was an 'Ess-Dek' and used to f-fight—" pursing her lips, she repeats the "f" sound to emphasize her contempt for her husband's heroics— "he always came home from the debates all scratched up. When he turned actor, they wouldn't let him play any serious roles; the other actors said that the audience burst into laughter as soon as he appeared on the stage. When he became a printer, the typesetters laughed at him, called him a bungler, and gave him a new nickname every day: hemorrhoidnik, Hotz-mah, 'payet,' Social Democrat—what didn't they call him? When he saw what he had done to Yudka, he went off to Latvia to give performances for his relatives there. But there, too, they soon recognized him for what he is, and he came back here as a village idiot."

"If Yudka had only learned to dance," Mottele philosophizes, "he wouldn't have been thinking about making revolutions, and he wouldn't be slaving away now in a Donbas coal mine. They say they keep the chaps from Vilna deep underground. All the world's troubles start because people don't know how to enjoy themselves."

"If Yudka had put all his wits and energy into his feet, he would have become just such another circus-horse as you," laughs the father. The start of an argument so delights him that he begins to scratch himself with pleasure.

"It's better to have one's wits in the feet than in the tongue, like you," retorts Mottele. "Yudka also had his wits in his tongue. He spoke

* I.e., SD, for "Social Democrat (ic)."

at mass rallies and repeated what he heard in the Party cell—that Poland was about to go to war against the Soviet Union, because Poland wanted to grab western White Russia and the western Ukraine for herself. And at night he painted slogans on walls: 'Hands off the Soviet Union!' When I'm dancing with some small-town creature and my hand wanders down below her waist, she also says, 'Hands off the Soviet Union!' . . . On the night before May Day, Yudka did a solo dance. He had a can of paint, and he tore pieces of canvas from sacks, dipped them in the paint, and threw them over telegraph wires. He was a painter like the rest of us, only he painted everything red. For that the politruks* promised him that in Moscow he'd be able to study at the Academy of Fine Arts. And Yudka promised me and him—" he points at Aizikel—"that as soon as he had settled in Minsk, or Kiev, or Moscow, he would send a message to us to join him. And as soon as we arrived, he assured us, the State and the Communist Party would fully support us, as though we were their own children, and let us study painting. We would dedicate ourselves to Art and help to glorify the name of the Soviet Fatherland. Those were his very words as he went off to study at the Academy of Fine Arts— and so Yudka, be well! That's why I'd rather dance, there's more wisdom in dancing than in making speeches. You mustn't get too close to your partner, you mustn't sweat, or look down at your feet, or throw yourself about like an epileptic. You have to hold yourself straight as a violin string, but not stiff as if you had swallowed a pole. You have to hold the girl gently, but like a man, so that she feels an electric current passing between you. I've developed such a sweet little step that as soon as I get close to a girl, knee to knee, she begins to tremble. That's how you have to dance!"

And Mottele bends his arms in a semicircle, as though embracing a girl. He stands tiptoe on one foot and on the heel of the other, and puffs out his broad manly chest so that his imaginary partner may lean her curly head against it. Then he begins to rock his broad porter's shoulders and to hum, whistle, and click his tongue as resoundingly as if he were beating a drum.

"The most important part," concludes Mottele, "is to stay in step with the rhythm, and to dance as if you were swimming."

"The most important part," says Fayga ambiguously but pointedly, "isn't the dancing but the cooling off."

"Mottele Press the dancing-master spends all his money on the girls," little Aizikel interjects as he strings a bunch of keys on a piece of cord. "Mottele takes his dancing partners, his plumed birds, to restaurants, and they make sure he treats them generously."

* Political instructors.—Trans.

"That's better than being a rag-picker." Mottele pirouettes on one foot, as though he were standing in the middle of a dance hall and looking to see which of his scores of plumed birds he should seize for the next dance. "Aizikel has always had the vile habit of burying everything in his little boxes, like an animal that scratches holes in the earth with its paws to bury everything it finds. A rusty penknife, a smoked-out old pipe, a bottle for catching flies, a child's cast-off toy—for Aizikel they're all treasures, and Mother takes great pride in him, to boot."

"Of whom, then, should I be proud—of you?" asks Fayga wearily. "Aizikel brings money into the house, while you take it all out for your girls."

"When it comes to my pleasures, I don't count the money." Mottele walks over to arrange his tie in the mirror above the decrepit dresser. "I work hard for my money carrying the sacks, and when I feel like going to a nightclub, I go. If a sock is a real garment, then Aizikel is a real man. Does he know what it means to live? Does he know what an 'English waltz' is? He's a grouch! A kill-joy! If you so much as touch anything in his trash-and-rag collection, he screams as if you were ripping a bandage and skin together off his scrawny body."

"And who dances with you?" Aizikel taunts. "Chicken-pluckers dance with you. They sit on a bench next to the wall, like birds on a fence, and wait for Mottele the dancing-master to twirl them around the spittle-covered floor."

"He's bursting with gall," laughs Mottele, "because no girl ever gives him a second look, miserly grouch that he is, no bigger than a fig."

"You see what it's like here, Vella." Fayga shakes her head. "Even the River Sambatyon rests today, but these two hurl stones at each other on the Sabbath as well as during the week, both by day and by night. Our ballet-master here inherited his dancing from his dear sweet father, who used to caper about on the stage. Even Aizikel's junk-collecting reflects his dear father's nature. My good-for-nothing always used to search for antiques in the trash. A misfortune! A family of 'artists'!"

" 'In a quarrel, one of the two must curb his tongue,' " responds my mother, who has been sitting there all this time, deeply grieved over the impudence these modern children display toward their father, and ashamed for the Sabbath that has been so callously desecrated. "If neither side is willing to swallow the insult, there will never be an end to the fighting."

"Their mother taught them that one must always have the last word," interjects Zalman, clearly all too eager to add fuel to the flames. "Comrade Fayga taught her sons not to respect their father."

" 'They don't respect their father!' " Stepping once again to the center of the room, Fayga mimics her husband. "For you they should have respect? Perhaps because you stand out there in the street and sing out your poems like a beggar? The truth is, he doesn't care in the least about selling his stockings—he cares only that people look at him and listen to his rhymes." And, as though she has just this moment caught sight of me, Fayga asks me sternly:

"Is it really true what this braggart says, that you yearn to copy his poems and have them published in your own name? Did you come to see him, or to see my sons?"

I look at Zalman, who does not so much as blink an eye. He has no fear, apparently, of my branding the whole story an outright lie. Aizikel, who has bent down to rummage in his boxes, calls out to Fayga:

"He came to visit our father, the 'payet.' Us he doesn't even recognize when he sees us on the street."

"Why should he bother to talk to the likes of us?" chimes in Mottele, in support of his brother. "He doesn't associate with people who deal in old sacks."

"It seems to me that you're the ones who always walk by with your heads turned away, pretending you don't see me," I retort, angry and thoroughly bored; I give my mother a reproachful look for having dragged me here.

"What do you expect—that we'd wait for you to give us the cold shoulder? As far as we're concerned, you're not so high and mighty." Hatred glitters in Aizikel's moist black eyes.

"You don't need to look down on my children," says Fayga sourly. "After all, they once taught you how to draw human figures. And you've made good use of that."

"You really mustn't be angry with him—" Mother speaks up in my defense—"often he's so absorbed in his thoughts he doesn't hear anything I say to him. Thinking up poems, it seems, is hard work."

"I don't have to think at all," Zalman interjects. "Rhymes come to me so easily, I barely manage to grab them by the tail. And not worn-out old rhymes like 'bread/ read/ dead.' I work with brand-new ones— for example:

> *"Enough of you, community leaders,*
> *And community bleeders.*

"As for just who's done the leading and bleeding, that makes no difference. You can stretch the lines like rubber bands and fill in whomever you want—the blood-sucking bosses, the communal leaders of Vilna, the old writers who don't let the young ones get ahead, the young who make life miserable for the old—you could even fit Fayga, my wife, into those lines. The important thing is the rhyme, 'leaders/ bleeders.' Mottele, your feet bounce up and down like rubber balls even in your sleep, so now tell us yourself: Have you ever seen a couple dance together as light-footedly as my verses dance with each other?"

Zalman laughs, obviously overjoyed to see that the storm which has been raging all this time within the family, is now beginning to engulf the guests as well.

"Synagogue loafers!" Mottele shrugs his shoulders contemptuously. "If I'd listened to you, I too would be warming a bench today, hatching out rhymes. And as a reward you would one day leave me as my inheritance that tattered bow-tie you're wearing today in honor of this snob."

"I thought you might have changed—" I stand up—"but you're just the same as when you were schoolboys, kicking the other boys under the desks while the teacher was explaining the lesson. Come, Mother, let's go."

"What did I tell you?" Mottele turns to Fayga. "I told you—'Don't invite him. He's as arrogant as they come.'"

I look impatiently at my mother, who sits as if in a daze and seems herself to regret having come. Yet she makes no move to rise.

Mottele, already a picture of honeyed elegance, suddenly begins to rub his cheek, peers into the mirror over the decrepit dresser, and then pulls out from one of the drawers a brush, a piece of soap, and a razor. So there should be no mistaking his intentions, he takes the blade out of the razor and tests its sharpness on his fingernail. He is quite obviously trying to force my mother to leave. And at this she does rise, deeply upset:

"On the Sabbath?"

"So what?" With two fingers he picks at a pimple on his pasty face. "Doesn't your own son do the same?"

"Bastard!" screams Fayga. "Couldn't you do that a little later? But you, Vella, don't you pretend to be such a saint. First pluck out the weeds from your own garden."

"He must shave—he must!" Mottele's father comes to his defense. "Otherwise his girls won't be able to press their fresh cheeks against his scratchy mug while they're dancing."

Head bowed, Mother runs out of the house. I follow.

III

"GEHENNA!" Mother rushes headlong down the crooked iron stairs. "The neighbors were right: the Press home is truly a hell on earth. That sons should kick like that at their own father. But then, do I get more respect from you? When I tried to tell that dancer he shouldn't shave on the Sabbath, the insolent fellow answered that my son is no better."

"You're complaining?" I run down the steps ahead of her. "It was you who asked me to go visit Zalman with you. And those vicious louts carried on like that on purpose, to make sure we couldn't stay."

"Exactly so," says a voice behind us. "They were fighting on purpose so you couldn't stay." Zalman has caught up with us; gleefully he shouts: "Now you know them for what they are."

"That's not something my life depends on," retorts Mother angrily. "I didn't even have time to read this week's Torah portion today."

"The weekly portion won't run away—but you," Zalman says, taking hold of my sleeve, "come along with me."

"What do you want of me now?" I ask, impatient and annoyed.

"I want the two of us to go for a walk." He hops up and down like a schoolboy. "I invented that bit about your liking my poems, because I knew that Fayga would run to ask your mother about it. I was certain that your mother wouldn't deny it, and also that she would talk you into coming with her to our chicken-coop."

"If you wanted to see me, you could have come to my house. Your sons put on a proper show for me."

"But that was just what I wanted." He hops about with still greater glee. "I wanted you to hear how my family insults me. Now you'll understand why I never became what I might have been. Today they were scratching in the dirt to find something to fight about. They refused to let their dear mother straighten the house. Just today, this once in a jubilee year, she wanted to clean, but her dear children told her to stay by the stove and scour pots. However it looks to you, it's only to me that she has a big mouth—them she obeys."

"But why?" Mother cries out in anguish. "It was your Fayga herself who asked me to come."

"It wasn't you, Vella, it wasn't you they were aiming at, but him"—Zalman points at me. "Fayga said he'd be coming with you, and immediately they began to scream: 'Naturally he thinks he's honoring us by coming here, but we'll show him how little ice he cuts with us.' And, though Fayga now pretends to laugh at the dreams we had long ago, she's really seething inwardly because her sons didn't turn out to be painters, but only dealers in old sacks. And it's all my fault, of course. So, are you coming with me? I give you my word of honor as a stocking-peddler that I won't discuss ideologies or spout rhymes at you."

After the splendid welcome we have just received in Zalman's house, Mother has no wish to tell me what to do. But when I do agree to accompany our former neighbor, she is clearly very pleased: she has always

maintained that often the greatest favor one person can do another is just
to be willing to listen to him.

"Where shall we go?" asks Zalman after my mother leaves. "To
Teliatnik Park or along Nowogrodzka Street? Polkowski's Courtyard
on Nowogrodzka is also a kind of park for me—" Zalman smiles a
secretive smile—"but let's go to Teliatnik."

Along the entire way from Szklanna Street and past Gaona Street,
his mouth does not close for a moment. He stops frequently to point out
buildings:

"The Gaon of Vilna conquered the world with his learning, and
Blind Avramele wished, blindness and all, to conquer the world with his
music. During the war years he used to stand right here on the street,
play his fiddle, and collect alms. When he grew up, he started performing
at parties. He took what he had earned, as well as money some charitable
ladies gave him, and went off to study with a professor. He dreamt of
becoming a great artist and no longer needing to rely on the charity of
do-gooders. 'When I hear people say how they pity me, my face turns
red with shame,' he, Avramele, used to say. I myself have heard him say,
'A pretty girl,' or 'An ugly girl.' Apparently you can get so used even to
blindness that you forget about it. Or perhaps he really didn't forget but
just wanted us to forget that he was blind, and so he talked like all the
young fellows: 'A pretty girl,' 'An ugly girl.' Since I returned from
Kreuzburg and Jakobstadt, I haven't seen him. Maybe you know what's
become of him?"

"He lives in Antokol, in a home for the blind. Once in a while I
see him in the company of other blind people. They hold each other's
hands and feel their way with their canes."

"And what's come of his playing?"

"I haven't heard."

"That means nothing's come of it," sighs Zalman gloomily. "And
over there, you see, Napoleon lived in that palace when he was on his
way to Moscow. And just so that I, Zalman the stocking-peddler, shouldn't
forget it, they've cemented a marble plaque into the wall: 'Napoleon lived
here.' Nothing came of him, either, they smashed him like a radish."
Zalman becomes more cheerful, as if drawing comfort from the thought
of Napoleon's downfall. "And here, just across the street, is Stefan Batory
University. My sons, though, were supposed to study at the Academy of
Fine Arts in Moscow. My Yudka used to say: 'In a warlord's Poland, it's
impossible for a poor boy to become an artist'—and so he went off to
Russia. And you know what?" He stops once more in the middle of the
street. "I don't turn a hair about my Yudka slaving away in Russia, in
a coal mine or wherever. I don't turn a hair about him! If he dreamt of
becoming a painter, he should have managed to achieve it. If I myself

had achieved something, I would now feel pity for those who failed. But since I myself have remained a good-for-nothing, as Fayga calls me, I despise others who are failures. If you undertake something, then go ahead and show you can do it."

Zalman bites his lips. His hands tremble and flutter, as if trying to escape from him, to fly off by themselves.

"Do you ever go to the Grand Synagogue to hear the cantor?" he asks suddenly with a wild fury and, without waiting for an answer, he shouts, "I never go. I don't want to hear him. Let him come hear me!"

"But you can't sing."

"So who needs it!" he shouts still louder. "If he can sing, let him rejoice, not me. I must congratulate the cantor, I must applaud the actor, I must doff my hat to the writer puffed up with his own importance, but who will make way for me? Who will congratulate me, who will applaud me, doff his hat to me? When I peddle my stockings in the streets and sing my songs, at least I know that people hear me, even though they laugh at me. You'll probably say that I'm willing to act the buffoon just so people will pay attention to me. So go ahead and say it. I don't care."

WE HAVE ARRIVED at one of the broad promenades in the City Park. Zalman sits down on a bench and looks across to a bench on the other side where a young couple are seated. The woman has one hand on her husband's knee; with the other, she rocks a baby carriage to and fro. The child inside sits propped up with pillows; he stretches out his soft round hands with their pink little fingers and tries to catch hold of the mother's nose or her cheeks. Just as he is about to do so, the carriage rolls backward. The child claps his hands and laughs, the mother is delighted.

"That's the life!" Zalman points at the group with his finger. "But when the child grows up, and the carriage begins to roll backward, and the smiling mother is no longer sitting there, then he won't laugh anymore, but will cry and gnash his teeth."

An elderly woman—wearing a small hat, her head half-hidden by the fur collar of her long coat as though it were the midst of winter—strolls by slowly and wearily. Behind her comes her husband, dressed in black. He wears a black fedora, carries a cane, and walks slowly, as though he were guarding his frail, aged wife. Zalman gazes after them and mumbles, more to himself than to me, "Fayga is right, after all. To this very day she throws it up to me that when we were first married, I used to leave her home alone to take care of Yudka and come here to the park to engage in debates. I didn't go anywhere with her then, and now she won't go anywhere with me. That young couple over there, with the baby—you'll see, they'll be walking together in their old age too, like the old couple who just went by."

"Zalman, you're torturing yourself for nothing," I say to him, seeing the sorrow that literally drips from his beard. "I don't know anyone who would say he has achieved all he once wanted, yet people don't consider themselves failures. Nor do I see that you've lost out on such great happiness just because you haven't become an actor or a writer, in other words, because your work hasn't appeared in print."

"I can't even print what others write," he laments abjectly, staring gloomily into the distance. "When I was a typesetter, my fellow-workers called me 'cripple.' And do you think that I was even a real revolutionary?" He turns abruptly to me, once again aflame with fury. "Fayga doesn't know yet what sort of hero I was before she married me. If she had known, she would have spat in my face already then, thirty years ago. You might as well hear the whole story, and after you've heard it you'll understand why I love myself like a pain in the eye. I won't even ask you not to repeat it to Fayga or my children. If you want them to laugh at me, go ahead and tell them.

"I was then a young fellow, an Ess-Dek, with long hair, and I always walked around with a book under my arm. To make a long story short—" He begins to shout and wave his arms about, as though trying to hurry an annoying bore who is pestering him with some long-drawn-out tale. "Once I walked into the shop of a Turkish baker to buy a roll. On the floor I notice something glittering—a silver ten-kopeck piece. So the question is: what should a proper Ess-Dek do if he sees a ten-kopeck piece on the floor? What should a 'world-liberator,' as my sons call me, have done? I'll tell you what I did: I covered it with my foot. But the baker notices this. So he comes out from behind the counter, bends down next to me, and tells me to lift my foot. I pretend not to understand— in other words, I don't know what he's talking about—and I step aside. He picks up the coin and looks at me with a caustic smile. Ordinarily, he would probably have just spat at me and chased me out of the shop. But then he sees that my hair is long and I have a book under my arm— that is, that I am one of the intelligentsia who want to overthrow the Czar and take his, the Turk's, bakery away from him. And so he decides to teach me a lesson, to show me what a worm I am. He stations himself at the door, doesn't let me leave, and yells for a policeman. The policeman comes in, listens, looks at me, and bursts out laughing. The same thing again: If it hadn't been for my long hair and the book under my arm, he would probably have given me a kick in the rear and a 'poshol von.'* But there I was, a member of the intelligentsia. . . . To make the story

---

* Out with you (Russian).

short—they threw me into a hole of a cell, together with drunks and pickpockets and bagel-snatchers. I was stuck there a whole week, and then they kicked me out. All the time I was there, I lived in dread of some political prisoner stumbling in and starting to question me about what heroic deeds had gotten me arrested, what high official I'd tried to throw a bomb at. . . . You're laughing? Well, it's true, I am a louse."

"Please don't be angry—" I cannot contain my laughter—"but it is a funny story. And why, indeed, did you put your foot over the coin?"

"Don't ask me, don't ask me." He becomes agitated. "I said, didn't I, that I'd tell you a story which would explain why I love myself like a pain in the eye. I could give you an 'intellectual' explanation, of course. I could tell you I was wrestling with my fate, that I was fighting—" He is mimicking himself, just as his wife often mimics him. "Even before I met Fayga, I already knew I was good for nothing. During discussions the others would outshout me, on stage they laughed at me, in the print shop everything slipped out of my hands. So I wanted to see whether there was anything at which I could succeed: here, I'll pick up the ten-kopeck piece and the owner won't notice; afterwards I would have returned the ten kopecks to him—that's what I might tell you. But I won't tell you that, even though there may be some measure of truth in it. The whole truth is that I'm a paltry, catch-kopeck soul. For me, as far back as I can remember, a kopeck has always been a treasure. I've always yearned to escape from my vile nature, but how can you crawl out of your own skin? And because I was an Ess-Dek, that is, a materialist, I used to comfort myself: Economics, it's all economics. Social conditions make a man what he is. After all, I grew up among herring-sellers and always had to 'sweat green worms' to earn a groschen. So I put my foot there because I wanted the ten kopecks. That's the real truth. I had a beggar's soul even then, in the good times, and now I'm a right and proper beggar, complete with beard."

"I don't see the point," I object, trying to calm him, "of your tearing yourself down this way. Forgive me for saying so, but it's a perverse kind of self-indulgence to flog oneself like this till the blood flows. You're searching for more faults in yourself so as to despise yourself even more. Here you are, running around day and night selling stockings, and yet you call yourself a beggar."

"Yes, a beggar!" Zalman jumps up from the bench. "And an impudent beggar, at that. Don't think I want to be a goody-goody, ever-so-pious beggar with tear-filled eyes, and that that's why now I'm making this breast-beating confession of my sins. And I'm not, either, one of those who like to reveal their swinish deeds and who think that the mere fact of openly admitting them excuses them, and that they even deserve admiration for their courage. But even such open-hearted swine, who will freely tell you all about their sins, won't admit their cowardice and misery as I'm doing. I'm not bragging about it, you might as well brag about a hernia in the groin. But for once in my life I want to be—myself! Without the pose and pretense of a street jester. Now I'll tell you something that will make you clearly understand who and what I am. . . .

"Recently I was standing on a certain street, selling stockings. Around me there's a crowd, shoving, laughing. For every frump who buys a pair of stockings I immediately make up a rhyme to go with her name, and spout my witticisms. I get so excited that I let go of my basket and begin to perform a song-and-dance, just like last week near your mother's gate. It's not for nothing that Fayga says Mottele inherited his dancing from me.

"When the performance is over, I look around—the basket's gone. My first thought is that some street urchin is playing a trick for the fun of it. I begin to search—it's gone, gone like yesterday! I scream for help, but the crowd only laughs louder, they whinny like horses. The clods think my calling for help is part of the show. I start tearing my hair. Now the crowd grows quiet; they begin to move away. So I scream at them: 'Don't leave! I sang and danced for you!' You hear? I bargained with them, because I'd sung and danced for them without charge. 'I can't afford to take the loss,' I moan. 'That basket is everything I own,' I cry. 'Take up a collection! Take up a collection for me!' Those were my very words: 'Take up a collection for me!' And they did take up a collection— everyone contributed. Ever since then I've avoided that street. The truth is that without that basket of merchandise I'd have had to throw myself into the Wilja. And most of all, I was afraid of Fayga and my sons finding out about this. They drag me through the mud as it is, for my singing and prancing in the streets. Can you imagine the sort of reception I'd have got if I'd come home without my basket and told them how some crook had robbed me? But if I didn't have the soul of a beggar, could I have started yelling in public that people should take up a collection for me? That's why I call myself a true beggar with a beard. . . .

"And yet, that's not what I really wanted to tell you. I wanted you to go with me to Nowogrodzka Street, to Polkowski's Courtyard. That's where my second Teliatnik Park lies buried—my second youth, you might say. After we left your courtyard, we moved again and again, from one house to another—but the only one I remember is the one on Nowogrodzka Street. What took place there is what I really want to tell you. Everything till now has been only the prologue, as they say in novels. Now the real story begins."

IV

THE YOUNG COUPLE across the way rise from the bench. Father and mother together push their baby carriage before them and leave the park. Zalman looks at the now empty bench with clouded eyes, as though his heart, too, has grown emptier. He draws his head down between his shoulders and in the gathering dusk his great beard seems even longer, as if it too were growing along with the shadows of the chestnut trees.

"So far you've heard only the prologue. Now I'll tell you about a love of mine." He breaks out into wild laughter, like a madman gibbering at passers-by from behind a barred hospital window. "When we were living in Polkowski's Courtyard, we sublet one of our rooms to a young couple. The entrance to their room was right off the hallway. The husband was short, like me, but he was a good provider—a bookkeeper. His wife, her name was Olga, was two heads taller than he, a blonde with light-blue eyes, a long marble neck, and slender hands, like the necks of swans, as they write in the poetry books—a real fairy-tale princess. For days on end she sat in her palace with its spacious garden—that is, in a rear room on Nowogrodzka Street, the home of thieves, dog-catchers, carcass-skinners, and just plain riffraff. Every evening the forest brigand who held her prisoner, that is, her husband the bookkeeper, came home with a sack full of booty; he was loaded down with parcels. Then he would set about preparing dinner with his own hands for his princess.

"At that time Fayga and I were quarreling even more than usual. This was not long after Yudka had left for Russia. We heard nothing from him, and she screamed that he'd left home because of me. By day and by night a cauldron seethed in our home, but the room where our tenants lived was always quiet—a graveyard.

"Both Fayga and I realized that the young wife did not love her husband. So we began to include them in our quarrels, though quietly, lest they hear us. Fayga insisted that the beautiful blonde would soon dispose of her little rooster of a husband, like a sacrificial Yom Kippur chicken. 'Not everyone is a kosher cow like me,' she would argue, 'not everyone is willing to go through life blindfolded.' But then I would say, 'Don't worry, the blonde will warm up to him. Tall women like short husbands who are good providers.'

"Once, when I was home alone, Olga came into our room. She was wearing a loose house-robe, her unbound hair fell down to her shoulders, and her eyes were filled with fear, like a child's. She seemed to me like someone just emerged from the sea, as the poets sing, so bursting with life was her full, white-fleshed body. Her slender hands glowed with such radiance that my eyes were blinded. She asked me whether I had any book she might read. It occurred to me that the captive princess must like poetry. I gave her a small, tattered volume, the poems of Lermontov. She stretched out her hand for the book with such joy, as if it could rescue her from her boredom, her melancholy, and all her troubles.

"I had once read a story about a lone-wolf—a crusty old bachelor. He falls in love with a woman who lives in an apartment facing his, but she never has any inkling that the man with the sunken cheeks who is always staring out his window might be in love with her. Now I became just such an imbecile. And so, just in case a dwarfish husband wasn't enough for our neighbor, she now had another suitor, the good-for-nothing Zalman Press, who already had three children and a wife who cursed him ten times a day. It was Olga's good fortune—or rather, mine—that she had no idea I was so infatuated with her.

"I began to hate her husband, the midget who was such a good breadwinner. I suspected that he had intentionally hidden his wife away in an unfamiliar neighborhood, among the poorest of the poor, so as to make sure there'd be no competitors to snatch his treasure away from him. Then I hated him even more for his placidity. He can't even chain her to him through his suffering, since he doesn't suffer, I thought. He's just waiting patiently until she becomes entirely dependent upon him, until she despairs and surrenders.

"I borrowed several more books of poetry from a library, and also began once more to write short poems, lyrical ones, of course. In my writing I did not lay my cards on the table, but only sighed and moaned with innuendoes, signaling to her with my moist little eyes. So as to appear like a real writer, I wrote my compositions down on paper. I arranged to be at home when no one else was there, and waited for her to reappear. But she never came out of her room. One day I got dressed up with the same wide black bow-tie I'm wearing today in your honor, and knocked on her door.

"She came out and looked at me in surprise. I began to mumble, to stammer: Had she finished reading Lermontov's poems, and would she perhaps like some other books of poetry, of heavenly songs? She smiled and went into our chicken-coop with me. She did not invite me into her own room.

"We began to converse as though in a salon. No, says my lady, she hasn't yet finished Lermontov. That is, she explains, she is already familiar with the poems, and is now renewing acquaintance with them. But that is just why she cannot now begin to read another poet—for, while it is possible to sympathize with the sufferings of many people, one can live with and love only one. Lermontov, the man of genius, she tells me, was a spoiled child with an overweening pride that devoured him altogether. He cursed with bitterness and gall the women who left him, and prophesied that they would never be able to forget him. He never understood that even at the moment they broke away from him, it was very difficult for them to leave him, but they had no alternative. . . . That is how she speaks to me, and the thought comes to me that my lady, too, must have her Lermontov, her 'krassavetz molodoy'*—some poor student or other lowlife who has stolen his way into her heart and of whom she still dreams.

"Now that, besides her husband, there is still another rival, and one whom she really does love, I say to myself: 'Watch out, Zalman Press, or you'll give yourself away with a careless word. Then she'll realize you're infatuated with her and will be deathly insulted by your presumption. Don't show her your poems. She'll burst out laughing at the thought that you, too, want to be—a Lermontov.'

" 'Of course,' I say to her, 'it wasn't very nice of Lermontov to refuse to understand that his countesses had no other choice. However, these young Russian women were willing to forgive his egotism, and not only because he was a genius. The beautiful princesses left Lermontov the officer for princes and generals, and therefore the romantic young women who read his books sympathized with him. But if his beloved had left him for a printer, let's say, or for an unsuccessful actor or an unfulfilled writer—that, for Lermontov, would have been not only a source of pain but also a disgrace. Then those same young ladies, his readers, would have smiled in mockery at their great poet. If men without distinction, without rank or money, had been able to pluck out the genius's mustache and steal away his noblewomen from under his nose, he would have been a comic rather than a tragic figure. But Lermontov suffered beautifully, and so it was fitting for young lady intellectuals or generals' wives to suffer with him. He sat in an arbor, his handsome head resting sorrowfully upon his hand, as if posing for a picture postcard. In an arbor, mind you—not on a torn sofa in a room whose windows look out upon a garbage heap. He stood upon the mountains of the Caucasus, a lonely, despondent demon, and looked down upon lakes and towers and ancient monasteries. Had he described, instead, how he stood upon the hill of Nowogrodzka and looked down upon the Wood Market, with its mud puddles and its slatterns, would the young women,' I asked Olga, 'also have read him with such delight and been so enthusiastic about his suffering? More than once he sings that, to forget his disillusionment, he will mount his horse and ride headlong into battle, sword unsheathed in his outstretched hand. But who would sympathize with a great hero who, instead of warring against the wild tribes of the Caucasus, battles with his own wife? Such a fellow arouses nobody's sympathy.'

---

* Beautiful young man (Russian).

"This is the way I hold forth to her, and I see she's smiling. She realizes I'm trying to ingratiate myself with hints at my own sorrows. I put on coquettish airs, like a woman long past her prime who can no longer persuade the world that she is young, and so constantly reminds people of her age to show that she has given up all pretenses. And yet— perhaps there will still be one chivalrous gentleman who will categorically deny that she looks like a great-grandmother. . . . My neighbor, however, doesn't deny that she hears the quarreling between me and Fayga. She begins to speak soberly and calmly, not at all like a dreamy-eyed captive princess.

"She knows, she says, of something much worse than quarreling: when there are no arguments at all, when husband and wife are always silent—not together, but each one apart. And not because they are angry at each other but because one of them—let us say, the woman—cannot and will not pretend to her husband that she loves him. The husband finds that he shares a room—not with a woman, but with an iceberg that blinds the eyes with its whiteness but is cold and silent, silent and cold. So the husband, too, grows silent and swallows the ice. 'He swallows his wife's silence,' says the cold blonde angel in the house-robe; she looks sharply at me, and I see that it was not for nothing that she reads Lermontov.

" 'Is there no possibility that later, perhaps years later, there will come a time when the ice will begin to melt?' I ask.

" 'No,' she answers sternly. 'The woman can't change, even if she wants to. She can't respect a man with so little pride that he marries a woman who tells him, day in and day out, that she doesn't love him. She cannot forgive him the foolish self-deception that's let him convince himself that she will gradually get used to him. Earlier, you said—' she turned to me—'that refined young women delighted in Lermontov because he suffered beautifully. But the person who is actually suffering feels the pain of ugly woes as much as beautiful ones—even more when they aren't beautiful!' she cries, and runs quickly back to her own room.

"What she meant was that her suffering was caused by a bookkeeper, and not by a highwayman or a count or a knight who is holding her captive.

"As for myself, both heart and mind were turning over within me. I no longer hated her husband. From her words about the husband who swallows his wife's silence like ice, I understood what agonies he was suffering. And yet, despite this, my infatuation grew even stronger, just because of her iron, unyielding character. At the same time, I desperately wanted her husband to overcome her. I wanted it out of pity for him and for my own sake, too. I longed to see a downtrodden, insignificant little man, just like myself, winning out over the unseen handsome lover who lorded it over her heart.

"Even though Olga claimed she envied me and Fayga for our quarrels, now for the first time in my life I pleaded with Fayga that we stop tearing each other apart. I burned with shame at the thought that she, in her room, might hear how we insulted each other—and envy us . . . I lived in fear that Fayga might become too friendly with our neighbor and tell her I'm a hemorrhoidnik, a buffoon, a 'payet,' a Social Democrat. Till now these epithets had bothered me about as much as last year's snow, but now I felt them clinging to me like rags. I began to try to ingratiate myself with Fayga, and to preen myself before the mirror. Fayga noticed that even on ordinary weekdays I took pains to comb my hair, carefully tied my bow-tie, and walked around the room with measured holiday steps. This made her furious, and she began to sputter like fat on a fire. There had been no letter from Yudka, and yet here I was playing the dandy, like a young man a-courting. 'Who is there here you want to impress?' she screamed. Fortunately for me, Fayga was not as insane as I, so it never once occurred to her for whose sake I might be preening myself. But I began to quake with fear, and the dread ate into my very bones; I began to pray to God that our tenants would move away as soon as possible, before I ended up an object of public ridicule.

"And, indeed, the princess now began to go out—often for the whole day. I would watch her husband come home at night, burdened with packages, and stand there as though paralyzed. She would return late in the evening, and even from behind the wall I could hear their silence. The stillness penetrated the walls of their room and covered me, too, with ice. Once I waited for our tenant in the courtyard and told him without ceremony to move out: 'My wife and I set a bad example for a young couple, especially when their life together is not entirely smooth.' He showed no surprise at my speaking to him so openly. And he told me that he had moved in with us because he was ashamed to live among people who knew him; he did not want them to see what was going on in his private life. When I heard this, I felt like slapping myself for ever suspecting him of hiding with us just so no one would steal his treasure from him. He told me that her parents were dead. They had been wealthy—had owned estates in Russia—but had fled when the Bolsheviks seized power. It struck me then just how much it had cost this ordinary young man of Vilna to go crawling after his Russian countess. He looked totally played out, his voice was lifeless, he sighed so heavily that I couldn't help but see the truth: he deeply regretted having ever persuaded himself that Olga would learn to love him, and he was praying to God that she would leave him.

"But Olga didn't leave him. She stopped going out and again spent days on end in their room, from which one heard neither laughter nor any other sound. A graveyard. I for one had not the least doubt that when she'd been running about, she had been meeting her Lermontov— and that this fine hero of hers, the blackguard, now had another woman, or else had simply told her he no longer loved her. In short, in short—" Zalman begins to shout through the darkness of the park, as though realizing at last that his tale has already stretched out too long— "one evening when I came home, I saw a crowd of people around the steps of our house. At once I thought that something terrible must have happened to Fayga or our children, and I began to scream. People spoke up to calm me down: 'It's not your family, it's not your family—your neighbor hanged herself. . . .' When I ran up to our apartment she was already lying on the sofa, covered with her robe. Her long hair hung down and dragged on the floor. Her husband had found her hanging in their room. Now he was standing over her and sobbing: 'Why did you do it? Why did you do it? Why didn't you simply leave me?' And the neighbors who had run in were dividing up the rope. A suicide's rope brings good luck."

Zalman is silent for a moment. Suddenly he begins to weep with a thin, drawn-out, choking sound, as though he has been abruptly transformed into Olga's husband as he stood and made his protest to the dead woman. Zalman's slight frame is convulsed by his sobs, and he speaks hurriedly, hurriedly, as though trying to overtake the tears streaming from his eyes:

"You see now how fate has always brought me together with people who are failures. My heart weeps not so much for her death as for her life. Her death proved how much she wanted to leave her husband but couldn't. But how could she not have taken pity on her long, wheat-colored hair, on her blue eyes, on her full body like a slab of alabaster, on her long marble neck, on her slender white hands? How can one be so merciless towards one's own beauty and youth? . . .

"Her husband disappeared after the funeral. I'm certain he's still wandering through the world and can't even remember his own name. He was such a dried-out little creature, no spark of vitality in him, and if a person can't be philosophical about his misfortunes, he must grow dull and withered. I, too, found I could no longer live in the apartment where Olga had hanged herself. The quarrels with Fayga became even fiercer, and so I took off and went back to my family in Latvia. But you know, no matter how much Fayga and I may fight, neither of us will ever mention that incident. Fayga had said that the blonde woman would eventually leave her husband, I had said she would never leave him—in the end we were both right. And today you were disgusted by my fighting with my family. What you don't understand is that if I were to be silent as she was silent, then I, too, would have to hang myself."

Amid the dark-green leaves of the treetops the electric lamps glow starkly, like the whites of enormous sightless eyes—as if the blonde woman were peering out from behind the trees and listening to Zalman talk about her. Huddled inside his clothes, Zalman shivers from the cold; his beard smells of dampness, like a rain-soaked tree in autumn.

"I love you, Zalman—" I put my arm around his shoulders—"and yet you've convinced yourself that you disgust me. I remember very well how you used to spend time with me when I was a boy. You treated me like one of your own children—except in one respect: you didn't want me to learn the secret of painting from your sons. Every Sabbath afternoon you took me along on your walks in the Zakret Forest and to the 'Forest Shacks.' Along the way you always stopped to look at the shop windows and explained to me the things displayed in them."

"Yes," he says, nodding in agreement. "I've always had to content myself with looking at the world through a window." He gets up to leave.

"Where are you going?"

"To the Synagogue Courtyard. Don't imagine I've become devout. It's just so comforting to sit next to the oven in the study-house, among beggars who tell idle tales and jostle each other with their elbows. Oh, how good it is to sit among your fellow paupers and scratch yourself! I don't need to pretend I'm a saint, a lamed-vovnik. I belong among these misfits; there, in fact, I'm a person of distinction—not a word now! When they want to collect ten men for a minyan, I'm just as great a personage as the Chief Rabbi or a Gabbai of the Grand Synagogue. Even standing on their heads, they couldn't put a minyan together without me."

He rushes off, but I catch up with him.

"I'll go with you."

"No. If I'm to be a beggar, let me be a true beggar. If you come with me, I won't be able to forget that once upon a time my name was Zalman Press."

He feels for his black bow-tie, hurriedly unties it, pulls it off his neck, and disappears among the trees.

A Second Marriage

NEAR DUSK on a Sabbath toward the end of summer, as I enter my mother's home on a visit, she abruptly informs me that she will be going under the wedding canopy with Reb Refoel Rosenthal, a widower who keeps a greengrocer's shop in a basement on Broad Street.

Her news delivered, she lowers her head and is silent. Dumfounded, I too sit without speaking, until at long last I stammer:

"Do you really know him?"

"Of course I know him," she answers slowly. "That is, I haven't talked with him very much, but we've taken a good look at each other. I don't know whether he ever talks much even to his own married children. He's by nature a silent person, every word 'weighed out like a gold ducat'—but the matchmaker says he's a very fine man."

"It seems to me, Mother, that you once liked Reb Mayer the egg-peddler very much."

"Why must you remind me whom I used to like once?" She looks at me in surprise, as though she would never have expected me even to remember the egg-peddler. "Let's say I really did like him, does that mean I'd let myself become involved in such things? Even when I married your father, I was no wild young goat. Oh, what a handsome man your father was!" Her face suddenly glows. "He was already a widower and the father of several children, but he still looked splendid as a prince! His beard was pitch-black, his eyes large and wise. During the time our marriage prospects were being discussed, a time of bitter cold, he would come to see me on Friday evenings dressed in a fur-lined coat with a big fur collar. When I was single, I kept a little shop on the Nowy Świat . . . and my life was always dark and bitter," she concludes unexpectedly, her face abruptly drained of life.

She is silent for a while and then, in deeply hurt tones, she adds:

"You shouldn't have reminded me of Reb Mayer."

"I didn't just bring him up for no reason. All I meant was that if you'd married Reb Mayer, I could have understood it. After all, you did like him. But now . . ."

"What did you think?" she interrupted angrily. "Did you expect Reb Mayer to just sit around and wait for me? When he wanted to get married, I didn't want to. I didn't want to set up the canopy for myself as long as you weren't married, I didn't want you to have to live in one house with a stepfather. Well, Reb Mayer found somebody better than me. . . . Truth to tell," she adds pensively, "Reb Refoel may not be as much of a scholar as Reb Mayer, or as cheerful, but he's a very fine and decent man. And how much longer should I continue to struggle alone with my baskets? You're married now, and living in your own home with your wife, and I can't expect you to be at the gate every day just when I need you."

"Mama, I've begged you so often to move in with us. We could all live together."

"I won't even consider it," she answers sharply. "You're letting your tongue run away with you—move in with you, indeed. And your kitchen: is it kosher? Your wife, you see, is a lot smarter than you are. When I come to visit you, she doesn't serve me a thing except tea and cookies. And I don't know, either, how you observe or don't observe the Sabbath. Well, there's no use talking about it. But since you don't ask me how you should live your life, don't, then, try to tell me what I should do. I want to make things a little easier for myself now."

"I don't see how it's going to be any easier for you. You'll be living on Broad Street and you'll have to come running here to the gate every morning. Surely you're not going to give up your stand at the gate?"

"What is the gate to me, a god? After I marry Reb Refoel, I'll work together with him in his basement shop. . . . You're still a child!" she suddenly cries out. "When you were little, you caused me no end of trouble, so now you want to make up for it with all this concern for me. You've even gotten into the habit of kissing and caressing me in front of Frumme-Liebche. I'm not saying, God forbid, that it annoys her, but she's got a right to be annoyed. God have mercy on you if you do it again—you don't even notice how she blushes every time. She's the sweetest person in the world, but she too tends to keep things to herself, she's a silent one like her brother Moshele, may he grow like a cedar tree over there in the Land of Israel. Every time you start up with your 'Mama, come to live with us,' she looks down at the floor. She knows that your words have no real meaning. You yourselves live in a room that you've sublet from someone else. But even if your home were a palace, I wouldn't come live with you. I don't want to be dependent in any way on my children!" she cries in great agitation.

In my heart I know that Mother is right; I am ashamed to admit to myself that I simply don't want to see my mother giving her love and loyalty to a total stranger, and such an extremely taciturn one to boot.

"We'll be married in a small town not far from here," she says, speaking more calmly. "For older people like us, it's more fitting to do it without a fuss. We've already set the time and place."

"You have? But I'd like to get to know him."

"Why do you suddenly want to get to know him?" She laughs softly. "I didn't express any opinions about your choice; don't you go giving me your advice now. It's not even proper for you to get involved. You should keep your distance until after the wedding. Later, if it be God's will, you and your wife will come to visit. But there is one thing you must do: You must take the little bookcase with your father's books to your house." Her tone is once again grave and stern. "Your father, peace be upon him, will be offended if his books are anywhere else but in the home of his son."

From her long lashes hang golden teardrops, which seem to contain within them the last, lost rays of the sinking Sabbath sun. Her pale face glows in the deepening darkness as, with the fall of dusk, the sacred whiteness of a tall and slender memorial candle glows unlit from the cantor's lectern in the synagogue.

AFTER THE WEDDING, Mother moved her belongings bit by bit into Reb Refoel's house. Watching this, Lisa, widow of Alterka the goose-dealer, gave vent to a deep sigh:

"As long as you were living across the way from me, I didn't feel that I was sleeping alone in my house. What will happen now? Who knows how long your apartment will remain empty, or who will move in in your place?"

"No one could be such a bitter enemy of mine that I'd wish on him my little room behind the smithy," replies my mother. "As for yourself, Lisa, you should take in some quiet woman to live with you; then you won't feel so lonely at night. That's one reason why I got married—I could no longer bear to be alone at night."

Even Shaya the grain merchant, who has lately had more than his usual share of worries, shakes his head sadly as he watches my mother walking down the street with two bundles; he turns to Hatzkel the grocer:

"Here today, there tomorrow. That's life for you. We move from one dwelling to the other, until at last we reach our eternal dwelling-place. There you never have to worry again about finding the money to pay the rent. And why are you looking so down in the mouth, Reb Hatzkel?"

"They say," answers the latter, eyes filled with fear, "that that Haman in Berlin has been yelping again over the radio: 'The Jews!' . . . It gives me the cold shivers."

"We hang by a hair, Reb Hatzkel. War could break out any day now—may God have mercy upon us."

To transfer to her new home all the poverty she has accumulated over so many years, Mother has to go back and forth several times a day. Reb Shaya, deeply despondent as he is, yet manages to keep an eye out to see whether Reb Refoel Rosenthal will come to help her. But Reb Refoel does not appear.

"That husband of hers gives himself the airs of a great lord. It's not for nothing he has such an imposing name: Reb Refoel Rosenthal."

"It seems to me that Vella has exchanged a good shoe for a wooden clog," says Ḥatzkel.

At last there appears on our street one day a broad-shouldered man of medium height, wearing a peaked cloth cap. Hands shoved inside his sleeves, he walks slowly, ever so slowly, and my mother walks behind him. All the shopkeepers stick their heads out their doors.

"He looks to me like one of those people whose age you can never tell," says Shaya.

"I don't understand why Vella walks with her head bowed so low," says Ḥatzkel disapprovingly. "What does she have to be ashamed of? She's slaved hard enough all her life."

"They say he's a silent one," says Shaya, pursuing his own train of thought. "Some people are silent out of great piety, but others because they're tough nuts, or because they want to seem simple-minded—one can never tell for sure."

And the two shopkeepers draw their heads back into their stores.

Just as my mother and Reb Refoel are leaving the courtyard, both laden with baskets full of household goods, they are greeted at the gate by the landlord, Reb Nossen-Nota the Gabbai. Smoothing his long, well-curled beard, he begins to speak to them with great earnestness. Actually he addresses the empty space between my mother and her husband, for he is not yet sure which of them is the decision-maker.

"No doubt," he says, "the smithy is no apartment and the gate is no shop." But what then? Vella still has old debts to him outstanding, for both the stand at the gate and the apartment. It would be only right, therefore, that she settle accounts with him. He won't say how much, but at least fifty zlotys . . . well, let it be forty . . . or, to make an end of it, once and for all, thirty-five. But not one groschen less! The remainder he is ready to forgive and forget, right then and there.

Mother is speechless with shame. Reb Refoel, however, unhurriedly sets down his bundles, tucks his hands inside his sleeves, and smiles with half-closed eyes.

"What do you want of Reb Refoel?" says Mother, her face flaming. "I'm the one who owes you the money and I shall, with God's help, pay my debt."

"If you didn't pay until now," retorts the landlord with suppressed fury, "then later, when you've taken away all your belongings, you surely won't pay." He turns abruptly to Reb Refoel. "The way I see it, no respectable man will want his wife indebted to anyone."

"Hmmm." Reb Refoel nods his head, evidently in agreement.

The landlord knows Reb Refoel Rosenthal and knows that one can rely on his word. As yet, however, Reb Refoel hasn't actually said anything. . . . And so Reb Nossen-Nota asks once more:

"Do you mean to say that you will pay?"

"Hmm." Again Reb Refoel nods his head.

"May God help me from this day forward as surely as I shall pay you to the last groschen," pleads my mother with tears in her eyes and her lips dry. "I'll get the money from my son and pay you. I'm not, after all, running away. I still have to come back several times to fetch the rest of my belongings. I'll pay you then."

Reb Refoel—who has been standing throughout this conversation with face turned skyward and eyes half closed, as though warming himself in the sunshine—turns to my mother and at long last utters a few words:

"Well, so be it." He shrugs his shoulders as if to say: If you insist on paying by yourself, I won't argue. But if you find that you can't, you don't need to get upset either. In that case, I'll settle the account.

On the palm of his hand Reb Nossen-Nota weighs a lock of his long, smoothly curled beard, as if weighing his own thoughts: He would prefer to have Reb Refoel take the debt upon himself. The fruit-seller's son might not have the money, or might have it but not want to pay. Since becoming an unbeliever, he has become impudent as well, and has even insulted him—him, Reb Nossen-Nota! On the other hand, he knows that Vella is an honest woman; she will not swear falsely, and it would shame her before her husband, besides, if she failed to keep her word. . . . Reb Nossen-Nota remains uncertain how best to deal with this situation.

Reb Refoel bends down, picks up his bundles, and walks off. Mother eyes the landlord with great trepidation: will he let her pass? But Reb Nossen-Nota is still at a loss as to what to do. And so Mother sets off after her husband. She now walks no longer with her eyes fixed on the ground, as before, but with face aglow, thinking to herself that Reb Refoel is indeed the soul of goodness and kindness—even if also a little odd.

MOTHER IS EVEN MORE ASTONISHED by the manner in which Reb Refoel conducts his business and sells his wares.

On her first night in her new home, she falls asleep, exhausted from carrying bundles all day long. Reb Refoel stands motionless at the window and recites the evening prayers. In the morning, when she opens her eyes, she finds him still standing at the barred window, as if he hasn't lain down at all, and under his peaked cloth cap she can see the head-piece of his phylacteries. He does not sway back and forth, barely moves his lips, and looks as though frozen stiff by the cold. After breakfast he takes a key off a hook on the wall and goes off to his cellar shop, directly adjacent to the courtyard where he lives.

Mother follows him, puzzled: why isn't he going to the market to buy merchandise?

When they get to the shop, she sees that there isn't much merchandise, and what there is is all thrown together in one pile—vegetables and fruit, fresh produce and withered. A garbage dump, God forbid she should say it aloud. Beginning with the furthermost shelf, she starts to sort the goods out, while Reb Refoel remains standing on the steps that lead down to the basement, gazing back out into the street. Doesn't he go to the market at all, for vegetables, for fruit? she cannot stop wondering. But she does not say a word, as though she too is now enmeshed in his silence.

Some time later, a woman porter arrives with two full baskets. Still panting, she begins to transfer the merchandise into Reb Refoel's baskets, talking all the while:

"The wholesaler sent you only the choicest and most beautiful of his wares. Whosoever finds grace in the eyes of men finds grace also in the eyes of God, so I have heard people say. The peddler women pushed and jostled to get close to the sacks, but the wholesaler yelled: 'Don't touch that—it's for Reb Refoel Rosenthal.' I cut open a radish, but it wasn't a radish—it was a slice of prime meat. The potatoes melt in your mouth—that's how juicy they are. The wholesaler won't send any dry, starchy stuff, not to Reb Refoel."

Reb Refoel glances at the merchandise, nods, and turns his gaze once again to the street.

"And when the wholesaler sends you onions, they're straight from onion-land—none with green beards, nor too large, nor dried up." All this while, the porter has never once taken her eyes off my mother, still busying herself in the furthest corner of the cellar.

Reb Refoel gives the woman a coin. She is obviously very pleased with the tip.

"May you have great success," she says wholeheartedly, and it is not clear whether she is wishing him success in selling his wares or congratulating him upon his marriage.

As soon as the porter has left, a customer arrives and begins to pick over the just-delivered radishes. She is obviously disappointed:

"They're tough, they're wood!"

Reb Refoel's only response is a shrug, signifying, more or less: "What do I know? Don't buy."

The customer is apparently used to his ways, but she notices that the stranger now bustling about the shop as though she owns it is looking at him with some astonishment. She turns to Reb Refoel:

"Is this your wife?" And then she speaks sternly to my mother:

"You shouldn't be surprised. It's not for nothing that people come to Reb Refoel—everyone knows he'll never try to cheat anyone. You seem to be new to this business."

"Actually, I'm not new at all to this business." Mother balances in her hand a large radish with a hard, brown, wrinkled skin and many small roots. "I can't crawl inside the radish to inspect it, but I don't think this one is wooden."

"You have a lot to learn yet," the woman says sourly, and directs a pitying look at the silent shopkeeper, as though wondering whether he has been as deceived in the choice of a wife as in the quality of his merchandise. "Where can I get a good radish?" she asks Reb Refoel, intending thereby to demonstrate to my mother how honorable a man he is, so that she might learn to follow his example. "For the Sabbath, I have to prepare a radish with chicken fat for my husband. If I don't, as far as he's concerned, the Sabbath just isn't the Sabbath."

Reb Refoel nods to indicate a point down the street, where can be seen another cellar shop with fruit and vegetable baskets out in front: there she can get what she wants.

"And how much will two kilos of carrots cost me?" the customer asks him.

Reb Refoel removes his hands from his sleeves and points a finger at my mother, meaning: Talk to her.

"So how much will that pleasure cost me?" The buyer, in a very dry tone, now puts the question to my mother.

"Fifteen groschen a kilo," Mother answers. "Everything is sky-high today."

"I'll pay twelve." The customer again addresses Reb Refoel.

With a smile in his half-closed eyes, Reb Refoel points once again at my mother. Speak to her—she, she will answer you.

The woman capitulates and Mother, as she is weighing the merchandise, thinks to herself: The very soul of kindness and sensitivity! He insists on people accepting me as the mistress of the shop. Master of the Universe, may I only prove worthy of all this.

The Other End
of the World

It Has Begun

I

AFTER BARELY TWO WEEKS OF WAR with the Germans, while the devastated Polish armies were still facing west, there suddenly came up behind them, from the east, the Soviet army. The Russian vanguard crossed the border in light tanks. By evening, long rows of glossy black cars with lamplike eyes stretched along the roads. After these came heavy tanks with protruding cannon mouths, like antediluvian creatures with wide-open snouts full of shiny sawteeth now crawling forth upon the earth. By the next morning, hosts of infantry soldiers in gray overcoats stiff as corrugated tin were marching along every road. The soldiers' faces were weary and drained after their long march, but atop every hat shone a red star, and high above the billowing tens of thousands of heads there hovered, as in a mist, a face with the smile of a tiger and a long, black mustache. . . .

The working-class neighborhoods, the markets, and even the narrow, shop-lined streets looked festive. People ran to greet the troops with open arms; some even wept with joy: If not for the Soviets, we would surely have fallen into the hands of the Germans. We have been saved!

On Zawalna Street stood agit propagandists—young Russians of average height with thin, bony shoulders, wearing visorless caps shaped like boats, with creases down the middle. As young fellows and girls crowded around them, the propagandists spoke of the good and free life in the Soviet Union.

"We have brought you," they said, "liberation upon our Russian bayonets."

A much larger crowd had collected around the tanks. Young men stroked the cold steel as a rider might stroke the back and velvety coat of his horse which has just carried him out of danger. The tank crews, wearing "pirozhki," braided little black caps, stood beside the guns and sang Russian songs. A girl with a flushed face shouted in a high voice:

"We knew those songs long before you came. We used to listen to them on the radio, secretly, so our Polish *pans* wouldn't know. We realized that a land that can sing so gaily must be a very happy land."

"How long did the march take from the Soviet border to Vilna?"

inquired a lad in a black peasant shirt, with still blacker hair. "I mean, how long did it take you to get to us?"

"We've been on our way to you for twenty years, ever since the October Revolution," gruffly answered a blond Russian with a turned-up nose, and everyone understood the implication: Don't ask questions about military matters!

This reply spread throughout the city. "For twenty years they've been on their way to us. All those years they worked day and night, getting ready to set us free. But we here weren't asleep either. We prepared the ground," young fellows and girls triumphantly proclaimed as they sauntered arm in arm through the streets. Whenever a glossy black automobile passed by, the girls stopped and smiled—with their eyes, their mouths, their teeth—at its curtained windows. True, they didn't know exactly who was riding in the car, but they understood that the passengers must be either commissars or senior officers.

Once one of these cars stopped, and a tall man in a leather coat climbed out. After him came another, in military uniform, shorter in stature than the first, and clearly of lower rank as well. Speaking in a loud voice so those standing nearby were sure to hear, the leather-coated commissar asked the chauffeur, in tones at once good-humored and stern:

"Will our gasoline last till Bialystok?"

The chauffeur, with an air of indifference, nodded his head in assent, but the military man, with a meaningful smile, said:

"Our gasoline will last till Warsaw."

"Maybe even till Berlin!" laughed the commissar.

They said nothing more and quickly drove off. The very fact that they had said so little, and paid no attention at all to the girls staring at them in open-eyed wonder, greatly enhanced the importance ascribed to their brief conversation. It was clear that to the Soviets the new German border inside occupied Poland, or even the old East Prussian border, was no border at all! People repeated to one another the remark of a soldier:

"I'll put up the Soviet border-markers wherever they tell me to."

But on Jatkowa Street, on Szawelska and Rudnicka, narrow thoroughfares noted for their many shops, long lines were becoming very noticeable in front of all the food stores. Even more conspicuous were the long queues of Soviet soldiers at the yard-goods shops. It seemed as though the whole Russian army had lined up at these Jewish shops to buy gifts for their wives and children, from bolts of fabric and suits to hairpins and spools of thread.

.   .   .

JATKOWA STREET: Shaya the grain dealer and Ḥatzkel the grocer are chatting away. Shaya is full of admiration for the men of the Red Army, but Ḥatzkel, a shopkeeper "to his tenth rib," retorts:

"If you gave me a million, I wouldn't have a suit made today. It's all I can do to get through from day to day, until the war is over. The Reds simply don't leave the shops. How come, since they claim they have everything?"

"Of course they have everything," answers Shaya. "They have tanks, guns, gasoline, and those little birds—little birds of steel, plentiful as the sands of the sea. So they simply haven't bothered their heads about things like yard-goods and haberdashery!"

"They seem to have too much money, too many ten-ruble pieces," mutters Ḥatzkel.

Several trucks stop at the intersection of Jatkowa and Rudnicka streets, near the large textile stores. Instantly word spreads from mouth to mouth that the Soviets are confiscating merchandise.

"Now it's going to be the same story as twenty years ago," sighs Ḥatzkel despondently.

"They certainly won't be giving us any honey to lick." Shaya casts his troubled eyes down at his goatee.

Walking down the street are some half-dozen Russians in blue caps. The napes of their necks, Shaya notes, are clean-shaven, rather than trimmed in the Vilna style. He notes as well that their coats are neatly hemmed, whereas the coats of ordinary Red soldiers are unhemmed and seem to have been simply cut from a piece of cloth. The blue-capped Russians walk up to the queue of soldiers in front of a yard-goods shop and say something to a few of the men. Within the twinkling of an eye, the entire queue melts away—though they have been standing on line for hours, the soldiers walk off in silence, heads bent low. Never in all his days has the storekeeper seen or heard such a large group of soldiers dispersed so quickly, with just a word or two.

"Those are NKVD men," Shaya whispers to Ḥatzkel, and both of them shiver with gloomy forebodings.

IN THOSE LATE-AUTUMN DAYS I wandered about the parks of the city. The broad walks with their old chestnut trees had suddenly become very dear to me, those very walks where often, before the war, Polish students with thick clubs had lain in wait for Jewish passers-by.

Castle Mountain was covered, as with glowing embers, with scarlet-red, dark-brown, and saffron-yellow leaves. After several days of rain the sky had cleared, lifted itself higher, and now glowed with a translucent, sickly hue. Dejected, brimful of autumnal dampness and gloom, I roved about for long hours in the neighborhood of the Wilja and the gardens, until at last I came to Cathedral Square, near the white cathedral with its six-pillared colonnade.

The square was packed with a dense multitude of Poles, all with somber, stern faces. I pushed my way to the cathedral entrance and peered in. The long wax candles upon the altar, together with the lamps at each of the shrines, produced a rose-colored mist that hovered throughout the church. It was filled end to end with worshippers kneeling bareheaded in deep silence. Great waves of organ chords flooded the high-vaulted space, chords as solemn and mournful as a requiem mass for an unseen corpse—for Poland laid waste.

Marching down the street came a company of Red soldiers. Some stared at the crowd around the church with curiosity, some with astonishment, others smiled. The Poles just then emerging from the cathedral in great numbers stood outside with bared heads and stared after the soldiers with lips tightly clenched.

At the Bernardine Cathedral, built of red brick in Gothic style, like a web woven of sharp-pointed rays, Poles young and old knelt together on the sidewalks and in the middle of the street. Here, too, they prayed in frozen silence, their heads bent low as though the unseen corpse were hovering above them in a silver coffin.

At the little bridge that spans the Wilejka, I noticed a crowd which had collected around a tank. Its driver, a youngster with flaxen hair and pale eyes, was telling a story that evoked gleeful laughter from those around him. I walked past them to the bridge, where I halted facing the tank. Should I go over to it? Should I try to laugh and rejoice together with the others?

But I did not go over. Instead, I entered the Bernardine Gardens and sat down on a bench. The wind had shaken clumps of leaves from the trees, but their tops were still densely covered with foliage, and the trunks looked as though they were engulfed in flames. Whenever the wind died down for a time, branches trembled and groaned, like a sick man after an exhausting, fever-tossed night. I recalled a line by Julius Slowacki: *"Smutno mi, Bože!"*—"I am sad, O God!" No matter what Poland was like, in my mother's tiny room behind the smithy I could be whatever I wanted to be. Now they would not leave me alone in my room; now no one is permitted to be sad.

II

AR DOWN THE TREE-LINED WALK a man sat on a bench, his face turned toward me; from the way he was stretching his neck in my direction, it was apparent that he was trying to see who I was. Probably a drunk looking for someone to talk to, I thought, and turned away impatiently. But as it happened, I turned toward him again, and noticed his resemblance to Zalman Press the stocking-peddler, who had once sat here with me for hours and told me of his love for the blonde neighbor who later hanged herself.

I rose from my bench and walked toward him. But the closer I came to him, the more certain I felt that I was mistaken. The stocking-peddler boasted a full, curly beard, while the man on the bench had only a sparse, graying goatee.

"I recognized you right away," exclaimed the man on the bench. "Right away! But I didn't want to go over to you, in case you're afraid. These days it's healthier not to have as an old acquaintance a Social Democrat who supported the Mensheviks and not the Bolsheviks."

"I didn't recognize you." I sat down next to him. "You've cut off your long beard."

"Cut it off!" he cried gaily. "My beard wasn't a pious beard—it was a Social Democratic, a political, a 'payetic,' you might even say a Tolstoyan, beard—but not a pious one. It was my greatest ornament. But then it began to get gray and, from my sitting in the Gravediggers' Chapel every night, it became a tangled, matted clump—so I chopped it off. I don't need a Social Democratic beard that hits the Bolsheviks right between the eyes."

From his excited speech and mordant tone it is clear that he is still the same as when, after talking and reviling himself all evening, he had torn off his artist's bow-tie and rushed from the park to the Gravediggers' Chapel.

"You tell me—what do I need a 'payetic' beard for now?" He tugs at his trimmed whiskers. "There were two things I used for getting the little slatterns and housewives to buy stockings: my beard and my poems. Now that I no longer sell stockings, I need neither the beard nor the poems."

"You don't sell stockings any more?"

"I'm through selling!" He laughs. "You can't buy stockings anywhere. As soon as the Bolsheviks, our liberators, arrived, I went out into the streets with my stock-in-trade. They bought up everything: women's stockings, men's socks, children's anklets—everything, everything! They paid honestly and properly, according to the newly established rate of exchange—that is, a Russian ruble is the exact equivalent of a Polish zloty. When I'd sold out, I went back to the dealer for new merchandise. But he only stared at me as though I were a foreigner unaware of what was going on, and swore that they had grabbed up all of his wares as well—again, paying a ruble for a zloty—by the tens of dozens, by the hundreds of dozens, and he had been left—so he said—with nothing. And so I was finished as a businessman. Finished! Now Fayga and my sons are once again mocking me: 'Schlemiehl! Oaf! Bungler! Where did you leave your wits?' "

I make a grimace to keep from bursting into laughter. But Zalman's small, sharp eyes have already picked up the hidden smile in my own eyes, and his glances now spurt piercing slivers of glass. His trimmed beard makes his face look even bonier and more shriveled, and the muscles beneath the skin of his cheeks shuttle back and forth:

"Go ahead and laugh! I'm very glad I'm not peddling anymore— glad as can be. What point is there in selling stockings without my little songs? None whatever! For our liberators I don't need any songs. The women, on the other hand, those little slatterns I used to draw with my singing—they don't even want to look at me anymore. The liberators are better singers than I, and handsomer too. That much, you see, I'm ready to admit. Besides, my Fayga made me swear that I wouldn't open my mouth. No matter how much she proclaims her hatred for me, she still takes pity on me. And so she pleads: 'Have mercy, don't sing any more of your songs!' You understand? My rhymes don't come from Moscow, so they might be considered counterrevolutionary propaganda disguised as happy songs."

"One isn't permitted to be sad," I say.

"Or happy either. On your own initiative you're not allowed to be happy. Do you remember my songs? One of them I sang at your mother's gate, and everyone enjoyed it. I excerpt, as the critics say, just one stanza:

> *"Dance you tailors, dance you cobblers,*
> *Dance you workers from the masses,*
> *But watch out that while you're dancing,*
> *You don't show your naked* ———.

It's a parable. The world is a wedding party. Inside sit the rich in-laws and the fat potbellies, and outside at the windows stand the poor who also try to wangle a little dance. That's how it was when I wrote the song. Today it's the other way around, but the song is even more appropriate: the fat potbellies stand outside and laugh at the poor workingmen who dance inside with their bare behinds—" He is all but choking

with laughter, and I can see the wild rage tearing at his guts. "I tell you
. . . they're tricksters! What am I saying? Tricksters? First-class actors!
I used to do a bit of acting myself, in the theater right here in Teliatnik
Park. It's no accident that I keep coming back to this park—it's to recall
my days as an amateur actor, when I turned Fayga's head with my great
talents. But how can I compare myself to them! They're the true actors."

" 'They' who?"

"They, the liberators—" his rage mounts still higher—"they've got
the world's greatest stage director. I could understand taking ten peasants
and teaching them to sing and act, even twenty or a hundred peasants—
but that thousands, tens of thousands, of peasants should all sing the same
song: *'U nas vsyo est'*!' 'We have everything!' . . . And yet, they seemed
to think my stockings were a good buy. Even my Fayga's sacks are a
good buy—Fayga was carrying a load of empty sacks, sacks that had
held flour or potatoes, and one of the liberators stopped her in the street,
examined a sack to see how deep it was and whether it had any holes—
and bought it. In case he got an opportunity to buy anything, he needed
something to pack it in . . . It's a pity, a great pity, that their old
intelligentsia is gone." Zalman's head sinks down and he begins to speak
slowly, ruefully. "Oh, their intelligentsia! Even a shlimazel like me, when
I was among them, felt like a human being, like one of them. In fact, it
was they who persuaded me that I could act and that I was a 'payet,'
even though they didn't understand a single word of my songs. 'The
rhythm,' they would say, 'we like the rhythm.' But now they have a stage
director—oh, do they ever have a stage director!" Zalman is once again
choking with rage, with a fury that threatens to burst out of him and
that he manages only barely to keep under control. "He's even taught
the Russian intelligentsia to play it smart and keep silent. He's even
taught me! Now I, too, at last keep silent!"

"But you're not silent." I gaze at the short shadows that stretch from
tree-trunk to tree-trunk but do not quite succeed in touching.

"I am silent." He looks round the empty park. "But of you I'm not
afraid. You too have remained on the other side of the barricades, as my
Yudka used to say to me. But how did you happen to come to the park
on such a windy day?" He turns to me abruptly, as though this question
has only now occurred to him.

"Just like that."

"I understand." He laughs. "You're sick at heart. The local Party
people no doubt keep a list of your sins. Surely at some time or other
you've said a word more than you should have. And your poems probably
don't measure up either. You were a yeshiva student once upon a time,
and some long beards have crept into your verse, the beard you shaved

off yourself has worked its way inside your poems . . . Nu, have you changed your colors yet? Or, as they put it, have you reconstructed yourself yet?"

"Not so far. They haven't yet demanded it of me."

"That's no good either. That's called 'antagonistic withdrawal.'" His tone is biting, and I cannot tell whether he is serious or speaking in jest. "Keeping too quiet and doing nothing—that isn't good either. That's what Fayga has been arguing all along against me: 'Either your mouth never closes or you're as silent as a robber in the woods. Anyone looking at your face can tell right away that you're dissatisfied,' she says."

"You're still quarreling at home?" I draw my head in between my shoulders; I feel chilled, as though a cold wind is blowing from his words.

"No, there's no more quarreling," he answers, delighted with this excuse I've given him for a new stream of words. "Now Fayga only has to point out the window at the tank crews standing around their tanks and singing. That's all she needs to show me what I've done to our Yudka. You know, of course, that during the time when running off to the Soviets was all the rage, our Yudka too ran off, to become a painter. We've known all along that he wasn't studying at the Academy of Fine Arts in Moscow, as he dreamt he would. We've assumed he was toiling away in some coal mine in the Donbas. Still, we thought that somehow, sometime, he'd show up again. And ever since the liberators came, I've had the fantasy that suddenly our door will open and a Red officer will enter—Yudka. I said nothing to Fayga, but I was tossing as if in a fever day and night: the door opens, an officer walks in . . . Yudka. And if not an officer, then at least a soldier in a gray overcoat. Fayga, though, didn't just dream: she sent my other sons chasing through the city to see what they could find out. On me she doesn't rely—I'm an idle babbler, she says. Till my sons came home with definite news they'd got from our local Party people, who had found out in turn from the newly arrived political instructors: *Razgromili*—Annihilated! The Polish party, according to the Soviets, had been practically eaten up by spies and Trotskyists. And so, at the time they were cleaning out the big reptiles, they also got rid of the little ones—the little fellows from Vilna. *Razgromili!* And so, I don't quarrel anymore with Fayga."

Zalman Press turns his face upward, bites his lips, and starts to rub under his chin, scouring the skin so hard he seems to be trying to tear out the roots of his now-vestigial beard:

"But my Mottele, you know, deserves even more pity than Yudka. Yudka used to go out at night with a bucket of paint and smear slogans on the walls: 'Hands off the Soviet Union!' As he saw it, Poland wanted to make war on White Russia and the eastern Ukraine. But my Mottele, now, never meddled with White Russia or the Ukraine. My Mottele always said that the only way to liberate yourself from all sorrows is . . . to go to a dance-class. But now the darkness of Egypt has descended upon him: The bourgeois dances have fallen out of favor with the girls, along with the petty bourgeois dancers. They now dance only folk dances, and only with Red officers. And so my Mottele has been left without dances, just as I've been left without my little songs. Unless, of course, he wants to twirl about with his mother—but she's got the gout and generally aches all over. In his great distress he's taken to baiting my Aizikel. Aizikel, as you know, has a habit of filling boxes with burned-out tobacco pipes, discarded children's toys, and other such junk. So Mottele mocks him, calls him a 'private entrepreneur,' a kulak, and keeps warning him that any day now the Soviet authorities will find out about him and confiscate his stock."

It is already dark in the park, but the sky is still light. I conjure up a fantasy: somewhere among the trees someone is walking barefoot through the wet piles of leaves, stealing closer to me, and presently will seize my neck with cold, slippery fingers. . . . I shudder. It's the wind, I tell myself, and get up to leave.

"Don't you go to the synagogue anymore?" I ask Zalman before bidding him farewell. "That other time we sat here, you went off afterwards to the Gravediggers' Chapel."

"Even the Gravediggers' Chapel isn't what it used to be," he answers despondently. "The people there are all sunk in a pit of gloom. Even the shnorrers sitting around the stove, who were always cursing the congregants, have run out of steam. If the shopkeepers have nothing to give them, they'll die of hunger. To the Soviets, paupers who don't know how to work are garbage."

As I am walking away, he calls me back:

"Your mother got married?"

"Yes, married."

"I know. To a man who's a grouch, a loner, who never speaks. Your mother has also had some great luck! Now, what was it I wanted to tell you?" He begins to squirm on the bench, gets up, sits down again, and I realize that he has called me back not to ask about my mother, but for something else. "What do you think? Was she right to hang herself? Was she right? You know whom I'm talking about!" Zalman shouts angrily, as though he suspects me of pretending not to remember the story of his love for the blonde woman who had been his tenant. "She came of a family of landowners who had fled Russia twenty years ago, and she married that hunchback, the bookkeeper, because her family was now poor. So she did the right thing when she hanged herself. Things would be going very hard for her now. Even her love of Lermontov wouldn't have helped her. Nu, go, go . . . wait—I'm going too. I'm going to the synagogue; if you like, you can come with me. That time I went by myself, but today you can come too. Sitting by the stove in the Gravediggers' Chapel, with the paupers, you're still allowed to be sad."

In the Later Years

REB REFOEL stands on the steps of his cellar-shop, gazing out into Broad Street—encased within his silence, as my mother is encased within hers. A second marriage, she muses, isn't the same as a first. Since he has already raised his children with another woman and she has had a son by another man, they are like two strange birds roosting in one nest. And so she sits hunched over on her stool deep inside the tiny cellar, her meekness shining mutely in her eyes; within her head she feels a roaring and a ringing, as though of wind and snow swirling about together; and in her mind her thoughts unravel one by one.

For years her neighbors had been debating among themselves: Would "he" start a war or would "he" not? Now he has started it. One Friday morning, as she opened the cellar-shop and Reb Refoel planted himself just where he is standing now and was gazing out into the street, she saw people rushing about, clearly panic-stricken, stopping for a moment to exchange a few words, and running on. Unable to bear Refoel's silence any longer, she asked him what was happening, and why was he always as silent as though he were reciting the Eighteen Benedictions, even when he wasn't praying at all?

He removed his hands from his sleeves and replied that the war had begun.

For Reb Refoel to remove his hands from his sleeves and utter a word, war had to break out.

Next she saw a woman tearing her hair right in the middle of the street, and screaming that her son had to leave for the front. His father had gone away just like that in the last war, and had never returned. "I won't survive another war!" the woman screamed.

Only then did she properly grasp what was going on. At once she rose and, leaving Refoel in the shop, rushed straight to the cemetery, to "storm the graves" on behalf of her son. She stretched herself upon the grave of her first husband and screamed to him that he must protect their son. His sons by his first wife had not had to be soldiers; he must, therefore, win Heaven's consent that the son she had borne him would not have to, either. The merit she had earned through her years of suffering must now stand in her defense. The gate at which she had sold her wares for so many years could bear witness that every Friday afternoon, as soon as the sexton had knocked three times with his wooden gavel, she had closed her stall, abandoned all thought of gain, and rushed home to light her Sabbath candles.

The Almighty heard her prayers: her son was not drafted into the army. In less than two weeks, the war was over. She knew well enough, of course, that there was little reason to rejoice. For other countries, the war had only just begun and Jews there were suffering severe hardships. Into Vilna, however, came the Russians—warmly dressed this time, not barefoot as they had been twenty years earlier. And because they were warmly dressed, and riding through the city with all sorts of weapons, she assured herself that all would be well. But in this, it turned out, she erred grievously. Soon there was hunger in the city, long lines for bread, and the merchants walked about as though an eternal solar eclipse had plunged Vilna into total darkness.

A week before, Refoel had let drop a remark to the effect that the Russians were leaving Vilna and handing it over to the Lithuanians.

The mere fact that Refoel had taken his hands from his chest and said something—that alone sufficed to show that this was no routine matter. And yet she could not grasp it: just the day before, Vilna had been under Russia like Minsk, and now Vilna was under Lithuania like Kovno. Still, the most important thing, she told herself, was that there be no war.

Peace, however, was not destined to be her lot in her later years.

Moïsey's only son, Aronchik, had seldom approached her produce baskets even when she kept her stall at her own gate; since she had come here to the little cellar-shop, he hadn't shown his face at all. Even with her son, his uncle, Aronchik had had no contact during the last several years. But she had been told by Taybel, his mother, that he had come to a parting of the ways with his erstwhile political comrades, that he was now working for his Uncle Issak in the pharmacy and was a good husband to Yudes and a devoted father to their son, Moshele.

A few days earlier, Taybel had come and told her that Aronchik and Yudes wanted to go to Bialystok with the Russians and were insisting that she accompany them. Wringing her hands, Taybel wailed that, no matter how much she pleaded with Aronchik not to go, he refused to listen. He was not even afraid of his former comrades, who were now his deadly enemies.

"Why are his former comrades his deadly enemies?" she asked Taybel, as she thanked God in her heart that her son and daughter-in-law had no desire to leave with the withdrawing Russians.

Aronchik's old comrades, Taybel replied, were angry at him for having once argued that an injustice was being committed against the Chinamen, because a revolution had not been brought to China as it had to Russia—whereas his comrades maintained that for the Chinamen the time was not yet ripe.

"Why," she asked Taybel, "did Aronchik need to meddle in the affairs of the Chinamen when he himself is a Vilner?"

Taybel answered that, indeed, he had had no reason to meddle in that, but, being his mother, she had understood what this was about: he wanted to settle down and become a responsible householder like other young husbands and fathers, but he was ashamed before his comrades to simply walk away from "the cause," as they called it. So he told them he disagreed with them about the Chinamen. Now they still held this against him, and called him a "Laybele."

Again she had to ask: "And what does that mean—a 'Laybele'?"

"Laybele," Taybel explained, was actually the nickname of a man* who had once held a high place among the Bolsheviks, but had been driven out of Russia for saying that it was necessary to do everywhere in the world what had been done in Minsk. In Russia nowadays, to be a "Laybele" was much worse than being a highwayman.

She would have liked to question Taybel further: Why had it been such a matter of life and death to the outcast Laybele to introduce everywhere the same system as in Russia? As yet, one could not see that it had brought such great happiness there. But she had remained silent, so as not to pour salt upon Taybel's wounds.

STRIDING ALONG BROAD STREET are the two merchants, Shaya and Ḥatzkel. On their own Jatkowa Street, long queues of housewives are lined up in front of the bakeries. Shaya and Ḥatzkel still have a little merchandise of their own, but have hidden it away to await better times. And, out of fear of being torn limb from limb by would-be customers, they stay away entirely from the vicinity of their shops. Instead, they stroll about the city to hear the latest news. One place they stop is Reb Refoel's cellar.

Mother, overjoyed to see her old neighbors, rises and invites them both in.

"We may congratulate each other—now we'll be able to do business freely again," says Shaya to Reb Refoel, alluding to the Russians' imminent departure.

"Hmhm," answers Reb Refoel.

"The 'Great Ones' keep their word," says Shaya, radiant with joy. "Twenty years ago they already gave Vilna to the Lithuanians, but then the Poles grabbed it."

"Why are you so happy?" asks Ḥatzkel. "Because you're becoming

---

* Leon Trotsky.—Trans.

a Lithuanian, or because the 'Great Ones' keep their word?''

"For both reasons," answers Shaya, who is now in high and festive spirits, a holiday mood. "We should recite the Blessing for Deliverance, first because the 'Great Ones' saved us from the Germans and second, because they're keeping their word. What do you say, Reb Refoel?"

Reb Refoel shrugs his shoulders; he doesn't know what to say.

"They're not leaving yet," sighs Ḥatzkel. "People say they'll be keeping a lot of airplanes all over Lithuania."

"Then we have a third reason for reciting the Blessing for Deliverance." Shaya is melting with joy. "They'll keep watch so the Germans don't invade."

"Well, Poland, after all, is Poland, a big country," says Ḥatzkel. "But Lithuania is like the smallest type in the smallest prayerbook. They say there's no express train there because before it could get up a full head of steam, it would already be pulling into Hotzeplotz, in Latvia. Isn't that so, Reb Refoel?"

Reb Refoel smiles, as if to say: It doesn't really matter to me how big Lithuania is. All I need is the steps of my cellar, where I can look out into the street. . . .

When Shaya sees that even this adamantly silent man agrees with him, he begins to laugh at Ḥatzkel:

"And what good did it do you that Poland was a big country, when any little shaygetz could throw stones at you? Have you forgotten already?"

"I've forgotten nothing." Ḥatzkel is getting angry. "It's you who've forgotten that when the Lithuanians were here twenty years ago, they came wearing wooden clogs. You, Reb Shaya, are always on the side of the top dog. Two days ago you were for the Poles, yesterday for the 'Great Ones,' and today you're all for the Lithuanians."

"And you, Reb Ḥatzkel, have a knack for siding precisely with those who are about to die. You're attracted to the corpses every time, without fail! I can see right through you—" Shaya shoves his finger under Ḥatzkel's nose. "And don't you worry your head any about the Lithuanians. What they were in the past, is in the past. Today they export a million pigs a year. I only wish I went to Kovno twenty years ago with my first cousin, I wouldn't have had to work like a slave here for so many years. You'll soon see what joy and happiness there'll be when families are reunited. Do you have any relatives in Lithuania, Reb Refoel?"

"Hmhm."

"And how are your married daughters?" Shaya is determined to get some response out of him. "Are they well, your daughters?"

"Hmhm."

Shaya feels as if he's about to burst. He can make even a stone talk, but this grumpy bear simply will not open his mouth, not to save his life. Nonetheless, Shaya tries again:

"And your sons-in-law—what do they do? They didn't have to go into the army, your sons-in-law?"

Reb Refoel shakes his head.

Well, thinks Shaya, at last he's gotten something, even if only a shake of the head; but it's not enough. Never mind, if Balaam's ass could speak, then this grouch too should be able to utter a word:

"And your grandchildren? How are they, your grandchildren?"

"Hmhm."

Now Shaya is totally baffled. He cannot tell what this means: are the dearly beloved grandchildren hale and hearty, or are they bedridden with Abele's disease? And so he shouts into Reb Refoel's ear, as though the latter were deaf:

"It's not for nothing that people say: When you've talked things over with a friend, your burden feels lighter. . . . A good day to you, Vella."

The two men take their leave, convinced that living under one roof with a man like Reb Refoel must be like being imprisoned in a cell with a highwayman.

My mother remains seated, deeply shamed by Refoel's lack of friendliness toward her two old neighbors. Even when her son pays them a visit, Refoel stands in the middle of the room facing the door, silent as ever, looking as if he either wants to leave or is waiting for her son to leave. And when her son comes together with his wife, Refoel stands right on the doorstep, gazing out at the street through the window in the door, just as though someone wished to drive him out of his own house. This is why her children never want to eat anything in her house, although she has told them more than once that she is earning her own living and can well afford to treat her children.

TAYBEL AND YUDES are bending their heads over the cellar entrance. Their faces, as Mother can clearly see, betray great fear; Yudes is holding the hand of Moshele, who is already a strapping youngster with coal-black eyes.

Breathless, the two women ask Mother to let them in, and she realizes that they are afraid to talk in the street. As for herself, she is glad that Refoel is away: he won't scare her relations away with his silence. Hunched over like an old crone, she follows them back into the house—no longer now the woman who had for years stood at the gate in heat and in frost, who had rushed to the market early every morning.

As they enter the chilly apartment with its low, vaulted ceiling,

Yudes bursts into tears. She weeps so bitterly that Moshele begins to cry as well.

Aronchik has been arrested.

Mother looks about her. The walls and the ceiling dance before her eyes. She feels dizzy and, in order not to fall, grasps the table with both hands.

Taybel, Aronchik's mother, who stutters, is now so numb with fear and anguish that she cannot utter a word. Yudes cries still louder:

"When the Poles arrested him, he went off proudly, his head held high. But this time he had tears in his eyes, because his own comrades informed on him, over the Chinese question . . . His former friends want to clear themselves and rise to the top at his expense. But it won't help them!" Yudes erupts in fury. "They've sinned against the Party even more than he did."

My mother feels unable to move a muscle. All her limbs have turned to stone. But the ringing and dizziness in her head have stopped, as though the entire world were already buried beneath deep snow.

The room is filled with a deep-cold silence. Moshele huddles close to his mother, who rasps, in tones more of laughter than of weeping:

"And we had already sold everything and were ready to leave with the Russians."

Eclipse of the Sun

A S UNEXPECTEDLY as the Russians had left Vilna so, barely a year later, did they return and declare that from that day forward, Vilna would be the capital of Soviet Lithuania. They stayed on for half the summer, the fall, the entire winter, and then, in the new spring, in honor of the first of May, red banners fluttered and waved in all the streets of Vilna, by day and by night. Red Army soldiers marched and sang:

> "Esli zavtra voina, esli zavtra v pokhod,
> Esli chornaya sila nagryanet,
> Kak odin chelovek, ves' sovetskiy narod
> Za svobodnuyu rodinu vstanet."*

The young people who marched along responded with jubilant shouts:

"Da zdravstvuyet krasnaya armiya! Long live the Red Army! The enemy will not dare to seize one inch of Soviet soil!"

But in the city, people whispered of a report by London radio that Germany was massing troops at the Soviet border and was likely to invade Russia any day now.

On Sunday morning, June the twenty-second, the first day of summer, I was alone in the house. Frumme-Liebche was at work in the hospital. I looked out through the window and saw the distant yellow sand mountains, the Mountains of the Cross, dozing in the sun; tall buildings dazzled with their whiteness; rooftops sparkled like silver; church-spires blazed with their golden crosses. And it was still, peacefully still and calm, as though the world were freshly created.

But the airplanes were flying higher than usual that morning. "Why are they flying so high?" I asked myself, and my lips suddenly felt dry. "Maneuvers—" I reassured myself—"the Russians are holding maneuvers." I wanted to turn on the radio, but my hands were trembling and I shouted to myself: "I don't want to know any news!" I was hungry

---

* If tomorrow war comes, if tomorrow we march,
If the forces of evil attack us,
As one man will our Soviet people arise
To defend their free fatherland.

and wanted to go out to buy bread, but I shouted to myself again that I was not hungry. I turned away from the window: I no longer wanted to look outside.

Suddenly I heard a metallic, grating screech; a whistling pierced my ears. Somewhere there was a deafening clap and the windowpanes began to quiver. The explosion paralyzed me and left me bereft of speech. A minute later the factory sirens began to wail with their voices of death. Somewhere another explosion shook the air. The windows trembled more violently, and I roused myself from my stupor:

War.

. . . I will not flee. The Russians will not retreat, and even if they do, I shall not flee and leave my mother behind. I shall not become a refugee and curse the day I left my home, as the refugees from Poland are doing. The Russians won't let people flee, they'll shoot those who try for creating a panic and for impeding the movements of the military on the roads. Good! I'll shave, today is a day like any other.

I shaved. I stood before the mirror and hummed a prayer-chant, keeping my eyes with deliberate effort on the brassy brightness that gleamed on the ceiling and floor. I gazed at the bands of sunlight that danced on the walls, and on the wine-colored mahogany bookcase filled with books. "Now I am completely calm," I told myself. "Now I can go down to buy bread."

Outside I saw large trucks in front of many houses, and Soviet women, wearing coarse, fuzzy berets, were hurriedly carrying bundles of clothing out of their apartments or, together with the truck drivers, were lugging chairs, tables, chests of drawers, and loading them on the vehicles. Now suddenly, the owners of the buildings in which Red Army officers and their wives had been quartered sensed the suspicion, alienation, and indifference of the Soviets toward them, the old, lifelong residents of Vilna. The Jews huddled together in small groups and spoke heatedly among themselves, but now entirely without fear:

"Why are they running? They've always said the Red Army never retreats—" one man shouted aloud.

"A broken old chair is more important to them than saving human lives. People they have enough, but not furniture!" shouted another, still louder.

"It's impossible that the Germans would kill all the Jews," stammered a third. "In the First War the Germans did business with the Jews."

"On the roads the Germans shoot at the refugees with machine guns, and the peasants kill them with their hatchets," screamed a fourth.

"I'm not afraid of bombs, I'm not afraid of peasants with hatchets— I'm afraid of the Germans," I said.

And the next day, as the Russian army began its retreat from Lith- uania, I—with a knapsack on my shoulders and a small Hebrew Bible in my pocket—fled, together with Frumme-Liebche.

First, we both hurried to my mother to say good-bye. The streets were full of people rushing in all directions, leaving the city singly or in pairs, carrying small children in their arms and bundles on their backs. It was quiet in the streets, awesomely quiet—as though all the people had been transformed into nocturnal shadows on the walls of a dark room illumined from without by a blood-red glow.

At the apartment of my mother and Reb Refoel, all the courtyard neighbors had assembled. The walls here were thick, the windows were barred, the ceiling was low and vaulted, and so this was the place the neighbors had selected as their shelter against bombs. They sat on chairs, on the sofa, on empty fruit-crates—sat in despairing silence, like a family of mourners gathered in a cemetery purification-house where the shrouds for the dead are being sewn. Mother, wrapped in her shawl, sat at the table as though she too were a stranger, and when we entered, Frumme- Liebche and I, her wandering eyes did not recognize us. Reb Refoel stood at the window staring out as always, as though there were no war at all. I was unable to utter a single word; it was Frumme-Liebche who spoke to my mother, told her that we were fleeing, that the trains had stopped running, and that we would have to go on foot. Very slowly Mother rose, and for a long time her lips moved soundlessly, like a deaf-mute's; then, weeping aloud, she clasped me round the neck:

"I'm going with you!"

Suddenly Reb Refoel loomed up beside us. He removed his hands from his sleeves and, in tones at once of laughter and wailing, rasped:

"On foot?"

Those two words, and nothing more. Mother instantly sat down again, her fate sealed. Now I embraced her to bid her farewell, but she tore herself free of me and pointed at her husband:

"First take your leave of Reb Refoel." Her face was suddenly as stern as when I was a child and she was instructing me in the proper way for a Jew to behave.

I bade Reb Refoel good-bye, then said good-bye to my mother, quickly, quickly, and rushed out. Mother ran after me across the courtyard and, at the gate, she grasped my head with both her hands:

"My child, never forget you are a Jew. Keep the Sabbath."

Then she herself pushed me out through the wicket of the gate, and Frumme-Liebche came out behind me.

. . .

AFTER WE PASSED THE CITY LIMITS, Frumme-Liebche began to lag behind. The Soviet army trucks, laden with furniture and with officers' wives, flew by like demons. In vain did the hordes of those on foot attempt to stop the vehicles by crying, shouting, or falling on their knees; the trucks just detoured slightly and raced on. Now the refugees began to tell each other that the motorized German divisions would soon overtake us and shoot us down. On the roads, death was certain, but if we returned to Vilna we might manage to stay alive. The golden grain in the fields rippled gently, the surrounding forests rustled, the leaf-covered branches swayed piously, and seemed to be asking: "why are you panicking? Your fears are unfounded. . . ." And many of the refugees did begin to turn back. One encouraged the other; each was glad that his fellow was going back home with him:

"We'll be back in the city even before the Germans reach it."

I, however, pushed on ahead, dragging Frumme-Liebche along with me, despite her cries that her feet were swollen, until we reached the village of Rukon, where a few years earlier, after our wedding, we had spent the summer. We were now on the very same footpaths on which we had then taken strolls; we recognized the stump of a tree on which we used to sit and rest; and out of the surrounding trees our familiar cottage with its thatched roof winked at us like an old friend. And so we turned aside here for a while, only a while, to get a drink of water and to give Frumme-Liebche a chance to rest her feet.

Beside the cottage stood our erstwhile landlord, barefoot and looking as though he had just awakened. The peasant gaped at us in astonishment. He took us into the house, gave us milk to drink, and tried to convince us to stay with him. His wife felt sorry for us; wiping the tears from her eyes, she argued that no matter how bad things were for someone in his own home, he would be much worse off if he left home to become a wanderer. Frumme-Liebche and I went outside to talk it over. And nature once again misled us, deceived us. . . . A breeze was blowing and cooled our feverish thoughts; the dense crowns of the trees billowed above us; the full stalks of wheat swayed to and fro, and so, too, billowed and fluttered Frumme-Liebche's hair. My eyes wandered over the surrounding fields and woods. In my mind a dream arose of a hut in the forest where we might be able to wait out the war. Oh, how happy we would be if we were to find such a deserted hut! We would eat chestnuts and herbs and roots, if only no one would discover our hidden nest; even if it were only a hollowed-out tree trunk, or a pit covered by a layer of moldy leaves—only to stay alive.

Frumme-Liebche awakened me from my dream. She had decided to remain with the peasants overnight and to return to my mother in the morning.

"Women and children 'he' won't touch," she said. "But for you there's danger—you must go."

And I left. And as soon as I left, night fell. It was like entering a subterranean cave. I walked along the path that cut through the forest, expecting every moment to be pounced on by a wild animal or a robber, or overtaken by a German—by whom or what didn't matter, I would never escape . . . never, never escape. . . .

"Who goes there?" I heard someone shout, and I didn't know who had shouted—whether I to someone else, or someone else to me, or I to myself.

Around a truck stood several Red Army soldiers equipped with battery lights and rifles. They were waiting for any passing Soviet vehicles that could give them gasoline. They asked me who I was and where I was going, and when I answered that I was running away from the Germans, one of them confidently sang out:

"*Shyroka strana moya rodnaya** . . . The Soviet Union is great and there is room in it for all!"

They paid no further attention to me. These were silent, crestfallen men, covered with mud from head to foot, their breath coming in weary gasps; it occurred to me that they must have fled from their battered regiments without an order to retreat. I offered them cigarettes, and they promised to take me along. Our wait was rewarded with the approach of a laggard truck racing away from Vilna at top speed. The soldiers lined up across the road with all their rifles aimed at the driver.

"Give us gasoline!"

The driver climbed down, gave them a few liters of gasoline, and drove off. A little later another vehicle came by, then a third, and our own truck's tank at last was filled. One of the soldiers said to me:

"Climb up."

I was standing facing the direction from which I had come. If only it were not so dark, I thought, I should still be able to see Frumme-Liebche standing somewhere about the village where I had left her. It's only a verst or two from here, after all; it's not even an hour since we parted. I will tell the soldiers and beg them to have pity and wait. . . .

The soldiers were already standing on the truck's back platform; the driver climbed into the cab, where he was joined by two soldiers carrying submachine guns. The engine started up. I realized they wouldn't wait, not for an instant. The Germans could overtake us at any moment. I barely managed to jump up at the last second as the truck roared away, hurtling headlong into the darkness.

A fatalistic calm descended upon me. I stood pressed in among the

* "Broad is my native land": first line of a Soviet patriotic song—Trans.

soldiers, locked into their closeness, and felt myself one of them, though without a greatcoat or a gun in my hands. The ashes of their cigarettes glowed in the darkness, their unshaven mouths emitted smoke; all were silent. From time to time one of them would spit out, with an oath, the bitter aftertaste of the cheap tobacco. A head was poked out of the cab, and ordered the cigarettes extinguished: enemy planes might spot the specks of fire.

"Naplevat'!"* answered the soldiers, and continued smoking.

The truck raced uphill and down, its headlights dimmed with a screen that let only a reddish glow shine through. Forests rushed by like great black nocturnal birds with wings outspread. Here a village was burning, there a small town. The fire slashed open a thick slice of darkness, and in the illumined space shadows of people and shadows of trees raced past, as though the trees, too, were seeking a hiding-place from destruction. We sped past a train depot littered with overturned railway cars. Gasoline tanks blazed like bundles of straw as oil spurted from them, and it seemed to me that the oil was spurting from my cheeks as well. The wind fanned and spread the conflagration, drove the smoke and the flames into our faces, saturated our clothing with the smell of gasoline and smoldering ashes. But we broke through the wall of smoke and fire. Behind us stalked the night that with her darkness covered the human habitations and fields of grain plowed by lead—covered the traces of agony and death.

* "Spit on that!"—Trans.

On Alien Soil

I

"MY LITTLE MOTHER, my little gray dove, I left you, left you behind and ran away," my lips mumble as, staggering like a drunkard, I drag myself along, one of a great horde fleeing on foot through the White Russian night.

This morning, before dawn, just after we crossed the old Russian border, the truck on which I was riding had stopped dead in the middle of the road: out of gas. The Red Army men had jumped off the back platform, rifles in hand, abandoned the truck, and left me alone amidst the vast and unfamiliar expanses of White Russia. I had stumbled on as God led me, fallen asleep in a cowshed, gotten water to drink in a village. Wherever I appeared, peasant women and children ran to inform the local militia that a suspicious-looking man with a knapsack on his back was loitering in the vicinity. My appearance, my clothing, my accent all betrayed my foreignness, and so I found myself being constantly stopped and then promptly released.

By now I know what to do whenever I am asked who I am: I show my passport, let my knapsack be inspected, and say, "*Ya yevrey*—I'm a Jew—and I'm running away from the Germans." I said that I wanted to go to Minsk, but was told that Minsk was all in flames, that I should go further, to Borisov; there they would place me with a transport of refugees, for evacuation deeper into Russia. So it is to Borisov that I am now making my way, together with the great throng I have met tonight on the road.

Soldiers from decimated regiments, peasants from burned-out villages, workers from destroyed factories, all mingle together in this multitude—one body with many hands and feet, with bearded faces, caps tilted back. A barefoot peasant from a kolkhoz walks beside a Red Army major, also barefoot, his boots tied together and slung over his shoulder to make walking easier. Next to a soldier cradling a lowered rifle is a peasant woman cradling a suckling infant. As though a storm wind has broken off half of a tree and is now dragging the crown with all its densely foliaged branches across the ground, so does this human throng move all entwined in one mass. Shoulders and arms jostle each other, feet step on other feet, but no one, whether in the front rows or in the rear, separates from the throng; each is afraid to be left alone. The enemy has sent down "angels of destruction," airborne advance units, and stabbing through the tangled forest blackness are steady flashes of blue, red, and green flame—flares that the newly landed German parachutists are sending up from the dense woods to show their planes where to release their bombs. The planes themselves, droning on in the darkness high above, also emit their own flares to help them spot their targets. The sky is suddenly lit by flames of all colors, flames of a cold, calm immutability which remain for a long while suspended between earth and sky, like enormous lamps set against the background of a dark-blue ceiling.

"Get down!" comes the shouted order from the front rows.

Everyone drops instantly to the ground. I throw myself down among a heap of bodies from which rises a salty, sweaty stench. Somewhere, near or far, there is a thunderous roar, a tremendous bang. A peasant lying to my right shudders all over, as though he knows that the bomb has hit his village, his house. To my left a woman lets out a sob, a wail, and presses her mouth against the earth to keep from screaming. Someone behind me emits a short, abrupt laugh and curses himself and his ancestors unto the tenth generation; someone else heaves a deep sigh, as though the very guts were being ripped from his body:

"Gospodi, pomiluy!" "God have mercy upon us!"

"Get up!" comes the command and all get up, their backs bent. The planes have hurled down their loads, the flares have burned out, and one can now go on. I alone remain on the ground, listening to the night's stillness hovering over me. The metallic hum of the unseen airplanes now returning to their bases—growling with malicious satisfaction, sated like beetles swarming back from a meadow at dusk—bores into my ears. "Beetles, beetles," murmur my chattering teeth. I feel them crawl across my back under my clothes. How good it would be if only I could remain lying here, fall asleep, and let myself be overgrown by grass and nettles. "Little mother, my little gray dove, I left you alone and ran away. . . ."

"Get up!" I am prodded in the back, and someone bends over me. "Who are you?"

I raise my head and make out the form of the soldier in the long greatcoat with his lowered rifle. I know why he is asking me who I am: I may be an agent, an infiltrator, who has spied out everything and now intends to lag behind, to vanish into the nearby forest and there signal to the enemy.

I get up quickly and press forward once again with the others, amidst tall, motionless trees whose gigantic shadows make our path even darker. Our only illumination comes from the narrow strip of sky above our heads, dark blue, with the silvery glow of distant stars that shimmer and twinkle in sleepy silence. I move ahead with long strides, but my head is drifting in a fog, in my memories of the days just past:

"First take leave of Reb Refoel," Mother said. Why did she demand that of me—Reb Refoel, after all, is only her second husband, not my father? And what did Reb Refoel say in parting? I do not remember. Perhaps he said nothing at all; he was, after all, a man who rarely spoke. Nor can I recall whether I kissed my mother, kissed her sunken cheeks or her high forehead. Whenever she used to come to visit us and I gave her a kiss, she would scold me, always she would scold me with the same words: "Don't kiss me—I'm not a Torah scroll." She was afraid it might annoy Frumme-Liebche. . . . She ran after me across the courtyard, she embraced me and spoke to me with a shy smile, spoke with the shy smile of a maiden who begs her betrothed not to forget her: "My child, never forget that you are a Jew. Keep the Sabbath." That was what she had said to me. I shall remember! I shall remember, my little mother, I shall remember your steps in your heavy shoes as you walked across the crooked cobblestones. Even as the clods of earth are falling upon my coffin, I shall remember your steps—if, that is, it be vouchsafed me to be buried in a coffin, if I do not fall by the wayside, victim of a bullet or a bomb, or of hunger and thirst.

"Water! I want a drink—I'm dying of thirst!" I seize the arm of a tall man with a full beard who is walking next to me.

"Funny fellow, where would I get water for you? I would also like to drink." He laughs good-humoredly.

"What's the matter with you?" Someone behind me gives me a shove. "Where are your eyes, under your forehead or in the back of your neck? Are you going forward or back?"

I do not answer and keep walking. In truth, my eyes have moved to the nape of my neck and bored two holes there, and are gazing back through the darkness at the way we have come. A voice is pursuing me, a voice is pulling me back. I plunge on ahead; I want to tear myself away from my memory, but the voice catches up with me:

"And what of me?"

It is the voice of Frumme-Liebche. For I have left her behind also, there at the crossroads outside Vilna, at the village of Rukon—I have left her and now she demands to know why I think only of my mother, not of her.

"And what of me?"

I cannot! I cannot think of both of them at the same time. My mother has long and narrow eyes and high cheekbones, and Frumme-Liebche, too, has long and narrow eyes. But my mother's eyes are light-green, while Frumme-Liebche's are black. She, Frumme-Liebche, has rosy cheeks and a full, well-shaped figure. Mother always took great delight in this buxomness of Frumme-Liebche's . . . Cursed fate! If only she'd stayed with me another half-hour, until I came upon the truck, we would be together now.

"Don't cry." A hand is laid on my shoulder. "It will pass."

I am weeping, shaking with stifled sobs, yet I myself do not hear it. I turn my head: it is the Russian with the full beard, keeping in step with me.

"What will pass?" I ask him.

"Everything will pass." He takes his hand off my shoulder. "Don't cry."

"What is it with you?" The same man who had given me a shove in the back before, now jabs me in the shoulder. "Why are you always underfoot and yet keeping yourself apart from the rest? Maybe you're a spy?"

"You're a spy yourself!" I turn toward him with clenched fists and see before me a small, thin peasant. He is frightened by my anger and steps aside. My accent has revealed that I am not a Russian, yet I may be some important official of one of the new Soviet provinces.

The argument sobers me for a while. I begin to march like a soldier in the ranks, swinging my arms: One, two! One, two! Gradually, however, my head sinks down again to sway like a bell hanging on a rotted rope. Soon my head, the swaying bell, will fall off and sink into the earth, soon the tongue of the swaying bell will grow silent. For now it still moves inside my mouth, that swollen tongue: "Little mother . . ."

SUDDENLY IT GROWS LIGHT, as in a house where someone opens the shuttered windows from the outside. The sky, without a single cloud, is transparently clear, deep, calm, with a greenish tint. From the fields on one side of the road arises a silver mist, and the treetops of the forest on the other side are already aglow with the light golden hue of sunrise. Somewhere in the distance, blue smoke curls upward from a burnt-out village that had already ceased to smolder the day before.

Our entire host comes to an abrupt halt. On the forest side of the road lie several parachutes with tangled cords: Germans have left their parachutes behind and crawled away amidst the trees, like snakes that shed their old skins and slither away, filled with venom. From the depths of the forest can be heard a strange, protracted cry, a hooting and a despairing wailing, as if of fragile forest creatures being torn apart by the claws of beasts of prey.

"What's that?" I stammer to the broad-shouldered Russian with the blond beard.

"The Germans are trying to scare us," he answers calmly.

The Germans are screaming and shouting in the forest to frighten and confuse us. The Red Army men among us fix bayonets on their rifles, and march alongside the civilians in a long, extended row, their weapons pointed toward the forest—our protection against attack. We start to move forward again, even faster and with greater urgency than before.

I am completely drenched in sweat. Big drops roll down my cheeks, over my lips, glue my eyelids together so that I cannot even see the light of day. I rub my face clear with both hands and, as though to refresh and revive myself, I gaze at the checkered fields, at the distant stretches of land crisscrossed by roads and bordered on all sides by forests. Not far from the road a tiny village—a cluster of freshly whitewashed huts with crooked windowpanes that glitter in the gold of the just-risen sun—nestles amidst tall trees. Just at the edge of the road stands a well with a long pump handle, from which a bucket is suspended.

"Water!" A joyous murmur courses through the crowd. All thrust themselves forward with necks outstretched, with thirsting, wide-open mouths and bulging eyes, and in an instant the budding fellowship among us is rent and shattered. Each races with all his might to be first at the well.

II

THE CROWD RUSHES toward the well with heavy steps and clings to it on all sides. Shouting and arguments resound against the pure stillness of early morning. The pump handle creaks up and down; heads are thrust into the bucket and gulp thirstily; others scoop up water by the handful, until shoved aside by those standing behind them. Ahead of me in the line stands the little peasant who has been walking behind me all night and jabbed me in the back. Now, in the daylight, he looks me over and seems to decide that he has no cause to fear me. He drinks his fill and, when my turn comes, holds onto the bucket with both hands. The hairs on his wizened, wrinkled face stand up stiffly like sharp needles.

"I'm a Soviet citizen, a bookkeeper in a kolkhoz. And who are you?"

I shove him aside with my left elbow and seize the pail with my right hand. Suddenly there is a shout:

"Germans!"

An airplane descends from the sky and swoops toward us. Within a second, its wheels and front section loom gigantic above us; in another instant it will hurl a bomb into our midst, cut through us with its wings. But already we've scattered, jumping into nearby ditches. Our soldiers shout to one another:

"Get the engine! The engine!"

Our machine guns open up with a heavy cross-fire; the bullets whistle above our heads. The sky seems to explode and fall blazing down in pieces. The plane, after having circled its target and begun its descent toward the well, suddenly lifts itself again and shoots up into the heights, like someone who jumps on the edge of a springboard and is instantly bounced back into the air. Caught in a hail of bullets, the plane turns toward the forest. Its tail is smoking and it is twisting, whirling, as if overcome by dizziness. It emits an eerie, metallic screech like the gritting of lifeless teeth, and begins to circle downward on one wing behind the treetops.

Next to me, in the ditch into which I have jumped, lies the peasant with the prickly face. He watches with evident pleasure and a twisted smile as I huddle close to the earth and try to burrow myself ever deeper into it.

He bares his teeth:

"You're afraid?"

"No more than you," I retort.

On the other side of me lies the tall Russian with the full blond beard. He gazes after the plane, just now vanishing behind the trees, and again tries to calm me, as he had done before daybreak:

"It will pass." He stretches out the words with sleepy indolence.

We crawl out of the ditches. Our faces are smudged; we are disheveled and covered with dust. I fall upon the well, thrust my head into the bucket, and gulp down the water left over by my enemy the kolkhoznik. Another group has collected behind me. But the soldiers who accompany us drive the crowd away from the well and refuse to let us walk together any longer, lest another enemy plane make us a target. The throng breaks up into small groups and, bending low, we creep through the fields toward the nearby forest.

There we are quickly surrounded by soldiers in green uniforms—border guards. They will not let us pass until our papers have been checked and we have been interrogated. This is the Soviet front line. In a thicket stands a large tank covered with leafy branches, with its crew circling around it. Deeper within the forest is a cannon with a long, raised gun barrel, and on a nearby hill a crashed plane is burning like a haystack. No one pays it any attention.

"Is that the one that attacked us?" I ask one of the soldiers of our group who is standing near me.

"That's the one." The soldier nods indifferently. There is an air of gloomy desperation about him: after the interrogation we, the civilians, will be permitted to go on, but the Red Army men who have accompanied us will be held back and formed into a new unit, which might soon have to go into battle.

I am awaiting my turn to be interrogated. I take off my knapsack and untie it, and pat the passport in my inside coat pocket. "*Ya yevrey*— I am a Jew." My lips whisper the phrase that till now has gotten me past all Soviet guard posts, and which I will soon have occasion to pronounce once more.

The closer I come to the officer in charge, the interrogator, the harder I find it to breathe. I notice that the crowd around me is thinning out; my companions are edging away, as though afraid to be associated with me. The kolkhoznik, my self-appointed arch-enemy, points to me as he whispers to the officer: he is denouncing me. I feel my limbs grow numb; a lassitude overcomes me, and at the same time I experience a strange feverishness, a warmth such as is felt in his last moments by someone freezing to death. Until now I have been stopped by Soviet militia patrols; now I am facing front-line soldiers who have orders to shoot anyone who seems suspicious. The commanding officer is no longer looking at the rest of my group; his fiery eyes bore directly into me. Two soldiers with hand grenades dangling from their belts shove me closer to him.

"*Ya yevrey*," I say and hand him my passport. He leafs through the pages covered with writing and official stamps, looks at the passport picture and then at me:

"Why were you, all along the way, looking about in all directions? Were you trying to hide in the woods?"

"I thought . . . it was hard for me to walk . . ." My tongue stumbles. I was about to explain that I thought my mother and my wife were calling me back. But I realize just in time that such an answer would probably evoke derisive laughter and make them still more suspicious.

"We know." The officer nods, as though he had expected my explanation. He begins to rummage through my knapsack and orders one of the others to search my pockets. The soldier pats me all over and feels a hard object in my coat pocket.

"I found something!" he calls out and pulls my small Hebrew Bible out of the pocket where I had put it when I left home.

"And what is this?" The officer leafs through the pages of the small volume.

"It's the Bible."

"Are you a German? A German pastor?" The officer pushes his cap visor back on his head; his narrow, overgrown forehead is furrowed, and grows still narrower.

Both the soldiers and the civilians, my fellow wanderers, stand around us with downcast eyes and wry smiles. I cannot tell whether they are smiling because they know the interrogator is toying with me to amuse himself, or because they are astonished at my failure to realize that I am already a condemned man.

"I, a German? I, a German pastor?" I touch my face, and a thought
strikes me: Yes, it is possible that I do look like a German pastor—my
sparse, disheveled hair, my unshaven blond beard, the Bible, my accent
. . . a pastor. I know that I must say something, shout; but instead of
giving an explanation I burst into wild laughter. I know that this could
well be the end of me: even if, up to now, the officer has not been all
that serious he may now, enraged by my laughter, give the order to finish
me off. But my guts are churning within me—I have to laugh. An officer
in a blue uniform springs at me in a rage, pulls out his pistol, and presses
the cold barrel against my forehead:

"I'll give you something to laugh at! Saboteur! Spy!"

The interrogator remains cool and calm. He hands my passport and
my Bible to one of the soldiers and says brusquely:

"The passport is forged. Take him to Headquarters."

Soldiers surround me, one on either side and one behind, and the
steel of their bayonets flashes before my eyes. I am no longer laughing.
Deathly silent, I heave the knapsack back on my shoulders and stride
off, hemmed in on three sides. The patrol leads me out of the woods,
along a footpath into a field of grain. Everything around us is golden,
luminous, still—the ripe, tall, yellowish stalks sway as high as my head.
It seems to me that the earth has rotated like a wheel and that the fields
of grain I now see before me are those of the village of Rukon, outside
Vilna where I left Frumme-Liebche. . . . The officer's order was to take
me to Headquarters. At Headquarters there will be generals and commissars. They will know what a Hebrew Bible is, they will realize I'm
not a German. But then, maybe they're only fooling me? Maybe they're
taking me to . . .

"Where are you taking me?" I scream at the patrol.

"Keep walking!" yells the soldier behind me.

"What do you need your shoes for? Give them to me," laughs the
soldier on my right.

"And give me what you've got in your knapsack—I'll send it home
for you," says the one on my left.

They want me to take off my shoes, to go barefoot. One who is
barefoot is not taken to Headquarters, but to be shot. It must be terrible
to die with your shoes on. They will shoot me, and there will be no Jew
to witness my death. My mother and Frumme-Liebche will never find
out what happened. They will think I'm still alive, that I'll come back
one day, and I'll be rotting away in a field somewhere. Mother! Frumme-
Liebche! Now I can think of both of them at the same time. Before I
was unable to think of them together. . . .

We come out of the tall grain into a meadow surrounded by forests.

A rider on a brown horse heads toward us at full speed. When he reaches us he reins in his horse, which is seething and foaming, stomping its hooves, barely able to hold still. The rider—who wears a hat edged with red and has red stripes running down the sides of his trousers, as though he were engulfed in flames—bends down from the saddle and measures me with his eyes:

"Who is this?"

"A suspect," answers one of the soldiers.

One of the patrol hands my passport and my Bible to the horseman. Even before glancing at the passport, he begins to inspect the Bible, which is very thick, small, and square, bound in black, with gilt letters on the spine. Then he leafs through it slowly, turning the pages with a bemused and somber expression. He casts a sidelong glance at me and immediately lowers his eyes to my passport. I sense that this man will save me and fling myself toward him:

"I'm a Jew. I'm escaping from the Germans, and they think I'm a German. The book the comrade commander is holding is the Old Testament in Hebrew. I took it with me from home."

"What kind of nonsense is this?" the horseman shouts angrily at my guards, as he hands me the Bible and passport. "Let him go!"

"We were told to take him to Headquarters," says the soldier behind me, stepping forward.

"Go back! On the double! Return to your posts!" The officer lunges at them with his horse, as though to trample them; then, head bent close to the horse's mane, he gallops toward the forest from which we have come. The soldiers leave me standing there and run back to their post, as if understanding from the horseman's shout that the enemy is approaching.

I remain alone in the meadow—passport in my left hand, the little Bible open in my right—and gaze about me in amazement, as though I were seeing the world for the first time. Birds are chirping amid the dense tree branches, summer flies buzzing in the tall green grass; around me all is still, a humming stillness, and the air shimmers gold and blue. My glance falls upon a verse in the Bible, and I read as if in a dream:

"For I am with thee, saith the Lord, to save thee: though I make a full end of all nations whither I have scattered thee, yet I will not make a full end of thee: but I will correct thee in measure, and I will not leave thee altogether unpunished."

I put the Bible in my coat pocket, the passport in my inside pocket, and walk quickly away. Where I am going, I do not know; I know only that I must get away from that place. I must also avoid meeting up with my companions of the previous day—the kolkhoznik might denounce me again to some other army patrol. I move to the left, across the meadow, to the woods. Within my mind, now broken free of its deathly stupor, my thoughts whirl about in a jumble:

The horseman was a Jew, surely a Jew! He had Jewish eyes, and he took his time leafing through the small Bible, turning the thin pages with trembling fingers, while he avoided looking directly at me. He did so intentionally, so the soldiers wouldn't notice that he saw in me one of his own and had pity. ". . . but I will correct thee in measure, and I will not leave thee altogether unpunished. . . ." In Jeremiah is this verse, in Jeremiah. I know this verse, yet I've never thought about it. Who opened my little Bible just to this verse, I myself or the horseman? I must take care not to lose my passport, not lose the Bible, and not forget the verse. "I will correct thee in measure . . ." Is this a miracle? I've left my mother, left Frumme-Liebche, and fled away alone, fled with the Bible in my pocket.

Parents and Children

I RUB THE SLEEP from my eyes and find myself in a wood; it is already past noon. The sun drips down among the dense branches like hot pitch. White trunks of birch trees gleam around me, light-green leaves glitter at their crowns. A few steps away, in the shade, lie my new traveling companions, a group of Jews from Minsk. Instantly I recall the events of that morning.

I was wandering aimlessly through the woods, not knowing whether I was going forward or backward, and so I decided to head toward a place where blue sky could be seen through sparse branches. I came out upon the asphalt highway that connects Minsk and Moscow. There I met a small company of Jews who were fleeing from Minsk, and continued on with them.

The sun baked us, drenched us in sweat. Our feet sank into the melting asphalt, which had been cratered and tunneled by the bombs dropped upon it. Scattered all along the way were overturned vehicles and the corpses of men slain by bomb fragments or bullets. One of the dead lay face down, crumpled into a ball; he seemed to be trying to crawl into the earth to hide from the bombardment. Another corpse leaned back against a rock in a half-sitting position, the face waxen, the large, yellowed head totally bald as if singed by fire; he stared with open, unmoving eyes and clutched at the ground with cramp-twisted fingers, as though making an effort to rise. By the side of the road lay a third corpse, stiffly stretched out and covered with a layer of branches—perhaps by passers-by who had thus taken pity on him, so that he should not be kicked about on the road; or perhaps it was a wife who had so covered her dead husband, or a son his father.

We marched on until we heard a metallic drone—the herald of death. High up in the sky, forming a slowly moving triangle, were nine planes. The bombardiers, we realized, did not intend their heavy load for us—a tiny clutch of walking refugees did not make a worthy target. But suddenly one of our company screamed that a plane was racing toward us. Frightened by his despairing cry, we all left the road and ran crouching toward the forest. Once in the thicket, we recovered from our momentary terror and fell upon the one who had screamed: Where had he seen a plane coming toward us? But, still trembling and weeping, he insisted he had heard the rattle of a machine gun: clack-clack-clack.

This earned him jeers from the other Minskers. Nonetheless, they decided that, though the danger this time had been imaginary, there was always the possibility of a real attack. And so it was determined that we would rest in the forest until it grew dark, and then set out for Borisov. We went deeper into the woods and the Minskers stretched out on the grass. I, too, exhausted from my long journey, crept off to the side and fell asleep.

I CRAWL ON MY ELBOWS toward the Minskers, who all wear short, narrow jackets, flat canvas caps with stiff and rounded visors, and high boots with unpolished tops. It is only a day since they fled their homes, and raw fear still shows in their eyes. They regard me with a certain wariness, a curiosity edged with suspicion—as though we were long-estranged brothers who, upon their reunion, carefully look each other over before recognizing at last that they are the sons of one father. In my disheveled, dust-covered clothing, unshaven face, and rigid silence they can discern their own imminent fate. Yet they wish to demonstrate to me their Soviet patriotism, and one of them tells me, his words punctuated by hard Russian r's:

"As soon as you get to Borisov, you must report to the Military Commissariat for service in the Red Army. You Zapadniki* were oppressed for years by the Polish *pans*. Now you should be the first to defend the Soviet fatherland."

My companions had waited until the very last moment, when the city was already in flames all about them and the trains had stopped running, and they had fled without their families. There is only one family group among us: a small, shriveled old woman with her son, daughter-in-law, and grandchild. The young man—it was he who had imagined a plane pursuing us—is short like his mother, with large, frightened eyes that wander constantly from one person to another. His wife, with a long, embittered face and stooped shoulders, holds her baby in her arms, rocking and feeding it. But the young man never looks at his child, as though he were still unaware that he is a father. At every rustling in the forest, every distant muffled cry or drone of a plane, he shudders and moves closer to his aged mother, nestling against her and trembling like a child. His wife sits with downcast eyes, not looking at any of us, apparently out of shame for her cowardly husband; she does not speak to him but, with barely contained anger, mumbles something

* "Westerners"—i.e., people from lands bordering the Soviet Union proper in the west, lands annexed by the Soviets in 1939 or later.—Trans.

to her mother-in-law. The old woman tugs at her son's sleeve and speaks to him softly, calms him, reassures him that he has no more to fear than the others.

"And when will we return to Minsk?" he asks in a tearful voice. The man who had warned me to report for army service in Borisov spits in disgust:

"And what will happen to you when you go to the front and get your first whiff of gunpowder?"

The frightened young man remains seated, his eyes dark, his face ashen-gray, rusty, like someone who has already been lying on a battlefield for weeks, rotting in the rain. His mother, the shriveled old woman, sighs softly and his wife begins angrily to rock the infant in her arms to quiet it, though the child has been silent all the while—as if it, too, were ashamed of its father, the coward.

THE SUN BEGINS TO SINK behind the trees. The tree trunks glittered as if molded of copper; the earth is dry and hot; the air is glowing, heavy, suffocating. A noxious breeze carries to our nostrils the odor of pitch, along with the sharp smell of pines and of steaming tree-foliage. The branches, which have throughout the day been hanging limp with heat, now begin to rustle their leaves uneasily, whispering into our ears that we shall soon be able to creep stealthily away. At night, airplanes are blind. Our small group prepares to move on.

Suddenly we hear soft, furtive footsteps, and a large crowd of people abruptly materializes before us: an entire kolkhoz has uprooted itself. Peasants, men and women and young girls, all rush by, all empty-handed. No one wants to stop even for a moment to tell us what has happened. Only one girl, with full rosy cheeks and a head of blond hair, whispers hastily to us, as though fearful lest the trees overhear:

"The Germans are coming! A German scout patrol!"

I jump up and begin to run. The dying sun dances toward me from all sides, its flames darting among the branches; it seeks to distract me, engulf me with its fire. Uncovered tree roots catch at my feet. I slide down a hill, trip over a tree stump, jump up, and run on. But I cannot run away from the thought that the Germans have succeeded in breaking through the Red Army's front lines in the forest. The green-clad soldiers who had taken me off to be shot were perhaps already all dead. And the Jewish officer on horseback, the one who had saved my life—was he dead as well? . . .

Many others are running with me, in front of me, behind me. We reach a meadow overgrown with tall vegetation. I see the kolkhozniks moving to the right, then to the left, and I follow in their footsteps. I know I must not lose sight of them—they are natives here and know the way. Just ahead of me is the old woman, weeping. She is shouting something, but I run past her, come abreast of the son, and struggle to overtake the daughter-in-law, who is in the lead with the child in her arms. I hear the old woman's cry:

"Where are you abandoning me? My children!"

"I don't want my child to be left an orphan!" shouts the younger woman, who does not even turn her head, so as not to lose a moment's time.

"My son, where are you abandoning me?" The old woman's wail catches up with me, like the echo of a mourning cry in a deserted graveyard . . . "My son!"

"Farewell, Mother!" shouts the younger woman into the wind that is blowing against her. "If it is our destiny to remain alive, we'll yet meet again."

I stand frozen, rooted to the spot, unable to move hand or foot. The young man, running behind his wife and ahead of his mother, again catches up with me. Seeing me standing there, he stops too, tears at his hair, claws his face:

"What should I do? What should I do?" He flings his head to one side, toward his wife; then to the other, toward his mother. "What should I do? What should I do?"

"Come on, I tell you!" His wife turns to him with the infant in her arms. "My child has had no life on earth yet, and neither have I."

The son no longer looks backward, toward his mother, but flings himself forward, to catch up with his wife. I feel the veins in my temples swelling, bursting. I spring at him and with both hands seize him by the throat:

"Are you going to leave your old mother alone?" I gag on the words, as though he were holding me by the throat, as though he were choking me and not I him.

For an instant he stands still and lets me shake him. Abruptly his upturned eyes flame with rage. He tears himself away from me and, gnashing his teeth, snarls:

"And you? Where's your family? You ran away without them."

His eyes glitter in vengeful triumph at my confusion, and he races on ahead. I lunge after him, not knowing myself whether I want only to overtake him or to seize him by the throat again.

"Run, children, save yourselves!" I hear the voice of the old woman. I turn my head: impossible that this could be the cry of the same woman who has just been pleading not to be abandoned. But it is she, it is she, the old woman. She is already far behind me, has grown smaller, more shriveled. But I can still see the strands of white hair fluttering about her head, and her voice rings out across the meadow:

"I'm a dead shard—it's a sin before God for me to compare myself to you. Run faster, my children, faster! Fa . . . a . . . a . . ."

Her voice is swallowed up amidst the tall bushes, and the surrounding silence. In the west a huge glowing sun is setting, deepening the silence of dusk. On one side the fields are already sunk in shadow, while on the other, the tall, gracefully curving plants are still illuminated with a dark-red hue, like fiery tresses of the setting sun. The last rays cut across each other, crisscrossing like bloody hatchets, assuming the shape of a swastika. From the crimson clouds now gathered on the horizon a great black aircraft darts out, silently, stealthily, and sinks down with a muffled sound upon the darkened plain.

A landing.

I start to run along the path on which the kolkhozniks, the Jews from Minsk, and the husband and wife have fled, but I see no one— somewhere amidst the tall vegetation, they have made an unexpected detour. A surge of pounding fear: soon the Germans who have just landed would surround me, submachine guns at the ready. I look back toward the place where the old woman had last stood. But I can see her no longer, as though she has turned herself into grass, or become a stone sinking into the moss. Where she had been there is now another abandoned one—there, wearing a shy smile, her face suffused with the last glow of the sun's rays, stands Frumme-Liebche . . .

I close my eyes for an instant and open them again, prepared to meet my fate—and see, quite close by, my group. They are running with heads and shoulders bent, so as not to be seen above the vegetation. I quickly catch up to them. The kolkhozniks, in the lead, bring us out upon the broad asphalt highway, the same one we had been afraid to use in daylight. Now that darkness has fallen, the planes can no longer attack and strafe us. The hidden enemy now rages like a fever in the forests, and we can walk along the main road.

The Moscow Highway

THE HORDES OF REFUGEES now surge along like wind-torn clouds, in far greater haste and in denser masses than the night before. My companions are constantly changing. I have fallen behind my former comrades-in-flight, the Jews from Minsk. One after another, new groups come abreast of me, keep pace with me for a little while, and then rush on ahead. The day I spent lying in the forest has made me realize how tired I am. My limbs feel like lead, I can barely lift my feet; again and again I am left behind.

Only one person, a scrawny little young man from Poland, stays beside me all along the way. A noxious smell emanates from him—the dank moldiness of rotting clothes, the stench of a swamp. In my nostrils his foul odor is poison to the fresh fragrance of the plains that stretch far and away all around us. I feel nauseous, close to vomiting, but I cannot get away from him; he dogs my every step like a shadow, chuckling malevolently:

"No butter and no meat, no clothes and no housing; they had to build factories and tanks and airplanes so they could stand up against the enemy. But now the war has come, they have no tanks, no planes, and they run like mice."

Since crossing into Soviet territory proper, I have till now heard no one speak against the Soviet authorities—although it is easy to read in people's faces the bitterness caused by the retreat of the Red Army; I can hear it in their silence, in their sighs. It occurs to me that this Polish Jew may be testing me: he is staying with me in order to find out what I am thinking. So I tell him we must hurry on, the Germans are hard on our heels.

"I'm dying for some bacon," he answers. The Germans, he says, will give him a piece of pork, something he hasn't tasted since he fled from his Polish shtetl to the Soviets. And once he's eaten a proper portion of pork, it won't matter if they shoot him.

"You're a Jew and the Germans won't give you any pork—a bullet in the head is all you'll get," I gasp breathlessly and rush ahead. He catches up with me again, and again the salty stench of urine hits me in the face:

"You probably had enough to eat under the Bolsheviks, so you're running away. I've been starving for two years already, I've been sleeping in my lice-infested clothes, I stink, and I myself don't know why I'm running away. From what I've heard, the Jews in the Warsaw ghetto 'are living and making a living.' "

A lunatic, I tell myself. Who knows what he's capable of? I mingle with a group of people who have caught up with me from behind. Soon we come up to a larger throng who have halted on the highway, unable to move forward. Lying in the middle of the road is a smashed truck, with a tall, broad-shouldered Russian beside it screaming hoarsely, wildly:

"Get back! The Germans shall not pass!"

The earlier arrivals explain to us, the newcomers, that the truck driver has been struck by a splinter in the brain and gone mad, and now will let no one pass. He is covered head to foot with blood and holding something in his hands—a stick of dynamite, perhaps, or a hand grenade or a bomb. If they try to move past him, he might throw it. But they're just as afraid to leave the highway: German paratroopers lurk in the woods. What a devil of a fix!

"What are you holding there, countryman?" asks someone in the crowd, seeking to pacify the madman by addressing him in tones of camaraderie.

"The motor. I took the motor out of my truck, so the enemy won't be able to drive it. They're not going to get to Moscow in my truck. The Germans shall not pass!" Holding the motor high with both hands, he advances toward us.

"May God have mercy on him, they ought to shoot him," someone near me murmurs. The crowd, finding the madman has no dynamite after all, fears him no longer, and the Russian who has just questioned him in comradely fashion now shouts like a general on a battlefield:

"Fellows, let's go!"

For a moment the crowd forgets the ever-lurking danger and, laughing boisterously, presses forward on all sides, as though pushing their way into a theater without tickets. The giant growls, bellows, tries in vain to hold the crowd back, and then, confused, like an animal at bay surrounded by hunting dogs, throws himself upon me:

"Where are you going?"

He raises the motor high with both hands, ready to bring it down full force onto my skull.

I scream, turn, run the other way. I hear him running after me, roaring: "Stop! Stop!" My eyes are clouded; I cannot see the road; I remember only that my feet must not become numb with fear. The knapsack on my back begins to bob up and down—one of the straps has broken. Still running, with my left hand I throw off the other strap and the knapsack. Perhaps he'll reach for it, perhaps he'll trip over it and fall; but no, he remains close behind me. Already I can feel his panting breath. I draw my head down between my shoulders, so as to lessen the impact of the descending motor . . . and find I have penetrated a new throng advancing toward us. My running, his screams, and the heavy object in his upraised arms confuse and scatter the crowd, as a storm-wind scatters a pile of withered leaves. I become entangled with the hands and feet of strangers, turn and run together with them, until I fall into a deep ditch, stretch out flat, and try to dig myself into the ground.

Above me I hear the sounds of snorting, of clambering, of wild running, howling, wheezing, many hurried steps, the stomping of boots. The earth above and beneath me is heaving, as though I were swimming under water. I can still hear the madman screaming: "Stop! Stop!" Now he is chasing someone else down the highway . . . At last his screams grow faint and muted, the whirling clatter of footsteps fades into the distance, and all other sounds ebb away. My heart is pounding, pounding as though it wants to burst out of my chest; it quakes and pleads: "Let me end here—what's the use of all this torment, this struggle? No matter what, you won't save yourself."

Slowly, slowly, the pounding of my heart ceases, and is replaced by the mysterious, uncanny silence of a deserted road. The silence burrows into my brain; the pre-dawn chill pricks me with thousands of darts; I roll myself tightly into a ball; I am weary, I want to sleep. But now a thought begins to flicker in my near-extinguished mind, like a small flame in the attic of a darkened building:

"The Germans!"

I crawl out of the ditch—and into the full light of day. The highway is deserted; between me and the relentlessly approaching Germans there is only empty space, with nothing and no one to hide me from them. The shadows that had enveloped the surrounding fields have vanished, and everywhere I look the earth lies naked in the light of the fresh new morning. I stride forward with eyes fixed on the ground, like someone climbing a steep slope who fears to look down into the abyss behind him or up toward the peak above, lest dizziness overwhelm him.

For some minutes I press on, just barely managing to drag myself along, until suddenly I stumble into the Polish refugee. He is standing in the middle of the road, and in his hands is—my knapsack. In the steel-gray light of day, he looks to be a man of about twenty-five; he is short, skinny, dirty, his face covered with pimples, and the foul stench that rises from him is even stronger now in the freshness of early morning.

"I knew this had to be your pack," he exclaims joyfully, and holds the knapsack out to me.

"You were waiting for me?" I stare at him: he clearly doesn't realize the danger we are in. "Throw away the knapsack, we'll be able to move faster."

Silently he flings my pack across his shoulder and starts walking beside me. Before long, however, he begins to lag behind. I turn toward him once, then a second time—he is falling further and further behind. I stop to wait for him, but he shouts at me:

"Go on, go on, I'll catch up with you."

I am possessed by a strange sense of calm, of indifference; nothing troubles me any more. I stride onward, laughing to myself: Let him take the knapsack with my underwear, the lunatic. He told me he's been rotting in the same rags for two years already—so now he wants to change his underwear once more before he dies.

Walking becomes more and more difficult for me and, looking down at my feet, I see that I am limping. Apparently I injured one foot when I jumped into the ditch, but in my panic-stricken state hadn't felt the pain, hadn't realized I was hurt. Well, that settles it, then: I will never escape.

In the middle of the road stands a soldier—coatless, weaponless, belt unbuckled, uniform unbuttoned; his feet are wide apart as he urinates. When he catches sight of me, his cheerful, ruddy face breaks into a laugh; inhaling deeply through his short snub of a nose, he shouts jovially:

"There's nothing to fight for!"

A deserter, I think indifferently, and stride on. He's certain the Soviet state is collapsing, and that nothing will happen to him. It won't matter to him if he falls into German hands. Soon it won't matter to me either. *Naplevat'!*

On the left side of the road is a forest, its treetops glittering in the sun. On the right side, broad expanses of land stretch before me: neatly bordered vegetable gardens, fences, here and there a cottage, a tall open-sided wagon without a horse, an open barn, ricks of hay dotting a meadow. No peasants or animals are in sight, not even a dog. They either have run off or are in hiding until the Germans arrive.

Directly ahead of me, in the middle of the road, walks an old woman in a long winter-coat. I catch up to her. But she does not notice me, as though either she or I were only a shadow, a figment of the imagination. She is silent, despondent, and I too am silent, feeling nothing, thinking nothing. She is old and I limp, and so we both—are lost.

The snub-nosed soldier with the red, drink-sodden face comes abreast of us on her other side. He is marching, singing gaily, waving his hands about:

"Where you off to, Granny?" he shouts into the old woman's ear while giving me a wink. "What's wrong? Did your daughter-in-law chase you out of the house?"

The old woman gives no answer; hunched over, stupefied, hands clasped within her coatsleeves, she walks painfully on. I glance at her again—and in my benumbed mind something wells up. I am overcome by an uncanny dread, I start to run! It is she—the same old woman whose son and daughter-in-law had abandoned her last night in the field near the forest. Now she was searching for her children. . . .

I look back several times, to find each time the soldier still at her side. He seems to be trying to convince her of something, gesticulating vigorously, laughing cheerfully. I must be mad, I tell myself. The Russian with the motor and the Polish refugee have infected me with their madness. That old woman fell behind in the first ten minutes; this is a different woman, one who lives nearby, and the Russian soldier, a stranger to her, a deserter and a drunkard, refuses to abandon her. I turn around once more: both old woman and soldier have vanished. A hallucination.

"Go on, go on, I'll catch up to you. I won't take your pack away." The Polish refugee appears yet again, behind me on the highway that winds its way uphill and down. But now I want to wait for him, I want to ask him whether or not he has seen an old woman with a soldier.

Behind the refugee are soldiers on motorcycles—riding slowly, row upon row, spread out across the highway. They sit stiffly on their cycles, as if hewn out of stone. On their helmets, pulled low over their foreheads, the swastika sparkles blindingly in the sunlight, and they are smiling: They look neither to the right nor to the left; they look only at me and grin like specters: You won't escape.

"Germans," I say to myself with frozen calmness; I am astonished by my composure. I leave the highway and turn to the left, to the forest only a few steps from the road. From among dense, low-hanging branches of the trees a head and a hand emerge and signal to me. I step toward the beckoner, beginning to feel that I too am hewn out of stone, like the cyclists up on the road. The man who has signaled to me stands with a broken-off branch in his hand in place of a stick. Under his jacket he wears a Russian peasant blouse that falls loosely over his trousers.

"Who's riding up there on the road?" he asks.

"Germans," I answer.

He stands silent and gives me a long look, amazed at my calmness. He clearly does not believe me.

"A Jew?" he asks in Yiddish.

"A Jew."

"Come," he says curtly, and starts to crawl back into the forest. I crawl after him, but from time to time I turn around.

Following us at a short distance is the Polish Jew, my knapsack slung over his shoulder.

Road Companions

EARLIER IT HAD SEEMED TO ME that the old woman on the road wearing a long coat was the same old woman I had met the day before, the one abandoned by her son and daughter-in-law; now the forest too appears to be the same one in which I had lain yesterday till dusk. The forest, I fantasize, has traveled with me all along the road, and during the night has grown older, denser, darker, primordial. Century-old tree-trunks crowd one upon the other; evergreens intertwine with leafy trees; branches entangled, they stare at each other like bewildered strangers. We too, three fleeing refugees, gaze at one another suspiciously, sniff at one another cautiously, huddling close together like animals pursued by hunters.

The Jew in the white peasant blouse has a good-natured face, full, well-fed cheeks, warm brown eyes. He is from Bobruisk, he tells me, and had been working for the Party in liberated Lithuania. He then turns to the short, shriveled Polish refugee, who looks like a young boy.

"Why do you stink so?" he asks. "Don't you ever take a bath? There's a public bath in every Soviet city."

"It's you Sovietchiks who stink!" retorts the other.

The man from Bobruisk turns back to me in surprise and asks in sign language what sort of fellow this is I have brought along. I touch a finger to my temple to indicate that our companion is unbalanced, and wink to him to leave the lunatic alone.

"You're certain the men on the highway are Germans?" asks the Bobruisker, as though suspecting me also of having lost my senses.

"They're already putting up markers along the road." I point through the trees at silhouetted figures moving about on the highway.

"I can see people," says the Bobruisker, "but I can't see that they're Germans." But he is afraid to crawl out from our hiding-place to get a better view. For a moment he sits with head bent, then he takes out a packet of folded papers from inside his blouse, looks through them, and tears them into small fragments. As he does this his brow becomes furrowed, seeming almost to swell, as though he were making a strenuous effort to repeat to himself and remember everything written in these papers.

"You'd better tear up your documents too." He moans and sighs as deeply and heavily as if he were flaying the very skin off his own body.

"If we're caught, the Germans must not find out that we're Jews. I'm a White Russian, and we don't know each other."

I take out my passport and turn to the page with my photograph pasted on it: before I tear it up, I want to take one more look at my picture. Suddenly the Polish Jew—who has kept silent all this time, sunk in the decay both of his own rags and of the wilderness around us—lets out a scream:

"Don't tear up your passport!"

I put my passport back in my inner pocket. He is right: if I'm caught, I won't be able to fool the Germans, to make them think I'm not a Jew; but if I do break through their lines, I won't be safe for even a day among the Russians without a passport. The Jew from Bobruisk is holding a thin, narrow, rectangular booklet in his hands, turning it this way and that; he looks at me in evident confusion and finally asks the Polish Jew:

"And you—do you have a passport?"

"I am an 'unreliable element,' " the Polish Jew replies, mimicking the official Soviet jargon. "Me they didn't give a passport. And now I don't need one anymore."

"I won't tear up my Party identification," mutters the Bobruisker to himself, as though the Polish Jew's avowal of not having a passport has made it clear to him, the Communist, that it is better to risk his life than to go without his Party card. He pulls off his right boot, places the slim rectangular booklet inside it as a padding on the sole, and, while struggling to pull the boot back on over his leggings, speaks to the Polish refugee:

"If we're caught, don't say anything about what we said here or what you saw. I have a long knife; if you say a word, I'll kill you with it." But he issues this threat with a wistful smile on his face, which is not the face of a knife-wielder.

"You don't have a knife, and I'm not afraid of you," the younger man answers. "It's you Sovietchiks who are informers, not I."

The Bobruisker does not respond. He looks dejected, and clearly has no wish to start up with a madman. Leaning on his elbows, he stretches out on his stomach, and whispers to me that after nightfall, we'll try to get through to Borisov, which is quite close by. "And in Borisov," he says, "our boys will put up a resistance."

By nightfall, I tell myself, the Germans will have overrun the whole area. But I say nothing. The thought that I will be shot stabs through my brain with a dull ache, as though all my limbs have already died and only in one temple does a pulse still beat. I look at the Polish Jew and am seized by a conviction I cannot explain: that precisely because he does not grasp the danger, he will survive.

"I'm from Vilna, and I have a wife and a mother there," I say to him, and repeat my name several times. "If they shoot me, remember my name and that I'm from Vilna."

"Very well," he answers.

We hear the crackling of dry twigs under someone's feet. Two hands push aside the leaves above our hiding-place, and a tall young fellow in a blue peasant blouse, with a long, pointed head and no cap, jumps back at the sight of us, as though he has come upon a den of wolves. From his obvious fright we know he has not been looking for us; he, in turn, can tell by our appearance that we are hiding. Speaking rapidly and disjointedly, he explains to us that he is a White Russian who lives in this area, and that he had been walking through the forest when he was set upon by two strangers who took his money, his jacket, and his cap.

"Scoundrels! If I ever run across them, I'll settle accounts with them soon enough," says the Bobruisker, delighted to meet someone from home, and he proceeds to tell the White Russian about the highway's being overrun by the Germans.

"Germans?" says the White Russian, showing neither much surprise nor much fear. "When I left Borisov this morning, nobody knew anything about that."

The Bobruisker leaps to his feet, squares his shoulders, and assumes a severe expression:

"I'm a member of the Party and a political instructor in the Army. Comrade, you must lead us through the forest to Borisov."

"I don't want to stay here with the Germans, either." The White Russian starts to move deeper into the forest. I scramble hastily to my feet, the Polish Jew behind me carrying my pack on his back, and, together with the Bobruisker, we creep softly behind our guide, until we reach a well-trodden path in the middle of the woods. Suddenly our guide becomes a whirl of hands and feet, scampers off, and before we can recover from our surprise is already a good distance away. He turns to face us, raises a vein-covered fist, guffaws, and disappears into the thickets. The Bobruisker looks at me with eyes turned completely white, as if the pupils have deserted them in terror.

"A spy—a White Russian spy!" My lips twitch and begin to mumble of their own accord: ". . . But I will correct thee in measure, and will not leave thee altogether unpunished." I put my hand into my coat pocket, where I keep my little Bible . . . where the verse is . . . But the Bible isn't there.

"What are you looking for?" asks the Bobruisker.

"I'm looking for my little Bible. You don't know what a Bible is? You're a Jew and you don't know what a Bible is?" I scream, all disheveled and drenched in sweat, and turn pleadingly to the Polish Jew: "Maybe you saw my Bible?"

"I'm not one of your pious thieves." His glowering eyes shoot sparks. "If I had a piece of pork, I'd gobble it up."

"A pistol would be more use to us," says the Bobruisker sadly, his voice quavering. "I'd have finished off that spy with the first bullet."

"My little Bible saved my life. Because of my Bible a Jewish officer on horseback saved my life, and you don't even know what a Bible is," I shout at him, and continue searching in my pockets: Nothing. I must have lost it early that morning when I jumped into the ditch, or even before then, when we were all sitting on the ground. I am about to turn back to look for it when . . . God in Heaven, it's here! It's lying just where I had put it, deep down inside my pocket.

"We mustn't stay here even one second longer," I shout to my companions. "That spy will bring his chums back here."

The Bobruisker hastily leads the way; I fall in behind him, and the Polish Jew behind me. Around us the fir trees are swallowed up in darkness. Scattered amidst the evergreens are stray oaks, stiff and numb, withering in the middle of summer—their trunks gnarled and knotty, their branches drooping, their hairy dark-green leaves hanging flaccid as limp fingers. An uprooted tree, lacking the space to fall flat, has remained at a slant, its crown caught in the branches of another tree. The forest is dark, cold, gloomy, numbly silent. I hear no birds singing, no woodpecker tapping, not even the buzzing of flies. I call out to the Bobruisker, who is getting further and further ahead:

"Wait for me!"

"I can't wait for you—you're limping!" In evident anger and distaste he turns around and then away, and strides off. Clearly, he no longer wants to stay with the two of us. I look behind me—the Polish Jew too has vanished.

I crawl on, amidst thorny bushes, over tall piles of fallen leaves and evergreen needles, into a thicket of ferns, until the woods become sparser and I can see the highway in the distance. From behind the thickly matted darkness there breathes upon me the breath of death, which drives me steadily toward the highway, bathed in noonday light.

When I emerge onto the highway, I see ahead of me a hilly area, the roofs of tall buildings, the chimneys of factories: Borisov! But where are the Germans! . . . No, I had not imagined them. They had been an advance guard which had reconnoitered the terrain and then withdrawn.

In front of me are two people moving slowly, wearily. Catching up to them, I can see that they are Jews—an old woman and a young man. He is carrying a huge bundle of bedding on his back. In his right hand he holds a large tin kettle, and I can hear the water splashing inside. I feel a dryness in my throat, a choking; a mound of sand is piled up in my gullet.

"Good people—a drink!" I rasp out. "Give me a drink."

The young fellow—who cannot lift his head under a pile of bedding twice as tall as he is—gives me a dark look from beneath his eyebrows: "I'm not even taking a drink myself. It's only for my mother."

The old woman, barely able to lift her feet, walks doubled over. Her drooping hands almost touch the ground, as though she were feeling her way with her fingers. She stops, gives me a sorrowful glance, and speaks to her son in a trembling voice:

"Don't begrudge a drink of water. Help a human being in need."

I look at the kettle in terror, as if blood, not water, were splashing about inside. Do you hear? He himself drinks nothing—it is only for his mother. . . .

"Throw away your pack," I cry out. "I saw a German reconnaissance unit on the way. I swear to you—it wasn't my imagination."

"Where did you see them?" He turns slowly around, with his load on his shoulders, and looks back at the road along which we have come. It is sleepily quiet: not a living soul in sight.

"My son has been carrying our belongings all the way from Minsk." The old woman begins to weep. "God has helped us this far, and we're already so close to Borisov, should we throw it away now?"

"There's no one on the road—you must have dreamt it," the young man tells me, as if convinced of this precisely by my insistence on not having imagined it. "I can see you're a Westerner, so you don't understand what it means to set off in Russia without bedding or clothes."

"Go on ahead, young man—don't wait for us," says the old woman. And once again she pleads with her son: "Give him a drink of water."

But I am no longer willing to wait for a drink. Defying my stiffened body, I stride forward at such a vigorous and rapid pace that I even stop limping. I clamber up a hill that leads to a suburb of Borisov. Here and there, under trees, small groups of Red Army soldiers are clustered around machine guns, but none of them pays me any attention.

I enter an outlying district of small wooden houses—ramshackle, misshapen, neglected. Small detachments of soldiers move this way and that in no apparent order, here dragging a small cannon across a crooked bridge, there following slowly behind covered farm wagons pulled by tired horses. The wagons rattle, street-corner loudspeakers play military marches, dense clouds of dust swirl everywhere, and the Red Army men, grimy and crestfallen, drag themselves along in disarray. And I, unsteady of foot and mind befogged, thrust myself among these shattered army units, among the wagons; and all the road I have traveled—bathed in sunlight, silent and mysterious—follows behind me.

Back on the highway, the young man with the huge pack on his shoulders is still trudging on, carrying the kettle and keeping close beside the bent form of his mother, not even permitting himself a drink of water. Behind these two, on the other side of the forest and its mossy darkness, another small old woman inches her way along the road, with a little soldier, a stranger and a deserter, staying loyally at her side. On the other side of the night, in a field outside Minsk, a woman with a child in her arms, her frightened husband, and an old abandoned mother pursue me. And behind those three, behind another day and another night, near the village of Rukon, Frumme-Liebche—stands smiling. And behind Frumme-Liebche, in her small house in Vilna, sits my mother, so tiny, so gray—a little dove. Even as I move further and further away from her, she remains the same, like a star in the heavens.

I hear someone call my name, and a hand grasps my arm. It is the Polish refugee.

"Here—" he hands me my knapsack—"and you thought I'd steal it from you."

"How did you know my name?"

"You told me that in case you were shot, I should remember your name. So I remember it."

"I told you that if I were shot, you should remember my name?" I stare at him as if he has come from another world to tell me what I did in a previous incarnation. "And why have you been carrying my pack all this time, if you're giving it back to me now? I thought you wanted to—I'll give you a set of underwear."

"I don't need your underwear and I don't need your Bible!" His eyes begin to glow again with an insane rage. "I want a piece of pork, I want to eat. I don't even know myself why I've run away. They say the Jews in Warsaw are living and making a living."

He leaves the knapsack at my feet and walks away, head swaying from side to side, feet stumbling wearily. To me it seems as if this gaunt youth in his tattered rags is going back—back to the quiet, sunny, deserted highway, back to the dark, overgrown forest in its mossy putrefaction.

The Train

FOLLOWING THE TRAIN is a wooden leg: to the long line of shadows that never leave me, this too has now been added.

In Borisov, on the way to the railway depot, I caught sight through an open window of a Jew with a clipped black beard. Burning with heat, covered with dust, I entered the house and asked him for a drink. He pointed toward a hallway with an earthen floor. There I found, standing on a bench, a tub filled with ice-cold water, into which I plunged my head. In the mirror of the water I confronted an unfamiliar face, unshaven and wild-looking. I continued drinking till at last the mirror crumpled and the water turned to ice, to lead, within me. Exhausted, I returned to the room where the master of the house was sitting, to thank him and to rest a few moments. The room was almost completely bare, with little furniture. On the table, which lacked even an oilcloth, lay some pumpernickel bread and a knife, and on the wall hung a picture of the Politburo reviewing a parade on Red Square in Moscow. I asked the Jew to sell me some bread. He cut off half the loaf and when I offered him thirty rubles, he took only ten—only as much as the bread had cost him. He shook his head sadly and told me he had two sons, both of them already at the front. I said that the Germans were just outside Borisov and asked him why he wasn't running away. At that, from behind the table where he was sitting, he stuck out a wooden leg, and sighed:

"How can I run away?"

He limped out from behind the table, climbed up on a chair and took down from the wall the picture of the Politburo reviewing the parade on Red Square.

Now that same wooden leg is following me, at the head of a long line of shadows trailing behind it. I hear it in the turning of the wheels, the clatter of the buffers, the heavy clanking of the chains between the cars; its measured wooden thud, reverberating above all other sounds, never ceases, never relents.

All the freight trains with closed box-cars have already left, packed with refugees, and we, the new hordes from Minsk and Borisov, from Vilna and Kovno, are riding on open platform cars such as, in more peaceful times, are used for transporting rocks or bricks, scrap iron or coals. We lie piled atop one another, hands and feet, heads and shoulders.

Those who have been unable to take anything with them push their way into any small free space. But those laden with bundles must fight tooth and nail for some room for their stuffed sacks. Each time the train stops, the battle breaks out anew: Those who are cramped or uncomfortable attempt to shift position. Eyes flash, faces twist, mouths foam, hands clench into fists, until the locomotive whistles, the train begins to move, and the close-packed refugees, restored to calm and to quiet, sway once again in time to the rhythmic clatter of the rails.

As I lie amid the crowd on the wood plank floor, my knapsack under my head, my attention is drawn to one particular group of men on our platform, all intertwined in a single heap. These are *zaklyuchonyie*, the bearded inmates of labor camps—burned by the sun, their hands rough and work-worn; dressed even now, in the middle of summer, in quilted cotton jackets and trousers, in winter caps with earflaps, and with dirty bundles beside them. Abject, tense, bewildered, they sit in total silence, seeming even to hold their breaths—fearful lest someone suspect them of rejoicing at the disastrous course of the war. Their guards have been forced to retreat with the Soviet army from the camps, and so they have been freed and permitted to go home. They look like animals that have escaped from a burning forest together with their enemies, the hunters, and the inhabitants of the surrounding village huts. All are now making their way together, driven by the smoke and flames.

A cheerful, shrill-voiced fellow in high boots and a ragged jacket, a factory worker, is roaming about the platform. Never staying in one place, he moves about from one group to another, seeking to ingratiate himself with those refugees who have food. The refugees, well aware of why he is currying their favor, calmly continue chewing their bread and cheese or onions and make no response to him. Finally he edges over to me and asks whether I have anything to eat; a Westerner, he says, must surely have a sackful of appetizing morsels.

This reminds me that in my knapsack I have a large paper bag of granulated sugar, put there by Frumme-Liebche. I take it out and place it before the factory worker. His eyes light up; he sticks a finger into the bag and licks it cautiously.

"So help me God," he shouts, "it's granulated sugar!" He heaps a fistful into his mouth and grinds away with jaws that quiver and twitch as if they were grinding pebbles.

One of the labor-camp inmates—a youngster with thick, curly blond hair and the face of a *durachok*, a simpleton—sticks out a hand and likewise grabs a fistful. The hand is promptly seized by the worker:

"Where are you sneaking? What did they put you away for, anyway?"

"Lost my passport," answers the young fellow with a grin that shows most of his front teeth missing.

"You're lying like a dog." The worker lets the ex-inmate take his handful of sugar and whispers softly to me, so no one else will hear: "Do you understand? Here, losing a passport does get you a little five-year stretch, but that low-down bum was locked up for panhandling. You can see for yourself he's a beggar, and here in the Soviet Union begging is forbidden. Everyone can work and earn a living." This last with a malicious gleam in his eyes.

He takes another fistful of sugar, slaps half of it into his mouth, and offers the remainder, still on his palm, to another convict, with a pock-marked face:

"And what were you in for?"

"Absenteeism."

"So, a devil-may-care attitude. Our government did the right thing when they locked you up." Beaming with delight, my companion favors me with a mock-serious explanation: "Do you understand? Here in the Soviet Union there are no bourgeois to exploit the working class. Here the working class owns the factories, and if you miss a day's work, well then, make up for it in a labor camp, and to the devil's dam with you!"

I see the rage burning within him; even as he hurls curses at himself, he is delighted with his inspiration of artfully disguising his atack on the regime under the appearance of praise. Yet again, he plunges his fingers into the bag of sugar as he asks a third prisoner why he was jailed. This one, however, has no appetite for either sweets or talk.

"Do you understand?" snickers my neighbor to me. "Here, in our stores, you can buy anything your heart desires at the official price. But this fellow, this speculator, did business at the bazaar bartering bread for cheap tobacco. Or maybe he got plastered, the lush, and slandered our Soviet Union, hooligan that he is. He must have complained that he has no boots, no workclothes, and that his guts ache with hunger. The liar! Here we all have boots, everybody has a nice place to live, everyone has enough to eat, and if you want to go to the theater, you can go, as often as you like."

"But now they've been freed," I say, just to say something, anything.

"Don't you worry," he laughs, with still greater gall and venom, "they won't get far. When they get home, the local NKVD will know exactly how much longer they're still supposed to serve, the vagabonds, and if by any chance their case records have been lost, they'll get twice as much. Don't you worry! The political prisoners, the enemies of the people, the counterrevolutionaries, those weren't set free. If they couldn't drag them along, then they surely shot them on the spot. To the devil with them!" He spits out the sweet aftertaste remaining in his mouth.

The refugees lie sprawled across their bundles, all entangled together and yet strangers to one another. Some eat, heads buried in their food baskets, swallowing more than they chew, as if choking on every bite they take in the face of the hungry people beside them. Others, however, are not the least bit bothered; they gnaw at their biscuits with visible relish, smack their lips, and rinse it all down with cold water. Those who have no food sit with eyes fixed on the floor, or stare up at the sky, so as not to sharpen their appetites further, and so their neighbors should not think that they, the hungry ones, are waiting to be offered a share of food.

The factory worker never takes his eyes off a young woman with a soot-covered face, who looks as if she has just escaped from a fire. Beside her are her two children, eating bread and herring, bread and sausage. She herself eats nothing and never lets her fixed stare wander from a glass pitcher filled with water that stands next to her. The children begin to fight, grabbing food from each other; startled out of her stupor, she slaps their hands.

"A commander's wife!" laughs my companion softly in my ear. Then he calls aloud to the woman:

"Give me some bread and herring and I'll give you some Western sugar to drink your boiled water with."

"And since when is it your sugar, scoundrel?" She hurls the words at him with loathing, as if she were shaking off a bullfrog that had leaped onto her lap. Then she turns to me, a dark glow in her eyes:

"Why do you let this impudent wretch eat up all your sugar?"

"I don't like granulated sugar. In Orsha I'll buy lump sugar," I answer, confounded by her piercing glance.

She looks at me with a surprised smile in her suddenly brightened eyes, but immediately lowers her head again; her fixed stare rests once more on the glass pitcher, as if the water that sways within it were the swaying scale of her fate. Other people also look at me—coldly, with contempt and even hostility, as one might look at a fool when one is in no mood for jests.

"You see," the factory worker roars in pretended anger at the commander's wife, "this man, even though he's a Westerner, is a good comrade and has faith in our Soviet state. He knows that as soon as we get to Orsha, he'll be able to buy as much sugar as he wants at the station refreshment stand."

In his shrill tones and mocking eyes I recognize his delight at making me out a fool, but I am even more chagrined at myself for having acted like a fool.

"Take the rest and move away from me." I point at the bag of sugar. "I know your game!"

"What do you know?" He jumps up, more frightened than angry. "You're a Western spy! Show us what you have there in your knapsack."

"Land him one right on his jaw, the scoundrel!" the commander's wife screams wildly, and the other refugees also turn on him:

"First you eat his sugar and now you're such a swine? We have people to protect us against spies, it's not your business, you loudmouth!"

"I didn't mean it, I was joking." The worker laughs a soft, ingratiating laugh; he crouches and then lies down, still and mute.

I put the paper bag with the remaining sugar back into my knapsack, place the bundle under my head, and begin swaying in unison with the other refugees on the platform, all now steeped once more in gloomy silence. Suddenly the locomotive shrieks, the wheels reverse, the chains between cars clank—and the train comes to a stop.

To THE RIGHT of the tracks there is a forest, to the left a station—a small shop inside a wooden hut, a water faucet, and several unfinished small houses. From all the open freight cars, those ahead of mine and those behind, people jump down with tumultuous joy. I want to drink, to eat; I grab my knapsack and start to climb down over the wheels. The commander's wife stops me:

"Young man, bring us some water, and you'll be able to drink, too." She hands me a tin kettle and promises to watch my pack so I needn't carry it with me.

I run quickly to the water spigot. When I get there, there is already a long line ahead of me and within a moment it has doubled in length behind me. The water flows rapidly in a full stream, and the line moves quickly. Some collect it in dippers, others in pots. One man drinks out of his cupped hands, another fills his cap, a third encloses the iron spigot with his fleshy lips, a fourth places a big pail under it, shouting as he does so that he is taking water for a whole car. "A supply officer," people mock, and refuse to let him fill his pail more than half full. I manage to fill the kettle and then rush over to the wooden hut, which is beleaguered by a throng of passengers.

"*Chto dayut?*"* I ask someone who is pushing forward with all his might.

"*Nye znayu,*"† he answers, not ceasing to elbow his way vigorously to the front.

* What are they giving out (or selling)?
† Don't know.

"There's nothing left!" comes the shout from those standing close to the shop door, and in the wink of an eye the crowd vanishes. Those who have succeeded in getting into the shop and making purchases now emerge with match boxes.

"There's no tobacco," they say.

Some carry small round packages wrapped in blue paper in their hands. I see my companion, the factory worker, coming out with such a package. He winks at me in a friendly, comradely way, as though there had never been a quarrel between us, breaks off half of the package, and hands it to me:

"Taste it, this minute, taste it!"

What he's given me looks like a piece of stale, dark honey cake. "Perhaps it's some kind of Russian gingerbread," I tell myself. I am hungry and the worker is looking at me provocatively, ready to take mortal offense if I don't accept his gift and eat this delicacy favored of all Soviet people. I take a bite, grimace, and spit it out:

"Chicory!"

"That's what they had and that's what I managed to grab. You gave me Western granulated sugar before, I give you Soviet chicory now. Never mind! You've eaten enough sweets in your life. 'We have everything.'" In his mouth the familiar Soviet slogan is suffused with undisguised hatred. "Aren't you going to eat the chicory?"

"No."

"Then give it back!" He pulls it out of my hand.

The locomotive whistles and I run back to our car with a full kettle of water, but also with an empty stomach twisting and writhing with hunger.

The Convicts

THE TRAIN NOW ENTERS A MILITARY ZONE, where the evacuees are forbidden to leave their platform-cars. On both sides stretch open areas surrounded by barbed wire. Behind the wire fences are munitions dumps, buildings, canvas tents, and many Red Army soldiers milling about. Guards are posted alongside the railroad tracks, protecting the stores of gunpowder. One soldier stands erect, head held high, boots close together, the butt-end of his gun close to his heel, as if he were at "attention." A second soldier smiles at the passing train and winks brazenly at a girl with a peasant kerchief, while a third gazes with envy after the civilians who are moving further and further from the front.

"Our heroic Red Army!" exclaims someone on our platform, with pride and affection. Someone else sighs, while the face of a third brightens. My neighbors gaze at the military encampment joyfully, as at a parade, yet sadly, as at a parting. The sight of front-line troops comforts the uprooted wanderers with the thought that, in the end, the Red Army will repel the enemy.

The train jerks forward and back, and before it comes to a full stop I see people everywhere jumping from the platforms, like a broad stream that has reached the edge of an abyss where its waves hurtle noisily downward. "Planes are attacking the ammunition depots, soon we'll all be blown up," I think suddenly, and I too jump down. But the mob is yelling and roaring like hunters giving chase, not like people running in fear. I learn that, just a minute before, while the train was slowing down, several men had jumped off one of the platforms and vanished into the barbed-wire enclosures, amid the arsenals.

German paratroopers in disguise.

The crowd races in all directions, searching in the bushes, crawling under the wire fences. The guards—excited, confused, embarrassed at having let the paratroopers get through—dash about with rifles at the ready. People shout to them: "Over here! Here! . . . There! Over there! . . . He ran this way! . . . That way! . . . ," bewildering the soldiers still more. A short, stocky officer runs up and thunders at the civilians:

"This isn't the Civil War now. We'll manage without your help. Get back on the train!"

Several pursuers have separated from the scattering throng and disappeared among the buildings—impossible now to tell whether they have gone so far in pursuit of the spies or are spies themselves. The soldiers open fire, bullets whistle overhead, and our crowd huddles together, uttering wild screams of terror. But other civilians turn red with rage and throw themselves upon the soldiers, fists flying:

"Idiot! Who are you shooting at?" . . . "I'm a major myself. I'll soon teach you how to shoot!"

"This isn't the Civil War!" bellows the officer with all his might. "Get back on the cars!"

We clamber back onto the train. My neighbors are heatedly telling one another where and how the spies got away. Yelling loudest of all is the factory worker: "They didn't manage to shoot anyone, the soldiers. Not a single one!"

He looks all around, as though trying to find on our platform the one the soldiers hadn't managed to shoot; and his gaze locks on the group of liberated convicts, who have all this time remained in their places.

"One of the convicts is missing!" he roars.

It is the young fellow with the curly blond hair and sparse teeth who is missing, the same one who had earlier claimed to have been imprisoned for losing his passport.

"There he is!" shout several of my neighbors.

The convict now appears from behind a clump of bushes. He is walking slowly, sleepily lost in thought, tugging at the trousers he has just pulled up, as though he were alone amid an empty field and had no cause to be embarrassed.

"Where have you been?" our whole platform howls at him in unison.

Even those on other platforms devour him with their eyes, and from dozens of throats arises a vengeance-thirsty scream—a roar like that of a wild beast, as with its paws, its claws and sharp teeth, its whole taut and massive body, it falls upon the crouched back of the prey it has run to ground:

"Spy!!!"

The simple-minded inmate halts beside the train, thunderstruck. He neither speaks nor moves—but his squarish jaws become squarer still with the strain of clenching his teeth to keep them from chattering. The little officer, together with several soldiers, pounces upon him and orders him to raise his hands. The convict raises his hands high, as high as though he were sinking into a deep abyss and stretching himself to his full height in a last effort to keep his fingertips above water. Pulled up with his arms is his short jacket, baring his sunburned shirtless torso, and the coarse string that holds up his quilted trousers. The entire transport holds its breath as the officer searches him, turns out his pockets—

and at last pulls out, from a rear pocket, a long, wide comb made of bone!

"A dandy." He smiles at the ragged, curly-haired inmate and returns the comb: "*Idi s Bogom*—'Go with God.' " A short while ago this officer was shouting angrily at people to return to the train; now here he is, as if to spite everyone, displaying friendliness toward a convict. The crowd is outraged, and they erupt into screams: The convicts are enemies of the Soviet Union. They could be spies bribed to sell their country out, they could be hiding real Germans among them.

"The paratroopers jumped off from among the convicts!" roars a voice from one of the platforms.

"Some officer!" comes another cry from within the refugees' close-knit ranks. "His father was probably a kulak, or maybe he was a White Guardsman himself, so now he's siding with the enemies of the people!"

The officer gazes at the densely packed throng with lips clenched tight, as though barely able to restrain himself from ordering his men to aim their rifles at the frenzied mob. What he does order is that the soldiers climb up and check the evacuees' documents, and that they stay aboard the train until it leaves the military zone. Anyone who tries to jump off—shoot him on the spot!

The soldiers spread out along the entire length of the transport, while the officer rushes up to the locomotive and waves his arm—the signal to start the train. The soldier who climbs up on our platform is young, with a bony face, gray eyes, an unshaven, stubbly chin. Clambering up behind him is the inmate with blond, curly hair, who seats himself at once in his old place among his fellow convicts.

The moment the soldier—stiff in his long coat, rifle in hand—mounts our platform, dozens of hands holding passports are stretched out toward him. He glances at the first passport and is about to return it when other refugees, not trusting him to inspect it properly, thrust their eyes and noses into it. Whereupon the man thus subjected to scrutiny shouts at those who have scrutinized:

"I showed you my papers, now you show me yours."

The train begins to move. The soldier and his volunteer assistants spread their feet wide to keep their balance on the swaying platform, and the inspection continues. The factory worker, who has shown his passport to everyone, waves the tattered booklet about triumphantly and then points at me:

"What about him?"

"Present your documents." The soldier stops in front of me, and my heart stops with him. I see that they are looking for a victim, and I—I am a Zapadnik, a Westerner. Even as I was boarding the train in

Borisov, I had overheard mutterings about Zapadniki in the "liberated territories" helping the Germans drive out the Red Army and wreaking bloody vengeance on any Russians who hadn't got out of the new provinces in time.

The soldier looks over my passport. Surrounding him are my neighbors—cold, alien, as if no one among them remembers that we have been traveling together all this time. Even the "commander's wife"—who earlier had come to my defense during my quarrel with the factory worker, and later had asked me to bring her a kettleful of water—now wears an angry frown, ready to deny instantly any acquaintance with me, should I try to cite her as a witness on my behalf.

"Yevrey," murmurs the soldier and hands back my passport. The commander's wife raises her head and looks at me in a friendly, familiar, even kindly way.

Now the examiners surround the convicts, who explain that they have no identification papers. These had been taken from them at the time they were arrested, and when they were freed there was no one to give them new papers. They had been released only when the Germans were already in the vicinity of their camp, and the officials in charge had been the first to run away.

"Every German spy can claim he has no papers because he's a freed convict," says the factory worker.

"Stand up!" orders the soldier. "We'll take a look at what you've got with you."

Slowly, lazily, the camp inmates rise—on their faces, a look of hardened despair. Only the convict with the curly blond hair remains seated, his back propped against a small square box that previously, when the others were also seated, had not been visible.

"Get up!" says the factory worker. "What have you got there behind you?"

The convict remains seated, his legs stretched out on the now-vacant wooden floor; he throws back his head, pricks up his ears, stares intently at the telegraph poles rushing past the train. Over his blank face there passes a tremor, a twitch—and with his arms flung out before him he hurls himself off the platform, faster than an arrow in flight.

Everyone freezes—stupefied, speechless, riveted to the spot. The soldier lunges toward the edge of the platform with the factory worker, eyes glistening greedily, close behind. I cling tightly to the floor with my hands: Don't jump up! Don't look! They may think I, too, want to jump off . . . The soldier fires, and I can tell from his expression that he has missed. He fires again, and the factory worker all but turns a somersault for joy:

"Got him!"

The soldier fires a third time and the worker laughs aloud:
"Finished!"

The fugitive lies dead.

The soldier stands motionless, pale and calm, a cold glitter in his gray eyes, a cruel smile of triumph about the tight-pressed corners of his mouth. My neighbors have been abruptly transformed; no longer do they shriek or shout in exultation, or clench their fists; their faces are dry, serious, their foreheads furrowed. The other cars—which had also had a view of the fugitive's end—have grown still as well, so still I can hear the train wheels groaning, as if the slain man's death-groan has entered into them.

The soldier walks up to the petrified inmates and in a rasping voice orders them to open the satchel which the fugitive had been hiding behind his shoulders. But before any of the convicts can move, the factory worker leaps over to the small parcel, tears it open, and rifles nimbly through its contents—a dark-blue shirt, a pair of trousers of the same color, a flashlight, a folded map, and a short, broad hunting knife in a leather sheath.

"This proves it: a paratrooper." The worker smooths out the blue shirt as though he wished to try it on. "I didn't like his looks from the moment I laid eyes on him."

"But he was together with us in the camp in Lithuania, so how could he have been a paratrooper?" a heavy-set inmate calls out—the same who had earlier refused to tell the worker why he was imprisoned.

"He was a *durachok*, and he found the satchel on the road," says another inmate. "He jumped out of fear, the poor fool."

"Did you know about the satchel?" asks the soldier, whose lips have turned white.

"We knew," answers the first convict. "We asked him: 'Where did you get it?' and he answered, 'A man lost it and I picked it up.' That's what he told us. What was inside we didn't know."

"And you guarded it all this time, hid it with your backsides, because he promised to give you a share?" The factory worker thrusts his head forward like a bird of prey.

"Yes," replies the first convict. "He promised that when we got to Orsha, he'd give each of us an equal share. But what was actually in it—that we didn't know." He speaks wearily, softly, sadly, as though he too has already bade farewell to life.

The refugees standing about have become deaf and dumb; they avoid looking at one another, and assume an air of indifference. But the commander's wife is unable to control herself. She turns to the factory worker, her face contorted with loathing and hatred:

"Damned scoundrel!"

"You shut your mouth!" The worker steps toward her. "I'm a Russian and I protect the Soviet Union against spies."

"A dog is what you are, not a Russian!" she spits out. "My husband is at the front while you run to the rear to save your dog's hide."

"Quiet," hisses the soldier from between clenched teeth; and the word holds such an ominous threat that the refugees return at once to their places and sit down. The commander's wife cuddles her children close to her, strokes their little heads, and rocks them to sleep.

The wind snatches tufts of smoke from the distant locomotive and chases them above our heads. The tufts become steadily denser, blacker, and mingle with the low clouds now scudding toward them. The refugees are silent, each steeped in his own thoughts. They all keep their distance from the factory worker, who lies in a corner by himself. And from the soldier, who stands in the center of the platform leaning on his gun, there emanates the heavy stillness of a dark thunderhead.

Rain

NIGHT FALLS. The train has again entered a military zone, and slows to a stop. From one of the distant cars comes a peremptory shout for the guards to descend and take up positions alongside the transport, to see to it that none of the evacuees gets off. Our guard climbs down without a word; he does not need to repeat the warning.

I nestle my head against my knapsack, cover myself with my coat, and try to stretch out my legs. But all around me lie tightly huddled bodies and I, too, must remain curled up into a coil. In my knees rises an unbearable pain: screws of iron have bored their way inside them, cracking the bones, then burrowing ever deeper within, and forcing the gray matter of my brain out through the nape of my neck. How well off I had been on the road between Minsk and Borisov! In the fields, in the forest, even in the ditches, I was able to stretch out. That empty, sunny highway now lives its own secret life inside me. It has become dear to me, that road of my countless dangers, as dear as the shadows I met there—shadows silent and lost in thought, and upon their faces the sad smiles of those resigned to their fate. The shadows follow me, calm me; I am not, they firmly assure me, not responsible for the death of the *durachok*.

The other refugees curled up all around me are, I sense, not sleeping, either; they, too, are likely thinking of the innocent youth who was shot. Yet not one of them will so much as aim a kick at the accursed factory worker who was an accomplice in the murder. He, that provocateur, is lying in his corner, probably vexed that I wasn't shot as well. The convicts surely had to know their comrade was innocent—after all, he'd been in the same camp with them in Lithuania—yet they had been too frightened to restrain the soldier.

The *durachok* had been with them in Lithuania—that was what they said. I had always known that there were labor camps in far-away Arkhangelsk, in Irkutsk and Yakutsk, but in Lithuania? The Soviets, after all, had been with us for barely over a year—when had they managed to set up camps in Lithuania? In Vilna there had been whispered rumors about their constructing secret airfields, building new highways, reinforcing the borders, but who it was that was doing all this work, no one knew. Now I know! Those who were arrested in Vilna were sent to

Siberia, and from Siberia prisoners were brought to Lithuania. I had wandered about those familiar towns and walked in those woods unaware of what was going on around me, unaware that I was treading on a concealed pit.

From somewhere overhead comes a clap of thunder that scatters my thoughts. I peer out from under my coat: the sky is wholly covered by clouds. A gust of wind hits the transport, tugs at and balloons the refugees' clothes, pulls off their coverings. Coppery raindrops begin to bombard the taut tarpaulins. Heads rear up, hands stretch out, trying to hold down the fluttering garments as the wind pulls and tugs from all sides. The heads are lowered, drawn back again between hunched shoulders; bodies collapse into a coiled and tangled heap, and we lie once again stiff and frozen to the marrow, all piled together yet each burrowed deep within himself.

Now the thunder comes more often, louder; between one clap and the next a flash of lightning flays the cloud-covered sky from one horizon to the other—and instantly vanishes. A dense rain begins to pound, heavy as lead, sharp as knives. The wind pulls the rain sideways, from right to left, left to right; sheetlike streams of water beat upon our heads. The water floods under my clothes, fills my shoes, my ears, flows over my neck and back, swirls around as in a whirlpool.

"God in Heaven!" groans someone next to me. "Why aren't they moving?"

"The rail lines are jammed," gasps someone else, choking on the downpour that all but engulfs him. "Or maybe the tracks have been torn up by an air attack."

The two children of the commander's wife begin to cry softly, then in a thin, long-drawn-out wail, like wolf-cubs: "Mama, I'm afraid!," "Mama, I'm wet!" Their crying saws through my veins, through the tissues of my brain, it aches and gnaws within my heart. It seems to me as if they are sobbing and howling to spite me. Let the thunder roll and the lightning flash, let the entire transport be washed away—only let them stop crying! I tear the coat off from over my head and sit up.

The commander's wife sits opposite me, holding the children close to her. She has already covered them with all her shawls, she shields them with her hands, with her body, while she herself—head bare, hair disheveled, defenseless against the rain lashing at her face—shouts into the darkness at the soldier standing guard beside the tracks:

"Comrade Red Army soldier, allow us to take shelter underneath the car, the children will get bronchitis."

"Can't," comes back the answer in a dead voice, as if from the bottom of an abyss.

"Take pity on the children." She bends over the edge of the platform, gasping with a hard, dry cough amidst the downpour, and her lament merges with the children's drawn-out, wolf-like moans. "My husband is at the front, Comrade Red Army soldier."

"Quiet," hisses the soldier, just as he had after shooting the convict. "Quiet!" he bellows suddenly, and the commander's wife and her children at once fall silent, as if his roar has choked off their voices. "Quiet," he rasps and rattles hoarsely, drenched with rain and with darkness, as if the spirit of the man he has killed has entered into him and is now torturing him to madness.

The rain stops as suddenly and unexpectedly as it began. From the sky a yellowish ray of light sifts its way through the now-sparse clouds to fall upon the huddled refugees, who resemble heaps of wet, slippery stones. A deathlike silence hovers from end to end of the linked cars. The clothes on my back begin to freeze and stand away from my body, as if I were encased in a block of ice.

THE LOCOMOTIVE suddenly begins to whistle, it cries and wails in the darkness of night: The slain man was a *durachok!* A *durachok!* . . . The train jerks forward and the wheels beat out the rhythm: dura-chok . . . dura-chok . . . dura-chok . . . I listen intently: the wooden leg of the Jew in Borisov who could not flee is following me again. In the clanking of the buffers I can hear him pacing, with a measured and soldierly tread, across the edge of a sand pile—and he does not fall. He squeezes himself between the train and the railing of a bridge that spans a river—and he is not crushed. The wooden leg strides on the left side of the rails, while on the right side a blood-soaked silence follows me. . . . It is the field with the slain man that follows me.

The throng of those who keep me company grows larger and larger.

But our platform guard has not come with us. He has taken the *durachok*'s satchel with him and remained in the military encampment where we stood half the night. Only his eyes, like the lights of a locomotive, burn in the cloud that floats low over my head, and the sound of his hoarse, rasping voice stabs and burrows into my ears:

"Quiet!"

Wanderings

In ORSHA I was drafted to dig trenches to stop the German tanks. I ate army-ration biscuits, drank water out of discarded tin cans, and slept where I worked, in the trenches that had already been dug. My beard and hair grew together into one matted clump, covered with dust and sand. A soldier shaved my face and my head, which revealed my hollow, sunken cheeks. Shells exploded all around me. Medics screamed into field telephones, "People are dying!"; but there were no ambulances or stretchers. The native Soviet youths in my section were taught to shoot, to attack with bayonets, to hurl themselves with grenades against tanks. But because I was from the West, a Zapadnik, I was not taken into the army. With all the trenches dug and the German tanks approaching, I was discharged, and moved on to Smolensk.

Smolensk was burned out. But I did not leave the city until I had bathed in the Dnieper, tearing the encrusted filth off my body with my fingernails. On my way back to the train station, I was enveloped once more by dust, smoke, and soot from the bombed-out buildings. The skeletal remains of houses hovered above my head, a lattice-work of metal beams, concrete, and wood . . .

Once again, days and nights on open platform-cars making their way east. We have already passed Bryansk and Orel, and are approaching Kursk, on the way to Voronezh. My fellow passengers no longer interest me. After long wanderings, each has lost his own face. They all crawl over one another like the gray clouds that pass over each other at the horizon's edge. I lie sprawled half-naked on the platform, drying myself in the sun like a log that has been pulled out of the water, and dream a sweet dream of Jatkowa Street in my Vilna of time past, on just such a hot summer's day as this.

A woman sits hunched next to a large keg filled with herring. On a stoop nearby a porter with a rope tied around his waist is taking a nap. An old-clothes dealer drags himself lazily through the quiet, empty street, bearing his entire shop on his back: a pair of red trousers, a velvet jacket, a green hunter's cap with a feather—the outfit of a street performer. A woman with an infant at her breast stretches out her hand to beg, but not a single living soul appears on the street and the beggar woman remains standing with hand outstretched as though paralyzed. My mother is dozing next to her baskets, dreaming of ripe currants with juice like wine, of sweet, fuzzy gooseberries and plump, glistening-black cherries. Her lips are moving; she is praising her wares to her customers: "These are currants? Grapes is what they are! These are cherries? Chunks of beef is what they are!" In her dream she gives herself too vigorous a shake; she opens her eyes and, instead of a swarm of customers, beholds around her all-but-empty baskets a swarm of flies. Above her head hangs her scale, the pointer at dead center, a witness before God and man that she has never used a dishonest weight . . .

I open my eyes and see the refugees baking their sooty bodies in the sun, and my gaze wanders far across the fields. A village rushes by and hides amidst the trees, as if frightened by this vast horde of wanderers. Laborers with crowbars and pickaxes, working on a side-track, look after us for a long time, silent and sad. A peasant woman standing on the threshold of her cottage, her fist dug into her chin, stares at us and then up at the sky: so far no German planes have flown over her house, but who can tell whether on the morrow she, too, might not have to flee from the bombs? . . . A well with a red cover stands by the wayside, and the refugees stretch their necks, their thirsty lips, toward it—but the train does not stop. Suddenly a group of barefoot children come running across the field, happily waving their hands, like a flock of storks with white wings. No one on the train waves back at them. The children halt, bewildered and embarrassed; their little hands drop.

The tracks are wider now—several main lines, and some smaller ones as well, here meet and intersect. Kursk, with its electric-power station, its factory chimneys and huge storage tanks, is already signaling to us. Stretching along one side of our transport is a freight train made up of tall, closed boxcars with machine guns on their roofs, and guarded by armed soldiers stationed on the small platforms between the cars. It is heading in the direction from which we have come—toward the front. On the other side of our train, on a hill, stands a Russian Orthodox church with its white walls, cupolas, and crosses. Clustered beside it are horses and wagons. Soldiers are carrying bales of hay out of the church's wide-open doors and loading them onto the wagons. None of my neighbors on our platform pays any attention to this church transformed into a barn; all eyes are fixed on the train station ahead. As soon as the train comes to a stop, a mob of people floods the station, seeking to buy food and get water.

I spot a barber shop and rub my chin; my beard has grown quite heavy again. I walk in—a different world! Quiet, cool, the customers army officers and government officials, the barbers young girls wearing white smocks. I sit down in a chair and a young girl begins lathering my face. She does her work listlessly, lazily, without so much as a glance at me. I look her over in the mirror: she is tall, dark, with a longish nose, pale skin, the fixed stare of an owl. She notices me scrutinizing her, and smiles.

"In this heat and especially on the road, a man's beard grows quickly," I say, trying to excuse my wild appearance.

She asks me to sit quite still and not move, so that the razor won't cut me. She shaves me in a leisurely way, rinses off my face with lukewarm water, and, without asking me, applies a cooling ointment to my cracked skin. I close my eyes, remembering how Frumme-Liebche had persuaded me to take my shaving kit along—I hadn't wanted to, had thought that I would never shave again . . . The Russian girl's fingers carefully massage my cheeks, smoothing away the puffy bags under my eyes. I am intoxicated by her fingers. My head grows heavy, my eyes are clouded, my lips tremble; I thrust my face under her hands as under a light springtime shower mingled with sunlight. How long has it been since a gentle feminine hand rested upon my forehead, how long? And she, as though feeling the tremor of my hot lips on her palms, does not pull away her hands, and smiles directly into my eyes:

"Don't worry, I'm watching your train through the window, and I'll tell you as soon as it gets ready to move. All the passengers are still outside, in the station."

"I didn't know that in Russia the barbers are women. What's your name?"

"Katya," she answers after a long, thoughtful pause, as if selecting one name out of dozens that had come to mind. I ask whether she is a native of Kursk, and whether she has a fiancé. The girl wipes my face with a towel, removes the sheet from around my neck, and replies reluctantly that the girls are not permitted to speak about personal matters while working. I observe the other white-smocked girls chatting quite freely with their customers, and understand that she is afraid to talk to me because I am a Zapadnik. Stepping down from the chair, I hand her two ten-ruble notes. For a moment she holds the money at the edges with the tips of her thin fingers, as if uncertain whether she has a right to touch it.

"You're giving me too much," she says softly. "Won't you need it for your journey?"

"No, thank you." And I leave. From outside I see through the window that another customer is already sitting in my place and that she is smiling at him exactly as she had smiled at me. But she keeps her eyes lowered, as if she were still thinking about me. So I tell myself—and then I begin to laugh, with a pang in my heart: I must be desperate indeed to be having such thoughts.

I manage to buy a string of hard ginger snaps sprinkled with powdery sugar, at which I promptly start nibbling away. But just then a man's voice rises in a wail so anguished that I choke on the hard morsel I have bitten off: A robust, broad-shouldered Jew, surrounded by militiamen, is tearing with both hands at the full head of hair visible beneath the tilted visor of his cap. His money has been stolen, and with it his passport. His wife stands beside him, wild with rage and despair, screaming at him as if he has lied to her and ruined her life forever:

"Where is your passport? Search! Search! Search!"

"I've looked and looked for it, it's not here! My passport, it's gone!" The man tears at his face with his fingernails and weeps before the militiamen, as though beseeching them to protect him against his own wife: "Comrades, help me! Help me find the thief! Let him keep the money, but my passport, let him give me back my passport!"

The militiamen stand silent, a hard glitter in their eyes. I cannot tell whether they are thinking of the thief who has thus ruined his fellow man, or whether it is the Jew sobbing like an old woman whom they find repugnant. The locomotive sounds its whistle. I rush to my platform-car, holding the string of ginger snaps in one hand as with the other I clutch at the breast pocket where I keep my passport.

IT IS JUST PAST NOON. Our train twists and turns its snaky way toward Voronezh. Upon us the sun pours down its fire; a kettle seethes in the entrails; opening one's mouth to exhale the heat, one inhales still more fire. The sun's rays pierce the flesh with red-hot darts, drain the blood from the veins, fill the limbs with tar and fever. Salty sweat cascades down the face, drips onto the chest; each drop of sweat sticks to the hairs over the heart like a lump of pitch. A dust-filled dryness spreads into the corners of the mouth; sand fills the spaces between the teeth and coats the palate. The skin peels and cracks, and the heat-flayed body oozes like a raw wound. Bodies twist endlessly, turn from side to side, find no resting place. The sky is molten brass; in all the surrounding terrain, not a single plant rustles; not a bird flies by; the foreshortened shadows of trees wind themselves around their trunks, as if the shadows too were seeking refuge from the heat.

The train comes to a stop in an open field, not far from a forest where the evacuees can cut branches for shading the platforms against the sun. But the branches of the outer rows of trees have already been lopped off by earlier transports. Only at the very tops have they left crowns of leaves which look down sadly at their denuded trunks. We have to go deeper into the forest, spreading out among the thickets, and soon there rises on all sides the dry, crackling sound of snapping branches.

I start breaking off the branches of a tall, slender aspen. Its leaves, round, smooth, with serrated rims, ceaselessly quiver and vibrate, like sunbeams. I fling the branches onto a pile, then pick them up, and am about to return to the train when I stop dead, abruptly overwhelmed by stillness and mystery.

The forest is listening—immersed in silence, pensive, full of wonderment—as though unable to believe that it is being destroyed. The trembling leaves of the broken branches in my arms fill me with horror, as if they were bizarre forms of life brought up from the ocean depths. Somewhere in the thicket someone is moving about, as if rising, overgrown by moss, from a sleep of many years. I look up and see, on a dark, narrow footpath beneath a lattice-work of trees, a small woman walking barefoot and carrying her shoes. She keeps looking uneasily about her with a baffled smile, as if she were both pleased and frightened at having lost her way. Eyes wide, I stare at her and my heart stops; I know I must not make a sound, lest I frighten her. Suddenly she turns her face toward me—and disappears. There is no one on the path, no one.

I have imagined, walking there, my mother.

I grasp the pile of branches more firmly in my arms and return to the train. Together with my fellow passengers I push the branches into the cracks of the boards at the edges of our platform, bend the tips at the top, braid them together—and when at last our train resumes its journey, it has become a moving forest.

I bury myself in my corner under the shade of the leaves and think about my little gray dove. She has come to me now as unexpectedly as she had once before, some years earlier, shortly after Frumme-Liebche and I were married. We were then staying in a hamlet near Rukon— the same one where I had left her behind in our flight from Vilna on the second day of the war. There the two of us, during that first summer after our wedding, wandered in the forest for days at a time, splashed about in the shallow brook, and helped the owner of our cottage cut the grass in his meadow. Every time out host drove into the city, he passed by my mother's stand and brought us a package of fruit and sweets from her. In the early fall, when the woods were covered by the bloom of purple sage, I would clamber about in the thickets, far from the hamlet, to gather King Boletus mushrooms. One day, whom did I see but my mother, barefoot and carrying her shoes, walking down a narrow footpath in the woods. She hadn't heard from us in two weeks—a time when our host, busy in the fields, had not gone into town—and so she had left her baskets and taken the bus to Rukon. There, at the house of a Jew, she had asked the way to our hamlet, and then started out through the forest in the direction pointed out to her. She had removed her shoes and stockings and, like a peasant woman, walked barefoot on the grassy, velvet-soft path—walked on and on until she lost her way.

"If only the Almighty would help me move to a village," she said to me. "In a village you can walk around barefoot, like Eve in the Garden of Eden. In the city I have to wear my flat shoes and run about on those sharp, crooked cobblestones."

And when I asked how she could have permitted herself to set out alone through an unfamiliar forest where she might have wandered lost the entire day, she answered with a little laugh:

"I wasn't at your wedding in Warsaw, so I want to have the joy of seeing the two of you together now. It's still your honeymoon."

When Frumme-Liebche saw us emerging from the forest, her face turned pink and her earlobes flamed hot, just as in our courting days, on her first Friday-evening visit to our smithy. But Mother refused absolutely to stay with us for more than an hour. When I urged her to remain longer, she became angry:

"When you have children, you'll tell them what to do, not me. My merchandise was taken on credit, and in this heat it'll spoil by evening. You have a wife, so be happy with her. For me it's enough to see that you're both well, thank God."

THE LOCOMOTIVE PUFFS AND PANTS, as if exhausted, across the broad Russian land. The further east we go, the sparser become the forests and the vaster the steppes. Dusk begins to fall, the sky clouds over, and through the clouds creep the rays of the setting sun, like the red legs of crayfish through the water. A wind blows in from the steppe and tugs at the interwoven branches above my head; the aspen leaves which just a few hours before still quivered with life now flap inertly, like the corpses of hanged men. The body, which during the day had glowed with heat, quickly cools off. Shivering with cold, I curl up, close my eyes, and, in a half-waking doze, see my mother once again before me, as if she has drifted out from the forest of Kursk along with the broken-off branches. I want to call out to her, to embrace and warm her, but I have no voice. I want to jump down from the train and run after her, but the shadows falling from the branches above my head bind me like ropes. I know I am dreaming, yet cannot rouse myself. I see her, small and shriveled, walking through the dark forests of Kursk back to Vilna, just as when she visited us for an hour and hurried back to her borrowed merchandise; she walks on without looking back, though she knows I am still following her with my eyes. And the wind in the leaves over my head rustles and whispers in a human voice—my mother's voice: "Poor little branches, they broke you off from your trunk and now you wander across foreign lands . . . poor severed branches. . . ."

A Night on the Banks
of the Volga

FROM THE MIDDLE OF SUMMER into late autumn, I worked in the "Red
Banner" Kolkhoz near Kistendey Station in Saratov Region, cutting
rye and binding sheaves. The young men had gone off to the front and
there were not enough hands for the harvest. The days were growing
short, the evenings long; rain soaked the rich black earth and the grain,
partly in sheaves and the rest still on the stalk, was rotting in the fields.
Trains filled with wounded soldiers returning from the front rolled past
us. Often the trains stopped and the bodies of men who had died on the
way were carried to the village cemetery. Those less seriously wounded
laughed at the village girls, threw them chunks of bread, and called out
to the older kolkhoz workers: "Keep cutting that grain!"

From time to time the chairman of the Kistendey City Council
would come out to exhort us in amicable tones: "Help us, my children!
This is war!" After he left, the kolkhoz manager would fall upon the
peasants with his fists: "You curs! If you don't do two days' worth of
work every day, I'll let you die of hunger this winter!" And so we worked
by lamplight, from the darkness before dawn to the darkness of night.
Only when Big Vasily, who was taller than his horse, every once in a
while called out, "Take a smoke!," only then would we abandon work
for fifteen minutes, to rest as we smoked. At mealtimes black bread was
distributed—sour, mushy, containing more water than flour—and sometimes even some meat, a few hardened morsels and bones. The peasant
women would snatch at these stone-hard bits of meat with happy peals
of laughter, gnaw at them greedily, and even lick their fingers afterwards.

I slept on a straw mattress in the village school; on the wall hung
a square of canvas with the embroidered slogan: "Thank you, Comrade
Stalin, for our happy life!" On the nights when no storm raged, I could
hear the transport trains rattling past the kolkhoz fields, rushing, ceaselessly rushing, the locomotive sirens bewailing the lot of ever-new hordes
of refugees. I was seized by a feverish longing to resume my wandering.

The kolkhoz discharged me, paying me for my days of labor with
dried fruit, some jars of honey, and two loaves of bread. With a full
knapsack on my back I set off for Kistendey, to wait for a transport.

Also at the station, accompanied by their wives, mothers, and children, were peasants who had been called up by the army. Weeping, the peasant women repeatedly made the sign of the cross over their husbands and sons, invoking God's protection. The men stood with heads bent, arms dropping, and muttered with annoyance at the women's laments.

I had no one to bid me farewell. But in my memory, too, the image of a cross remained inscribed, the cross of the ruined village church. Broken and rusty, the cross had been worked into the railing of the little iron bridge that spanned the brook in "Red Banner," and I had seen it every day on my way to work in the fields.

I jumped on the first freight train that passed; it carried a cargo of scrap-iron, and I dug myself in amidst the chunks of metal. The conductor, accustomed by now to such uninvited guests, shone his flashlight directly into my face and chased me off at the next stop. I immediately clambered up one of the other flat-cars of the same train and continued on my journey until, at one train-juncture stop, I managed to change over to a transport and melted into a new wave of refugees, Jews from the Ukraine and Bessarabia.

I find myself in a car together with a group of Jews from Konotop. For the first time in my life, I behold the Jewish Ukraine: broad-shouldered, black-eyed men, with heads of hair like wads of pitch. The women, too, are fleshy, heavy-bodied, with faces like risen dough. They travel in family groups and carry multitudes of bundles: bedding, clothing, and food. When they push their way into the lines for hot water, bread, and cigarettes, they shout: "We are Soviet people!" But among themselves they are simple, good-naturedly quarreling Jews. About them still is an aura of wind and of steppes, of old-fashioned inns and taverns, of the vigor of small-town merchants, of the warm reek of manure that envelops peasants who work around cattle, of green vegetables, of milk and cheese and butter. The women quarrel among themselves in Russian with a Yiddish intonation, as if they were chanting passages from the Women's Bible, and from time to time the men throw in a mangled word or two in the Holy Tongue of their now-forgotten heder days.

From me, the Zapadnik, they keep their distance. The only one who has befriended me is Lev Kogan. He wears a khaki shirt with a leather belt, and boots with heavy metal tabs on the soles. He is short, with very broad shoulders, a short neck, a large bald head with a square chin sharp-edged as a polished stone, and a wide slit of a mouth, the mouth of a born public speaker, an orator to the masses. He is the secretary of the Communist Party in Konotop.

He turns out, however, to be a quiet, crestfallen man who keeps apart from the other Konotop Jews; they for their part, out of a mixture of fear and respect, stay away from him. Whenever one of my fellow passengers gets into an argument with me about the amount of space I'm occupying, or about my opening the door of the freight car to get more fresh air, Lev Kogan always takes my part. With an angry glance at the refugee who is quarreling with me, he snaps brusquely, "That's my order!"—and the other man at once gives in.

Lev Kogan has no big bundles with him, and no family. His wife and two children, he tells me, have stayed in Konotop—his wife absolutely refused to go with him, because she did not believe the stories being told of the German massacres of Jews. And he seeks to know from me, as a Westerner, whether all that is said about the Germans is true.

"Why doesn't your wife believe in the German massacres?" I ask.

His only answer is a sigh, and he asks me again whether the stories are true. I tell him of one incident which had been related to me by Polish refugees in Vilna: When the Germans invaded Poland, they rounded up four hundred Jews in the city of Hrubieszów and force-marched them to Chelm. In Chelm they rounded up four hundred other Jews and made them march to Hrubieszów, and on the way they had shot and killed half of each group.

"That means my wife has stayed on to face certain death. . . ." He begins to shudder, quietly. "And my children too."

"No, no—they won't kill the women. I never heard anything about Germans going from house to house and shooting women." I begin to scream. Perhaps the intellectuals, I say, or prominent people denounced as having spread atrocity stories about the Germans.

"There are always informers," murmurs Kogan. He remains silent a moment and then breathes a little more freely. "But they won't kill women or children?"

"No, no, ordinary women and children, that I don't believe! What would they want of women and children?" I shiver as in a high fever. I tell him how my own wife remained behind with a peasant we know in a village outside Vilna. Now I want him to tell me: did she manage to get back to the city and rejoin my mother before the Germans arrived, or not? My greatest fear is that she might have walked through the city at a time when there was not a living soul in the streets except German soldiers, with helmets pulled down low over their foreheads and sub-machine guns in their hands. What does he think?

"I think your wife managed to get back to the city and find your mother before the Germans came in," says Lev Kogan, not looking at me, lest I discern by his expression that he is saying this only to calm me. "But for men active in the Party, you think, it would be dangerous to stay behind?"

"Yes, for active Party members it could be dangerous, but for women and children alone, I don't think so. Well, perhaps there is some danger for women and children too, but that the Germans will go from house to house looking for them, that I don't believe—" I am shouting at him in terror, in anger, and at the same time pleadingly, as if I were begging him not to strip me naked.

OUR TRAIN, originally headed for Saratov, now detours northward to Penza: Saratov will not admit us, out of fear that some people might stay on in the already overcrowded city. But Penza, too, chases us away like a plague of locusts. We detour once again, eastward, and stop overnight between Syzran and Batraki on the Volga.

On the same track, in front of us and behind us, stand other trains filled with refugees, while on the opposite track is a long military transport full of soldiers going to the front. It is a luminous autumn night. In the gold-yellow moonlight the Volga, dark-blue and broad-flowing, rolls on serenely. Great hulking barges lie at rest in the water; tethered rowboats bob up and down; the shores are dotted with wooden warehouses, with nets, with balls of coiled rope, hatchets, pieces of metal, wires, wooden planks.

The women dismount from the freight cars, collect kindling wood, and build fires on which they cook dinner for their families in huge pots. Around these bonfires the men sit and smoke and talk softly, companionably, as though they have been wanderers all their lives. The refugees in our car also descend to prepare the evening meal; only I and Lev Kogan remain seated near the door, gazing out. Facing us are soldiers of the troop train, sitting on the steps of their cars, some with boots off and white wraps around their feet. Several scores of men have stretched out in a nearby field and are singing. The *zapevala*, the leader, sings slowly, stretching out the words:

> *"Izvela menya kruchina*   (I'm worn down by my sorrow,
> *Podkolodnaya zmeya—"*   Stealthy snake beneath the tree)

And the chorus of men around him join in:

> *"Dogoray, gori, moya luchina,*   (Burn, my wood-brand, there's no morrow,
> *Dogoryu s toboy i ya."*   And I shall burn out with thee.)

The *zapevala* takes a higher register, his voice becomes thin, shrill, and the soldiers accompany him, with a wild abandon which has yet beneath it an undertone of sadness. In their voices I seem to hear the cloud-darkened, thousand-year-old Russian patience, the inurement to suffering, the raw strength in brutal battle, the fatalistic calm when taken into captivity or dying of hunger.

"Maxim Gorki's boatmen are no more in modern Russia, but the Volga is still the same and she still bears the spirit of Stenka Razin."* Lev Kogan speaks without taking his eyes from the people clustered around the bonfires, as if he were watching his wife and children in Konotop beside the cozy fire of their stove. "The Great War for the Fatherland! The war against Napoleon was the first national war and now, it seems, this is the second, the great national war. It's no longer in the name of Communism or the International Proletariat, but in the name of Mother Russia . . ." Lev Kogan is speaking more to himself than to me; he is summing the figures in an account of long standing. "And if it is for Mother Russia, then what need is there now for Communists? And indeed they do hate us—and us, the Jewish Communists, most of all."

Briefly he is silent; then, head bent low, he speaks again, mournfully stretching out his words, as if he has fallen in with the melody of the soldiers singing in the nearby field:

"You said they won't touch women or children. I'm not so sure of that. Even if they won't kill all the women and children, they won't spare the wives and children of active Communists, especially the Jewish ones. I can't go on. With every day, every hour the train moves farther from Konotop, another piece of my heart is torn away. I shall stay here in Syzran, or go back to Penza or perhaps to Saratov."

He steps into the depths of the dark car, returns quickly with a small bundle, and softly bids me good night. I am sorry to see him go: among my fellow passengers, he is the only one who has become a friend. But before he leaves, I want him at least to tell me one thing, at least this one thing:

"What do you think: did my wife manage to get back to Vilna before the Germans came? And my mother? Will I live to see her again? My mother isn't an old woman, she's not even sixty."

"I don't know," he answers in a weary voice, as if he were setting out to return to Konotop on foot and the thought of the long road ahead has already exhausted him. "You asked me why my wife didn't believe that the Germans were slaughtering people. Now I'll tell you. From the time Hitler came to power, we constantly heard and read that Fascism aimed at enslaving the proletariat of the entire world, that they would attack the Soviet Union and massacre all the Jews. Suddenly Moscow and Berlin concluded a peace treaty, and even though the war's been going on all this time in the west, here nobody was writing anything

---

* A leader of the great peasant rebellion in Russia in the eighteenth century.—Trans.

anymore about how Hitler treated workers or Jews. It was only when
the Germans attacked us that they began talking again about his atrocities.
And so my wife said it was all just propaganda, and she didn't want to
leave."

He climbs down from the freight car and walks alongside the train
until he comes to the end of it. I remain seated alone at the door, listening
to the soldiers' song. Their voices seem to fuse with the calm flow of the
Volga, with the flames of the bonfires. And I, too, begin to sing—a song
I had whispered often in the dark nights when I lay on my straw bed
in the kolkhoz:

> *She is thin, she is small,*
> *She barely reaches my shoulder*
> *But in her sorrow*
> *She's grown taller than all.*
>
> *Little mother, little gray dove dear,*
> *With eyes full of meekness and fear*
> *In wind and in darkness I lie*
> *And I sing you a lullaby.*
>
> *On my heart rests her head,*
> *I dry her tears as they flow.*
> *As with her hand she strokes*
> *Beads of sweat from my brow.*
>
> *I hear from afar her soft moan;*
> *"You must endure all, oh my son!"*
> *On her face I count each furrow:*
> *"Do not die, Mother, of longing and sorrow!"*

Suddenly from the Volga is heard a distant, drawn-out cry. I watch
as the people around the bonfires lean toward and question one another,
then turn their heads toward the river. A few minutes later the men of
my freight car return to the train carrying hot pots wrapped in cloths,
followed by the women holding their stirring spoons. As they approach
the door, I hear them saying that people camped on the riverbank had
seen someone throw himself into the water.

"Lev Kogan—" the cry tears itself from my throat—"Lev Kogan
has thrown himself into the river!"

The Konotopers stare at me, puzzled and curious; where, they ask,
did I get the idea it was Lev Kogan? Disconcerted by their calm indifference, I tell them that Kogan had taken his bundle and left in a depressed
state of mind.

"And here I thought he'd told you he was going to drown himself," says one man, grimacing with annoyance at my attempt to spoil his pleasure in first eating his fill and now going to sleep.

"A Party secretary doesn't jump into the water so easily," interjects another, adding that Lev Kogan has chosen not to drag himself off to Central Asia, but to remain instead in one of the larger cities on the Volga. With his Party card he will easily manage to settle down anywhere.

"Our Party secretary is a good swimmer—I've heard him say so more than once," jokes a third man; and all join him in hearty laughter.

The Steppes of Kazakhstan

IT IS NOW THE SECOND DAY of our southward journey through the steppes of Kazakhstan. Our last stop in the north had been at Chkalov. There, at the threshold of Asia, a poor Russian peasant woman had called me *synok*—"little son."

On an empty stretch of track between two transport trains, a passenger train from Central Asia, on its way to Chelyabinsk and Sverdlovsk, pulled quickly and merrily in—and within a few moments found itself besieged by the women of Chkalov, all wearing winter clothing and high felt boots. In their outstretched hands they carried chunks of salty lard, lumps of butter, or tens of eggs in baskets. "Salt, salt, salt!" they called out to the train windows. Down from the train came senior officials— *nachal'niki*—in paramilitary uniforms, holding bags of salt, and there ensued a lively round of bargaining and bartering. The women offered meat, lard, and dairy products in exchange for salt, and the *nachal'niki* carefully fingered and examined the proffered wares.

Directly opposite our freight car, a Russian with a big, round, good-natured face, carrying half a bag of salt, clambered down from the passenger train. A woman with full, rosy cheeks, light-blue eyes, and rouged lips looked on from the train window above him. An elderly peasant woman pushed her way up to the passenger and meekly held out a lump of butter wrapped in a thin piece of linen. The man, smiling, handed it up for inspection to the woman, who stretched both arms out of the window to receive it, as far as her bare white elbows. She sniffed at and examined the butter at some length, but remained dissatisfied. The peasant woman, fearing that her merchandise did not please, fell upon the Russian with pleas and tears, calling down blessings upon him and his wife, until at last she wormed out of him his half-bag of salt. Clutching her treasure with both hands, the woman now thrust herself in our direction, calling out plaintively: "Sugar! Raisins! Raisins! Sugar! Sugar!"—more, it would seem, out of habit than any real hope of doing business with us, since none of the other peddlers had even approached the evacuees' transport.

"And what will you pay for the sugar with?" someone asked her placidly.

"With money. Whatever you say, that's how much I'll pay." The peasant woman set down the bag of salt and pulled a wad of paper money from her bodice.

My fellow passengers, the Jews of Konotop, did not budge. In my knapsack, it occurred to me, I still had the paper bag of granulated sugar into which the factory worker had dipped his dirty fingers. Out of anger and disgust at him for having provoked the shooting of the *durachok*, I had not touched the remaining sugar since, yet I hadn't had the heart to throw it away. Now I quickly untied my knapsack, took out the sugar, and handed it to the old woman.

"How much?" she asked breathlessly, ready to start counting out the money. But of the eight hundred rubles I had taken with me from Vilna, I still had more than five hundred. In the kolkhoz I'd had no need to spend any money. Now there seemed no point in trying to wangle a few rubles out of an old woman.

"Take it, Granny," I answered.

"Synok, synok!" She began to kiss my hands, and when our train suddenly jerked forward, she stood there calling after me: *"Synok, synok . . ."*

"This is truly 'the bread of affliction,' " murmured a man with a black-stubbled face and heavily veined arms, the former manager of a food store in Konotop . . . He was, he told me, one of those Jews who still prayed regularly, and in packing his belongings he had not forgotten his prayer shawl.

THROUGH ENDLESS EXPANSES covered with a broad-leafed, cabbagelike weed the train speeds nonstop, except for an occasional brief pause in the middle of an open field. Relentlessly pursuing it are hungry dogs of the steppes with sharp, protruding ribs. They neither howl nor bark, but continually run, panting and baring their teeth, at the open freight-car doors, in the hope of being thrown a piece of stale bread or a dry bone.

Atop the telegraph poles ruffled-feathered birds of prey sit in frozen gloom, as if sunk, like the refugees, in melancholy thoughts. Suddenly a sparrow hawk breaks free of his stupor and, eyes aglitter with bloodlust, shoots skyward. His wings flap with a dry, snapping sound as he turns from side to side. Now he hangs suspended a moment, wings outstretched and taut; then plummets like a stone toward some point on the distant horizon.

On the railway tracks opposite, a group of Kazakh women are working with crowbars, spades, and hammers to repair the cross-ties. They wear threadbare men's clothing—grease-stained trousers and patched jackets. Even from their faces, yellow and wrinkled with high cheekbones and narrow Kalmuck eyes, it is hard to tell that they are women. Only two things reveal their sex: their small stature and, especially, their rhythmic gait, a gait as infectious, as feminine and coquettish, as if they were dancing on carpets, castanets in hand. When they catch sight of our train, they drop their tools and run after us with a cry of *"Chai, chai, chai!"* They sing out the word with longing and a gentle softness, and one can tell from their pronunciation that it is the only Russian word they know. Their greatest passion is drinking green tea made from large-cut leaves. The more affluent Kazakhs barter for this tea at train stations, paying for it with watermelons, with round, flat, big, hard cakes, with goat cheese. But the poor women laborers working on the tracks beg for it from the transport trains that pass by the regular stations. *"Chai, chai, chai!"* The word rings out with both feminine charm and a helpless, childlike plaintiveness, until the women tire and fall behind.

It is growing dark. The train picks up speed, as though attempting to escape the night. In a corner of our freight car someone lights an oil lamp, and the refugees begin drifting off to sleep, exhausted by the long hours of doing nothing at all, of staring unremittingly at the steppes, of silence. I alone cannot sleep. In my brain a darkness crouches, as if two electric wires have become entangled and caused a short-circuit. I have convinced myself that if Lev Kogan had not thrown himself into the Volga, then Frumme-Liebche had managed to get back home before the Germans entered Vilna, and she is safe; but if Lev Kogan actually had thrown himself into the river, then Frumme-Liebche on her way back had met the Germans, their helmets pulled down low and submachine guns in their hands. To connect the fates of the two in this way is to sink, as I know all too well, into dismal superstition, into mad absurdity; yet I cannot shake free of the thought, and I need to talk to someone about it.

But the Konotopers are all asleep. Some have already stretched out on their bundles, while others have dozed off sitting up, as if just taking a short nap. One sways to and fro, while another is motionless—no matter how violently the car shakes, he sits straight as a post that has been firmly driven into the ground; a third smiles in his sleep, dreaming, while the limply hanging head of a fourth shakes back and forth, and a fifth, his face covered with sweat like a lump of raw, as-yet-unkneaded dough in water, blows bubbles with his lips, snores, and groans from out of sweetly languorous depths.

Through the open door of the freight car, blue water sparkles in the distance like a many-faceted block of ice. A moment later, through the darkness, I catch sight of a long row of people as they jump with bearlike clumsiness toward the train, carrying heavy sacks and shouting, *"Salt! Salt! Salt!"* The store manager from Konotop opens his sleep-swollen eyes and, befuddled, makes an effort to rise, but at once sits down again.

The train is moving at top speed, as if fearful lest any of this outside horde jump up upon it. The long row of people along the tracks has no end. *"Salt! Salt! Salt!"* they repeat, pouncing like specters.

"The Aral Sea," says the store manager to me. Here, he explains, is where workers and peasants come out to sell bags of salt. It was here that the passengers of the train we'd seen in Chkalov had bought their salt; but we are refugees, and the train will never halt on our account. The Konotop Jew closes his eyes and begins to sway, preparing to go back to sleep. But I do not let him. Moving closer, I whisper:

"I think that members of the same family share the same fate. Do you understand? It can't be that one of the family should escape to safety while the others perish."

"Why can't it be?" He stares at me, fully awake now. "You see all these Jews here? Every one of them has one or more relatives who died in the Ukrainian pogroms during the Revolution. This one lost a brother or a sister, the parents of that one were killed, another one is the only survivor of an entire family. Whoever is destined to live, lives."

"No, no, that can't be . . . What do you think: did your Party secretary return to Penza as he told me he would, or did he throw himself into the Volga?"

"He is alive, our Party secretary—he is alive!" The Konotoper speaks with measured emphasis, plainly impatient and annoyed at me for not letting him sleep. "He is alive, and he'll manage things so he won't have to go into the army, either."

"Right, right!" I exclaim, cheered by his words—but then quickly move away out of fear of his saying something more, something that might contradict my fixed notion of a link between Lev Kogan's survival and Frumme-Liebche's. I bury myself in my corner, hearken to the dark steppe's eerie silence, and dream of my return home . . .

It would be just as it had been after the First World War. I recall how one of our neighbors, a soldier in the Russian army, came back from his captivity in Germany wearing a long overcoat. In the evenings the neighbors would gather in his house and he would describe all he had endured in the army and as a German prisoner-of-war. His stories were inexhaustible and I, a small boy then, listened to them open-mouthed. Just so, when this war comes to an end, shall I sit together with Frumme-Liebche in a small room—small, because that is cozier—and on the table will be a small lamp; in the lamp's reddish glow our shadows will merge as I relate all that has happened to me. And my mother? Will she still be there? . . .

Again I begin looking around our car; again I am searching for someone to talk to.

On a pile of bundles sits a tiny old woman with a wrinkled face who rocks back and forth with her eyes closed. She bears no resemblance to my mother, none at all; but in profile her shadow on the wall looks just like my mother's. In the shadow I see that Mother is feverish, that she is lying in bed ill, and is gazing out into the street through the barred window in Reb Refoel's house, just as for years she had gazed out of the window of our smithy room every Sabbath night and awaited the appearance of the stars that would tell her she was again permitted to light a flame. Now she is waiting for me to push my head in through the bars of Reb Refoel's window and say, "Mother, I'm alive!" . . . I know it is only a shadow on the wall, the shadow of a woman who is alien to me. I know the woman—she is ill-tempered and spiteful; both her sons are at the front and she is traveling with her daughters-in-law, with whom she has been quarreling for days. I will soon chase the shadow away.

I get up and creep carefully over the tightly packed mass of contorted bodies until I reach the corner where the lamp is hanging, and move to extinguish it. But at that precise moment, as if she has been awake all along, the old woman opens her eyes. She hisses angrily at me, in the same tone as when quarreling with her daughters-in-law, that I must not turn the lamp down: In such a crowded place you can't make a move in the dark without getting hurt; and besides, it's so depressing without some light—she feels as if she's being led about with her eyes bandaged and she doesn't know where.

"The guard said that we mustn't light any flame, because the cars are made of wood and there might be a fire." I extinguish the light and creep back to my corner. It has to be dark, totally dark . . .

Stalinabad

AFTER A YEAR AND A HALF of wandering across the Soviet republics of Central Asia, I arrived in Stalinabad,* the capital of Tadzhikistan, close to the borders of China, Afghanistan, and India. All the Jewish refugees from the west were streaming toward Central Asia, ostensibly because it was warm there. But in their eyes there glistened the fervent dream of getting across the border to Iran or Afghanistan, and from there somehow reaching the Land of Israel. In the end the refugees realized that nothing could penetrate the wall of Russian bayonets, no, not even a shadow. At the same time we already knew that in the west the Germans were leaving no survivors.

Always before my mind's eye is the courtyard where my mother lives with Reb Refoel Rosenthal. It is the day after my departure, or perhaps the year after, or perhaps now, this very moment. . . . In the courtyard there is utter confusion. People run to the gate that leads to Broad Street, but find it closed off; now to the gate on Jatkowa Street, but it too is closed, and patrolled by guards I cannot see but whose voices and heavy footsteps I hear. Shouts come from the besiegers without while the Jews within flit back and forth as silently, as eerily, as shadows across a lake. Only my mother stands unmoving, her face expressionless, seeing and hearing nothing of the tumult around her, her glazed eyes fixed on some point far distant. All the neighbors have now crawled into hiding places, but still she does not stir; she stands in the center of the deserted courtyard and listens to the blows against the locked gates, as though in the sound of the blows and the murderous voices she is straining to hear whether I am alive. . . .

This image has carved itself into my brain, it burns within my eyes, and I have only to lower my head to hear at once the sound of the blows on my mother's gates and see her standing in the center of the courtyard.

ONE GLOWING-HOT SUMMER DAY I was standing on line for beer in the Park for Culture and Recreation. Ahead of me were invalided soldiers returned from the front, each consuming up to ten half-liter jars of beer,

---

* Now again known by its original name, Dushanbe.—Trans.

and straining to guzzle down more and more. Next to a one-armed man tottered a disheveled woman with a swollen face who was stroking his empty sleeve. She never touched his face or the remaining arm—only the empty sleeve.

"Come, love, come home," she pleaded, with a hoarse laugh that fell into pieces like the rags that covered her emaciated, filth-encrusted body.

"Three more jars." The transparent, pale-yellow beer continued steadily down his gullet. "I'm not leaving until I'm soused—then I'll feel good, very good." He tore open his shirt and breathed deeply, as though the hot dusty air would help him get drunk.

"Come now, come—that's enough!" She pulled him by the empty sleeve she had just been stroking so gently. The cripple flew into a rage and began to beat her swollen face with his fist:

"Why do you stick to me like a scrubbrush to the skin? You're not my wife, my wife stayed behind with the Germans. You're a pest, a whore!"

"Beat me, but come with me!" The woman pulled at him still more forcibly and, already drunk, he lost his balance and fell. She swiftly bent down to lift him up, but he pushed her away and struck her again with his fist. But she stood her ground and, in quick succession, beat him, kissed him, and dragged him off.

When my turn came, I drank half a liter, and spat—the beer was thin and warm. Even so, I drank two more half-liters and then walked off to rest on a bench in the shade. After a few minutes, I was approached by Misha Troiman, a refugee from Lodz.

Troiman, a tailor by trade, works in a shop for the NKVD. He has nothing to do with the NKVD as such, but as an excellent craftsman is entrusted with the sewing for the top officials. He is short, quick in his movements, with a high-domed forehead, a white, finely chiseled nose, and a face as smooth as a porcelain doll's. Excitable of temperament, he speaks rapidly and volubly, the flow of words punctuated by the heavy r's of Lodz. His wife and child have remained in Lodz, but his brother's wife and child are living in Stalinabad and Misha has to support them, because his brother is in jail. He is always complaining to me about his earnings being inadequate to support his brother's family.

This time too, as he comes up to me, he begins at once to speak of his brother, who had imagined that the Soviets considered him one of their own. And so, when an army of exiled Poles had been formed here but Polish Jews with Soviet passports had not been permitted to join it, his leftist brother, with a whole group of other refugees, had staged a sitdown strike in the offices of the Stalinabad City Council. They demanded that the government take away their Soviet passports and give them back their Polish documents, so they could then join the Polish army. He wanted to return to Poland and help establish the Soviet system there—so he shouted, this leftist brother of his. And so he was clapped in jail. Now Misha needs between three and four thousand rubles a month to provide for himself, for his sister-in-law and her child, and for sending packages to his brother in jail. But he earns at most four hundred rubles a month, and he's afraid to steal anything from his shop—he could easily get five years for that. And wouldn't it be a fine state of affairs if the war were to end and he couldn't go back to his wife and child in Lodz because he was in a Soviet labor camp for theft?

From my silence and dark look, he can tell what I am thinking—and he starts to speak still more quickly, more heatedly: He is sure the Germans aren't treating everyone the same. The worst off are the Jews who have always lived in Soviet territory—those of Kiev and Minsk; them the Germans will not spare. As for the Jews in the new Soviet territories, such as Bialystok and Lvov, those the Germans will separate into two groups, those who supported the Soviets and those who opposed them. But the Jews of Warsaw, where the Russians have never been at all, won't be in any danger. And the Jews of Lodz, where many ethnic Germans have lived and been their friends and neighbors for many years, have nothing at all to fear.

"Is 'Troiman' really your family name, or did you make it up?" I ask him. "The name certainly fits you."*

"You're wrong. I'm not a dr-r-reamer." His rolling r's sound like ten pairs of wagon wheels clattering across a cobblestone road. "It's my brother who's the dreamer, with his crazy idea of calling a strike in the Soviet Union."

For a while he remains seated beside me, dejected, wrinkling his high-domed forehead. Suddenly he jumps up. He asks me to go with him to the Tadzhiks to drink wine and eat shashlik; he knows of a place in a cellar where they make good shashlik of horsemeat. I decline. Again he wrinkles his forehead, starts to say something, stops, and at last, deeply embarrassed, stammers out:

"I need a woman."

"So?"

"I know, there's no lack of shiksas in Stalinabad, and I'm no saint." His speech is once again rapid and animated: But he doesn't mean one of those who can be bought for a spool of thread. He means a real friend. And he knows such a young woman, intelligent and pretty, but his conscience holds him back. Every day he thinks about how it will be

---

* *Troiman* (or *Troim-man*) can be interpreted as "man of dreams" in Yiddish (troim = dream).—Trans.

when he returns to Lodz and has to look straight into his wife's eyes. She will have had to struggle there for her very life, while he has been enjoying the good life here. . . .

IN THE PARK a fight has broken out among the now-drunken amputees. Each lacking one or more hands or feet, they flail away all the more viciously at one another with their wooden crutches; the more disabled a man, the more fiercely he fights, growling like a maddened beast. A one-legged invalid leans on one crutch and with the other tries to beat over the head an amputee seated on the ground who is missing both legs. The legless man brandishes one of his own crutches to keep his enemy at bay. Unable to get near his opponent, the one-legged man launches his crutch straight at the other's face. The cripple on the ground nimbly catches the flying crutch and hurls it back, striking the one-legged man with tremendous force in the stomach. He falls. Two other amputees, each missing his right arm, grasp each other's left hand so that neither can get at the other one's throat, and use their heads, butting from below, to batter each other's noses, teeth, and jaws, until both are covered with blood. A few paces away other one-legged and one-armed men, all en-tangled in a heap, jump up and down like demons and scratch each other's faces with their fingernails, while crutches are crossed and rammed against each other until they break.

"A real 'Park for Culture and Recreation' this is," laughs Misha.

I leave him and drag myself to the exit. Near the gate stand several militiamen, watching the fight from a distance. They're afraid to get any closer because they know that if they do, the battling cripples will instantly form a united front against them—as has already happened more than once—and hurl themselves ten upon each militiaman, screaming: "You rear-guard rat! We gave our lives at the front, and here you are, hiding like a mouse, where it's safe!"

I walk along Lenin Street, which is sunny, deserted, and quiet. On one side is the fence that stretches along the entire length of the park; on the other, the whitewashed walls of the small, flat-roofed clay houses gleam in the sun. What with the heat and the beer I have drunk, a heavy sweat breaks out on my brow, I feel dizzy, my feet falter, but I plod on so I will no longer have to hear the drunken voices behind me. Another melody is coming to me now, and it is in order to listen to it that I have left the park. Quiet and radiant, with no beginning, no end, the melody stretches through my memory like a ray of sunlight, and I follow the unending, luminous strand back to Vilna, back to my mother's house. From my earliest childhood I remember how, on the Sabbath preceding the New Moon, my mother, before she left for the synagogue, would chant a Yiddish prayer in the front room of the smithy near the work-bench, and I, still sunk in sleep in the back, would hear it:

"I beseech Thee, O God most praised, that Thou shalt send me my sustenance, and shalt feed me and my household and all Israel, in joy of spirit and not in sorrow, in dignity and not in shame. Deliver me from all terrors and misfortunes, and save me from slanders and all evil encounters. For this I do beseech Thee . . ."

I whisper the words, with the feeling that the melody is creeping out of a grave. I sense about it the stillness of a cemetery. My mother, I feel, is no longer chanting it. . . . I turn to go back to the park. I will find Misha Troiman and go with him to the Tadzhiks to drink wine, to eat shashlik made of horsemeat. All I will ask of him is, not to speak to me of home.

Just then, coming toward me, I see a Jew with a grayish-black beard, wearing a black frock-coat. He walks at a sedate pace, hands behind his back and a white kerchief around his neck, just like any urban Jewish householder taking a late Sabbath afternoon stroll after his nap, and now on his way to the synagogue for the Minḥa and Ma'ariv prayers.

"Good Sabbath."

"Good Sabbath and a Good Year." He stares at me, astonished. "Where is the young man from?"

"From Lithuania—I'm a native of Vilna. And you?"

"It doesn't matter," he answers grudgingly, but then, apparently deciding that I pose no threat to him, he adds, "I'm from White Russia, originally from Mogilev. But I was living elsewhere, not in Mogilev."

"When I saw you wearing that kerchief, I realized at once that this is the Sabbath," I blurt out joyfully. "It never even occurred to me to wonder whether there's an eruv in Stalinabad."

"And before you saw me, you didn't know it is the Sabbath?" He gives me a sidelong glance, and his long, pointed beard, his sharp nose and smoldering eyes, tell me that he is a Ḥassid, a zealot.

"Indeed, I did sense that it is the Sabbath," I murmur, thinking of my mother's prayer which had so suddenly come to mind. "But you know, here one lives in surroundings that do not remind one of the Sabbath. How do you know the proper time for lighting candles, or when to recite Havdalah? There are no Jewish calendars in Russia, are there?"

"Where there's a will, there's a way," he replies with a conspiratorial smile. "There's no law that says a calendar must be printed."

"Oh, a handwritten one? But tell me, how do you avoid violating the Sabbath, since the only day of rest here is on Sunday?"

"Where there's a will, there's a way." And he explains that he is a bookbinder, an independent artisan who works at home and is paid by the piece.

I see that he is about to walk on, but I am unwilling to end the conversation. I tell him that I once studied in a yeshiva. He reacts with evident anger and displeasure, looks all about him, and, seeing that the street is deserted, addresses me sternly, slowly, emphasizing each word:

"Since the young man once studied the Torah, he surely knows that the Sabbath is a secret token between the Jewish people and the Master of the Universe. And if the young man has reasons not to reveal his Jewish faith, he should conduct himself like a newly wed couple. When they're among strangers, they communicate with each other by secret signs that no outsider understands, but they understand each other very well. They have their own private tokens of love and affection."

He falls silent and fixes his gaze on the snowcapped mountains. I, too, look at these peaks and am reminded of the people who dwell in those mountains. The refugees would tell stories about the mountaineers of the Pamirs—that they know a secret path that leads to India, and that they regularly make pilgrimages to their holy shrines there. But I cannot believe that the Soviet border guards are unaware of this and unable to stop it.

"The Pamir Mountains border on the Himalayas, the highest mountains in the world," I inform the bookbinder from Mogilev. "And the name of this particular mountain range is 'Silselayi Koohi Hissor.' Can you pronounce such a difficult name? 'Silselayi Koohi Hissor.'"

"I neither can nor want to." He shrugs his shoulders. "It seems to me that if I should ever, God forbid, forget when it is the Seventh Day, I would feel the approach of the Holy Day of Rest in my very bones. A good Sabbath to you."

I remain alone on the empty, darkening street and gaze at the crags that tower one above the other. The golden sunset now illumines with a magical glow the blue sky, the crystal-white snow, the green ice on the mountain peaks. Everything melts and burns together in a blaze of diamonds. The purple clouds, the snowcapped mountains, and the bare rocks look like a gigantic city with walls of glass and white towers, where the Sabbath has been rekindled after having been extinguished on earth.

Refugees

I

THE STALINABAD CITY PARK is already carpeted with the yellow leaves of autumn. The refugees who habitually stroll about the park have likewise developed a yellowish, parched, and transparent skin with prominent veins on their hands, as if they, too, are burning with autumnal fever. Many have malaria, others are sick with dysentery. In the evenings an orchestra plays in the park, and on the dance platform girls dance with other girls: the young men have been sent to the front, all gradually scooped up like live fish from a fish-monger's tub. And the healthy young men who have gone away have been replaced by a steady influx of maimed and crippled men who during the day go on rampages in the marketplace as they wait in line for tobacco and beer, and in the evenings gather around the orchestra in the park.

The amputees whistle, laugh, and with their armless or legless bodies enact a lewd mimickry of the girls' dancing. Some of them climb up on the platform and catch hold of girls around the waist, one with his remaining hand, another with the stump of a hand that has a metal hook instead of fingers, while a third deliberately presses against his partner a shoulder from which dangles a bare, withered, truncated bone. The girls are afraid to refuse and so they dance with pained smiles, eyes half-closed, trembling with fear, disgust, and yet a secret pleasure. Among those refugees who have managed to obtain work and are earning money, there are also some who dance, drink, and generally carry on, as if to show that nothing matters to them anymore.

"Carthage!" says Orenstein to me. He is a lawyer from Warsaw whom I know from Vilna, to which he fled immediately after the outbreak of war between Germany and Poland. Two years later, I met him again in the capital of Uzbekistan, Tashkent, which he called "Hong Kong" because that sounded more Asiatic. In Tashkent, Orenstein was still wearing a white linen suit and white shoes. Now, however, he is head to toe in tatters and walks about virtually barefoot; of the advocate of old, the distinguished counselor-at-law, nothing remains except his black, glittering eyes.

"Stalinabad is Carthage. And the god of Carthage, to whom human sacrifices were brought, was called Baal-hamon. Carthage, you must know, was a colony of Tyre, of the Phoenicians who brought human sacrifices to their idol Melkart. Baal-hamon, Melkart, and Moloch, they're all one and the same bloodthirsty god. Now do you understand?" This is Orenstein's way of explaining to me that Tadzhikistan is a Great Russian colony and that the same iron law governs here. "Come along with me to the marketplace, and I'll show you how to survive in this world. I survive by sampling."

The market is flooded with Tadzhiks who have led their small donkeys here laden with ripe fruit. Displayed on mats are mountains of watermelons whose rinds, the color of blue water streaked with green veins, look like chunks of marble. Next to them lie mounds of cantaloupes, round ones and oval ones, as transparent as fresh eggs. Orenstein stops at two baskets—one filled with peaches with flaming-red cheeks, the other with ripe apricots that shine like small suns. From each basket he takes a piece of fruit, the biggest one, and devours both in a trice.

"It's stones you're selling, not fruit!" he shouts at the startled Tadzhik, and before the latter can recover himself Orenstein has already dragged me off. We pass stands with apples, pears, tomatoes, sweet radishes, all of which Orenstein contemplates with gloom-filled eyes but doesn't dare try to sample. Women stand at these stalls, and women, he explains, are very petty: for a single apple they may scratch out both your eyes.

Next we stop at tall, narrow, woven baskets filled to the rim with grapes—some round and dark-blue like eye-pupils, others long and fingerlike, yellowish and sticky like honey. Orenstein tears off a large cluster and gulps the grapes down with great speed; when only two or three remain on the stem, he replaces it in the basket, saying to the Tadzhik with a grimace:

"Sour as vinegar."

The Tadzhik's eyes bulge: that anyone, in the fall, should call his grapes sour—such a thing he has never heard before in his life. But Orenstein is already striding swiftly away, hands deep in his pockets, as though to guard from theft the large wad of bills secreted there. We pass a little shop where all manner of spices are on display in small canvas sacks—pepper, bay leaves, cinnamon, and saffron. Nothing here, clearly, for Orenstein to sample.

"Do you know how they cook pilaf here?" he asks me with dry lips, and one can see from his face that his guts are churning with hunger. Pilaf, he continues, is always cooked by the Tadzhik men themselves; they do not entrust it to their women, because they consider it a great art. First a fire is built outside in the courtyard, and a bowl with oil is placed over it on a tripod. When the oil is quite hot, they throw a potful of peeled onions into it. The fire flares up, there is a sizzling and a seething, until all the onions' bitterness evaporates with the smoke and they become sweet as sugar. Then they take lamb, beef, or veal and put it into a large pot together with the onions, with rice, and with *kishmish*, as the Asiatics call raisins. They set this pot, as large as an army cauldron, over the tiniest little flame and let it simmer for two hours, three hours, four hours, or as long as they have a mind to. Only then do they wrap the pot with cloths, so that everything will stew together thoroughly. When the pilaf is finally done, every onion is as large as a goose egg, the rice and the raisins are puffed up, golden as sunshine, the meat is steaming and drips with fat. They eat it with their hands and accompany it with wine.

"With their hands?" I ask.

"What's the matter—you wouldn't eat it?" Orenstein bares his teeth. "I would eat it with my feet, if only they'd give me some. I've seen how they eat it. With two fingers they knead together rice, raisins, and a piece of meat and toss it down—and then they knead some more with two fingers and toss that down." Orenstein repeats these phrases over and over, like a broken phonograph record that keeps turning in the same groove and emitting the same shrill, piercing sounds.

Suddenly his eyes glitter: he has caught sight of a Tadzhik who is squatting on the ground in a corner of the marketplace with a watermelon between his knees, and is cutting slices from it with a knife. He takes one bite of the red, juicy melon-meat and throws the rest of the slice away. Orenstein sits down next to the Tadzhik, speaks to him, waves his arms about, and slaps him on the back. The Tadzhik stares at him, wipes away the seeds that have stuck to his chin, and then hands Orenstein the remaining half of the watermelon. He walks away, and Orenstein buries his face in the half-watermelon, bites into the sides with his teeth, gags on the juice, and finally offers me the broken pieces of rind to finish up. I decline—even an animal wouldn't eat such filth.

"Don't eat it if you don't want it." He stands up. "Now I want a smoke. I'll ask 'the saint' for a cigarette."

The man whom Orenstein sarcastically calls "the saint" is a refugee from a small town in Volhynia—Yankel Grot. He is short, with a high, raspy voice, swollen feet, hands like pieces of sodden wood, and so much dust in his hair you would think all the sands of the desert of Kara Kum have fallen upon him. Like Misha Troiman, he believes that he will find his wife and children alive at home, but he doesn't talk about it as much. Yankel Grot makes a living: he rolls cigarettes and sells them in the marketplace. But often, at the end of a full day of standing in the market, he still hasn't made enough to pay for the cigarette wrappers or the tobacco he has taken on credit, because the amputees have grabbed all the cigarettes right out of his hands. Nonetheless, every so often he gives Orenstein three rubles—never to be repaid—in return for Orenstein's submitting to a lecture.

"Herr Advokat," Yankel Grot pleads, "don't let yourself go, and you'll yet merit the privilege of entering the Land of Israel. Look at me, I don't even have the strength to lift my feet, and yet I make the effort. When a man lets himself fall apart like an old fence, everyone grabs a piece and carries it off."

Orenstein always promises to look for work, proceeds then and there to spend every kopeck of the loan, and returns to the cigarette-maker a week later. This time it is not even a week since he last took money, so he is going to ask Yankel Grot only for a cigarette. But when we find him, he is standing rigid as a statue, while from his half-closed fist protrude about two dozen pieces of empty cigarette-wrappers.

"Now you're selling wrappers without tobacco? Who will buy just the wrapper?" asks Orenstein, and looks at me as if to ask whether the cigarette-maker has lost his mind.

"The wind blew the tobacco away," Yankel Grot answers in deep dejection, with neither the strength to speak further nor the strength to move.

Silently we walk away and leave the marketplace. Orenstein suddenly bursts into bitter laughter. "In Carthage," he says, "even the wind is a bandit and blows the tobacco right out of Yankel Grot's cigarette-wrappers."

Tadzhik women, homeward bound from the market, ride by on small donkeys. They wear long red dresses with green silk capes around the shoulders, tall round hats that resemble rimless tophats and are hung with bells, and circlets of coins on their bosoms, while their faces are covered up to the eyes with black veils called *parandjas.* One, however, a young girl, wears no veil. Her face is dark brown, the nose curved like the beak of a bird of prey, the eyes hypnotically black, while her hair is red as fire. She sits upon her donkey with regal immobility, like an eagle atop a rock, and I cannot take my eyes off her.

"Come away!" Orenstein pulls me by the arm. "Do you want some Tadzhik knifing you in the back? The Asiatics don't like anyone looking at their women."

"It's the first time I've ever seen one of the natives here with red hair, they're all black." I look down at my shabby clothes, and the thought strikes me that the marvelously beautiful young woman with the dark-brown face would never take notice of such a ragged creature as myself.

"The Tadzhiks have boxes full of the ten-ruble notes that they got for their merchandise. . . ." Orenstein is thinking out loud. Again he tugs at my arm. "Come, I'll introduce you to 'the Prophet Elijah.' He's a

Bukharian Jew, a shoemaker, who shines the shoes of the refugees without charge. Lately he's found himself a spot in a side street with his little box."

Throughout the summer I had seen, on Lenin Street near the gate of the municipal park, a shoemakers' shop of Bukharian Jews, who worked outdoors beneath a long, narrow awning. They were black-haired young fellows with merry eyes, always talking and laughing heartily among themselves, yet working diligently all the while. The soles of my shoes were beginning to separate from the tips and I asked the Bukharians to repair them on the spot, as I had no spare pair to change over to. But the shoemakers, overwhelmed with work, told me it would be a few days before they could oblige me. But before my turn came, most of the group had vanished and of what had been a long line of cobblers, there remained only two at one end and two at the other; all the benches in the middle were empty. They had been drafted into the army. The few who were left ceased to talk or to laugh; they only sat bent over their lasts and worked, while large beads of sweat formed on their foreheads. And it was not long before the last of the shoemakers, along with their benches, also disappeared. Beneath the shop's narrow canopy drunken amputees now loitered. I am therefore overjoyed to hear about Orenstein's shoemaker—perhaps he will be able to repair my shoes on the spot.

THE SHOEMAKER SITS on a side street that I rarely pass. When I see him, it occurs to me that he must be the father or father-in-law of one of the men who have been mobilized, and that he is trying to earn some money to support the family that has been left behind. He appears to be past eighty; his long white beard covers his entire chest, down to the little shoeshine bench. He wears a multicolored robe and an embroidered skullcap in the Tadzhik style, a *tyubeteika*. The moment he sees us, his kind, black, grandfatherly eyes light up. He beckons us closer. Orenstein has already visited him several times before, and the old man recognizes him. But the lawyer's white shoes are now so torn and soiled they can no longer be polished. With a resigned wave of the hand, Orenstein turns to me:

"A slave in Carthage can do without shoes. I'm going to the park to stretch out on a bench. When you're finished here, come join me."

I sit down on the bench facing the old man and ask him to mend my shoes. But the Bukharian doesn't understand Russian. Pondering, I decide that he will surely understand the Holy Tongue. I take off my shoe, show him the torn sole, and explain what I want. I also show him money, to indicate that I'm not asking him to do it for nothing, that I will pay. The old man doesn't understand Hebrew either—he speaks only Tadzhik—but he does manage to grasp my meaning. With a sad smile he shows me that he has no leather, no cobbler's thread, no tacks, and apologetically spreads his hands: he can do nothing for me.

I put my shoe back on and start to rise, but he holds onto my foot and indicates with signs that he will shine my shoes. He pulls out a brush and shoe-wax, but as he is about to wipe the dust off my shoes with a rag, he looks intently at their tips and uppers, as though he can discern in them the long way I have traveled. I point at myself and say one word: "Vilna."

For a moment the old man is motionless, wrinkling his forehead as though trying to remember something. Then he begins fumbling about the foot-bench and pulls out of it a book with a tattered cover which he gives to me; he points at the title page to call my attention to it.

It was now shortly before Rosh Hashanah, and the book was a sliḥa, a volume of penitential prayers. On the title page it states in large letters that the book was printed in Vilna.

The old man finished shining my shoes and I reach into my pocket to pay him, but he shakes his head, his face solemn, his eyes closed. Yet again he rummages about in his little box, pulls out a large pomegranate with a hard, brown, wrinkled skin, and holds it out to me: "Sheheḥeyonu." It is the only word he has said all this time, and he utters it so prayerfully and with such devotion that I accept the pomegranate at once.

*"Afilu reiḳonin sheb'ḥo m'lei'in mitzvos ḳorimon,"** I exclaim, to gladden the old man's heart. I see that he doesn't understand, yet he nods, happy that I have accepted his gift and that I am speaking in the Holy Tongue. But then, he becomes deeply pensive and melancholy; his thoughts seem to have turned to the son or son-in-law who has gone off to war. I, too, sit as if turned to stone, with my old but now shiny shoes, with the sliḥa in one hand and the pomegranate in the other, almost like Yankel Grot in the marketplace with his empty rolls of cigarette wrappers from which the wind has blown all the tobacco.

The old man has given me the pomegranate so that I may pronounce the Sheheḥeyonu blessing in honor of Rosh Hashanah. My mother and Frumme-Liebche are . . . there; and I sit here, with a pomegranate for Sheheḥeyonu in my hand.

---

* "Even the least worthy among you are as filled with good deeds as a pomegranate with seeds" (Talmudic saying).—Trans.

II

ORENSTEIN, the Warsaw counselor-at-law, has decided to quit Carthage-Stalinabad for "Sodom and Gomorrah"—that is, Samarkand or Bukhara. These, he has heard, are truly Oriental cities, with mosques and minarets, and tearooms where the Uzbeks sit with their legs folded beneath them as they drink green tea. He himself couldn't ask for more: to sit in a tearoom with his legs folded under him, drink tea, smoke—and do nothing.

To me, Orenstein has always seemed a little mad, and even at times quite frightening—as when, for example, he would stand in the middle of the marketplace where he has gone to sample the Tadzhiks' fruit, and deliver long discourses on history. Once he stopped to tell me that the bloody games of the gladiators took place not only in Rome but in all the Roman colonies as well. He spoke in a deliberately loud voice, and laughed at me for trembling with fear lest some bystander overhear him and understand the true meaning of his parables. I both envied his ability to be so irresponsible and severely scolded him for it; eventually I began to avoid him. And yet, when he left, I felt sad. I wandered around the Stalinabad marketplace all alone. It was now the end of autumn: the overripe fruits were now to be had for next to nothing, and in the evenings, when the market was closing down, the Tadzhiks would give me two pounds of slightly overripe grapes for two rubles.

Late one afternoon in the marketplace, I saw a large crowd gathered around a half-blind singer-musician, who sang and strummed lazily, sleepily, on a two-stringed mandolin. Suddenly he let out a wild howl, as though the desert of Kara Kum and the snowcapped mountains themselves were howling, and his fingers raced back and forth over the two strings. Then he subsided once more into a quiet lament; his fingers on the strings died down as well. Just as I thought he was about to conclude, his wild, hoarse desert cry rose once more. He ended as suddenly as he had begun and announced that he would read everyone's fortune in his palm. All this time he had been surrounded by Tadzhiks with pious faces suffused with the copper glow of the setting sun, but the first to approach the half-blind fortune-teller was Misha Troiman. The fortune-teller felt Misha's palm with his fingers and chanted his prophecies in a mixture of Tadzhik and Russian. I turned to walk away; Misha threw a coin to the fortune-teller and ran after me:

"I'm making a fool of myself. What does that Tadzhik know of my wife and child in Lodz?" From his pocket Misha takes a handful of spools of thread. "You once asked me for some thread; you said the buttons of your jacket had come off. What do you need—black, white, brown?"

"Where did you suddenly get so much?" I look cautiously all around.

"Where I work. Do you think I can live on the three or four hundred rubles a month they pay me?" Troiman puts the spools back in his pocket and accompanies me to the City Park, the refugees' haven. On the way he tells me that, as long as his sister-in-law was well, he could argue that she should get work to support herself and her child and to send parcels to her husband in jail. But now she is in the hospital, ill with typhus, her little girl is being cared for by strangers, and both may die of hunger, just as many of the other refugees are dying. When the war ends and he and his brother return to Lodz, his brother will always throw it up to him: "You found your wife and child alive," he will say, "but while I was in jail in Stalinabad, you let my wife and child die of hunger." And so he has to help his sister-in-law.

"But you yourself told me you can easily get five years in jail," I say to him as we enter the park.

"Here in the Soviet Union, comrade, they have a saying: There are three categories of people—those who've been in jail, those who are now in jail, and those who will be in jail. Nobody can live on what he's paid. So what color thread do you need—black, white, or brown?" Misha again takes the spools from his pocket. "Don't worry! If I get caught, I won't tell them I gave you a spool of thread."

I choose one of the spools and with disdainful carelessness he stuffs the others back into his pocket. Then he transfers from one pocket to another a wad of ten-ruble notes, rumpling them in his fist as he does so, in the approved Soviet style. This—as opposed to keeping one's money in a wallet, with the bills flattened out and their edges neatly aligned—this, in Soviet Russia, is the hallmark of prosperity and affluence, and of a generous nature. And the refugee from Lodz, it is easy to see, wishes ardently to become a Russian.

From another pocket Misha now draws a small, embroidered velvet bag, from which he takes out a sizeable collection of Uzbek skullcaps, some six-sided, others square or round, with stiffened linings and borders colorfully embroidered with Oriental designs.

"I'm collecting these *tyubeteiki* for my boy," he stammers, somewhat embarrassed. Often, he tells me, he cannot remember what his son looks like—probably because at the time he left Lodz, the boy was still quite small and it is difficult to remember the faces of small children. He has heard people say that if misfortune befalls a person, a change comes over his photographs too—the face in them begins to shrink and turn yellowish, like that of a real corpse. He, Misha, doesn't believe this, and yet he envies a friend of his, another refugee, who possesses a photograph of his wife and his two little girls. The friend has told him that he keeps the picture on a table in his room, and whenever he goes out it's with the feeling that he's leaving his wife and daughters in his Stalinabad apartment, waiting for his return.

"That's why I'm collecting these skullcaps for my little boy—I look at them all the time, as if they were his picture." Misha gathers up his *tyubeteiki* and hastily leaves the park, before I can say a word about his dreams.

THE TREES IN THE PARK, which earlier in the fall were scarlet, have now turned yellow, and the wind carries piles of leaves across the ground, like a river that carries with it masses of fallen, drowned birds. At night the sky is still clear and dark blue, and the great stars seem like flaming, overblown flowers. But one night I notice that the moon, large and round and golden-yellow, is slowly becoming obscured by clouds. The sky no longer clears; the heavy rains of late autumn have begun: it pours and teems by day and by night, without let-up, until the sand blown in from the surrounding desert, the fallen leaves, and the grayish sandy ground have all become one solid mass of mud.

I am living in a narrow room which I share with my landlady and her twelve-year-old son. The landlady has taken me in because she is often away from home for several days during the week. She drives a large truck and brings produce from the surrounding kolkhozes to stores in the city. When at home, she speaks little to me and even less to her son, from whose father she is divorced; in place of words she prefers blows to the boy's face with a large, masculine fist. She has a broken nose with nostrils wide as a dog's ears. At night she entertains men, totally heedless of my and her son's presence in the same room. None of her one-night lovers is as ugly or coarse as she herself. Until she gets them thoroughly drunk, they are ashamed to undress before me and the boy. I lie in my bed, my face to the wall, and choke with disgust.

Once, however, the autumn rains begin to fall, my landlady's nocturnal revels cease to trouble me; my only concern is how to get into town in the morning and back at night. My shoes have at last fallen apart completely and the neighborhood where I live—a valley packed with tiny houses cheek to jowl—is like a crack in the earth's surface overflowing with mud. At night I must find my way in total darkness. The streets have no lamps or electric lights, and the local residents keep their windows tightly shuttered, as if begrudging the out-of-doors even the reflection of their small oil lamps. But the worst moment of all comes when I drag myself at last into my kennel, and the landlady sees me enter with soaked and muddy shoes.

I have stopped thinking about the war, about food—stopped thinking even about my mother and Frumme-Liebche. My one heart's desire is a pair of shoes. The mud is encrusted between my toes, it completely covers my heels, I can feel it starting to grow on my back. Mud seems to be creeping under my arms, spreading over my throat and the back of my neck, over my hair and my eyebrows, seeping into my ears, into my nostrils, between my teeth, under my eyelids . . . I feel I am going mad.

By day I pace up and down Lenin Street, or stand under the awning of what was once the Bukharian shoemakers' shop, and stare at the passers-by—not at their faces or their clothes, no, only at their shoes. I see a pair of women's feet walk by in high rubber boots; how they shine, those boots, as though polished just a minute ago. A second pair of women's feet parade past, in felt overshoes that button on the side. Then a pair of men's sport shoes with nails in the soles clatter past me; the trouser cuffs are stuffed inside the leather boot-tops. Next to march by are stiffly moving men's feet in high boots, with galoshes over them. Both boots and galoshes! Suddenly I spy a pair of feet wrapped in wet rags even worse than my own—and the feet come to a halt beside me. I raise my eyes: it is Yankel Grot, the refugee from Volhynia. His face, too, is sodden and puffed like a swollen cucumber.

"Are you still selling your homemade cigarettes?" I ask.

"In this weather, how could I sell cigarettes in the open market?" He looks at me in astonishment. "The rain would soak them through and through." Besides, he tells me, he's already been arrested and tried for speculating in tobacco. He had argued that he wasn't speculating, that he only charged a little extra to cover the cost of the wrappers and for his labor in rolling the cigarettes. So they let him go that time, though with a warning to stop doing that kind of business.

"Let you go?"

"Yes, the Jewish woman judge let me go," says Yankel Grot.

I know that Jewish woman judge. The courthouse is on Lenin Street, and I see her pass by quite often. She wears low overshoes with fur trimming alongside the buttons and around the edges. She is a rather tall, stoutish woman with wise, kind, youthfully sparkling black eyes— although when she walks by with brows knit in a frown, she appears much older and more severe.

"And where do you sleep?"

"In the courthouse," answers Yankel Grot. The judge, he explains, had talked to him privately after the trial and complained about the refugees who were breaking the law. In small matters, she said, she could close an eye, but when it came to more serious crimes she neither could nor wanted to let them off scot-free. Then she asked him where he slept, and when he told her he had no steady place, that he never spent the day where he had spent the night, she told him to come to the courthouse every evening—but he should make sure no one saw him when he entered or when he left.

"Grot, old friend, do me a favor and introduce me to this judge." I catch hold of his arm. "Perhaps she'll let me sleep in the courthouse, too. Let it be on a hard bench, or even on the floor—just so I won't have to crawl through the mud any more to my witch with the broken nose."

"That's no longer possible," sighs Yankel Grot. He gasps for breath. Once or twice he did take some other refugees in to sleep with him— and then someone stole the drapes, the green cloths off the tables, and even the courthouse chairs. He couldn't say that the refugees were the thieves, but when the judge heard about it she held her head, aghast. He himself was in serious danger of punishment, and the judge had mobilized the entire militia to find the thieves, so that he wouldn't get sent to a prison camp.

"Orenstein did well to leave Stalinabad," I say aloud to myself. "Perhaps life in Samarkand or Bukhara isn't as terrible as it is for us here."

"Orenstein? You mean the lawyer Orenstein?" Yankel Grot looks at me with his gentle eyes and seems to ponder for a moment whether he should say something more. "You don't know that Orenstein is dead?"

"Dead?!"

"Not very long ago." Yankel Grot is shivering with the cold and damp. "He couldn't manage to find a place for himself in Samarkand or in Bukhara, so he went off to an Uzbek kolkhoz, and died there. A refugee who came from Tashkent told me."

That refugees died of dysentery, of cholera, of malaria, that is no longer news to me. But I had known Orenstein from Vilna, from Tashkent, and it is hardly more than two months since we were tramping about the Stalinabad marketplace together. Now I stand motionless, silent and downcast. For this, I say to myself, Orenstein had to flee from Warsaw to Vilna, from Vilna all the way to Central Asia, to die in a half-barbarous Uzbek village . . . Had he known what the future held in store for him, he would have lain down in the middle of the road right outside Warsaw and let the German hordes trample him into the earth. Had he known it still earlier, he, like Job, would not have wished to emerge from his mother's womb.

"Now I regret the way I used to preach at him about letting himself go, and kept telling him to look for work—" Yankel Grot huddles within his wet rags. "Toward the end I no longer even gave him his three rubles a week, because I myself wasn't earning anything anymore. If he'd gotten sick here in Stalinabad, we could have gone to see him in the hospital—we might even have saved him. What do you think?"

"I don't know," I answer. I, too, feel remorse for having avoided Orenstein toward the end, out of distaste for his effrontery. "I don't know whether we could have saved Orenstein, but at least we would have been at the funeral. Ever since I left home, I've always thought that the worst fate of all must be to close your eyes for the last time knowing that you are surrounded by strangers who won't mourn for you or even remember your name after they've buried you."

Yankel Grot looks at me with an unspoken reproach in his gentle eyes at these words of despair. It is the same reproach he feels toward all the refugees.

"Sometimes I think there is a measure of comfort even in expressing one's despair," he says with a smile, and drags his sodden feet away. I resume my staring at the shoes of passers-by. Suddenly I observe a pair of wooden crutches which rise and strike the pavement in steady alternation, with a merry clacking sound, as if in mockery of Yankel's rag-wrapped feet and my shoes. The cripple is well off now—no need to worry about his wooden crutches getting wet or soiled.

Misha Troiman

I

IT IS SPRING IN STALINABAD. The trees are sprouting blossoms and the fragrance of jasmine is as intoxicating as wine. Misha Troiman abruptly informs me that he has given up hope of finding his wife and child alive, and that he is now in love with his young Russian sweetheart, Lydia, the girl he has known ever since he came to Stalinabad. Misha's sister-in-law—just recently released from the hospital after a bout of typhus, with all her hair shorn off—stops me in the street one day and accuses Misha of intentionally convincing himself that his wife and child are dead, so as to be free to carry on this romance with his shiksa: he is planning to marry her and to have the marriage officially recorded in the Civil Marriage Registry.

"Why can't he just have an affair without getting married?" I ask. "Many of the refugees have girlfriends here, but they don't plan to get married and they don't give up hope of returning to their families someday."

"That's my brother-in-law for you—all he knows is how to be a husband, not a lover." Misha, she continues, is spending all his money on the shiksa: he dresses her up, pays her rent, takes her out to wine-cellars, hosts parties in her room for her and her friends. As for herself, his sister-in-law, and her child, he no longer gives them any help, and has even stopped sending food parcels to his brother in prison.

"I beg of you—speak to him!" She is screaming now more than pleading. "Tell him there's no shortage of shiksas in Stalinabad, but he has only one brother, a brother who's in prison, and a sister-in-law who's come out of the hospital a sick woman."

It is noon. In the City Park, which has been closed all winter, a band, together with singers and dancers, is rehearsing a new program for the coming season. The refugees rejoice in the park's reopening. With nowhere else to go, here they sit gossiping and watching the rehearsal. I, for my part, find the grimaces and gestures of these vaudevillians grating on the nerves, and I choose instead to stride up and down Lenin Street near the park entrance. The passers-by, hearing the band's marches and dance music, begin to walk more rhythmically, moving their feet in time to the beat, their faces breaking into smiles. But suddenly there is an outburst of whistles and sirens—a signal for everyone, pedestrians and wagoners, to come instantly to a halt, as though a fire engine or ambulance were moving through.

Down Lenin Street marches a group of convicts, surrounded on all four sides by militiamen, most of them Tadzhiks, with tin whistles and with guns that they keep pointed at their charges. Within this rectangular enclosure the prisoners walk four abreast, in some half-dozen rows. They carry bundles of clothes, as though they were coming from the baths. They walk slowly, with an air of dull, listless indifference. Since they are being taken through the streets on foot in broad daylight, rather than at night in sealed cars, it is clear that these are not serious offenders, but minor transgressors, imprisoned for petty theft or hooliganism or talking too much. Yet every so often the guards set up a wild whistling, as if they were escorting dangerous felons who might at any moment break out of their chains and escape. Automobiles come to a halt at intersections; pedestrians stand motionless on the sidewalks. There is a deathly silence, broken only by the band music in the park, the militiamen's heavy footsteps, the weary shuffling of the prisoners' feet.

Only one man, a drunken Russian, ignores the order to halt. He walks unsteadily along the sidewalk and carries on a conversation with a female prisoner who has a folded blanket under her arm. She is in the row nearest the sidewalk, and is hidden from view by the Tadzhik guard who walks beside her.

"Valentin is getting very wild . . ." The drunkard moves his tongue with as much difficulty as his wobbly feet. "He doesn't want to do his lessons, the rascal. . . ."

"Belt him one on the chin," the woman with the blanket answers coolly. "You're the father—you have to raise your children properly. And make sure Lyuba doesn't run around too much with the boys."

"No talking!" roars the Tadzhik who walks between them.

"And our neighbor went on a rampage." The Russian, undaunted, continues his conversation with his wife. "He says to me, 'Timofey Vassilievich, you're alone now with only two children in a big room, while I'm crowded into a small room with my five children. You have to change rooms with me.' That's what he says, the swindler!"

"You tell him, Timofey, that when I come home in two years I'll knock out his teeth and scratch out his eyes," answers the prisoner calmly.

"I said, no talking!" the Tadzhik sings out again.

The Russian on the sidewalk stops walking and stands swaying to and fro, rubbing his face with the palm of his hand as if trying to sober up. Suddenly he spies half of an unsmoked cigarette lying near his feet. He bends down cautiously so as not to fall, picks up the cigarette, slaps it between his teeth, and slowly straightens himself again. In the meantime the prisoners and their guards have walked on, and not even his wife turns her head to glance back at him. Motionless, feet planted wide apart, he gazes after the already distant marchers, shakes his head from side to side, and gives vent to a long string of curses directed variously at his guts, his dog's-soul, his ancestors, the Mother of God.

Approaching me from the other end of Lenin Street is Misha Troiman. He stops and tells me in great agitation that he had almost been arrested that very morning as he was disposing of goods he had stolen from his shop. While thrashing out the deal with his fence in a corner of the marketplace, he had spotted a man in civilian clothes observing them. The fence had laughed it off, he was a war cripple and had nothing to fear, but Misha had felt a twinge of terror.

"Misha, you're playing with fire." I look cautiously about. "They just marched a gang of convicts down the street. You should have seen what they looked like. Last fall you said you were taking things only because you needed the extra money to help your sister-in-law in the hospital and her child, and your brother who's in jail. I know you're not helping them anymore, yet you're still going on with it."

"How do you know I'm not helping them? Oh, I see! My sister-in-law's been talking to you. She threatened to tell all my friends that I've deserted my family because of a shiksa."

Misha gets excited; foam forms on his lips, and he speaks even more rapidly and gutturally than usual: His sister-in-law had never objected to his taking stuff from the shop as long as he gave her all the money he made, but ever since he decided to live a life of his own, she's been trying to frighten him by saying he'll get caught. He would never forgive her! Nor would he forgive her for constantly repeating, to tear him away from Lydia, that his wife and child are alive and suffering in Lodz, while he is carrying on here with a shiksa.

"Would you do me a favor?" he finally asks, his face still red. "Please take this money and buy three tickets for the Leningrad Comedy Theater, for me and Lydia and for yourself. The three of us will go to the theater together. The box office is only open in the late afternoon, when I'm at work—that's why I have to bother you."

I promise to buy the three tickets. Red flecks of anger still blazing on his cheeks, he goes on to tell me that Lydia's fiancé was killed at the beginning of the war and she is still very sad. He admires her devotion to her dead betrothed, yet he would like to find some distraction for her. Since he knows she loves the theater, he's taking her the day after tomorrow to the local Russian repertory theater and has also promised her a visit to the famous Leningrad Comedy Theater, which has fled to

Stalinabad because of the war and is now performing in the Tadzhik Opera House.

We are accosted by a tall Jew with an unkempt yellowish beard, wearing a thin and threadbare surtout and large, shapeless shoes. He is a devout Ḥassid from a small town in Poland who was deported, together with his wife and seven children, to a settlement in Siberia. Since their release, they have wandered all across Siberia and Central Asia, burying three of the children along the way. This past winter they reached Stalinabad, where they are now subsisting on the alms he collects.

"I think of you when I pray. . . ." He stretches out a hand between me and Misha. "For myself it doesn't help at all, but when I pray for others I know my prayers are answered."

Misha gives the Ḥassid a five-ruble note, to which I add a few rubles, and he, towering above us, starts to sway in fervent prayer, expressing the wish that we might be privileged to see our families once more.

"I've already told you a hundred times, I don't want you to mention my family. I'll never give you another kopeck if you speak of them again!" In his agitation, Misha lapses back into the heavily rolled r's of his Lodz dialect. Being a workingman, he puts no faith in Biblical verses, no faith in blessings, and he most especially rejects any distinction between Jews and Gentiles.

"One must never despair," mumbles the Ḥassid through his matted yellow beard, and he hurries away. He has no desire to get into an argument with Misha and risk losing a benefactor.

"He's a humbug," rasps Misha angrily. "He doesn't believe himself that we'll find anyone alive there." And he reminds me once more about the Leningrad Theater. He asks me to meet him and Lydia on Lenin Street the evening after next, when they'll be coming out of the Russian Theater; I can tell him then whether I've gotten the tickets, and if so, for which date and which play. And he also wants me to meet Lydia, so I can see for myself how fine, intelligent, and devoted she is, that she's not just some shiksa out to take advantage of him, as his backbiting sister-in-law describes her.

II

THE LENINGRAD COMEDY THEATER was preparing for the premiere of a new play, *The Siege of Leningrad*. I bought the three tickets, for Misha and his girl and for myself. The theater lobby was empty, cold, and silent; only the tiny box office was open. The window was so narrow I couldn't see the cashier's face. After I told him what I wanted and shoved the money across, two hands holding tickets stretched out toward me—two skinny, wrinkled hands with long, restless, greedy fingers that twitched and had a life of their own, like the amputated legs of a spider.

I have often thought since that those hands never actually gave me any sort of premonition at all—that only in retrospect, in the light of what happened later that evening, have I convinced myself that I experienced a sense of dread and revulsion. What I am sure of is that I was sufficiently unnerved to push my head inside the narrow window to get a look at the ticket-seller—and my astonishment when I did so. He had a large round head and a round face, and wore large round eyeglasses. I couldn't see his eyes because he kept them lowered to the pages of a book he was reading; his shoulders, too, were lowered. That head, that face, those shoulders could not possibly belong to the hands that had stretched out toward me. . . . A bizarre thought entered my mind that made me shudder: he was just pretending to read so I wouldn't guess that he had substituted a strange pair of extra hands. . . . I realized instantly, of course, that this idea was insane, and I left the window before he had a chance to raise his eyes. Nevertheless, as I walked away from the theater, I imagined that I saw, across the glowing white sands, the shadows of the ticket-seller's long evil fingers. . . .

The rest of the day passed, as usual, in wandering about the marketplace, waiting for the public kitchen to open, where one could get a bowl of *lapsha*, a black noodle soup; and I spent the entire evening sitting in the City Park. About midnight I walked out to Lenin Street, toward the Stalinabad Russian Theater, to meet Misha and his girl. I found them on the theater's broad steps. The performance had just ended, and they had been the first to leave because they knew I'd be waiting.

Misha introduced me to his friend, as we started walking. Lydia was tall, a full head taller than Misha, with chestnut hair combed neatly away from her face; weariness showed in her walk and her smile, too, betrayed exhaustion. I got the impression it was an effort for her to be affectionate toward Misha, either because she did not really love him or because she was still mourning her dead fiancé. He held her by the arm and looked with great devotion into her eyes. I told them I had obtained three tickets for the premiere performance of *The Siege of Leningrad* on the fourteenth of April.

"Today is March twenty-seventh and the tickets are for April fourteenth?" Misha burst into loud laughter. "By April fourteenth I may already be in a labor battalion in the Urals. Just today I received another notice to report to the Military Commission."

In the streets of Stalinabad one often sees large crowds of Tadzhiks, swaying as they walk with heavy bundles on their shoulders, like laden camels over desert sands. These are older men who are being sent to the labor battalions in the north to replace the Russians who have left for the front. The Tadzhiks, it is said, can tolerate neither the Siberian climate nor the hard labor, and are dying like flies. "They have soft bones," the Russians say contemptuously. Refugees are also conscripted into these labor battalions; lacking a Soviet upbringing, we are not trusted to serve in the Red Army together with Russians. Misha has already been summoned to the Military Commission several times, but thus far has always been released.

"They'll let you off this time too," Lydia comforts him. "They don't have another worker as good as you in the entire shop. The higher-ups will intercede for you."

"Till now I didn't care whether they sent me to the labor battalion or not, but now I don't want to leave Stalinabad." This is Misha's way of telling Lydia how much he loves her. "But you hold on to the tickets anyway—" he turns to me with a forced laugh—"and if they should call me up after all, you'll go to the theater on April fourteenth with Lydochka and one of her girlfriends."

"My poor dear boy . . ." Lydia gently strokes his face.

Seeing how deeply absorbed they were in each other, I turned around to watch the people leaving the theater. Most of them were still well behind us, near the City Park. Suddenly, on the empty sidewalk directly behind us, there came hopping a dwarf—the head and torso of a legless cripple. The streets of the city were dry, and instead of crutches the cripple was using his hands, propping them on the sidewalk and then bouncing up very quietly, as though trying to steal by unobserved. I made way for him but Misha and Lydia, walking arm in arm in front of me, didn't see him. The cripple, accustomed to being noticed and having the way cleared for him, bounded to the very heels of the couple, shoved Misha from behind with his right hand, pushed Lydia aside with his left, and rolled himself through between their feet. Lydia screamed with fright. The cripple turned his head and laughed, revealing a full set of white teeth that glistened in the darkness, and propelled himself forward without a word, as if seeking to alarm us even more with his silence.

"Why so frightened, Lydochka?" Misha tried to calm her. "Haven't you ever seen an amputee before?"

"He jumped out so suddenly," Lydia answered weakly. "It seemed like a head without a body rolling past us."

We started to walk a little faster, and in a few minutes found ourselves on the sidewalk of a wooden bridge at the intersection of Lenin and another street. A large truck was coming down the road, and we stopped to wait for it to pass. I was nearest the truck, Lydia in the middle, and Misha beside her.

Suddenly the truck, instead of continuing down the center of the road, swerved its dark front onto the sidewalk. I flew up into the air as though on a swing, flew up easily but came down hard. I felt a sharp blow to my right knee, but quickly jumped up. "Am I alive?" I asked myself, with a strange calm and wonderment. The trouser-leg above my right knee was torn and some blood was trickling down, but otherwise I was whole, in one piece, and fully conscious. I even caught sight of the rear of the truck, which was twisting and swaying from one side of the street to the other, until the driver finally regained control of his steering wheel and drove off. I looked at the wooden bridge where Misha and Lydia had been standing a few moments before—and couldn't find them. I looked again, and then I saw them: both were lying on the pavement, hurled far apart.

Lydia was lying on her back, her eyes closed; she was not breathing. I began to shake her, but she remained as motionless as a piece of wood. I ran over to Misha, who was lying curled up and moaning: "Lydia . . . Lydia . . ." I called his name, and tried to get him to stand up, but he screamed with pain: "Oh, I can't! He's broken all my bones!" Then he fell silent.

From a long way back, theater-goers now raced up to us. Some of them, looking at Lydia's face, surrounded her and began to lift her. Others bent down to try to raise Misha, but then all drew back quickly.

"Help!" I cried, and lifted Misha up on my shoulders. Regaining consciousness, he clasped both hands around my neck, so as not to fall. He had regained his voice as well and now began to speak, loud and fast:

"I work for the NKVD, in the NKVD tailor shop. I have to finish a coat for a commissar, a commissar on the People's Committee." He was pleading pitifully, as though the importance of his employer could help him win the onlookers' goodwill. But when he realized that no one was lifting a finger to help him, that only I was carrying him, he started kissing me rapidly many times on my head. His blood was dripping over my face, my ears, onto my coat, and he continued to kiss me with lips that were hot and sticky.

At that moment a young man came up, with a pale, bony face, hatless, with tousled hair and a turned-up collar. "Take him to the Respublikansky Hospital—it's only a few steps from here." He pointed to the street along which the truck had driven off. Then he turned to the bystanders. "Let's take the girl, she's not bleeding."

The onlookers who had been standing around Misha all this while in frozen silence—as if they could neither offer help nor walk away—now, together with the newcomer, ran over to Lydia.

"Lydia, Lydia—is she alive?" Misha moaned on my shoulders. "Help her, friends, help her."

I don't know how I managed to find the hospital, or where I got the strength to carry the injured man, who was gritting his teeth all the way so as not to scream with pain. When I finally reached the closed gate, I rang the bell with such force that a commotion instantly arose within. The door opened and I saw several guards. The wounded man was lifted from my shoulders; someone led me to an office and told me to wait for the doctor on duty.

For a long time I remained alone in the room, numb, stupefied, breathing heavily; no doctor appeared. At last I heard slow footsteps. Quickly I wiped Misha's blood from my face and covered my torn trouser-leg with my coat. My knee had stopped bleeding.

A young woman—no older than twenty-two or -three, with thick, shiny black hair, full succulent lips, sleeves rolled up to reveal two dazzlingly white arms, wearing a snow-white smock that intensified by contrast her wondrous dark beauty—entered the room. She gave me a friendly glance but said nothing. "A nurse," I thought to myself, and watched as she spoke to someone on the telephone, her expression glowing, yet with a touch of shyness. At first I was certain that she was speaking to her parents, or perhaps a boyfriend, but soon I caught a few phrases like "broken ribs" and "severed arteries." She was evidently asking someone questions and then, with a smile of eager curiosity on her glowing face, listening to the answers. From time to time she interrupted the other speaker with a few words: "Is that so? . . . Then what should I do? . . ." I could barely wait for her to finish and put down the receiver.

"I brought in an injured man and am waiting to see the doctor in charge," I said, standing up.

"I'm the doctor in charge," she answered. "I've already examined the patient and will shortly perform the operation."

"He needs an operation? And a surgeon won't be present?"

"I'm a surgeon."

Her radiantly youthful appearance, her thin smile, and her asking for instructions over the phone left me stunned: I was certain she had no experience. I began to stammer that an older, more experienced surgeon was needed. Then I began to shout, angrily and wildly, that I would not let her operate on the injured man. "He works in the NKVD workshop!" I repeated, almost insanely, Misha's pitiful claim.

"There won't be any other doctor tonight. If you prefer, you can take the patient away." The radiant young woman was now all cold white stone. Having silenced me, she added, in a tone of calm superiority, "Do you want to see the patient before the operation?"

"Is he in any danger? Is his condition serious?" I broke down completely: she seemed to be telling me to bid Misha a last farewell.

The young doctor did not answer. She left the room, and I followed like a doomed man. She pointed to one of the closed doors, indicating that I should enter, and then walked away. In a large, semi-dark room, Misha Troiman lay on a narrow bed whose iron legs ended in wheels; a sheet covered him up to the neck. His head was bandaged. All that was visible was his sunken eyes and his nose, which seemed to have become longer and pointier. He recognized me and began to speak in a clear but hollow voice, like wind howling through broken pipes:

"Take my watch, it's in my vest pocket. It could be stolen here. Go to my sister-in-law and ask her to come. Oh, I won't come through this alive. . . ."

"You will live, Misha! You will live!" With trembling hands I started to search through the clothes that lay on a chair beside the bed, until I found the pocket-watch. "I'll go to your sister-in-law . . . you will live . . . you've only been injured . . ."

"What will become now of the pretty hats I've collected for my little boy?" His voice broke and he began to gasp for breath. "I didn't believe my son was alive because I couldn't remember his face. Now I see him clearly before my eyes. . . . I feel I won't live . . . I'm going to die. . . ."

"You'll live, Misha, you'll live! I'm going to your sister-in-law . . . You'll live." And I ran out of the room, out of the hospital, ran through the dark empty streets, to Misha's sister-in-law. Every few minutes I stopped. "God in Heaven, how will I tell her? God in Heaven, she might die from the shock!" Then I started running again, and as I ran I felt as if I were kicking a head attached to half a body, the head of the cripple we had met earlier that night. The head attached itself to my feet; it bit into my knee and, grinning, bared its white teeth: "He will die! He will die! He will die!" And I kicked the face of the head: "He will live, he will live! If only his sister-in-law doesn't die of shock when I tell her he's been run over by a truck. . . ."

MISHA'S SISTER-IN-LAW did not die of shock; it was Misha Troiman who died that same night, during the operation. We buried him in the cemetery of the Bukharian Jews, already half filled with the graves of refugees from Poland.

Other Jews told me, and I told myself, that I should recite the "Gomel" blessing, in acknowledgment of my own miraculous escape. But that did not give me peace of mind. I kept asking my Russian acquaintances: Why had the theater-goers declined to help me take Misha to the hospital? They all shrugged their shoulders at my naïve question and all gave the same answer: The theater-goers hadn't wanted to get their only decent suits smeared with blood. The proof: the passers-by did take home the girl, who wasn't bleeding but had only suffered a concussion. But as for the young man who had shown me the way to the hospital, all the Russians agreed that he was indeed a scoundrel for not helping me carry the injured man. They knew him, he was an actor with the Stalinabad Theatre troupe, and actors always have clothes—all they want!

I also wanted to know whether the woman doctor with the dainty little white hands, who had performed the operation on Misha, might not bear some responsibility for his death. And why was it that at no time had any militiaman appeared on the scene? And why had they never looked for and arrested the truck driver, the murderer?

"We don't know," my Russian friends replied gloomily. "Stop tormenting yourself and stop tormenting others—live while you're alive."

On the fourteenth of April, the day on which Misha, Lydia, and I were to have gone to the Leningrad Comedy theater, I went there to return the three tickets, which I was still holding. On the way the thought came to me that the driver who had killed Misha might be the very one to buy his ticket, and would never know that he was sitting on Misha's grave—and probably, even if he did realize it, wouldn't be troubled by it. I thought also of the ticket-seller with his hands of the Angel of Death. It now seemed to me that those long hungry fingers with their loathsome fidgeting had forewarned me of Misha's fate, and that, like a Hindu idol, he must have other pairs of hands as well.

This time, however, a different cashier sat at the box-office window. His hands were coarse and fleshy, and he gave me the money as soon as I showed him the tickets, before I had a chance to say a word. The production of *The Siege of Leningrad* had been canceled before the premiere, and the ticket-seller already knew to give refunds to all who had bought tickets.

Later I learned that the Central Committee of the Tadzhik Communist Party had ruled, after attending the dress rehearsal, that the play did not adequately express the patriotic Soviet spirit of the besieged citizens of Leningrad. The author—a member of the company who was himself from Leningrad and had personally endured the siege—had agreed to revise the play in accordance with the instructions of the Tadzhik Communist Party.

Lydia was bedridden for six weeks before she regained her strength. I visited her once, and she spoke to me at length about her first fiancé, who had died at the front, and about Misha.

"My poor dear boy. . . ." She shook her head quietly and sadly, and I could not tell of whom she was thinking—of her first fiancé or of Misha.

Whenever I saw Misha's sister-in-law passing by, I went over to her. She too shook her head quietly and sadly, she too spoke of two men:

"They were the Troiman brothers, two brothers from Lodz. Now one is buried in the desert, in the sands of the Stalinabad Jewish Cemetery, and the other one, my husband, rots in the Stalinabad prison."

While Misha's sister-in-law spoke, I remained silent. But after she had gone, I said to myself: To what purpose had Misha collected all those *tyubeteiki* for his little boy? Who now would wear the six-sided and the four-sided and the round skullcaps with their many-colored embroidery?

The Seven Little Alleys

Return . . .

SINCE MY RETURN TO VILNA, I have roamed through the seven little alleys that once made up the Ghetto. The narrow alleyways enmesh and imprison me, like subterranean passages, like caves filled with ancient graves. Orphaned, they cast a spell upon me; their emptiness hovers in my brain, they attach themselves to me like seven chains of stone. Yet I have no desire to free myself of them. I want them to carve themselves still deeper into my body, into my flesh. I feel the dark, icy stiffness of bolted gates and doors creep under my skin. Shattered windows stare out through my eyes, and someone inside me cries aloud:

"So be it! I want to become a ruin! . . ."

This inner cry comes from the dybbuk—the spirit of the ruins. Since my return, he has taken up residence within me, and I am no longer master of my thoughts, or even of my lips. The demon within speaks on and on, without end. I hear every word he utters, I implore him to be still; but his lamentations continue, at times as a wild outcry, at times with bitter calm, as of a mourner grown hoarse from wailing. And then, just when I want him to shout and lament, he falls silent, and his silence is so loud it deafens me—a terrifying silence, the furtive silence of a criminal, of an arsonist, as if it were he who had set all the fires in the Ghetto.

Now he speaks, the dybbuk within: Woe unto me that I have returned here. There, in Central Asia, there are snowcapped mountains; here, razed houses. I walk across paving stones, and it feels as if I am walking across a pavement of heads. Every stone has a different face, a different mask. How much better to have the sands of Kara Kum blowing in my face, or to look upon the saksaul tree of the desert, with its twisted branches and crippled trunk, than to hold in the palms of my hands the ashes of the Ghetto, or to gaze at a tall black chimney which, like me, stares up at the sky and, like me, asks: Why? If only just once a wind howled in the chimney! But even the wind lies poisoned, slaughtered—all is empty, still, dead. When I was a child I heard my mother say that in a ruin, evil spirits dance. Would that I might come upon a band of demons . . . at least then I would see that there is a Hell, then I would know that there is a reckoning.

All that is left is walls, roofs, pillars, cornices, tottering beams. All that is left is broken iron bedsteads, the rusty entrails of Primus stoves, twisted forks, knives, spoons—without the mouths. And I am left with eyes without tears, like window-holes with neither frames nor glass. I cannot squeeze even a single tear from my eyes, just as not even a single solitary Jew sticks his head out a window-hole. Behold! An entire row of shops, shuttered and bolted; an entire street with locked gates and doors. I think I hear laughter—behind one of the bolted gates someone is stifling his laughter, or perhaps choking on a consumptive cough.

"Open up, you brigand, open up!"

No one laughs, no one coughs, no one answers.

Thus does the demon within me rage without respite, cry out unceasingly, beat with my fists against the locked gates; and the slaughtered alleys answer with a moan, aggrieved at this disturbance of their deathly rest. For days on end, and half the nights, I drag myself through the same seven alleys of the Second Ghetto—the "Great" Ghetto. There had been a "Small" Ghetto, too—the First Ghetto, consisting of the Synagogue Courtyard and a few surrounding alleys. The Germans had slaughtered the Jews who lived there four years ago, and the entire area has remained desolate ever since. Even my dybbuk is afraid to drag me over there. That was where my mother lived.

More than once it has happened that, sunk deep in thought, I have come upon the Ghetto's exitway, where the gate had been; one step more—and I shall be on the other side. It is dusk. Here among the ruins it grows dark earlier than anywhere else. From here the darkness spreads into the city, where people are strolling, talking and laughing. Vilna is gradually coming back to life. In the distance I hear the heavy, measured steps of soldiers. A military band begins to play and the soldiers sing. Those marchers and singers are the victors, but the Ghetto has not lived to see the victory. Hastily I turn back into the narrow streets. I am the guardian who may not leave. I hear the eerie silence asking me: "Watchman, what of the night? Watchman, what of the night?" And the spirit of the ruins who dwells within me answers: "Here the day is as dead and desolate as the night. Here the week is made up of seven Sabbaths, seven Sabbaths for seven alleys. But the Sabbath here is the Sabbath of Retribution—a Sabbath accursed eternally."

"And what do you seek here? What more are you waiting for?" asks the mysterious stillness, and the accursed one inside me begins once more to wail softly: "I am waiting for the moon to rise and to spin, from its cold rays, the silvery beard of an old Jew who will lean his head out a window toward me. Or perhaps, fluttering down a broken staircase will come a young Jewish girl in a white nightgown woven of moonlight. With her long black hair unbound she will run out from her hiding-place, embrace me and cling to me. Or perhaps someone is still alive in a hide-out and cannot believe that the day of salvation has come. Let him, this man driven mad with fear, emerge now from his living grave to laugh with a hollow, subterranean laughter. He will laugh—and I will shudder. I want to shudder! I want to be shaken!"

But the moon avoids the Ghetto, and the nocturnal specters spun from my sickly fantasies do not reveal themselves to me.

The narrow alleys grow pitch-dark. From a street-lamp at the Ghetto's exit falls a red ray of light, pointing toward me like a bloody knife. Something rustles at my feet: a bunch of crumpled stray leaves from prayerbooks and Bibles, scattered pages from volumes of commentaries. The Ghetto has long since been exterminated, but these pages of sacred books are still strewn about, as though the dead return at night to immerse themselves in their tomes. After reading each page, the dead scholars tear it out and give it over to the wind, to bring to me so that I may see what has become of the People of the Book. I pick up the torn leaves and stuff my pockets with them. When I return to my lodging, I shall sort them out and smooth out each one. Perhaps I shall recognize the fingers that crumpled them. Perhaps I shall hear the voice of the scholar who involved himself in the Talmudic disputation between the sages Abbaye and Rabbah. Perhaps the tears that have been absorbed by the pages of the women's prayerbooks will glisten again for me. Perhaps my own childish face will glow anew for me, and I will be able once more to dream over a book of miracle tales.

Do you remember, I murmur to myself, do you remember that wondrous tale you read when you were a boy? A pious Jew loses his way in a forest late one Friday afternoon. The sun sets and the pious man begins to weep in sorrow, because he will be unable to observe the Sabbath. Suddenly he sees a palace standing amidst the trees. An old man appears and motions wordlessly to the lost Jew to follow him. The old man leads him to a fragrant pool, in which the Jew bathes, and then gives him luxurious raiment to wear in honor of the Sabbath. When the guest tries to ask a question, the old man signals him to be still. Then he leads the wanderer into a chamber that glitters with silver and gold, with pearls and precious stones. From there the guide takes him into a second chamber, where candelabra and chandeliers gleam with the radiance of the seven great lights of the Six Days of Creation. And so the guest wanders, enchanted and bedazzled, from room to room, each more beautifully and splendidly adorned than the one before—until, in the seventh and last chamber, he is approached by seven ancient men who with their white beards resemble a forest of snow-covered oak trees. They welcome him and tell him that with his arrival they now have a minyan. This bewilders the poor Jew: here are these seven elders, he is the eighth, and the old man accompanying him makes nine, but nowhere does he see the required tenth man. Yet he vividly senses the tenth everywhere about him, like the radiance of the Divine Presence. And he is seized by overwhelming feelings of fear, of awe and reverence, though of the ordinary kind of fear that makes the limbs tremble, there is in his heart not a trace. Now an elder wearing a royal crown takes his place at the cantor's pulpit and welcomes the Sabbath, chanting with such sweetness that one might think him to be the Psalmist himself. After prayers, the Jew is told to wash his hands, and he is then served meat that tastes like the Wild Ox which the righteous will eat in Paradise, and wine with the taste of the wine reserved for the coming of the Messiah. And thus does he spend the entire Sabbath in the elders' company, in prayer, in singing Sabbath hymns, in study of the Torah. And if he essays even a single word about profane matters, they silence him with a gesture. At the conclusion of the Sabbath, he is given spices to smell which have the fragrance of the Tree of Life. Finally, the old man who has been his guide leads him back out into the forest, and whispers in his ear that he has just been in Paradise. And the elders are Abraham, Isaac, and Jacob, Moses and Aaron, and David and Solomon, and he, the caretaker of the palace, is Eliezer, servant to the Patriarch Abraham. And the tenth for the minyan was the Holy One Himself, Blessed be He. . . . The palace disappears and the Jew finds himself no longer in the palace's seven chambers but instead in the seven bereaved alleys of the Vilna Ghetto. The Patriarchs who have come to welcome him are the shades of those who have perished. And the prayers he has heard are the torn pages of sacred books that rustle at his feet.

By now the dybbuk within me is weary unto death; I try to rouse him, but he seems too dazed and exhausted to answer. At last I can go home. I live on Giedyminowska Street, in a Gentile neighborhood that has remained untouched, the residence also of the other Jews who have returned to Vilna. I drag myself along the dark streets, followed by houses with windows that have no panes, by empty walls and smoke-blackened chimneys, by crooked roofs and maimed dwelling-places— a throng of cripples, a host of blind beggars who feel their way with their hands.

Across the cobblestoned pavement of one dark Ghetto street a shaft of light falls and bars my way. I spring aside as if I have stepped on the body of a living Jew who has just crawled out from some secret hiding-place. The light is seeping out from a cellar window, close to the ground. In the window hangs a black boot with a pointed tip—the sign of a shoemaker. I peer in: he appears to be a Jew. The slow, sleepy hammering in the cellar drifts toward me with a familiar warmth, and impels me to descend to see who this workman is. I feel for the door and walk down several slippery, half-broken steps. My nostrils are assailed by a smell of mildew, decay, and filth. I open the lower door that leads into the cellar, and the smoky kerosene lamp, suspended by a wire above the cobbler's workbench, becomes agitated. Its flame blazes up, begins to jump and quiver, as though it is happy to see me, the midnight guest.

The Shoemaker

I

ATALL, BROAD-SHOULDERED MAN sits on a stool, his back toward me, and works on a boot pulled over a cast-iron boot-tree. He turns one shoulder slightly toward me and waits, holding his small hammer suspended in mid-air.

"A Jew?" I ask.

"A Jew."

He utters the word hoarsely, angrily, giving no indication of even wanting to look at me, and resumes his hammering on the boot sole more quickly and loudly, to let me know he is very busy. I remain standing at the entrance, enmeshed in the shadows that hover stiffly upon the walls and the ceiling, speckled with the reddish bands of light emanating from the sooty lamp.

"It doesn't bother you to live here in this ruin?" I ask him.

"It doesn't bother me." The stool creaks beneath his weight as he bends still more intently over his work.

"I understand. You hear no echoing voices in the ruins. Neither do I." I look around me. "Yet it strikes me as odd that you live here, and not together with all the other Jews on Giedyminowska Street."

"And what about you? What are you doing, roaming around here so late?" With an effort he pulls the boot off and pushes the iron boot-tree aside.

"Something draws me here," I answer. "Were you in the Vilna Ghetto?"

"Yes."

"And you managed," I continue, "to save yourself?" and am myself surprised at my question: obviously he saved himself—here he is, alive. The shoemaker, as if he has heard my thoughts through the nape of his neck, responds:

"I didn't save myself. I just stayed alive."

"That's right," I say. "Neither you, nor I, nor anyone saved ourselves—we simply stayed alive."

The shoemaker stretches his left arm down to the floor, and begins rummaging about in a pile of old shoes. He remains sitting upright, his face to the cellar window, his back toward me, as his hand continues its search, until it finds a piece of leather. He then resumes his work, diligent and silent, as though between his lips he were holding wooden pegs for hammering into a shoe sole. I see that I am disturbing him, that he finds my curiosity annoying, yet I make no move to leave. I am glad to be together in a room with a Jew, and above all here in the devastated Ghetto. An empty stool stands near the workbench, and I walk over and sit down on it. I take a good look at the shoemaker: a broad face with unkempt sideburns, a head of gray hair cropped close, a long drooping mustache. He looks like a Pole.

"Balberishkin!" I suddenly shout. "You stayed alive? Yes, you're the shoemaker Balberishkin."

"My name isn't Balberishkin," he says irritably, yet without surprise, as though he had expected me to make this mistake.

"Really, your name isn't Balberishkin? What is your name, then?"

"My name isn't Balberishkin." He pulls a piece of cobbler's thread between his lips and then draws it through the eye of a large shoemaker's needle. But his hands, as well as the boot he holds clamped between his knees, are trembling.

"You look very much like him." I am even more astonished. "But I haven't seen Balberishkin since some years before the war. So it appears I've made a mistake. In my head everything is all mixed up—the heads and faces of those who've disappeared swim around in there like drowned bodies after a shipwreck. What's the difference, anyway? As long as you're one more Jew who's stayed alive."

I fall silent. But by now the dybbuk within me has shaken off his stupor and is talking to himself: Of course I should rejoice for everyone who's survived; yet I do not rejoice, or at least not as much as I grieve for every Jew who hasn't survived. If I had found them all alive, I would have rejoiced with each one individually, but now those who have been saved are strangers to me, as I am a stranger to myself. Each of us, it's true, had lived for himself, not for the community; but it was good to live for oneself when, on the other side of the wall, there was always a neighbor. Now there is no neighbor on the other side of the wall, and we ourselves are . . . lone-standing walls, soot-blackened chimneys, stairs that end in mid-air—in no case a building, either for ourselves or for others.

"I myself find it very strange—" I speak to the shoemaker as though continuing an already ongoing conversation—"I understand how a child that remained alive in a concentration camp can become very precious. I understand how you can love a woman who has just crept out of her Ghetto hiding-place, or who saved herself by escaping to the other side. A hero, a partisan from the forest, or a refugee who's returned from

Russia—these, too, become very dear. But have you ever in all your life heard of anyone falling in love with dead streets, with ruins? Wherever I go, the seven cobblestoned alleys surround me like seven orphans. Without Jews, they have grown so small, these alleys, that when I stand at a corner and stretch out both arms, they seem to encompass the full length of two streets and my fingers seem already to extend beyond the borders of the Ghetto."

"Where did you just come from?" asks the shoemaker.

"From Moscow. For several years I lived in Central Asia, and now I live in Moscow."

The shoemaker is no longer working. He keeps his head turned toward the lamp and gazes at the flame with half-closed eyes, as if he were warming himself in the sun. He is silent, and I too want to be silent. I want to sit sunk within myself as he does, this gloom-shrouded Jew. Yet I talk on without a stop, like a windmill that must keep turning in the wind.

"Balberishkin the shoemaker also used to live in a cellar, in a cellar facing the train station he lived. He was married for the second time. His first wife he never mentioned; apparently he was happy with the second one. And she, the second wife, was also happy. Small wonder: Before her marriage she was an 'older girl,' in terror of remaining a spinster, and then God had granted her a husband and two fine children. She was short and rather thin, with sickly eyes, but she had a daughter—a girl like a golden needle, a needle of pure gold. That was how she always seemed to me, the little girl, whenever I saw her father, a giant of a man, carrying her in his arms. And his big hands used to tremble, for fear he might lose her in his piles of old shoes, galoshes, pieces of leather and tools. It was even more interesting to watch the father holding conversations with his little daughter. After sitting a whole day bent over his workbench, his shoulders and the back of his neck would ache. So he would stand up, straighten his shoulders, and stretch his head up toward the ceiling. Just then the little girl would come in, and turn her little head toward the ceiling also, and start chattering away to her father, who would stand there and smile at her with half-closed eyes, just the way you're doing now. His shoemaking didn't bring in enough to support the family, although Balberishkin worked fifteen or sixteen hours a day. So his wife took in lodgers, poor students and teachers, and it was to visit these lodgers, who were friends of mine, that I used to come to the house."

"And what about the son—I mean, the other child?" asks the shoemaker in a low voice. "Didn't you say he had two children?"

"He was a very odd youngster." I am glad to find the shoemaker breaking his forbidding silence. Balberishkin's boy, I tell him, was about twelve or thirteen years old at the time. He was short and thin like his mother, but had a large head and wore spectacles like an old man. He was a timid, fearful child who never made friends with other boys, but only read books day and night. His mother wanted him to be like other boys—to go for walks, be mischievous, play games—and so she would chase him out of the house. But he'd come running back in immediately, crying that the other boys had hit him. "If somebody hits you, hit him back!" his mother would yell at him. She didn't want him growing up to be a coward, someone who would never make his way in life. The father, on the other hand, was positively overjoyed: just because he himself was such an earthy giant of a man, he was delighted that his son was a delicate, timid child, a future professor.

"What do you want of me? Why do you keep telling me about other people's sorrows? I have enough of my own," shouts the shoemaker, and the boot falls from between his knees. "You must have come in because you needed something. Do your shoes need repairing? Are you looking for someone?" And he starts searching for the boot on the floor, although it is lying right beside his foot.

"I'm not looking for anyone," I answer, ignoring his shouting. "I was simply wandering about the Ghetto, and when I saw a window with a light, and a Jew, I came in to take a look. I was surprised, because I know no one lives here. But you obviously don't care for company, though these days most Jews seek out one another."

I rise to leave. With both hands the shoemaker seizes me by the elbows and pushes me back down onto the stool.

"Sit, sit—don't leave, and don't take offense if I get a little angry. And even if I'm not Balberishkin, shouldn't you be glad anyway that I stayed alive? Please, tell me more about Balberishkin. I think I may have known him—after all, we have the same trade. And tell me especially about his family; I want to hear about them." He sits now with closed eyes, his face tense, like a man mustering all his strength to undergo an operation without anesthetic.

"No, it's late—I'll be leaving," I say in a preoccupied tone: something is stirring in my brain, and I strain to pry loose some dim piece of memory. "Oh, but I saw him! . . . It's a pity that you're not Balberishkin—I met his son in Tashkent."

For a few moments the shoemaker remains seated, with his ears pricked up as though he has seen a flash of lightning and is awaiting the peal of thunder which he knows must follow. Slowly he rises, spreads his hands wide; his mouth opens. Only now do I see how tall he is, and there can no longer be any doubt: he is indeed Balberishkin.

"My son—he's alive? . . . But they told me he died on the road, while fleeing from the city."

"I saw him with my own eyes in Tashkent. But didn't you say that you're not Balberishkin?"

"My son—he's alive? . . . Yes, I am Balberishkin! I didn't want you to pity me, I didn't want to remember that I'm the Balberishkin who once had a wife and two children. I am left all alone. . . he's alive, my little boy! Where?" He embraces me with his big, heavy hands.

"I already told you that I met him in Tashkent. That's a city far off in Asia."

"And when did you see him, there in Tashkent?"

"In 1941—that was when I saw him. It was sometime between Rosh Hashanah and Yom Kippur."

"Four years ago?" Standing in that cramped cellar, shaken, confused, bewildered, he looks like some gigantic creature that has crawled out from a subterranean pit. "And you haven't seen him since?"

"No, I didn't see him again. It could be that he went into the army," I say, lost in thought, and when I realize what I've said it is too late to take it back. Balberishkin sits down on his stool, his spirits clearly sinking.

"He went to fight in the war?" His face is drawn, his hands hang down, and he stares at the wall as if he were reading there some secret writing. "He went to fight in the war."

"I didn't say that. I said he might have gone into the army. Some men in the army work at headquarters, or in an administrative office. Your son, after all, is well educated." I force the words out of my throat. Just now, when I need to calm the poor man, I feel such a heaviness in my limbs that I would gladly stretch out on the floor, if only I could sleep.

"But a letter—he could have written his father a letter." The shoemaker's head is bowed.

"What, a letter?! Do you think some angel from Heaven informed your son that though all the other Jews were murdered, you were still alive? And to what address should he have sent this letter?"

My words serve to calm him somewhat. He begins to tremble with joy. A broad, pitiful, Golem-like smile spreads over his face. He picks up the unfinished boot which had fallen from between his knees:

"Even if he did go to fight, that's still not the same as here under the Germans. From the fighting you can return alive." He strokes the leg of the boot, as though contemplating his son's returning from the front with but one sound leg. "And how did he look when you met him?"

"It was only a few months after we left Vilna, so he looked the same as in Vilna." His questions are becoming a torment.

"My Itzikl isn't the same little boy anymore that you knew in Vilna. He's twenty-one now." Tears glisten in Balberishkin's eyes. "And what

did he talk about? Did he speak of his father and mother, of home?"
"Yes."

Resting my elbow on the edge of the workbench, my head leaning on the palm of my hand, I sit there exhausted, with my eyes closed. And I recall my meeting with Balberishkin's son. . . .

In the first year of the war, Tashkent seemed like a gigantic river caused to overflow its banks through the enormous influx of its tributaries. Every day, dozens more refugee transports arrived from the Ukraine, Bessarabia, and Great Russia. The evacuees slept on their bundles in the Uzbek tearooms or in the city parks and the streets, under the open sky. The refugees from Lithuania and Poland gathered in a small park opposite the train station. Some slept there, some sold the clothes off their backs to buy bread, others searched for relatives who had got lost on the way. There, early one morning, amidst all the noisy crush, I had come upon Balberishkin's son. Although I hadn't seen him for nearly four years and he had grown considerably, I recognized him by his broad-boned face and his spectacles with their brass frames. "You too?" I called out to him. "You also ran away from home?" Deeply insulted, it would seem, by being thus addressed as a child, he retorted with a spiteful smile: "And why did you run away?" This left me speechless for a few moments, unable to think of a response, and in the meantime a friend of his dragged him away. I never saw him again. But his smile had clung to me, as though he had pulled a black sack over my head. I had been peculiarly enraged by his impudence: How could he compare himself to me? He was only a boy! Yet his answer tormented me. Perhaps this impudent youngster, with his large head and thin, slight body, had understood the danger better than I? Later, when the dreadful reports of what was happening began to reach us refugees, I had often thought of my meeting with Balberishkin's son.

"Why did your son flee without you?" I ask the shoemaker, who is still staring at the boot in his hands.

"He was a member of the Communist Youth. His friends had gotten him involved, and people in Vilna were saying it was dangerous for a Communist to stay under the Germans. But that all the Jews were doomed, that nobody believed."

"And I don't believe it even now!" I cry out. "If I'd been told that they had driven all the Jews into the Ghetto and they had all died there in an epidemic, that I would have believed; that an earthquake had swallowed them all, that I would have believed. But that this was done by human beings, by men who have hands and feet as I do, eat and sleep as I do, that I do not believe. I know they did it, but I don't believe it. No matter how often it is told to me and explained to me, I still do not understand why they did it—I will never understand it."

"I once heard someone say that man was created in order to be devoured by wild beasts——" With the palm of his hand the shoemaker wipes the joyful smile from his face and the tears from his eyes, like one who notices that together with the green leaf which has fallen on him from a tree, there has also fallen a worm. Balberishkin tells me that when the Jews of Vilna were already in the Ghetto, and the mass executions in Ponary were taking place every day, the Jews still did not believe it. Even when a few who escaped from the pits returned to the Ghetto and showed themselves bleeding and bullet-riddled, and told how they had heard the death rattles, the dying moans, the seething of human guts from those who had fallen on top of them—people bandaged the wounds of these refugees from beneath the mountains of the dead, and were convinced that they were insane. Balberishkin himself hadn't believed it then. Only when there was no longer any doubt as to what the Germans were doing with those who were deported to "labor camps," only then did he begin to make plans for saving his family. Since he looked like a Gentile and spoke White Russian fluently, he smuggled his wife and daughter out of the Ghetto and concealed them in a "malina," a hideout, in the city. Having no ready funds, he often left the malina and made his way beyond Lipowka to carry on his cobbler's trade among the local peasants; and he would return with a sack full of food. He told the peasants he was a White Russian, with a hungry family in the city to whom he brought the bread, dairy products, and pieces of bacon which he received for his work. Once he stayed with a peasant family for several days, and the wife went into town and returned with the news that on Subocz Street, beneath a church, there had been discovered a hideout "full of yids." This was the very malina where his wife and little girl were hiding, along with other Jews. But he allowed nothing in his demeanor to give him away to his host and hostess. He finished stitching the boots, accepted his wages in food as always, and because he no longer needed to feed his wife and child he took the sack somewhere else, where he sold it. He was calm. He just wondered how the buyer could fail to see that, rather than a loaf of bread, he was buying a little Jewish girl. . . .

Then he went to a different suburb of the city, where no one knew him, and remained there among the Gentiles. It no longer mattered to him whether he lived or died, and it was precisely his indifference and composure that saved his life. No one suspected he was a Jew. He was certain that his only son had also perished. Some youngsters who had run off on foot together with his son on the second day of the war, had returned to Vilna the next day and reported that they had been overtaken on the road by the Germans, who had shot many of the refugees on the spot. They had said that his son was among the dead, and he had believed it. But his wife—both in the Ghetto and, later, in the malina—had always argued with him, insisting that her heart told her their son was alive. Sometimes he had let himself be convinced.

But after his wife and little daughter had been taken to Majdanek, he had lost all hope that his Itzikl might be alive, and after the liberation he had come to a decision: he would no longer be Balberishkin. No, he was not one of those Jews who, having survived through their non-Jewish appearance, now wanted to continue as Gentiles, because they were still afraid or because they wished to protect their children who had been saved, so that they would never again have to suffer for their Jewish origins. He, rather, would cease to be Balberishkin so that no one who had known him and might have remained alive, would be able to remind him about his family or to pity him; and he himself did not want to remember his former name. So now he lives in a suburb of Vilna, among Gentiles, has his workshop there, and mends shoes. And yet, there are times when he feels drawn back to the Ghetto. And so he has set up a workshop here, in the same cellar in which he once lived with his wife and little daughter, and here is where he comes to be the Balberishkin of old. But he does not wish to meet old acquaintances; that was why he had pretended not to know me, although he had recognized me at once. He comes here to sit shiva—a shiva that never ends. He sits here and works and when he wants to rest awhile, he looks into the flame of the kerosene lamp, at his little daughter.

"You see your daughter in the flame of the lamp?" I ask him. Clearly there dwells in him, as in me, a dybbuk.

"Whenever I look at the flame, I see in it my little girl, my Yentele." Again the shoemaker half-closes his eyes to shield them against the light of the lamp; his expression is blissful, as though he were warming himself in the sun. "A while ago, before you knew that I'm Balberishkin, you told me that Balberishkin's little daughter looked to you like a golden needle. During the years after you stopped coming to our house, my daughter grew a little, but she always remained small, taking after her mother. And when I look into the flame, I see her there—so small, so delicate, so thin, with her two glowing eyes. I remember how when she was very little, she used to climb over my knees, just as the little flame climbs up inside this smoky glass cylinder. She, my little girl, can't climb out over the rim, so she attaches herself to a thin wisp of smoke, like a bird tied to a string, and can't tear herself away, can't fly out. Here she jumps and frolics, there she grows sad and shrinks into a tiny ball, and suddenly she begins to shake her little hands, her little feet, until she sinks into the wick. Then I take down the cylinder and straighten out the wick so it won't smoke so much. And when I feel a burn on my palm from the rising flame, that burn is as dear and sweet to me as if I had stroked my Yentele's little head with my hand. Because, you see, they took her and her mother off to Majdanek and burned them there."

THE SHOEMAKER—who has been speaking all this time in the voice of a man buried alive, his words seeming to rise from beneath the cellar floor— at last falls silent. I am glad he has stopped, for now I will be better able to hear the mute outcry of the ruins without, my ruins. There they stand in the night, forsaken, huddling together in the darkness, and their frozen emptiness, their stillness of stone, is filled with sorrow and with dread. In the end they will be razed and all that will remain of the Ghetto will be a space even smaller than some poor peasant's plot. Any small city park, a children's playground, will seem larger than the cleared space of all seven of my alleys together. But for me, my seven narrow alleys, you are larger than that half of the world across which I have wandered. Your emptiness says more to me than all the cities and countries I have seen. And when they will tear down your rubble and I shall depart—as I surely will depart this blood-soaked earth—yet shall I roam forever about your vanished ruins week in and week out, year in year out, just as now I do not weary of dragging myself, for days on end and half the nights, over your crooked cobblestones. No matter how green the forest I may someday see from my window, nor how high the mountains I shall perhaps behold in my lifetime, you, my ruins, will overshadow all the forests, all the snowcapped mountains. When I speak, I shall hear your silence; when I sleep, you shall encircle me; when I laugh, I shall hear my laughter wailing amidst your alleyways.

"Do you believe in the Resurrection of the Dead?" I ask the shoe-maker.

"In the Resurrection of the Dead?" He repeats my words and from somewhere within his large, heavy body, as if from somewhere behind a wall, there comes a stifled sobbing; closer and closer comes the sobbing, until at last the tears gush from his eyes. "His mother, my Itzikl's mother, will not see him again. And he will not see his little sister again. His mother always worried that he'd grow up to be a recluse, a bookworm afraid of the world. Now she would have seen how he has grown into a man and traveled through the world. But she was not destined to live to have joy from her son, and I will yet have to justify myself before him, as to how I alone stayed alive, without his mother or his sister."

"I wasn't asking you whether you believe in the Resurrection of the Dead as regards your family, or any other family; it was in regard to the Germans that I asked you whether you believe in the Resurrection of the Dead." I whisper feverishly, with the uncanny stillness of the ruins without. "It is written that at the Resurrection of the Dead, the wicked will arise together with the righteous. And the wicked will die again, will be consumed once more and turn to ashes beneath the feet of the righteous. I used to dislike this concept intensely. It was proclaimed by the last of our Prophets, Malachi, and he said it in the very last verses of his prophecy, a pronouncement for all the generations to come. I used to think: How could a Prophet be so cruel? Why should the wicked rise, only to die once more? And what sort of joy will it be for the righteous to plant their feet on the ashes of human beings who have been consumed by fire? But now I understand. And I understand as well whom the Prophet meant by 'the wicked'! And if indeed there will be a Resurrection of the Dead and all those who have died will rise again, not a child from the orphanage will be missing, not one old man from the home for the aged will be missing, not a market woman will be missing, not one small bone will remain in the earth; then the murderers will also have to rise. All of them! Not one single murderer must be missing! All those who died a natural death, as well as those who died on the battlefield, or who drowned in some stinking swamp, but who haven't yet paid for their murderous deeds—so that all shall behold their punishment and they themselves shall know it, all of them must rise and die again, be burned again, become ashes before the eyes of their resurrected victims. The murdered Jews must see that there is at last a final Reckoning. For if not, then all the resurrected, together with the prophet who foretold their resurrection, will wander gloom-shrouded about the world as in a world with no sun and no stars, as in a world of eternal night. Even if the resurrected were to live a thousand years, or ten thousand, their life would give them no satisfaction, their despair and suffering would not be diminished, as long as Hingst, Weiss, Mürer, and Kittel, the executioners of the Vilna Ghetto, lie rotting quietly in the earth. They have burrowed into the earth as into a hiding-place. Each man, after all, must die. And so they lie there in the earth and laugh even in death, even as they rot, because they have evaded their punishment. A young Jew told me that when the malina where he and his parents had been concealed was uncovered, a German cried merrily, 'Come out, you Jewish dogs, there's plenty of room left for you in the earth.' But for him, the German, I say there is no room even in the earth! He must arise and be burned again! . . . And God, do you believe in God?" I shout at the shoemaker, and I feel my heart about to burst from my body. "You never answered me as to whether you believe in the Resurrection of the Dead. But do you believe in God?"

"Now I believe." Balberishkin does not take his eyes off me for a moment, as if he were beginning to suspect that I am not entirely sane. "If such a miracle could happen to me, then I believe in God. You did see my son, didn't you? You didn't just imagine it?"

"I saw him, saw him, I didn't imagine it!" I shout still louder. "You're thinking only of yourself. And all those Jews for whom there was no such miracle as for you, should they believe in God, or not believe? A few days ago I entered the ruins of the Grand Synagogue. There I saw one of those fine young men with a little black rabbinical beard, together with his young rebbetzin. I knew at once he was a visitor from America, that he had not suffered, had lost no loved ones. And here he'd brought along from America his little wife with her little matron's wig. So there he was, showing his rebbetzin the ruined synagogue. I speak to myself, to him, to the young rebbetzin, and to the devastated synagogue. 'It is empty now,' I say, 'empty now.' But this fine little rabbi answers: 'That's because it was empty before as well.' I ask him: 'What do you mean, empty? On the Sabbath and on the Festivals the Synagogue Court-yard was always crowded, filled with thousands of Jews.' And he replies: 'Those Jews came to hear the cantor, not to pray. Their hearts were empty.' And I ask him: 'What do you mean, "their hearts were empty"? During the Days of Awe the Courtyard was flooded with Jewish tears.' And he answers: 'You are an infidel.' And to his little wife he says: 'Come away—don't talk to him. The wicked never repent, even at the very threshold of Gehenna.' You hear? It was because of the Jews of Vilna that the city's Grand Synagogue was destroyed! One of those Jews who burned the corpses at Ponary and himself survived, told me that whenever they opened up one of the pits filled with Jewish corpses, he had to marvel: How was it that in that last moment before death so many had managed to wrap themselves in their prayer shawls? And these were the Jews of whom the little rabbi said, 'Their hearts were empty.' Do you remember Rabbi Levi Hurvitz, who lived in Shloime Kissin's courtyard? Did you know him?"

"Of course I knew him," murmurs the shoemaker, head bowed. "Every Jew in Vilna knew him. He was a very strict Jew."

"Very strict!" I scream, with sparks in my eyes, and I gnash my teeth, as though the dybbuk within me were defying a rabbinic tribunal that is seeking to exorcise him with curses and anathemas. "When Rabbi Levi Hurvitz was alive, and all the other Vilna Jews were still alive, he too used to say that the Jews of Vilna had empty hearts. He complained constantly of their insufficient piety. But he was a great scholar, of a most distinguished family, a Jew of the highest integrity, and above all, he had himself endured great suffering. His wife was in an insane asylum for twenty years and in the end his daughter went mad as well. Once a controversy arose that even caused him to leave Vilna for a time, to abandon the rabbinate because he no longer wished to bear responsibility for the Vilna Jews' lack of piety. Later he returned, and when the Germans entered the city and he was warned to go into hiding, because he was known throughout Vilna and would be one of their first victims, he answered: 'God will protect me.' When the murderers came to take him, he resisted, he resisted them with his fists. Then the murderers beat him, pulled bunches of hair from his beard, tore pieces of flesh from his body, kicked him with their feet, and when he fainted they threw him into a garbage truck and took him away to prison. From there the other Jews who went with him to Ponary had to carry him in their arms. The Jews of Vilna did not leave their half-dead rabbi behind on the road. They carried him in their arms, carried him like a Torah scroll. And so, in his last moments, this great master came to recognize what sort of people were these poor Jews, these people he had excoriated all his life. Then at last, he saw truly those in whose company he would die and with whom he would lie in a common grave. And I say to you, I swear to you, though I was not present, that this was Rabbi Levi Hurvitz's final consolation: the loving devotion and compassion shown him by the Jews of Vilna as they made their own way to the grave. So now this little rabbi from America enters the ruined Grand Synagogue of Vilna and tallies up the reckoning; that fine, silky young man has his verdict all ready and prepared; that frock-coated scoundrel knows all the answers. 'Infidel,' he calls me; 'wicked,' he calls me. . . ."

"But I don't speak like that. I was left alone, entirely alone—" The shoemaker stretches his broad palms toward me, and his hands tell me that they, too, would have carried Rabbi Levi Hurvitz. A choking sensation rises in my throat; any moment now, I feel, the tears will burst forth from me and burn out my eyes. But I hold back the tears, I press my lips tightly together and stand up:

"Good night."

"You're leaving already?" Balberishkin rises quickly from his stool and from his uneasy expression I realize how all I have said has reinforced his suspicion that I may be an unstable person subject to fantasies and delusions. "And you really did see my son? Really and truly?"

"Really and truly!" I shout angrily. "I'm not mad, not yet. I said things that you didn't understand or that don't interest you, so you think I'm not of sound mind. There are people who care only about themselves. The catastrophe struck everyone, but they can think only of themselves and their own families."

"You're right, absolutely right. You're my guest—and what a guest to be received in this ruin. When I come here, I bring nothing with me except the work I need to finish and some dry bread. Such a guest, such a guest!" He starts bustling about the cellar, but then abruptly halts facing me, as though he has finally come to understand why I am angry at him. "And have you found out anything about your own family? Have you asked around whether your belongings were left with anyone? Some people have discovered their things in the houses of Poles or Lithuanians."

"I wasn't trying to get you to ask me about my family, nor am I looking for my belongings. I had no great wealth."

"Even those who had no great wealth, or had but can't find it, still would like some sort of memento."

"I don't want any memento. I'm not looking for that," I cry out, feeling as though my skull is splitting like a cracked earthenware pot. "I never left the Ghetto; even though I spent years in Asia and in Moscow, I never left the Ghetto of Vilna and I don't need to move back into it, as you do. I shall never forget the Ghetto, and therefore I don't need any memento. Do you understand?"

"I understand," he mumbles, frightened and confused, and I can see he doesn't understand at all. "At the time of the liquidation, two years ago, when the Jews were sorted out on Subocz Street to the right and to the left,* I was no longer in the Ghetto. But before then, when I was still living there, I knew your wife. She was a nurse and worked in the children's ward of the Jewish hospital. My little girl was sick once and was in the hospital, and there I heard someone calling a nurse by your family name, so I realized she must be your wife. I told her that you used to visit our house when you were a youngster. Did you know that your wife worked with the children in the Jewish hospital?"

"I know."

"Later, with some other young women, she moved into the attic right here, above me." Balberishkin points toward the ceiling. "As I told you before, this is where I lived in the time of the Ghetto. The entry to the attic is from the courtyard, and the number 'nine' is written on the door in chalk. Did you know that your wife lived here, in this courtyard, when she was in the Ghetto—in Number Nine?"

"No, I didn't know that."

"You see!" Balberishkin exclaims, happy that he can in some measure return a favor. "Come, we'll force the door open and go up. Perhaps something was left behind there—then you'll have a keepsake." Balberishkin takes the kerosene lamp down from the wire that holds it.

"I told you I'm not looking for any memento." I run out of the cellar, as if Balberishkin were trying to set me on fire with his lamp. But he catches up with me in the entrance hallway, the lamp in his hand.

"And when will I find out about my son?"

"I'll ask around among the refugees who returned and among the Jewish soldiers," I say as I start to ascend the steps.

He catches hold of my arm and will not let me leave. The lamp in his other hand shakes and the flame inside the glass cylinder begins to

* To the right and to the left—i.e., for forced labor or for death.—Trans.

toss about, to writhe and struggle against the wind that is blowing outside. Balberishkin lets go of my arm and tries with the palms of both hands to shield the glass cylinder, his face betraying his terror, as though his daughter actually were inside the flame. Fearing that he will again insist on going into Number 9, I rush up the broken stairs. He runs after me, and I hear the clatter of breaking glass. The lamp has fallen from his hand and shattered, and now the cellar steps are entirely dark.

"And what if he—my son—is not alive?" he wails from behind me, out of the dark depths.

But I do not answer him. Running, I disappear into the empty streets of the devastated Ghetto.

The Pediatrician

I

THE PEDIATRICIAN ANNA ITKIN SURVIVED, together with one of her twin sons. Her husband and her other son perished. I know her from before the war, and her appearance has not greatly changed. She is tall, erect of bearing, with a dark complexion, brown eyes, and gray temples. On one cheek she has a wart that gives her an expression of grandmotherly kindness, mitigating the otherwise masklike quality of her face, which—in the deliberately masculine manner of women doctors at the turn of the century—bears not a trace of makeup, not even lipstick.

Her attire, too, has something of the character of a professional uniform. She wears mostly tailored English-style suits with a plain silk blouse, a straight felt hat, and somewhat heavy shoes with low "Viennese" heels. When she smiles, she appears at once younger and more tense.

Her calm, aloof manner had made her very popular with all the respectable young matrons in Jewish neighborhoods. Before the war I would often see her walking the streets, doctor's bag in hand, and pausing at street corners to talk with young mothers as they warmed their babies in the sun. Anna Itkin would recall in precise detail each child's illness or condition, which greatly impressed the mothers. What impressed them even more was the doctor's refusal to waste time in housewifely gossip or chit-chat. She would briefly ask one young woman about her daughter's digestion, another about her little boy's rash, a third about some chafed skin between her child's toes—and then continue her rounds. The young women were rather in awe of her, and if on occasion a mother became seriously overwrought, a sharp word from the doctor to "stop getting hysterical" sufficed instantly to calm her.

Since my return to Vilna, I have met her walking about with doctor's bag in hand, as calm and aloof as ever. Her eyes, it is true, no longer search out young mothers with baby carriages on the corner of Zawalna or Rudnicka or Stefanska Street. But she still works as a pediatrician, in the children's home in which the surviving orphans have been gathered. She goes there every day, and I've noticed that she makes a wide detour in order not to have to pass through the Ghetto.

At our first meeting she told me that in the Ghetto she and Frumme-

Liebche had worked together in the children's ward of the Jewish hospital. When I remained silent, Anna Itkin realized how painful this subject was for me, and never mentioned it again.

One morning, shortly after that evening when the shoemaker had offered to take me up to the attic in Number 9 where Frumme-Liebche had lived, I went to see the doctor. All I wanted was to sit and talk, nothing more, to the woman who had worked together with my wife in the children's ward. Yet, at the same time, the prospect of Anna Itkin's speaking of Frumme-Liebche filled me with fear.

It is the mistress of the house herself who opens the door and asks me to step into the office where she receives her patients. On the way I manage to get a glimpse of her private quarters. Anna Itkin is someone who could be expected to have her affairs always in perfect order, as much in her closets as in her mind; it comes as a surprise, therefore, that her room, partitioned by a screen in the center, is a scene of great disarray. Crowded together along the walls stand numerous étagères and cabinets; old and faded oil paintings lie in corners unhung, along with rolled-up carpets; and on the table in the middle of the room are stacks of dishes. She must, I decide, have found some furnishings of her prewar home and stored them all in her cramped present apartment.

Her office, by contrast, is spacious and rather bare. It contains a couch, a glass cabinet with medical instruments, a desk by the window, and, on a small marble table, a scale for weighing infants. With its freshly painted walls and sparse furnishings, the room gives off a blinding glare, as though frozen within a crystalline case of snow. The mistress of the house—as she sits at the desk, her back to the window and her face toward me—herself looks frozen. The masklike quality of her face intensifies. It is the face of a woman who conceals more than she tells. A heavy, oppressive feeling comes over me. What is this woman's real face? Does she herself know? What kind of face did she show Frumme-Liebche? Could the possessor of this mask ever have been a friend to Frumme-Liebche? If only Frumme-Liebche had been in the Warsaw Ghetto, at least, among her own family and friends! In Vilna she lived among strangers, all alone . . .

With an effort of will, I banish these thoughts. I gaze at the infants' scale, a large, white-enameled bowl: Only earth has remained to be weighed now—no children.

"Where's your son?" I ask.

"Bolek is still asleep, there behind the screen," sighs his mother, as though she had been sitting and thinking about her son even before my arrival. "When I lost my husband, only I, his wife, lost him. But when I lost my son, the world lost him too. He was young and could still have given the world much. Now I have only one son left. I plead with him to go back to his studies which he began before the war. But he has other ideas in his head now."

Anna Itkin's son, Bolek, is a swarthy, broad-shouldered fellow with a fine, intelligent face and the sportive eyes of a playboy. He retains the look, if nothing else, of the well-bred offspring of a wealthy family. From his murdered father he inherited a little money which he managed to hide while in the Ghetto, and immediately after the war he started "to do business." The strict Soviet laws against black-marketeering fazed him not a whit. "I've lived through much greater dangers and survived," he says, and he deals in everything that is forbidden. He fritters away his money on friends, on women; he plays cards and even drinks with Soviet officials in the newly opened restaurants. He never speaks of the Ghetto, never boasts about his earnings, never mentions how much money he has given away to friends, almost as though he doesn't even remember these things. He only talks about women and tells jokes, at which he himself laughs uproariously.

"Your son is doing the right thing," I tell the doctor. "Everyone now keeps saying: 'Do not forget what happened!' But that's only talk. There are only two options: to remember and be unable to live—or to live, and forget the Ghetto."

"But it's precisely because my son is still living in the Ghetto that I'm upset," sighs the doctor. If Bolek were truly himself, his mother insists, he would be a quiet student, not a businessman or, as the Soviets say, a *spekulant*, a black-market operator. Once his natural inclination was to love one girl, to have a select few tried-and-true friends, and to blush at an off-color joke. But the reckless way he throws money around, his undiscriminating choice of companions and of women, his risky business deals—all this is because he lives still in the Ghetto. It was there that he began to lead a life of dissipation, and that is the life he continues to lead. . . .

Again the same oppressive feeling seizes me: not every supposedly fine young man of good family who was in the Ghetto has become a playboy and black-market operator. But once again I forcibly repress such disquieting thoughts, and listen to what Anna Itkin chooses to tell me, to what she has chosen to tell herself. . . .

Even in the Ghetto, she and her husband had made every effort to maintain a normal life. Other people didn't get undressed at night for fear the Germans would conduct an *Aktion** and they'd have to run to their malinas; she, however, insisted on undressing and going to bed just like before the war. Now her thoughts focus on her life with her husband as it was before the Germans entered Vilna. And even when she does

* A roundup of Jews for deportation or immediate execution.—Trans.

think of the Ghetto, it is the normal times there that she calls to mind.

"Now I even avoid walking through the Ghetto, but you, I've noticed, wander about there for days on end." She laughs but abruptly cuts her laughter short, frightened, as though she senses that in her laughter, as in an abyss, her slaughtered husband and son lie buried.

It is true, I answer, that I spend whole days wandering around amid the ruins and there seek to comprehend that which she, Anna Itkin, terms the normal days, the normal moments, in the Ghetto. I know the exact dimensions of the Ghetto, which courtyards were part of it, and have even crawled down into some of the underground malinas in which Jews hid. I know as well the sequence of the massacres, the chronology of the slaughters. But what I do not understand is this: how did people live from one massacre to the next, singing songs, attending concerts, getting married, celebrating the Festivals? How people perished in the Ghetto—that I understand; what I cannot understand is how they lived there.

"Those who were in the Ghetto no longer understand it themselves," replies Anna Itkin, sitting rigidly, as though her entire body were in the grip of a chronic and painful rheumatism and she is struggling to sit erect and upright. "Since I've come out of the Ghetto, I also understand less and less every day how I was able to exist there, and eventually I will cease to understand it at all."

"You say you don't understand—you say you will cease to understand—and I, I don't want to understand! That is, I do want to understand, but I do not want to accept it!" I jump up shouting, but immediately sit down again. "I don't want to accept what you call the normal times in the Ghetto, nor the return now to a so-called normal life. Before I again enter into harness, before I again begin to live this accursed life, I must find a way to make my peace with what happened here."

"Those who have returned are even more hysterical than those who were actually in the Ghetto." The doctor smiles—a bitter, hostile smile.

"The very fact that we who have returned are hysterical proves that we are sane; it's those who are capable of passing straight from the Ghetto into what they call a normal life, it is they who are the real madmen. It is madness for them to be normal." I begin to speak rapidly, furiously, unable any longer to restrain the demon within who burns my lips with deadly poison. "Since you're a pediatrician, let me tell you some of the things I've heard here, just a few incidents, and just ones relating to mothers and children. I heard about one mother who screamed: 'This, this sacrifice! Three such children! O God! Let them shoot me first so I won't see them fall into the pit.' This is what I must understand before I can go on living. That is, I must understand how it is possible for me to know this and to go on living. I heard of a mother who with a bullet already in her heart could still cry out to her little son: 'Save yourself, my child, and tell Yankel to say Kaddish for me.' I heard of another mother who called out as she stood at the edge of the pit: 'Run, run, my child, I will guide your eyes!' I know of a little girl who asked her mother: 'Does it hurt when they shoot you?' A fourteen-year-old girl in your orphanage told me that when the Germans shot her parents, she ran away into a field and there fell asleep. The next morning, when she awoke, she heard the birds chirping and mocking her in their bird language: 'Look, she's still alive!' If this could happen, and I'm to go on living, it can only be in one of two ways: either I forget everything, or I and every other survivor must each kill at least one of the murderers. Perhaps then it might be possible both to remember and to go on living. To have settled accounts! But as long as all the murderers are still alive and neither I nor anyone like me has grabbed a hatchet and gone hunting for· them, and since I certainly can't forget all that's happened, I shall roam day in and day out about the Vilna Ghetto, even if Fate carries me off to the farthest corner of the earth, even if not one stone of the Ghetto is left standing on another! I have not the slightest wish to leave it, here is my place!"

"In the orphanage there are children who hid in the malinas, where they knew that they must never cry. To this day these children are afraid to let a sound pass their lips, they sit pale and silent, no matter how many times we tell them that now they're allowed to play, to laugh, even to cry." The doctor herself now lapses into a frozen silence; for the moment her face sheds its mask, and her eyes fill with clear quiet tears, as if suddenly suffused with the eerie silence of the deep pits.

II

BOLEK CALLS OUT from the next room, and the tears in his mother's eyes are immediately absorbed into the smile that spreads over her face. Anna Itkin excuses herself: her son is up, and she must go prepare his breakfast. She leaves the room, and after a few moments Bolek sidles warily into the office, as though taking care not to push the door fully open with his broad shoulders. Having just arisen, he is shuffling about with feet and chest bare, hair disheveled; he is wearing a pair of light-blue pants. He shakes my hand without a word and sits down on the couch near the wall, his bare feet on the floor. He stretches, yawns, runs his fingers through his hair, rubs his chin with the palm of his hand, and bursts out laughing:

"If women weren't afraid of getting pregnant and of the gossip of malicious tongues, they'd be a thousand times worse than men. They'd never crawl out of bed."

"What were you doing last night?" I ask. "Drinking?"

"Not a drop. I was playing cards at the Prophet's." He laughs still louder. When he sees I have no idea who the Prophet is, he explains that this is his name for Tzalka the stockbroker. A week before the war broke out, the Soviets had arrested and deported all the businessmen, Tzalka among them. And as he stood on the truck, guarded by NKVD agents, he had called out to the Jewish onlookers on the street corners: "Well, my little chicks, you'll be envying me yet!" Now Tzalka has returned from Siberia, and the Jews who had stood on the street corners are no more. And so he, Bolek, has nicknamed Tzalka "the Prophet." He plays cards well, the Prophet does.

"Did you ever go watch the Maccabee* rowing team in the old days?" He had recently, Bolek says, felt a longing to visit the Maccabee stadium on the bank of the Wilja. In the summertime the riverbanks had once been crowded with young people, even as far as Green Lake. There they sunbathed, swam, sang, strummed mandolins, and the boats filled with young women in swimsuits looked like troughs filled with red berries. So he had gone, and found—a desert. Never before in all his life had a river in full flow from one bank to the other seemed so empty, so desolate. But then he had looked again: yes, there was a single kayak with a long prow on the water, and in it sat Krymski, the former coach of the swimming team—Krymski, who had always sat in a kayak's prow facing four to six Maccabee team members, and intoned commands: "All raise your oars together! All lower your oars together!" Now he was rowing alone, working the oars so swiftly that the boat flew like an arrow upstream and downstream. Krymski himself is thin, tall, and pointy, like a pole, and one might think the Devil himself were driving the kayak forward and back. But as skillful as Krymski is with his oars, just so inept is he at the card table.

"Bolek, there's something I want to discuss with you." I move closer so his mother in the next room won't hear. He must know, I say, how many people would give years of their lives to be able to hear their mother moving about next door, to be able to place a hand on her shoulder, to stroke her hair, to watch her hands as she serves a meal or, a still greater joy, to be able to serve her a meal, to take care of her. But that's not really the heart of the matter—what I really mean to tell him is that, for his mother's sake, he ought to conduct himself a little more soberly, more discreetly, or at least restrain himself in her presence. As far as such a saintly person as myself is concerned, he may drink, play cards all night, and in general do whatever his heart desires. But to cause his mother grief just isn't right! Especially since, so she tells me, he is by nature a

---

* A Jewish athletic club in Vilna.—Trans.

quiet young man and his present behavior is simply a bad habit he's carried over from his life in the Ghetto, where everyone lived from one day to the next, from one moment to the next.

"My mother lives not only with the Ghetto—she lives with Ponary." Bolek bends his head closer to me, while keeping an eye on the door. "She accuses me of continuing the abnormal life of the Ghetto while she marries me off to dead brides."

"What do you mean, Bolek? I don't understand a word you're saying."

"I don't understand it myself," murmurs the strapping young man, and his face takes on the look of a frightened child. "My mother says nothing to me openly, but I understand her meaning from isolated words and even more from her silence. She speaks of my dead brother, and that one or another girl, with whom my brother kept company for a time, would have been, so she thinks, a suitable bride for him. She says these things to me, and then she asks me my opinion. Then I say that I don't understand why she asks, since my brother is gone and so are his girl-friends. Thereupon she remains silent and lost in thought for a long time, and finally she asks me which of my girls had I planned to marry. So I shrug my shoulders and say, 'What difference does that make now?' At this she gets very angry and tells me that one must not forget one's close friends."

"I still don't understand," I murmur in astonishment. "Your mother reproaches me for constantly roaming about the Ghetto and assures me that she herself tries to remember only the good times. How does that fit in with what you're saying?"

"But that's just it!" Bolek's expression again becomes cheerful, full of laughter. Here his mother chides him for continuing to lead the life he lived in the Ghetto, while she lives in her thoughts with those who perished at Ponary. Truth to tell, says Bolek, he doesn't plan to live this way permanently; he has other things in mind. He and his mother intend to leave for Poland, and from there will go to join their relatives in America. Once they're in another country, he will, perhaps, resume his university studies.

"Did you know my wife when you were in the Ghetto?" Suddenly I have asked the question I had thought never to ask.

"She was a very fine person," he answers. Once, he tells me, word spread in the Ghetto that the Germans were planning an *Aktion*. So he ran to the hospital to find his mother and take her with him to their prepared malina. Some of the staff, doctors as well as nurses, went into hiding. At first, Frumme-Liebche also wanted to run and hide, but then she decided that she could not abandon the children. As things turned out, the Germans caught the staff members who had gone into hiding, but did not enter the children's ward. Or perhaps they did enter it, but their orders didn't include taking the children or those caring for them. . . . He no longer remembers clearly.

"And, besides, I'll tell you the truth: it doesn't matter!" A moment of silence; then Bolek continues: "It's like putting your foot down in the sand: when you take your foot away, the sand instantly fills up the hole. We want to go on living. Those who were away and have now returned reproach us for not offering resistance; from what I hear, you too blame us. So here's my advice to you: In Vilna there are still plenty of the murderers, Poles, Lithuanians, walking around freely. Go and buy yourself a revolver—you can get one now for a few groschen, unlike the Ghetto days—find one of these murderers, and shoot him down right there in the middle of the street. . . . You see! Neither you nor I nor anyone else will do it, because it's dangerous and we want to go on living at any price."

"You yourself just told me that my wife did not leave the hospital and did not desert the children," I say softly. "So you see there are people who do not choose to live at any price."

"I'm hungry. What's taking my mother so long?" Bolek gets up. "How can you make any such comparison? In the Ghetto we still believed there was justice in the world, that it was only the Germans who were murderers. In the Ghetto your wife wasn't the only idealist. But now we see that for the whole world we're all dead and buried and forgotten. The night before last, I was drinking with some government officials. I needed them to shut their eyes to something, so I treated them to drinks and such a feast as they'd never seen in their lives. And after they were good and drunk they said to me: 'You Jews, you meddle in things too much. You didn't fight in the war, but you want us to lay down our lives for you. You Jews,' so they tell me, 'you're very bloodthirsty but you're afraid to die, so you want us to take revenge for your brothers. But our government has its own aims. The Germans killed us, too, so we paid them back, and that's that. *Nashe dyelo malen'koye*—it's over and done with. Now we need them—the Germans, that is.'"

Anna Itkin walks in and announces that breakfast is on the table. She invites me to eat together with Bolek—she has set the table for two. But when I decline, I can tell she is glad to have me remain behind in the office with her.

AFTER BOLEK LEAVES, Anna Itkin sits down again at her desk and I— deeply disturbed by what Bolek has told me about his mother's planning marriages for him with dead brides—begin to speak rapidly, with feverish vehemence, at times even bursting into laughter, a laughter of astonishment.

"My mother, you know, had a twin sister. I never used to think about it, but lately, since I've returned to Vilna, I can't get it out of my mind. When I was just a boy and my mother would collapse exhausted after a long day's work, she would tell me, apologetically, that it was no wonder she hadn't the strength to work so hard. 'I'm really only half a soul,' she would say. Her twin sister lived in Kreuzburg or in Jakobstadt on the Dvina, and, so we heard, was quite well off. She had a houseful of children, all of whom were musicians. And when my mother would tell me about her twin sister, I would think: It's strange—one half-soul, here in Vilna, rushes about the marketplace, while the other half-soul, in Latvia, listens to her children playing their violins. And since I had a good singing voice, I used to sing for my mother so that her half-soul here in Vilna wouldn't be less happy than her sister's half-soul in Kreuzburg on the Dvina. Then my mother would laugh and say that I and my cousin, the violinist in Latvia, would make a fine couple. The odd thing was that my aunt had the same idea. When my mother wrote her that I was married, her sister answered irritably that her daughter wouldn't remain an old maid either. In their letters to each other, neither had ever mentioned the possibility of a marriage between my cousin and myself, but it seems they had both been thinking of it."

Anna Itkin's pale, aging face is suddenly suffused with a rosy glow that makes her look younger, more gracefully feminine, with a touch of shyness; for these few moments, yet again, the mask falls away. But abruptly, I realize that I've talked too much—it must be clear to her from what I've said, that her son has told me of her speaking to him about girls no longer living. Gradually the glowing pink color fades from her cheeks; her manner is once more cool and stiff, and she speaks softly, gazing down all the while at her fingers, which rest on the edge of the table.

She reminds me of something I said earlier—that in order to go on living, one must choose between two alternatives: either to try to forget everything, or to take revenge, for only with a sense of vengeance satisfied would it be possible both to remember and to go on living. But she, Anna Itkin, does not believe that revenge can bring any lasting comfort, especially since we are too weak to properly punish the murderers. And if some courageous young man were to ask her whether he should risk his life to kill one of the butchers, she would tell him that so few of us are left alive that we must not, even for the sake of executing a murderer, risk our own lives. But neither can we, or may we, forget. And so we must live with our memories of those who have perished—not with the memory of their terrible deaths, but of their joys and sorrows in life. Those who were alone, who were strangers to us, who left no one behind, must receive a place in our hearts just as do our own loved ones. A young man must remember an old man, and an old man a young man. Whichever of them has remained alive must recite the Kaddish for the other—with his heart, not with his lips. She often tells Bolek that she thinks about mothers, strangers to her, who did not live to have joy in their children, the same way she thinks about herself and her dead son, Bolek's brother. A wife must not be jealous if her husband sees before his eyes the murdered brides of other young men; and if she is so enamored of herself and of her own peace of mind that it makes her shudder to know her husband is thinking of brides dead and unknown, then let her—cold, egotistical woman that she is—shudder with wide-open eyes. Let her know that she must pay for having stayed alive. She must be prepared to accept her husband's giving a part of his love to those who are no more, whom no one longs for or remembers, those poor, mute doves.

"What this comes to," I rejoin, grimacing sourly, "is that instead of taking revenge on the murderers, we should take revenge on ourselves. And what good will that do those who have perished?"

"You see, I believe—or, rather than believe, I feel—that those who died are comforted when we think of them." Anna Itkin speaks with a smile of indifference, as if to show me that she doesn't care what I think of her. She has a feeling, she says, that those who perished are wandering about, desolate and anguished, because we do not live out their lives, because we have abandoned them in their mass graves. It seems to her that our houses are filled with their shadows and when there is no one near, they come closer to us, they cling to us. But when others enter the house, when there is laughter and loud talk, the shadows feel insulted and withdraw into the far corners of the room. It is not to wreak vengeance upon ourselves that we must remember those who are gone. On the contrary, it is to ease our own burden so that we can go on with our lives, just as a mother who has lost a child goes on living for the sake of her other children, and even doubles her love and care for them, while the dead child continues to live in her heart. If we could learn to live such a double life, to live along with our memories, then our wounds would slowly heal. But trying to forget, and perhaps actually doing so for a while, brings us back sooner or later to even greater pain. Because to forget altogether and forever is impossible for anyone who has a heart, and so we go on for a time only to be brought up short, feeling even guiltier and more sinful.

"To live in a dream, to live with shadows—" I squirm impatiently on my chair—"that's an attitude of having no alternative. I too have no alternative, but I don't look for excuses. In the end everything will be resolved very simply: those who torment themselves will eventually die off, and so will cease either to suffer or to anger those who feel they've sighed and groaned enough and that it is only we, the survivors, who insist on reminding them of the horror and refuse to let them get on with their lives in peace."

"And among the survivors themselves," says Anna Itkin, "there are some who are always ruminating and philosophizing about the general tragedy, so as not to have to think of those who were closest and dearest to them." And though she is directly across from me on the other side of the desk, she seems to be sitting inside a glass box, or enveloped by some thin, transparent covering of ice. I am silent as I await her next words—knowing that she will now begin to speak about Frumme-Liebche.

"Your wife never doubted that you were alive." Anna Itkin cracks the knuckles of her fingers, which lie limply on the edge of the desk. "She always guarded a suit of yours, as well as a bundle of your manuscripts. She hovered and fretted over them, and no matter how often we had to run off to hide, she never forgot to take them with her. I advised her many times to sell the suit and buy things she needed for herself, but she wouldn't hear of it. 'When the war ends,' she would answer, 'and my husband returns from Russia, he's sure to need this suit.' That's how certain she was that you were alive." The doctor's face is suddenly bright and animated. "Your Frumme-Liebche came to full bloom in the Ghetto. I knew her before the war, but in the Ghetto she became even more beautiful, younger. Waiting for your return made her blossom."

Anna Itkin's words might have made the world go dark before my eyes, made my knees give way beneath me. Instead, her manner of speaking fills me with annoyance rather than sorrow. As I listen, I am convinced she is avenging herself on me for rejecting her insane theory about those who perished.

"What," I ask, "did Frumme-Liebche say to you about my escaping to Russia and leaving her behind? Did she bear any resentment against me?"

"How could I know that?" Anna Itkin shrugs her shoulders, her voice edged with what seems like disdain, and a certain note of condescension—as though I had come to ask the hand of her daughter in marriage and she, the aristocrat, is unwilling to surrender to me this only daughter.

"She couldn't have been angry at me. We left Vilna together, on foot, but the walking made her tired—and no one could have known then what was to happen later." I scowl at the doctor from beneath knit brows. "The Germans were at our heels, if they'd overrun us on the road to Russia, it would have meant certain death. Other refugees had panicked and were turning back. I too panicked, I insisted that Frumme-Liebche go back, I didn't want her to take the risk. The refugees were saying that the Germans would leave women and children alone. That made sense! Who could ever have believed what was going to happen?! In the middle of the twentieth century, in the middle of Europe, the Germans, supposedly a nation of humanists, slaughtering helpless old people, women, and children! Frumme-Liebche went back to Vilna. At that moment I was convinced she was safer there than on the highway with me. She returned to be with my mother. . . . Had my ailing mother expired in Frumme-Liebche's arms while I was away, it would have been a tragedy, but a human tragedy. What really did happen was inhuman! Who could have known it! And yet some people did. Why? Because of their own potential for extreme evil, or because of some extreme awareness of the evil in human nature? And how do you draw the line between the potential for extreme evil in one's own nature and an awareness of the extreme evil in human nature? . . ." These are the thoughts that whirl through my head. I suddenly realize that I have not in fact spoken aloud; not a sound has escaped my lips. Better that way: why should I justify myself before Anna Itkin, a fellow-sufferer, yet a complete stranger? Much more a stranger to me than the shoemaker Balberishkin. And how do I know whether Anna Itkin might not have some reason to justify herself before me regarding Frumme-Liebche? After all, she was the doctor, and Frumme-Liebche the nurse. No, Anna Itkin doesn't look like a woman capable of concern for anyone else but her own, especially in the face of mortal danger. It's so easy to utter that beautiful discourse about remembering those who perished, but to show humanity to a living human being is something else! And the truth of how she acted toward Frumme-Liebche is something I will never know. . . .

"And my mother—did she also believe I was alive? I'm not asking you this for myself, but for my mother's sake. If she believed that I was alive, it was easier for her to go on that last journey. But if she thought I had perished on the way, as people said, then it was hard for her, very hard. . . . What did Frumme-Liebche tell you about that?"

"She never talked to me about it. And what difference does it make to you now what your mother was thinking at that time? After all, you believe that the silent reckoning between the living and the dead is an invention, a hallucination, a disease." Anna Itkin sits hunched over on her chair, wrinkled and weary. "You ought to be looking for your manuscripts. When the rumor began to spread that the Vilna Ghetto was to be liquidated and its remaining people transferred to other camps, your wife hid the bundle. I remember her telling me about it, but I don't remember where she hid it."

"Believe me, I have no need now of those manuscripts."

I am hard-pressed to resist the leaden heaviness now spreading through my limbs.

"Maybe your wife hid a letter among the manuscripts; maybe she wrote something about herself and about your mother." Anna Itkin's voice comes to me from afar, from the ruins of the Ghetto. "In the Ghetto your wife lived in a garret, at Number Nine—maybe she concealed it in the wall there. Have you gone yet to Number Nine?"

"I'll look there," I answer slowly, in a muted, subterranean voice, the voice of Balberishkin the shoemaker, who sits in his cellar waiting for me to bring him news of his son. "Frumme-Liebche always dreamed of working with children. She used to tell me: 'I want to work with children, where life begins, not with old people, where life ends'; but somehow she could never arrange it. Only in the Ghetto, I see, did she at last manage to work with children, where life begins. . . ."

Anna Itkin does not answer. She sits enmeshed in the empty silence of her office, and the sad stillness that rests upon her face falls like a shadow upon mine as well. We both gaze mutely at the little marble table on which stands the infants' scale. The scale's white enameled bowl looks as though it has frozen while waiting for the little pink body of a living child to be placed in it.

Number 9

MY CEMETERY-ALLEYS SPEAK TO ME: "Why don't you go to eat? Why don't you go to sleep?" They ask this in the same voice my mother used when, while I was still a child, I sat next to her all night beside my dead father, who was lying on a layer of straw, covered with a black overcoat and surrounded by candles. Mother, who had not closed her eyes nor taken a morsel of food, had no strength left to weep; only her lips moved soundlessly, repeating the words of the two sleepy psalm-readers. In her dry eyes the candles that surrounded my father's body burned rigidly, and from time to time she repeated those same words to me: "Why don't you go to eat? Why don't you go to sleep?" As my cemetery-alleys are speaking to me now.

But just as then I could not tear myself away from the silence of my father under his black covering, from my mother's sorrow, from the chanting of the Psalms and from the nocturnal shadows on the smithy walls, suffused with the reddish glow of the deathwatch candles—so now I cannot tear myself away from my narrow streets. My heart keens bitterly over the ruins: A corpse is supposed to be covered, yet here you lie so nakedly exposed. How can I eat or sleep when I still cannot understand what happened here? If they had died during a plague, I would have understood; if they had been guilty of something, I would have understood; if they had had any chance to escape death and had not taken it, I would have understood. But the murderers didn't even give them the choice of conversion. And why do the Gentiles, our former neighbors, feel no compassion for us? Their brothers were also killed and buried in the pits of Ponary. Why do they hate us so much they are even ready to forget that their blood, too, was spilled?

"If you really could find an answer for it all," my cemetery-alleys reply, "you would no longer suffer such anguish—and why should you wish not to suffer?" And they remind me again that I should go to eat, should go to sleep, should go to Number 9, where Frumme-Liebche once lived.

And so I go back to eat and to sleep and the next morning, in my apartment on Giedyminowska Street, I hear what I hear every morning. On the other side of the wall live a young couple—Lithuanians, according to the landlord, who have returned from Russia. And every morning I hear the woman laughing. Their apartment faces on a different courtyard, and I have never seen the couple, but from her laughter I can tell that she must be young, pretty, tall, with a plump body, and good-naturedly simple-minded. How her lover looks I cannot picture, because he is always silent, and after a while she grows silent too. The silence burns through the wall with the heat of hidden passion, with flaming breath; all is still on the other side, hot and sultry, as when the sun blazes into a thicket of densely foliaged trees. After a while the laughter can be heard once more, no longer loud and wanton as before, but sleepy and satisfied, like the lowing of a sated animal. She is, no doubt, lying there now on the rumpled bed, her body big and bloated, her hands under her head, yawning and gazing out through the window at the sun that scorches her bare copper breasts with its rays. For me that does it! I've had enough of living on the other side of the wall. I get dressed and leave for the Ghetto.

I do not know whether even this time I would have had the strength to enter Frumme-Liebche's room—except that this day the early-morning laughter from the other side of the wall had intoxicated me more than ever before; it pursues me from Giedyminowska Street as far as the Ghetto and drives me into the courtyard of Balberishkin the shoemaker. I quickly find the entrance, on which a large "9" is scrawled in chalk, and ram the door several times with my shoulder until it opens wide. I rush up the steps to the garret. . . . Nothing! My fears had been unwarranted. Four bare walls. On the floor, splinters of glass, small pieces of broken bricks—not even a pile of rubble on which to sit shiva. I begin tapping the walls, whose paint has peeled off, and beating against them with my fists, but I find no sign to indicate that anything might be hidden there. I am just about to go back down when, suddenly, Balberishkin the shoemaker appears in the doorway, his big, burly frame barring my exit.

"Ah, it's you! Have you found out anything about my son?" he calls out all in one breath as with his right hand he takes from under his left arm the cobbler's long iron last he had been holding between his knees on the night I first visited him.

"Why are you holding that?" I jump to one side.

"I was in my cellar and heard someone forcing open the door, and so I thought some Gentiles had come to look for buried treasure in the ruins. They've broken in here more than once." He sets the iron foot down on the floor. "Did you find out anything about my son?"

"I found out something. I learned from a Jewish soldier who served in the Lithuanian-Russian Division in Balakhna, that your son was not there. The Jews there all knew each other. Since they didn't take young men from Vilna into the Russian army proper, it's clear that your son wasn't in the army at all." I never take my eyes off the iron last. "And what would you have done if you had come upon Gentiles looking for hidden treasure? Would you have attacked them with that piece of iron?"

"Yes, I would," he answers and then bursts into a lament: "But you said my son was in the army. . . ."

"I said it was possible your son was in the army—I never said I was certain of it. You ought to be happy that your son wasn't at the front—" And suddenly, against my will, I begin to scream at the shoemaker that in the Ghetto too he had had an iron last and a hammer, but had never used them to bash a German's head in.

"And do you think you would have attacked a German with an iron last?" The shoemaker assumes an expression of naïveté. "Just now you were frightened when you saw me with the iron."

"If I had been in the Ghetto, you could ask me that question." I begin to scream still louder. "But it was you who were in the Ghetto, not I. And so I ask you: Why did you do nothing when the murderer Kittel used to come to the Ghetto without a guard, without even a submachine gun, and walked around there with his hands in his pockets? Why could he be so sure that no one would touch him?"

"Is it my fault that you found nothing here?" bleats the shoemaker.

"That's just the sort you are!" I spring toward him, furious. "You think I'm angry only because I found nothing here? When your son returns from Russia, he'll ask you the same questions I'm asking!"

"My son won't ask me that. He knows his father and he knows I'm not a coward. He will ask only where his mother and his sister are. All those who return from Russia accuse us. Over there they spread slanders against us. . . ." Clumsily, as hurt as a child, this great hulk of a man wipes the tears from his eyes, and silently I curse the demon within me that springs thus to my lips, spitting fire and deathly venom. Instead of becoming an avenger, I am croaking like a toad. My complaints and accusations have made me as welcome as a bitter onion to the survivors of the Ghetto, and even to those who fought as partisans in the woods. They hurl insults at me and scream: "When are you going back to Moscow? There they'll tell you tales of heroism and you'll calm down!" Then I keep still for a day or two, only to start in all over again.

I begin to speak gently, placatingly to Balberishkin, telling him again that he should be happy his son was not at the front. Probably he is working somewhere in a factory or in a kolkhoz. Wherever he may be, he cannot leave his job without official permission, on pain of severe punishment. One must also have a special permit to travel from one place to another, and it is very difficult to get permission to enter Vilna, which had been an actual combat area.

The shoemaker doesn't believe me. It's in vain, he says, to try to convince him that his son could not have returned yet. He had gone to inquire at the headquarters of the Jewish community, which is now located in what had been the Choir Synagogue, and there he saw many Jews, as well as large piles of letters written by former inhabitants of Vilna who were asking for information about their families. But he had not found his son there, nor had any letter from him been received. . . .

Balberishkin sighs and falls silent; he picks up the iron last from the floor and moves to return to his work in the cellar. But I hold him back, and tell him I have been to see Anna Itkin, who had worked together with my wife in the Jewish hospital, and that she told me my wife had always been confident I was alive. But surely he must know more about her—after all, they had been neighbors here.

"Of course the nurse, your wife, was certain that you were alive," exclaims Balberishkin, "just as my wife was certain that our Itzikl was alive." His tone is joyful, as though the fact that Frumme-Liebche had been proved right has strengthened his hope that his son too lives.

"And my mother? Do you know whether my mother also believed that I was alive?"

"I don't know anything about that," answers Balberishkin, after pondering the question long and thoughtfully. "I only know that the nurse very carefully guarded a shawl of your mother's."

"A shawl? My mother's shawl? A black silk shawl?"

"I myself never actually saw the shawl, but my wife saw it," answers Balberishkin, and from the expression of bewilderment on his face I realize that I must now have the desperate look of a brigand. "When the nurse moved in here with her friends, we became acquainted. Whenever our Yentele wasn't feeling well, my wife would take her up to the nurse. And after each such visit she would tell me what a lovely person the nurse was, and that she treasured a shawl which had belonged to your mother. Whenever the nurse spoke of you and your mother, she would cry and hide her tear-stained face in your mother's shawl. That's what my wife would tell me, and then she would cry, too."

"The shawl—my mother's shawl—her black silk Sabbath shawl —" I stare about me in the empty room, as though the peeling walls have changed into ocean waves that rush at me from all sides, seeking to pull me down into the abyss. The doctor, I tell Balberishkin, had suggested the possibility that somewhere in these walls there might be a small bundle of my wife's and perhaps she had put my mother's black silk shawl in it too.

"It's not here." Balberishkin shakes his head sadly and tells me that the morning after I had run off, unwilling to come up here with him to search for a keepsake, he had come up by himself. His thought had been that if he did find something and brought it to me, I would not refuse to take it. So he had tapped all over the walls, but found nothing. A pity—a great pity. He wanted in some way to give me something in return for the good news I had brought him, even though he hasn't heard from his son yet. . . .

"So—there's nothing here. Come away!" I seize his arm and pull him outside to the stairs. I promise him that I will inquire about his son wherever I can, but he must promise me in return that he will close up the door downstairs with a board and nails and make sure that no one goes up there.

"When my Yitzhak* returns, I won't live here in the ruins anymore," Balberishkin says with a pathetic, imploring smile. "But please ask everyone about my son, my only son. You can see how Fate keeps throwing us together. Before the war you used to visit my boarders. In the Ghetto we were your wife's neighbors, and even in Russia God brought you together with my son."

"Yes, I will ask, I will keep looking. . . ." I cast one last glance through the open door at the empty walls. "Close up the door downstairs with a board and nails. I don't want people creeping around and rummaging in there. But don't do it before I leave—I don't want to hear the blows of the hammer."

Balberishkin nods his head: he understands. I drag myself down the garret stairs and into the street; I want to run, but my feet refuse to carry me. It's all I can do to totter off, trembling in fear of hearing the hammer-blows—and hear them I do, just as I drag myself to the corner of the alley. Through the mute and desolate silence of the devastated Ghetto the echoing blows pound their way straight into my temples. Yet simultaneously I have the feeling that, rather than running away amidst the piles of rubble, I am still there in that empty room as the shoemaker, with hammer and nails, boards up the entrance to my grave, the garret of Number 9.

* Yitzhak (Isaac) is the Hebrew name of which Itzikl is one Yiddish form.—Trans.

Spiderwebs

I

MY MOTHER'S HOME has remained intact. But over the entire entrance, where the door once stood, from the lintel down to the threshold, hangs a dense net of gray spiderwebs.

I fled, shuddering in all my limbs, feeling as if the spiderwebs had spread over my face and were interwoven with my hair, my eyebrows and eyelashes. For years I had prepared myself for the day when I would return home and find only ruins. Instead, I had found my mother's dwelling—whole. But a curtain of spiderwebs bars my way, like the angels with flaming swords who barred Adam and Eve from returning to Eden.

I stand motionless on German Street, between Jewish Street and Gitka-Toybe's Alley, and the sun, too, seems to be standing still directly overhead—a mild, serene, autumnally golden, and peaceful sun. I recall from Scripture that when the Prophets wish to image forth an impending catastrophe, they declare that the sun will set in the middle of the day. But I am fated to see the sun shining at all times. It shines now as it shone four years ago, on the day of my flight; now it seems hardly more than a minute ago that I bade my mother farewell. I still hear her running in her heavy shoes across the crooked cobblestones, to see me to the gate. . . .

Across the street from me, at the corner of Jewish Street, a short, stocky woman stands gazing down at the pavement. Before the war she had tended a stall in the marketplace, and she is one of the few survivors who knew my mother. I was aware that she had survived, but until now I have avoided her, been reluctant to question her.

"I heard that you'd returned from Russia," she tells me.

"How did you manage to save yourself?" I ask.

"Right here." She points at the pavement she has been staring at.

"Where—'here'?" I look about.

"Here in the sewer." Again she points at the pavement, at the grating over the sewage pipes. She had saved herself in the filthy waters of the underground pipes.

"Do you know anything about my mother? She was in the Small

Ghetto. Her second husband, Reb Refoel Rosenthal, used to have a fruit-and-vegetable shop in a cellar on Broad Street."

"Of course I knew Vella the fruit-peddler! Why, for years we bought our merchandise from the same wholesalers." The woman's voice is faint. "There were several *Aktionen* in the Small Ghetto. One of the first was on Yom Kippur. But exactly when your mother went, I don't know."

She went on Yom Kippur, I say to myself. Frozen, benumbed, she became one of the first to go. All her life she had lived with the Sabbath and with Yom Kippur, and she went to Ponary as she would go to the synagogue. While still in Asia, I had already decided that my mother's Yohrzeit must fall on Yom Kippur.

"Here was the First Ghetto—" I point to Jewish Street with one hand—"and right here was the Second Ghetto—" I point to Gitka-Toybe's Alley with the other hand—"barely two or three paces away. And yet I've heard that in the Second Ghetto people used to say: 'They say an *Aktion* is taking place in the First Ghetto, they say they're taking all the Jews out of there.' . . . 'They say'!"

"Yes, no more than two or three paces, but here on German Street stood real live Germans—" now the woman points—"and the distance from one Ghetto to the other was great, very great. . . ." She stretches out the words to show me how great the distance had been.

The short, stocky stall-keeper interlaces her fingers over her bosom as if a pair of heavy baskets were dangling from both arms; she lifts her head, and speaks up toward me with a hollow voice, as though she were still standing in the underground sewage pipes and addressing someone above through the grating:

Whenever she sees two or three Russian soldiers leading a band of German prisoners of war, she cannot believe her eyes—that these same prisoners, now so tattered and forlorn, could have been such murderers. When the Russians first entered Vilna, Jewish partisans had recognized one of the murderers and taken him to be hanged. She had watched the murderer as he was being led along, and never in her life had she seen anyone shaking so with the fear of death. He was so pale, his features so contorted, that she felt only disgust at the sight of his ugly face. All the hatred she had felt toward him had suddenly vanished and she wanted only to vomit.

"And how did Jews go?" I ask.

"The Jews went quietly," answers the stall-keeper.

She speaks in a strange, otherworldly voice, as though the sun above our heads had drained her last drop of blood, and in the frozen desolation that surrounds us her voice sounds still more frozen, more desolate.

Once she had gone out with a group to work outside the Ghetto and she had seen, among a group of Jews who were being taken to

Ponary, an old man and an old woman. Each was carrying a pillow under one arm; they were holding hands like two children, and they were walking so quietly—never in her life had she seen such quietness. Her eyes had been dim with tears, but yet she had noticed that the pillowcases for the old couple's pillows were carefully ironed, fresh and white, as though they had just been put on.

"Why did the old people take along their pillows?" I ask. "Didn't they know what Ponary was, or did they think they were being transferred to another ghetto?" And I feel that the sun high above is waiting with me for the stall-keeper's answer.

She doesn't know, the woman says, why the old people took their pillows with them. It is possible they didn't realize where they were being taken, but perhaps they did—at such moments, very strange thoughts can enter one's mind. Perhaps they had the notion that with the pillows they would lie more softly in their grave. She herself had several times been within a hair's-breadth of death and she knows that at such times wild, extraordinary ideas come into one's head. . . .

The stall-keeper falls silent, and her eyes rest once again on the sewer-grating: she marvels endlessly at the miracle of her survival down there. Then she turns to me and begins to tremble, like the net of spiderwebs over my mother's doorway.

"In the Ghetto," she says, "people used to sing this rhyme: 'The homes are empty and bare/ But in the pits—all are there.'" And she walks slowly away down Jewish Street, until she disappears behind the piles of rubble.

"The houses are empty and bare/ But in the pits—all are there," I murmur and stare dumbly at my own shadow which lies motionless on the pavement, not knowing where it should go or where it belongs—in the empty houses or in the full pits.

I start walking down Gitka-Toybe's Alley, inwardly glad that the sun has remained standing over German Street, above the sewer-grating, and does not follow me. But ahead of me now walks the old couple. I do not see their faces—only their hunched shoulders and the pillows under their arms. They wander amidst the ruins, holding each other's hand. . . . Jews went quietly, the stall-keeper had said. That is the answer to all the questions that torture me and with which I torture others. Now the dybbuk within me may die its own uncanny death. Jews went quietly. . . .

The sun, left behind above the sewer-grating, now seems to have caught up with me again, to hang suspended once more above my head. Suddenly, as if springing up from underground, Balberishkin the shoe-maker looms up before me. Amid the small, collapsed houses he looks even taller, broader, and he moves not a muscle, as though afraid he might burst the narrow street apart. His small eyes are wide open; he stares at me with the stillness of a murdered man who appears to his murderer in a nightmare. But he does not frighten me. Grasping my chin with my right hand, like a Talmudic scholar clutching his beard as he pores over a page of Gemara, I speak aloud in the traditional sing-song chant:

"Let us say, for example, that a winged angel came down from Heaven and announced to an old man and old woman that they had lived out their allotted days and the time had come for them to join their forefathers, but that, in order to enter at once into Paradise, they had to agree to go first to Ponary with pillows under their arms, and to be shot there. Surely, then, we may assume that, being in the fullness of their years, and having faith in God, the old man and old woman would agree to die as martyrs so as to be spared the punishment of the grave, of Gehenna, and to be admitted directly into Paradise. But this I simply cannot accept. Had the old people died a natural death—well, then, they would have died! Nothing new about that—especially since they had already lived out their time on earth. But here they were driven to the pit, with their pillows under their arms, and their executioners laughed at them for bringing the pillows, and I do not understand, then, how the sun can continue to shine. Perhaps for the old couple their death was not nearly so terrible as I imagine it. Perhaps they had never had faith in the justice of this world. But I, I did believe in the justice of this world, I did believe in mankind, and so the manner of their death is more terrible for me than it was for the old people themselves. Do you understand?"

The shoemaker does not answer. His gaze becomes even more piercing, the mute furrows in his brow scream still louder. I too fall silent, rendered momentarily as speechless as he; but the dybbuk within me, still unwilling to die, now bursts into wild laughter:

"Spiderwebs, my mother's doorway is covered by a dense net of spiderwebs. I remember that at Ḥanukah-time, when the rich matrons would begin to render goose-fat for Passover, my mother, too, would set about her Passover preparations. She would climb up on a stool and with a broom begin to brush away the webs that clung to the ceiling of our smithy-room. I used to watch this and laugh. 'By the time Passover comes,' I would tell her, 'we'll have had three times as many new spiderwebs here.' And now all the webs that she swept away from our smithy are hanging over the entrance of Reb Refoel's home. My mother remarried just before the war, and her second union turned out to be even more fortunate than her first. . . ."

Balberishkin is staring at me with the same expression I've observed on his face several times before: he thinks me a madman. I seize him by the elbow and shout directly into his face:

"I don't want to enter my mother's house! I regret having listened to you and gone up into the garret of Number Nine, where my wife lived. I didn't find anything anyway, but the emptiness there is still pursuing me. I will not go into my mother's house, I will not go in."

Balberishkin still does not answer. I leave him standing there and drag myself onward, as though he were not a human being barring my way, but only a pole. I immediately sink back into my thoughts about the old couple: It may well be that they had children living somewhere overseas, who supported them in their old age. Fine children! And when they find out what happened here, they will say: "So many young lives were cut short, how can we complain? Our parents, after all, were already old." Something like this is what the children will say, and little by little they will forget the old man and old woman. But I, I shall not forget them—for the sake of their walking with their white pillows under their arms, I shall not forget them.

"What did you have against me!" A protracted wailing cry overtakes me from behind. "I saw right away that you're a crazy man. You told me a tale of my son being alive, but all the others have returned and not my son, not my son."

I can sense the shoemaker following me with his eyes; something seems about to happen. I turn toward him and shout across the ruins, as though I were on the other bank of a wide and desolate river:

"I did see your son alive in Tashkent. Not everyone from Vilna has returned. Many haven't come back because they don't expect to find anyone here. Your son lives, but he doesn't know that you're alive."

"Your words have as much weight as spiderwebs," wails Balberishkin. He stops dead, turns abruptly silent and motionless.

I do not answer him, do not look at him, and walk on. I am a cause of misfortune: After the man has already given up all hope, I come along and raise him out of his despair, but only to suffer new anguish. His son may well have died of starvation or disease in Asia, as thousands of refugees had died, or he might have somehow incurred the authorities' displeasure and been sent off to a labor camp. But it is not my fault. I spoke the truth. And whatever may have happened to young Balberishkin, he is still better off than others. At least he has a father who will remember him.

II

O N THE EVE OF YOM KIPPUR, just before the "Kol Nidrei," I return to my mother's house. The spiderwebs at the entrance appear even denser. This time, however, I do not run away. I gaze at the web of circles so artfully interlinked with fine threads, and detect in them a likeness to the heavenly spheres. Here, on my mother's doorway, all the signs of the zodiac spin about in a circle, and peering out between them is the great wise golden apple of the setting sun—a flaming-red, blood-chilled sun, a sun always at dusk, always of the eve of Yom Kippur, a sun that never sets and never rises.

A sleek, well-fed gray cat steals out from behind the spiderwebs and stretches itself on the threshold while it stares at me with wild green eyes. A shudder passes through my entire body, as though those green eyes had sprung out of the animal's head and were rolling across my back, beneath my clothes. I try to chase the cat away; it opens its mouth and begins to spit, but it does not meow—a mute one. Then, hunching its body, it vanishes within the house, as though it knows I will not dare to tear the net and pursue it inside. Shortly, it appears once more on the threshold and rears up on its hind legs, its front paws against the spiderwebs, as if to taunt me, to threaten that if I do not leave, it will tear the net apart.

I go off to "Kol Nidrei" at the Choir Synagogue, now the sole remaining synagogue in Vilna. Once it was the synagogue attended by advocates of enlightenment and wealthy men of like views. Here the bima stood directly in front of the Holy Ark, as in a Reform temple, and the trustees' prayer shawls were small, hardly bigger than neckerchiefs. Now all the survivors are gathered here—the partisans who had fought in the forests, those who had crawled out from malinas, those who had returned from Russia. All are fused into one great wail of lamentation, as the flames of the memorial candles have fused into one flame. But before my eyes there hovers still a night-vision of the ruined Synagogue Courtyard and my mother's home. There she sits with her husband, behind the curtain of spiderwebs, and they do not wish me to enter, lest I disturb them now as I disturbed them when they lived.

For two years Mother lived with Reb Refoel, but they remained strangers to each other. Between them stood the years of their separate lives, the separate anguish and joy in their children. Over the long years of his widowerhood Reb Refoel, a taciturn man by nature, had withdrawn even more deeply within himself. As for my mother, she was vexed at herself for living in her thoughts more with her son and daughter-in-law than with her second husband. Once having married Reb Refoel, she believed, she owed him her total devotion, even in thought. She also felt guilty towards him because since their wedding she had begun to take sick, and so saw herself as having, at it were, deceived him. Of late she often felt dizzy and had a ringing in her head; her cheeks had become more gaunt and she was always feverish. Often I sat by her bedside all night, because she did not wish to trouble Reb Refoel with having to attend to her.

On Friday nights I would come to have dinner with them. I was there just two days before the war broke out. Mother said the blessing for the Sabbath candles. Between the outspread fingers covering her face, great tears rolled down. After blessing the candles, she softly wished me a "Good Sabbath" and glanced over to where Reb Refoel was standing facing the window; she would not, with any loud word, interrupt her husband's "Welcome to the Sabbath." Considerable time passed, and Reb Refoel had yet to speak an audible word or even to move. We could not tell whether he was still praying or, as so often, simply standing there.

Mother bent her head and, furrowing her brow, gazed lost in thought at her work-worn hands. This was her habit whenever something troubled her that she did not want to speak about: to look down at her hands. Finally she asked me why Frumme-Liebche hadn't come for dinner. Frumme-Liebche, I answered, was still in the hospital tending the sick. Mother sighed and made no reply. I could tell that she suspected Frumme-Liebche of intentionally accepting night duty at the hospital so as not to have to sit at table with the silent Reb Refoel.

After the meal, Reb Refoel stretched out on the sofa in the front parlor, while I remained sitting next to Mother's bed in the bedroom. She was feverish, breathed heavily, and groaned, but was otherwise silent. Leaning against the edge of her bed, I began to doze. Unexpectedly, Mother began to laugh, softly and shyly.

"My son, you used to study the Torah," she whispered to me. "So now tell me—whose footstool shall I be in Paradise: your father's, may he rest in peace, or Reb Refoel's, may he be granted many more years of life?"*

Mother had always wished to be my father's footstool. But it may be that when she went to Ponary together with Reb Refoel, he was in that hour closer to her than my father, who had died in his own bed in our smithy-room. So quiet, so small and shrunken, she had gone. And perhaps she and Reb Refoel had held each other's hand, like the old couple with their white pillows. Afterwards Frumme-Liebche must have run from the Second Ghetto back to the First, to Reb Refoel's house, and

---

* A reference to the folk belief that men who have devoted their lives to the study of the Torah will have seats of honor in Paradise, while their wives will serve as their footstools.—Trans.

found no one there. It was then that she had taken my mother's black silk Sabbath shawl. But that shawl is nowhere to be found—nowhere.

I rush out of the Choir Synagogue into the street; shadows tremble across the cobblestones illumined by the lamps in the synagogue's windows, and it seems to me that lying somewhere out there in the Yom Kippur night must be my mother's black silk Sabbath shawl.

That whole night long I dream of Balberishkin the shoemaker standing amid the ruins, erect, motionless, gazing at me with the dead eyes of a murdered man who appears in a nightmare to his murderer— just the way he had gazed at me during our last encounter in the Ghetto. On Yom Kippur morning, when I awake, it occurs to me that I hadn't seen him at "Kol Nidrei" the night before. The thought strikes me that in his despair he may have hanged himself. I hurry to his workshop, but the window, which is sunk halfway below street level, is shuttered on the inside, and the cellar door has been closed off with a board nailed on from the outside. Apparently the shoemaker Balberishkin has returned to the village where, among White Russians and Poles, he too is thought to be a Gentile, as he had told me. There, amidst the Gentiles, he wishes to forget that once long ago his name was Balberishkin and that he had a wife and two children—until, one day, the longing once more comes upon him to return to his Ghetto cellar and there sit shiva for his old Jewish life. But it is also possible that now he will never again make this return, because I have betrayed the hope, which I myself reawakened in him, that his son is yet alive; he will not return—and I will no longer need to fear him, to fear his sudden emergence from behind the ruins to demand that lost son of me.

Ruined Synagogues

THE FEW MINYANS OF JEWS who are all that remain of the Vilna community now rise in the Choir Synagogue to recite the Yizkor—the Memorial Prayer. Their lamentations entangle them as might the lines of a sinking ship, they are drowning in their own tears. But I, I am not reciting the Yizkor; around me all is still, peaceful, serene. I am standing at the iron gate of the Vilna Synagogue Courtyard and the sun, in the center of a clear sky, sprays all about its rays of fine gold, just as it had done four years earlier on the secluded forest path between Minsk and Borisov, that path of my perils which has left implanted in me a sweet dread, an unfathomable stillness, and a longing. Today the sun shines again exactly as it did on that other day in the distant Asiatic city of Stalinabad, when I nearly perished together with Misha Troiman, the refugee from Lodz.

From the walls around the Synagogue Courtyard slogans shriek at me, slogans dating from before the war. Painted red letters call upon the viewer to vote for this party or that in the communal elections. Living faces immured in the bricks vie to outshout one another:

"Long live the Jewish Workers' Party!"

"Through blood and struggle toward freedom in the Land of Israel!"

"Buy the products of the Land of Israel!" pleads a placard of the Women's League.

"Baths and tubs in the Synagogue Courtyard," advertises a small sign affixed to the iron gate.

I close my eyes: perhaps it is all no more than a bad dream? I open my eyes again, to behold an entire row of shattered windows in the Straszun Library, directly opposite the poster-covered walls. On these walls the library casts an enormous shadow, like a black cloth hung over the mirror in a house where there has been a death.

I climb over large piles of rubble and refuse, attempting to go up into the Synagogue of the Gaon of Vilna. But the stairs are broken, as though the ladder of Jacob's dream had toppled. I look up into the black void of the Gaon's house of study, above whose entrance there yet remains the inscription "Synagogue of the Gaon Rabboni Elijah, of Blessed Memory." The inscription hovers above the entrance like a bird that has returned to its nest and finds its tree . . . cut down. Frightened by the

silence of the forest at dusk, the bird utters not a sound, but remains
suspended in mid-air upon its weary wings.

Here is the Gravediggers' Chapel. It is itself now—a grave. Here,
too, the steps have collapsed. God wants his synagogues to be suspended
in the heights like clouds, so that no one can reach them. I look up: that
was where the bima once stood. Once, on Tisha B'Av, during my youth,
I had sat shoeless* on a low stool on the bima of the Gravediggers' Chapel
and read the Book of Lamentations for the congregants. Now the bima
is gone, and gone too is the pious young boy who had once lamented:
"The Lord is righteous, for I have rebelled against his word. . . ." High
up on the East Wall, there where the Holy Ark had stood, one solitary
word, formed of beaten copper letters, still hangs: *"Anoḥi."* I want to
scream, but my breath has congealed, my feet are benumbed, and the
numbness creeps closer, ever closer, to my heart. All around me is a
deathly silence, and above the ruins there burns the first word of the first
of the Ten Commandments: *"Anoḥi*—I am the Lord thy God. . . ." Then
again, could it be taken from the verse in Isaiah: "I am He that comforteth
you"? Or does it mean, rather: "I am the guilty one"? . . .

A tremor passes the full length of my body; it seems to me that the
Anoḥi is moving—soon it will swoop down like an eagle and peck out
my eyes for this blasphemy. I stand there as frightened as when I was a
child in the synagogue on Yom Kippur and the entire congregation would
fall to their knees at the intoning of the words "And we bend the knee
and bow down." I gaze upon the mounds of earth in the dug-up Synagogue Courtyard, and they seem like the bent backs of gray and ancient
Jews as they kneel during the recital of the Priestly Service of Atonement.
I turn, and behold the Old Synagogue.

Old Synagogue, it is for you that the Prophet laments: "The Lord
hath cast off His altar, He hath abhorred His sanctuary, He hath given
up into the hands of the enemy the walls of her palaces. . . ." Your façade
has been torn down, as has the curtain before your Holy Ark. Now the
unclean ones, the uncircumcised, can see how your unsteady pillars strain
to support your vaulted ceiling—and they, the unclean, laugh. Are you
not waiting, Old Synagogue, for another Samson to burst your pillars
asunder and bury those who blaspheme and plunder you? They climb
up to your windows to take away their wooden frames. They wrest out
the oaken doors of the bookcases built into your walls. They pull down
the carved lions and deer that adorned you, and use them for kindling
wood under their unclean pots. Whatever the Germans have left is now
carried off by our neighbors, the Edomites—the Poles and the Lithuanians. Old Synagogue, your ruins are for me as Mount Nebo, where

---

* Shoes are removed as a sign of mourning.—Trans.

Moses died. For me you are as the Temple Mount where the Holy Temple stood. Your crumbled walls block my way, so that I cannot get to the other part of the Synagogue Courtyard. Your tottering pillars may collapse without warning upon anyone who tries to steal into the forbidden, rubble-covered, martyred ground. Yet that ground reverberates with an eerie stillness which draws me toward it, an air of perilous mystery— like ice-covered mountain peaks that terrify the beholder with the abysses that surround them, and yet attract him with their snowy silence, with the hope that whoever attains them will behold at last all those eternally shrouded mysteries that only there lie revealed.

I clamber across piles of stones and iron beams, crawl through holes and crevices, until at last, covered with plaster and dust, I enter the second part of the Synagogue Courtyard—and halt, surrounded by wild, thorny weeds. Weeds climb upon the walls, wind and plait themselves around empty structures, conceal the Artisans' Synagogue, the Tifereth Baḥurim Synagogue, and the small synagogue of the Kaydanover Ḥassidim, so they shall not be shamed for nakedness. But the buildings' inscriptions will not permit the weeds to grow over them. The letters burn and fall like sparks upon my face: we were built—so say these houses of study and prayer—in the year 5641, in the year 5635, in the year 5505.* Here lie buried—so they scream, in silence—here lie buried all the prayers that Jews have uttered for hundreds of years.

The Old-New Synagogue: to keep you from collapsing, an external wall was erected to support you, while the congregants within upheld you with their prayers. The great philanthropist and man of wealth— Rabbi Judah, the Scribe and Judge—who built you, donated a fortune to the community on the condition that his son-in-law, Rabbi Shmuel, be appointed Chief Rabbi of Vilna. The community's leaders accepted this condition, but after the death of the father-in-law they became embroiled in a bitter dispute with Rabbi Shmuel, and so humiliated and persecuted him that he was at last compelled to leave Vilna. After his passing the community, out of remorse for the shame and disgrace it had visited upon its rabbi, placed in his memory a large stone slab in the Grand Synagogue, next to the Holy Ark—signifying that no one ever again should occupy the seat of Vilna's last Chief Rabbi. Now all of Vilna is a gravestone for its last Jew, and the Gentiles now sit in the Jews' stead, like owls amid the ruins.

It seems to me that just during the brief time I have been standing among the weeds, they have grown taller. They enmesh and entangle me, threatening to trap me here. I tear myself out of their net and attempt

---

* The dates according to the Hebrew calendar, corresponding, respectively, to 1881, 1875, and 1745.—Trans.

to crawl back to the first section of the Courtyard. But bricks have started to fall from the Old Synagogue, as though God has at last heeded the prayer of the desolate sanctuary and is now demolishing it, so that looters can no longer desecrate and plunder it. I experience a momentary pang of terrror: will I remain a prisoner here amid these collapsed walls? Then I notice, almost at ground level, the bottom windows of the Grand Synagogue. I crawl down through the empty window-spaces into the depths of the synagogue, from which I can make my way back to the street.

Through the Grand Synagogue I walk with head lowered. I do not want to see anymore—I have had enough of dust and ruins. On the great stairway leading to the exit, the brass railings glisten now just as they once did on festivals, when the congregants would press forward to hear the cantor and his choir. Confronting me in the lobby are the still-surviving alms-boxes for the sick, for the aged, for the scholars, for the charity fund of Rabbi Meir Ba'al Ha-Nes.* The stark emptiness of the synagogue blasts at my back with an arctic coldness that freezes my feet to the steps and bars my escape. Slowly I turn my head to look back, and discover that the synagogue has grown, as the hair and nails of a corpse continue to grow. Without the row upon row of pews, the Grand Synagogue looks twice as large and spacious as before. The four gigantic pillars around the bima and the colonnade of striped marble upon it resemble fountains whose spouting waters meet in semi-arches. High above the cantor's lectern, where David's harp and winged lions once adorned the Holy Ark, there remains a solitary, orphaned verse: "So shall they put My name upon the Children of Israel, and I will bless them. . . ." The verse gazes down upon the cement steps that lead to the Ark, the steps upon which the Kohanim once stood with hands outspread to pronounce the priestly blessing—Kohanim who will never again raise their hands to bless, those hands that have since been consumed by fire.

I hear a mysterious sound and look round again: raindrops are dripping from the ceiling, slowly and monotonously, as in some stone-walled cave high up in the mountains. There has been no rain in Vilna for months, so this must be water that accumulated on the decaying roof last year, or even two years ago. One by one the icy drops fall to the cement floor, one by one, and in that frozen emptiness their echo is so drawn out and mournful, so tinged with a grieving melancholy, that they might be the very tears of the Jews of Vilna—tears that have secreted themselves in the ceiling of the ancient Grand Synagogue and now speak aloud, giving utterance to their tales, lamentations, grievances, sighing softly, softly, in a still small voice:

---

* A charity fund for the needy in the Land of Israel.—Trans.

"You have returned from far away with hidden reproaches in your heart. You fled to the north, and lived among alien people skilled in the arts of war, who fought the German enemy attacking them from the west. The fierce valor of these victors has confused you, and now you demand valor of us as well: 'Why did you not resist?' You have saved your life and now you want us who perished to save also your imagined honor; you want to be able to proclaim yourself before the world a last survivor of annihilated heroes. In the presence of the arrogant, of the powerful, of those who live by the sword, you call us to account for failing to exact vengeance.

"Don't you know that they deceived us? The murderers sent traitors into our midst who persuaded us that by labor we could save ourselves from death. No one returned from the grave, and the forests around Ponary hid the secret of the bloody pits even from the birds. The police and oppressors within our own ranks, to keep themselves alive one day more than the rest, assured us after each new edict that no further steps would be taken against us. And we had children and wives and aged parents to care for. They tortured us, to destroy within us the image of God; they stripped us naked, to crush us with shame and humiliation; under a hail of blows and laughter we ran to our graves—willingly, we ran! For do you know what it is to lie in a field, surrounded by executioners, and watch others being led to their death while you yourself are left behind for later—for later? Can you conceive how great a deliverance it is then to die even one moment sooner? And still you demand heroism of us, our dead hands must uphold your honor in the eyes of the peoples of the earth, who bend the knee before power, never before suffering.

"And you, stouthearted fellow that you are, what did you do while we were dying? And your brothers living far away in freedom, what did they do? Did they fall at the feet of the nations and plead for our rescue? Why did you not besiege the leaders of governments? Why did you not lie down in the streets, so that the world could not have passed by so heedless of our murder? Why did you not starve yourselves to death, nor rend your garments in mourning every day, every hour, every moment? You failed to show for our sake a Jew's self-sacrifice, and of us you demand the valor of Esau? Whosoever heaps blame upon us for our weakness has no compassion in his heart. Whosoever says that we are punished for our sins, blasphemes against God. Today, on this Day of Atonement, you must pray for us. Our lives were cut short, our prayers were cut short."

Thus do the drops weep into my very being. Drop by drop, word by word. Every word echoes in my skull, every drop makes me shudder, as though a needle had pierced my body. But I do not leave; it is as though after long searching I have at last found the ghosts that have haunted me. "Let me go, let me go, torment me no longer," I murmur. "How many more yellowed scraps of sacred pages shall I devour? How many more times shall I cut my fingers on rusty nails and mold-covered dishes? How much more ash must settle upon my lips and enter my lungs? How much more mildew shall eat into my skin? How many more sacred verses shall be carved into the marrow of my brain and inscribed in the furrows of my face?" I turn my face upward in search of the letters left hanging from the synagogue beams, like the scattered limbs of a body torn apart. And in the Ghetto-prison I had to bend down to the ground, to the very ground, in order to decipher the writing that a little Jewish boy had scratched into the wall: "Yossele is preparing himself for Ponary. . . ."

By the rays of the sun penetrating from without, I see that it is past the time of the Additional Service. The latticed screen of the women's section, now illumined by the sun, is transformed into slats of gold. On the West Wall, where the clock that showed the time of sunset once hung, a wheel of light glistens like a polished mirror. A sheaf of sunbeams bisects the entire length of the Grand Synagogue up to the East Wall, and there vanishes into the dark recess from which the Holy Ark has been torn. In the black vastness of the shattered sanctuary the sheaf of rays dazzles like a diamond; gleams with all the hidden radiance of the plundered Torah crowns, sparkles and glows in all the hues of the mantles, embroidered with silver thread and studded with precious stones, that once covered the Holy Scrolls. Suddenly the sun-diamond emerges from its hiding-place and swings toward me, as though it were a fiery seraph sent to drive me out of the synagogue. I walk out backwards, over the steps and out into the open, overcome with dread, a fever raging in all my limbs as if the gleaming diamond had invaded them—the fever of the hour of Ne'ilah.

Ne'ilah

I RUN TO REB SHAULKA'S SYNAGOGUE on Jatkowa Street, opposite the courtyard of the goose-dealers' row where we used to live, and opposite the gate where all her life, until her marriage to Reb Refoel, my mother served God as she attended her baskets filled with rotting apples. Now, in the hour of Ne'ilah, it is fitting that I return to that same beth midrash where as a child I played among the benches, where in my youth I studied. Here every wall was covered with bookcases filled with sacred tomes, every bench occupied by pious congregants. Not for nothing was there a saying in Vilna: So much Torah is studied in Reb Shaulka's Synagogue by day and by night that its benches are trayfa from the tallow drippings that cover them, but the hearts are kosher.

There it is—Reb Shaulka's Synagogue! I lunge fiercely at the boarded-up door, which emits a muffled groan, like a wooden gallows when the corpse is cut down. In the death-emptied Ghetto the silence reverberates, as though the ruins are shuddering at my desecration of the Day of Atonement. With murderous force I continue pulling at the door, until at last the rotted boards give way. I go up into the beth midrash—it is in ruins, as in all the other synagogues. But on the wall, in the southwest corner, there still hangs a tablet whose inscription I remember from childhood: "The woman Lieba, daughter of Reb Azriel Hellin, has bequeathed three thousand rubles for the support and maintenance of the Torah scholars of the synagogue." Stepping further into the small prayer-house, I espy another wall tablet: "In memory of Reb Yosef Shraga Trakinitsky, who for nearly fifty years established his place of study and prayer in this synagogue, and served as its Gabbai for forty years. Reb Yosef Shraga died on Yom Kippur in the year 5692,* in the city of Seattle, in the United States of America, where he had stopped on his way to the Land of Israel."

I gaze at the bima, where the tall Gabbai, Reb Shraga, would stand on Sabbath mornings and give out the aliyoth. And then I call to mind another man who also once stood on that same bima—the sexton, Reb Dov-Ber Galein. Reb Dov-Ber, a ritual slaughterer as well as a sexton, was a passionate religious zealot. His full black beard and great black

* 1931.—Trans.

eyes were perpetually aflame with rage against the "worldly" Jews. His own sons had become rabbis under his tutelage, a source for him of inordinate pride and self-importance. After I abandoned my Talmudic studies, he would avert his face from me when we met on the street. On Yom Kippur he would stand on the bima and in a melodic chant auction off the honor of Opening the Holy Ark:

"Twenty gulden for the Opening of the Ark. . . ."

Reb Dov-Ber looks around: Who will bid more? A congregant at the East Wall raises a finger; the sexton understands the signal and calls out:

"Twenty-five gulden for the Opening of the Ark. . . ."

The first bidder now blazes up, and raises his whole hand. The sexton continues his chant:

"Thirty gulden for the Opening of the Ark. . . ."

The second bidder, infuriated in his turn, now leaves his seat and moves toward the bima; his rival does not lag behind. The two take positions at either side of the lectern and wave their hands at the sexton. When, however, Reb Dov-Ber sees that the bidding is rising too high, he pounds the desk with all his strength: he will not go on with the auction! When men thus outbid each other out of spite and pride, one has reason to suspect that afterward they will not fulfill their pledge. . . .

I stare at the bima and a gasp, a wailing, bursts from my throat, as though someone were strangling me:

"Twenty thousand Jews for the Opening of the Ark. But the Gate of Heaven did not open. . . .

"Forty thousand Jews for the Opening of the Ark. But the Gate of Mercy remained locked. . . .

"Seventy thousand Jews have perished. Communities outbid each other: Which would bring more sacrifices? But none could induce the Gate of Mercy to open. Reb Ber, pound the desk: Enough of sacrifices! Reb Ber, turn your fiery black eyes upon me and consume me for my taunts and blasphemies, Reb Ber. . . ."

The beth midrash is empty, silent. I descend the steps.

Where shall I go? Where can I find a place for myself? All the Jews have been exterminated; only their Yom Kippur still dwells within me, cries within me; yet I cannot pray—not for them and not for myself. . . . Another synagogue!

This is the small house on Szawelska Street where poor workingmen came to pray and weary shopkeepers would rush in to recite Kaddish. In my student days, this was a synagogue I rarely entered. I sat instead among the great scholars of Reb Shaulka's beth midrash and dreamed of becoming one of them. Now I drag myself up into Yogihe's Synagogue—and abruptly halt, overcome with amazement.

Out of the buckled floor has sprouted an entire field of sunflowers. Their leafy yellow heads tower over me, they radiate a golden brightness like that of a thousand suns revolving around one another. They tremble in such joyful ecstasy that one might think them the poverty-stricken congregants of Yogihe's Synagogue, gloriously transformed. They nod their heads toward the empty Ark, as if the open repository were still filled with sacred scrolls.

I close my eyes and sway silently with them, feeling drawn, woven into, that fervently sweet stillness. I make no sound, only smile to myself, and wipe the sweat from my forehead. It is with careful, quiet steps that I descend the stairs, so as not to disturb the silent devotions of these luminous flowers.

Once outside, I hurry quickly away: I need to see how the setting sun of Ne'ilah shines upon the spiderwebs in my mother's doorway, just as I had seen the sunset there yesterday, at the time of "Kol Nidrei."

Those are not spiderwebs, my little Mother, hanging in your doorway, but a curtain of gold for the Holy Ark, and behind it a Holy of Holies. In the Holy of Holies in the Temple, the Divine Presence hovered between two cherubim, and in your home the Divine Presence hovered every Friday night between two poor Sabbath candles in their copper candlesticks. In the days when we still lived in the smithy, you used to complain to me about being unable to afford more than ten-groschen candles for the Sabbath. The little candles burned down quickly, and for the rest of the Sabbath evening only the smoky oil lamp continued to sputter. Now, my little Mother, the glow of your ten-groschen Sabbath candles has been woven into a sunny, golden curtain for the Holy Ark, and it hangs before your door.

Once when I was a boy, I left Reb Shaulka's Synagogue with a gang of friends just before Ne'ilah, and we ran off to the church on Rudnicka Street to gather chestnuts. We climbed over the tall fence with its iron palings into the church courtyard, climbed up the trees, and from their heavy branches shook down the velvety-smooth brown chestnuts in their bursting, prickly-green skins. I returned home after my father had already said Havdalah; our post-holiday family celebration was quite ruined. For a long time my father could not forgive me for having left the synagogue at Ne'ilah. In later years my mother often told me how in the closing hours of that Yom Kippur she had peered out between the curtains of the women's section to look for me, only to meet my father's furious gaze, which seemed to accuse her of responsibility for my running off.

The church on Rudnicka Street still stands, untouched; even the tall fence with the iron palings is the same, and the branches of the same old trees are once again densely covered with ripe chestnuts. But there are no longer any little Jewish boys to run away from Reb Shaulka's Synagogue at Ne'ilah-time to gather chestnuts. Of all those boys, I am the only one left alive, and I am hurrying to your house, my little Mother, so that you may look upon me through the golden curtain of your Holy of Holies, look upon me through the spiderwebs over your ruined home, to see that I have returned for Ne'ilah. But where will I find the strength to reach you? I have wandered across half the world, but this path, through the ruins of this handful of dead streets, is longer and harder. God! I am even ready to make peace with You, for a while—just give me the strength to get there.

THE ENTRANCE to my mother's house is open; darkness stares out from within as from a deep and dried-out well. Someone has torn away the spiderwebs; or perhaps the wind has carried them off. I do not enter the house, but stand motionless in the courtyard until the mounds of rubble are covered with the shadows of night and the young crescent moon rises in the sky, waiting for me to recite the Blessing for the New Moon, as Reb Shaulka's pious congregants had always done following the Evening Service after Yom Kippur.

From the dark open house the cat creeps out and stretches itself across the threshold. I recall how on Yom Kippur, just before the Afternoon Service, my mother would always break off her devotions and return home to feed our cat. Now I approach this stray cat on the threshold, no longer with fear, as on the day before, but with friendly familiarity, as an old acquaintance. The cat, for its part, neither runs away nor hisses; it raises its head and, sorrowfully and sadly, looks straight into my eyes. I sense that my face is wet with tears and that I am whispering meaninglessly to this strange, forlorn cat, defending my mother for having allowed it, one of God's creatures, to go hungry this entire Yom Kippur day:

"Mother has gone to the synagogue and cannot return: she cannot return from Ne'ilah . . . she will not return . . . will not return. . . ."

Glossary

Abele's disease: A proverbial—and, despite the ostensibly grim implications, a humorous—expression for a hopeless or incurable ailment of whatever nature; derived from a man named Abele said to have been the first in Vilna to contract syphilis.

Agudah: Ultra-Orthodox faction in Jewish communal life. Before World War II the Agudah was vehemently opposed to Zionism, which in their view represented an impious refusal to wait for the coming of the Messiah, who alone was the proper, divinely ordained instrument of the people's redemption and restoration to the Land of Israel. In modern Israel, the Agudah fights against the separation of religion and state.

Agudahnik: Member of the Agudah.

aliyah: Lit., "an ascension" or "going up." A section of the Torah portion assigned to be read aloud in the synagogue on a given Sabbath or Festival. Each aliyah is bestowed upon an individual worshipper who ascends the bima (pulpit), in principle to read the section himself; the more usual practice, however, is for the section to be read by the Torah reader, with the worshipper reciting the appropriate blessings before and after the reading.

arba-kanfoth: Lit., "four corners." See *tallith katan*.

baal tefilah: Lit., "master of prayer." The leader of prayers at a religious service.

badhen: Lit., "a jester." A person hired as an entertainer and master of cermonies on festive occasions such as weddings, bar mitzvahs, and the like. One of the most renowned badhens in Eastern Europe was Eliakum Zunser.

bath-goy: A Gentile employed as a bath attendant.

beth midrash: House of study, or synagogue, where worshippers come both to pray and to study the law.

bima: Synagogue pulpit, on which the Torah scroll is placed for public reading and from which the reader sometimes leads the service. In Eastern European synagogues, the bima was normally located in the center of the sanctuary.

bread of affliction: The unleavened bread (matzot) associated with the Passover festival; so-called in reference to the slavery and oppression the Israelites were escaping as they baked unleavened bread in preparation for their flight to freedom.

cholent: A stew or ragout of meat and vegetables, traditionally prepared before the Sabbath and kept warm overnight for consumption on the Sabbath day, since Jewish law forbids cooking or the lighting of fires on the Sabbath itself.

dybbuk: In Jewish folklore, a spirit which possesses the body of a living person; an incubus.

East Wall: In a synagogue, the favored or honored location, since Jerusalem and the Land of Israel lie to the East. Seats along the East Wall were customarily reserved for the congregation's more prominent and influential members.

Elul: The last month of the Jewish calendar, corresponding to parts of August and September; traditionally a time of reflection and introspection, in anticipation of the forthcoming New Year.

eruv: A boundary marker surrounding a town or community, delimiting the area beyond which its residents may not travel on the Sabbath.

esrog: Citron; used together with a lulav, or palm branch, during services on the Festival of Sukkoth.

fonya: Derogatory Yiddish epithet for a Russian.

Forest Shacks: Term for the switchmen's booths along the railroad tracks in the vicinity of Vilna. Before the Revolution of 1917, the area around the Forest Shacks was the clandestine meetingplace for the local revolutionaries; after the Revolution, it became a popular area of recreation and amateur theatrical performances for working-class Jewish youth.

Four Questions: The traditional questions, asked by the youngest person present at the Seder (*q.v.*), as to the nature and meaning of the special observances or rituals associated with the first and second nights of Passover; the questions are then answered by the person conducting the Seder.

gabbai: A trustee; a lay congregant charged with assigning duties and honors to other worshippers and overseeing the general functioning of a synagogue. A position of respect.

Gaon of Vilna: Rabbi Elijah ben Solomon Zalman (1720–1797), one of the greatest Talmudic scholars of the Diaspora. As was not unusual among the rabbis in Lithuania, the Gaon of Vilna refused to assume an official rabbinical position. He led a vigorous, even ruthless battle against Hassidism, and also against the Haskalah ("enlightenment"), even though he wrote not only famous commentaries on the Talmud and other sacred writings, but also treatises on mathematics and the geography of Palestine; he was besides the author of a Hebrew grammar. The religious Jews of Lithuania (the Misnagdim) regard him to this day as their spiritual leader and authority.

Gehenna: The Hebrew-Yiddish term for Hell. Originally, Gehenna (or Ge-Hinnom, the "Valley of Hinnom") was a valley southwest of Jerusalem where in Biblical times children were sacrificed to the god Moloch. The horror and revulsion evoked by such practices led in later times to the name becoming the term for Hell.

Gemara: Same as *Talmud*; the vast body of elaboration, interpretation, and commentary on the Mishnah (*q.v.*), the codification of the Oral Law. While the language of the Mishnah is Hebrew, that of the Gemara is Aramaic. (*Gemara* means "teaching" in Aramaic.)

golem: An extremely foolish or "idiotic" person; a dolt. The original Golem was, according to legend, an artificial man of enormous strength created by a great sage, the Maharal of Prague, to protect the Jews of the city from their enemies.

Great Sabbath: The Sabbath preceding the Passover festival.

Haggadah: Lit., "telling" or "narration." In Jewish religious practice, the book which contains the order of the service for the Seder, or festive evening meal, on Passover—a combination of ritual observances, narrative description, songs, and philosophical reflections relating to the holiday.

ḥallah: A special kind of bread, baked in the form of a braided or twisted loaf, for the Sabbath and holidays.

ḥalutz (pl. *ḥalutzim*): A "pioneer." One of the pioneering settlers in the Holy Land during the late nineteenth and early twentieth centuries, before the establishment of the State of Israel. Most (though not all) ḥalutzim were of secular orientation, and held socialist or communitarian convictions that found their most notable embodiment in the kibbutzim, the collective agricultural settlements.

Ḥanukah: Lit., "dedication" or "consecration"; a holiday of eight days, also called the Feast of Lights, which begins toward the end of the month of Kislev. The holiday commemorates the rededication of the Holy Temple to the service of God in the second century B.C.E., after the recapture of Jerusalem from the Syrian Greeks by Jewish forces under Judah the Maccabee.

Ḥassid: Lit., "pious one," an adherent of a rabbinical spiritual leader, or rebbe, genealogically or spiritually descended from Rabbi Israel ben Eleazar, the Baal Shem Tov (1700–1760), who stressed joy and spontaneity in prayer, faith in God, and faith in a tzaddik—a "righteous" or "holy man," the rebbe—as the three cardinal principles of Jewish life. A Ḥassid subordinates his will to the will of his rebbe. Ḥassidism was at least in part a popular reaction against what was perceived as an excessive intellectualism in Jewish religious practice at the time, as a dry and legalistic approach to life based upon an all-absorbing study of the Talmud.

Havdalah: Lit., "distinction" or "separation"; ceremony that marks the end of the Sabbath and so distinguishes it from the rest of the week, which the ceremony ushers in.

Ḥayei-Adam: Lit., "Human Life." A volume of regulations and rituals governing the life of a pious Jew. Written by Rabbi Abraham ben Jeḥiel Miḥoel Danzig (1748–1820).

ḥeder: Lit., "room"; an elementary Hebrew school, most often conducted in a room in the teacher's (melamed's) house, where reading Hebrew, prayers, the Pentateuch, and the rudiments of Jewish law are taught.

Ḥofetz-Ḥaim: *Desirous of Life*, a famous Talmudic commentary by Rabbi Israel Meir HaCohen of Radun (1835–1933), a great Talmudist and legal authority, who is, in accordance with rabbinic custom, usually referred to by the title of his work.

ḥometz: Lit., "leaven"; by extension, leavened bread as distinct from the unleavened bread *(matzah)* prescribed for Passover, and, by further extension, any kind of food containing yeast or leaven and therefore forbidden during Passover.

Hotzeplatz: City in region of Silesia, in Germany; because of its remoteness from the chief centers of Eastern European Jewish life, "to get to Hotzeplatz" became a proverbial expression for getting lost, literally or figuratively.

Jethro's names: In the Pentateuch, Jethro, the father-in-law of Moses, appears under several other names as well; hence a proverbial expression for someone or something that goes by multiple names or designations.

Kaddish: Prayer recited by mourners at daily services for eleven months after the death of a family member, and thereafter on the anniversary (yohrzeit) of the death. Because of the great importance traditionally attached to being thus memorialized after one's passing, it became customary to refer to a man's or woman's son as his or her "Kaddish."

kapote: A full-length cassock-like gown worn by a rabbi.

kashruth: The process of making (or keeping) utensils, food, and a home kosher, that is, in conformance with the Jewish dietary laws.

kibbutz: A Jewish collective agricultural settlement in the Land of Israel, in which land and property are held in common and all members participate in governance and decisionmaking.

kibbutznik: A member of a kibbutz.

Kiddush: Lit., "sanctification"; a brief ceremony that ushers in the Sabbath (on Friday evenings) or a holiday, and is also performed prior to Sabbath and holiday meals.

Kislev: A month of the Jewish calendar, corresponding to parts of November and December. Hanukah begins on the 25th of Kislev.

kittel: White floor-length gown worn during services on the High Holy Days and at the Passover Seder, as a symbol of purity.

kolkhoz: Collective agricultural settlement in the Soviet Union.

Kol Nidrei: Penitential prayer whose threefold chanting inaugurates the evening service on the Day of Atonement, Yom Kippur.

Korban Minha: Lit., "Sacrificial Offering." A very popular volume of Hebrew prayers, which also incorporated the collection of Yiddish prayers known as the *Tehinah (q.v.)*.

Lag B'Omer: The 33rd day of the seven-week period of the "Counting of the Omer" (the seven weeks between the beginning of Passover and the festival of Shavuoth—see below). Lag B'Omer falls on the 18th day of the month of Iyar, in late spring. Legend has it that on this day an outbreak of plague stopped among the pupils of Rabbi Akiba in the second century c.e., and Lag B'Omer is therefore also known as the scholars' holiday. On this day is suspended the state of half-mourning that prevails overall during the seven weeks.

lamed-vovnik: From "lamed/vov," the Hebrew letters that in combination represent the number 36. In Jewish folklore, one of thirty-six just and saintly men living at any given time, who collectively form a pillar of the world's existence.

Lev-Tov: Popular Jewish work on ethics by Rabbi Isaac ben Eliakim. First published in 1620, it went through countless editions.

little red Jews (roite yideleh): In Jewish folklore, a proverbial expression for the Ten Lost Tribes, said to live in a remote land cut off from the rest of the world by the raging River Sambatyon. After the Bolshevik Revolution, the term "little red Jews" came to be applied facetiously or ironically to Soviet Jewish Communists.

lulav: Young palm branch, which is used together with the esrog (citron) and willow and myrtle branches during services on the Festival of Sukkoth *(q.v.)*.

maggid: Preacher, or deliverer of inspirational sermons, who might be an ordained rabbi, though often was not. Maggidim were usually itinerants, traveling from town to town, although a maggid might receive a formal appointment as the preacher in one town or synagogue.

mahzor: A special prayerbook for the High Holidays, as distinct from a siddur, the daily and Sabbath prayerbook—though a siddur, being more comprehensive, might be used on all occasions.

malina: Lit., "raspberry" in Russian. It became an underworld slang expression for a gang, and, during the years of the Holocaust, took on the meaning of a hiding-place from the Nazis.

melamed: Lit., a "teacher." Traditionally, one who gives elementary instruction in reading and in the Torah, or Five Books of Moses, to young children.

mezuzah: Lit., "doorpost." In Jewish religious practice, a small case containing Scriptural verses and affixed to the doorpost of a house or an individual room, in obedience to the Scriptural injunction "And thou shalt write them [the words of God] upon the doorposts of thy house and upon thy gates" (Deuteronomy 6). The verses embody fundamental elements of Jewish faith.

minyan: The quorum of ten adult males required for public worship, at the thrice-daily services; the term is also used to refer to a service itself (thus, the "morning," "afternoon," or "evening minyan").

Mishnah: Legal codification of the Oral Law, as compiled by Rabbi Judah HaNasi (135–220 C.E.) on the basis of previous collections; the Gemara, or Talmud, is the body of commentary, elaboration, and interpretation of the laws of the Mishnah.

mitzvah: Hebrew for "commandment" or "precept"; in Yiddish parlance, most often used in the sense of a good deed or praiseworthy act.

Musar: A school or movement of religious/ethical practice in Eastern Europe, which emphasized rigorous, unremitting self-examination as the means to attaining the highest standards of moral purity and righteousness.

Ne'ilah: The concluding, and holiest, service on Yom Kippur, the Day of Atonement.

Nisan: A month of the Hebrew calendar, corresponding to parts of March and April. It is the month in which Passover occurs.

pan: In Polish, the term for "lord" or "master." In radical circles, "pans" was a pejorative term for the feudal nobility.

Rashi: Rabbi Solomon Itzhak ben Isaac (1040–1105), French rabbinical scholar, one of the greatest commentators and exegetes of the Bible and the Talmud.

rebbetzin: The wife of a rabbi.

River Sambatyon: In Jewish folklore, a raging, impassible stream that cuts off from the rest of the world the land where dwell the Ten Lost Tribes; the river becomes calm only on the Sabbath.

Rosh Hashanah: The New Year in the Jewish calendar. Rosh Hashanah inaugurates the most sacred period of the Jewish year, the Ten Days of Penitence, which culminates in Yom Kippur, the Day of Atonement.

rosh yeshiva: Head of a yeshiva *(q.v.)*.

Sabbath of Penitence: The Sabbath that occurs within the Ten Days of Penitence, between Rosh Hashanah and Yom Kippur. Traditionally marked in the synagogue by a lengthy inspirational sermon by the rabbi and the reading of the call to repentance by the Prophet Hosea.

Sabbath of Retribution: The Sabbath on which the weekly portion of the Torah includes Deuteronomy 28.

sacrificial rooster: The rooster used in the ceremony of Kapporoth ("atonement") which takes place on the morning of the day before Yom Kippur. In this ceremony the rooster is waved overhead and symbolically assigned to bear the punishment that might otherwise be in store for the supplicant. The rooster is generally eaten at the meal just prior to the onset of the Yom Kippur fast. The ceremony evolved after the destruction of the Temple, where the lamb was the sacrificial animal.

Seder: Lit., "order." The ritual, accompanied by a festive meal, observed in Jewish homes on the first and second evenings of Passover (in Israel only the first Seder is observed). See also *Haggadah*.

Shavuoth: The feast of Shavuoth (Weeks), which occurs seven weeks after the beginning of Passover. Originally, Shavuoth was a celebration of the harvesting of the first fruits; after the destruction of the Temple, tradition added to it the commemoration of the Giving of the Law on Mount Sinai.

shaygetz: A contemptuous term for a gentile man or boy, especially a peasant; may also be applied, sometimes humorously, to a non-observant Jew.

Sheheheyonu: Blessing that expresses thanks to the Almighty for having permitted one to live long enough to have enjoyed a festival, a new fruit, or any personal occasion of joy and happiness.

Sheva K'ru'im Synagogue: A small synagogue on Vilna's Synagogue Courtyard which received this name—"Sheva K'ru'im" means "Seven Who Are Called" (to the reading of the Torah on the Sabbath and Festivals)—because it became one of the places where people went to receive an aliyah *(q.v.)* when the waiting list for aliyoth at the Grand Synagogue became too long. Information about Sheva K'ru'im is derived from the book *From the Vilna Ghetto* (1920) by Haykel Lunski, the distinguished librarian of the Straszun Library, who perished in the Holocaust.

shiksa: Contemptuous term for a gentile girl or woman, especially of peasant origin.

shofar: Horn of a ram, or of any other kosher animal except an ox. It produces a resonant, piercing blast. The shofar is blown on Rosh Hashanah (and at services during the preceding month), as a symbolic call to repentance and spiritual reawakening.

Simhat Torah: Lit., "rejoicing in the Law"; the autumn holiday that marks both the completion of the annual cycle of reading the Torah, or Pentateuch, and the recommencement of the cycle.

sukkah (pl. sukkoth): A temporary dwelling, or booth, with a thatched roof (in northern countries, of fir branches) in which Jews eat and sometimes also sleep during the Festival of Sukkoth *(q.v.)*.

Sukkoth: The Feast of Tabernacles, festival of eight days commencing five days after Yom Kippur. Sukkoth originated as a harvest festival, but later came to serve as a commemoration of the Israelites' wandering in the desert, when, according to tradition, they lived in booths, or sukkoth.

tallith: Prayer shawl worn by adult males, usually after marriage, generally covering the head during the more important sections of the service.

tallith katan: Small tallith, also called "the Four Corners," poncho-like garment worn under the shirt or in lieu of a shirt, on the corners of which are knotted fringes or tzitzit as commanded by Moses (Numbers 15:37).

Talmud: The same as *Gemara (q.v.)*.

Targum Shayni: Aramaic translation of The Book of Esther, with commentary that contains rich legendary material; translated into Yiddish and incorporated into the *Tzenah Ur'enah (q.v.)*.

Tehinah: Prayerbook in Yiddish, mostly for women.

Tishah B'Av: The Ninth of Av (Hebrew month around July-August); the anniversary of the destruction of both the First and the Second Temple, a fast day and an occasion of deep mourning. The Book of Lamentations (traditionally ascribed to Jeremiah) is read at services on this day.

Torah: In the stricter sense, the Pentateuch, the Five Books of Moses, the foundation stone of Jewish law and tradition; more broadly, "Torah" means learning in general, the entire corpus of Jewish law and tradition.

trayfa: Not kosher, unsuitable for consumption under the Jewish dietary laws; by extension, applied to anything unsuitable or improper.

tzaddik: Holy man, saintly person. Hassidim treat their rebbe as a tzaddik and believe in the sublime power of his will, of the blessings he bestows upon them.

Tzenah Ur'enah: A compilation of rabbinical commentaries and legends on the Pentateuch written in Yiddish by Rabbi Jacob Ashkenazi (1550–1626). "Tzenah Ur'enah" literally means "Go forth and see (ye daughters of Jerusalem)" (Song of Songs 3:II). It was a work especially popular with cultivated Jewish women.

U'nessaneh Tokef: A prayer recited on the High Holidays, Rosh Hashanah and Yom Kippur, which dramatically portrays God in His role as Judge of all mankind, weighing the actions and intentions of all human beings and decreeing their fate in the coming year. Tradition ascribes the origin of the prayer to Rabbi Amnon of Mayence, who is said to have chanted it as he lay dying a martyr's death in the synagogue on Rosh Hashanah.

yenta: A vulgar gossip, foolishly garrulous and sentimental.

yeshiva: An academy of Talmudic studies.

Yizkor: Memorial service for the dead, recited on Yom Kippur and on major festivals; "Yizkor"—"May (God) remember (the soul of . . .)"—is actually the first word of the central invocation of the service.

yohrzeit: Anniversary of a person's death, when the nearest relative or relatives recite the Kaddish, a memorial prayer, for him.

A NOTE ABOUT THE AUTHOR

CHAIM GRADE, who died in 1982, was the author of numerous works of prose
and poetry in Yiddish. His first prose work to be translated into English was
the philosophical dialogue *My Quarrel with Hersh Rassayner*, and among his
other writings to appear in English have been the novels *The Yeshiva, The
Agunah*, and *The Well*, and a collection of novellas, *Rabbis and Wives*. Born in
Vilna, Lithuania, in 1910, Mr. Grade came to the United States in 1948 and
lived in New York City with his wife, Inna. He received many prizes and
awards, including the B'nai B'rith Jewish Heritage Award for Excellence, the
Morris Adler Prize of the American Academy of Jewish Research, and the
Remembrance Award of the World Federation of Bergen-Belsen Associations.

A NOTE ON THE TYPE

THIS BOOK was set in a digitized version of Granjon, a type named in compliment
to Robert Granjon, a type cutter and printer active in Antwerp, Lyons, Rome,
and Paris, from 1523 to 1590. Granjon, the boldest and most original designer
of his time, was one of the first to practice the trade of type founder apart from
that of printer.

Linotype Granjon was designed by George W. Jones, who based his draw-
ings on a face used by Claude Garamond (c.1480–1561) in his beautiful French
books. Granjon more closely resembles Garamond's own type than does any
of the various modern faces that bear his name.

Composed by Maryland Linotype Composition
Company, Baltimore, Maryland.
Printed and bound by Maple Vail Book Manufacturing
Group, Binghamton, New York.
Designed by Virginia Tan.